A bibliography of
higher education in Canada

Bibliographie de
l'enseignement supérieur au Canada

Studies in the history of higher education in Canada
Etudes sur l'histoire d'enseignement supérieur au Canada
sponsored by the Association of Universities and
Colleges of Canada, with financial support from
the Carnegie Corporation of New York

1   ROBIN S. HARRIS and ARTHUR TREMBLAY
A bibliography of higher education in Canada

2   W. P. THOMPSON
Graduate education in the sciences in Canadian universities

3   ROBIN S. HARRIS
A bibliography of higher education in Canada: supplement 1965

4   D. C. MASTERS
Protestant church colleges in Canada: a history

5   ROBIN S. HARRIS
A bibliography of higher education in Canada: supplement 1971

6   LAURENCE K. SHOOK
Catholic post-secondary education in English-speaking Canada

A Bibliography of higher education in Canada

Supplement 1971 / Supplément 1971

Bibliographie de l'enseignement supérieur au Canada

ROBIN S. HARRIS

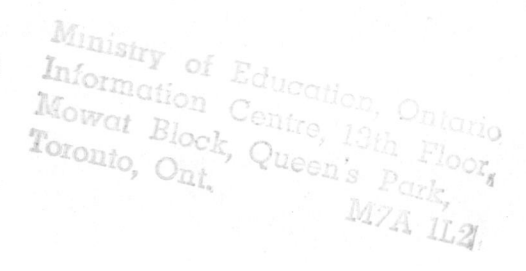

University of Toronto Press
Les Presses de l'université Laval

©University of Toronto Press 1971
Printed in Canada by
University of Toronto Press
Toronto and Buffalo
ISBN 0-8020-1777-0
Microfiche ISBN 0-8020-0030-4

Avant-propos

Le troisième volume dans cette série bibliographique en plus de s'ajouter à la collection des instruments essentiels pour la recherche sur l'enseignement supérieur au Canada, s'avère un portrait révélateur de l'évolution du secteur supérieur de l'éducation au Canada durant la seconde moitié de la décennie qui vient de se terminer.

Il témoigne à sa façon de l'expansion et du développement extraordinaire qui a eu lieu durant les cinq dernières années. La création des CEGEPs, des Community Colleges ou l'équivalent, le rôle croissant des gouvernements provinciaux et par suite la création de nombreux organismes au sein de chaque province, sans parler de tout ce qui touche à la participation croissante des étudiants, autant de phénomènes qui nous sont présentés dans cette collection de documents sur le secteur post-secondaire. Il est à souhaiter que les historiens et les autres chercheurs fassent état de cette poussée rapide qui a d'ailleurs été de pair avec une croissance comparable des inscriptions puisque en cinq ans les étudiants à temps complet au Canada sont passés de 158,000 à presque 300,000.

Nous encourageons les lecteurs à parcourir l'introduction du professeur Robin Harris dans cette perspective. D'ailleurs il y laisse percer sa touche d'historien de métier.

Nous devons donc féliciter le professeur Harris et ses collaborateurs qui ont mené à bien cette oeuvre à laquelle il travaille depuis le lancement de la collection. La continuité, accompagnée d'un développement interne et naturel, nous est donc assurée. Il est à souhaiter que la collection continue à croître et au nom de la communauté universitaire nous espérons que l'auteur principal continuera encore durant de nombreuses années à en assurer la direction.

Nous remercions enfin la Foundation Carnegie, principal bailleur de fonds de cette étude, de l'encouragement fourni à ce projet.

Roger Gaudry
Président, AUCC

Contents

Avant propos	v
Introduction	xi
Sources	xxi

I DEGREE-GRANTING UNIVERSITIES AND COLLEGES :
UNIVERSITES ET COLLEGES QUI CONFERENT DES GRADES

1 History and Organization : Histoire et organisation 3
  A General : Généralités 3
  B The Atlantic Provinces : Les Provinces Atlantiques 4
    Memorial University of Newfoundland 5
    University of Prince Edward Island 6
    The Universities of Nova Scotia : Les Universités de la Nouvelle-Ecosse 6

Acadia University, 7; Collège Sainte-Anne, 8; Dalhousie University: University of King's College, 9; Mount Saint Vincent, 10; Nova Scotia College of Art and Design, 10; Nova Scotia Technical College, 11; St Francis Xavier University, 11; St Mary's University, 11

    The Universities of New Brunswick : Les Universités du Nouveau-Brunswick 12

Université de Moncton, 12; Mount Allison University, 13; University of New Brunswick, 13

  C The Universities of Quebec : Les Universités du Québec 14

Bishop's University, 16; Collèges Classiques, 16; Université Laval, 18; McGill University, 20; Université de Montréal, 23; Université du Québec, 26; Université de Sherbrooke, 27; Sir George Williams University, 27

  D The Universities of Ontario : Les Universités de l'Ontario 28

Brock University, 29; Carleton University, 30; University of Guelph, 30; Lakehead University, 31; Laurentian University of Sudbury, 31; McMaster University, 32; Université d'Ottawa : University of Ottawa, 32; Queen's University, 33; Royal Military College, 37; University of Toronto, 37; Trent University, 42; University of Waterloo, 42; University of Western Ontario, 43; University of Windsor, 44; York University, 44

  E The Universities of Manitoba : Les Universités du Manitoba 45

Brandon University, 46; University of Manitoba, 46; University of Winnipeg, 47

  F The University of Saskatchewan 48
  G The Universities of Alberta : Les Universités de l'Alberta 49

University of Alberta, 50; University of Calgary, 52; University of Lethbridge, 52

H The Universities of British Columbia : Les Universités de la Colombie-Britannique   53
  University of British Columbia, 53; Notre Dame University of Nelson, 56; Simon Fraser University, 56; University of Victoria, 57

2 Current Trends and Problems : Orientation et problèmes présents   58
  A General : Généralités   58
  B University Government : Administration universitaire   64
  C University Finance : Finances universitaires   69
  D The University and the State : L'Université et l'Etat   74
  E The University and the Church : L'Université et l'Eglise   78
  F The University and the Economy : L'Université et l'Economie   80
  G University Planning : La planification universitaire   82

3 Curriculum and Teaching : Programme d'étude et méthodes d'enseignement   85
  A The Faculty of Arts and Science   85
  B Faculté des Arts   86
  C The Humanities : Les Humanités   87
    General : Généralités, 87; Archaeology : Archéologie, 89; Art : Arts plastique, 89; Drama : Théâtre, 90; Languages and Linguistics : Langues et linguistique, 91
      African Studies : Etudes africaines, 92; Byzantine Studies : Etudes Byzantines, 92; Classics : Langues anciennes, 93; East Asian Studies : Etudes sur l'Asie de l'Est, 93; English : Anglais, 94; French : Français, 95; German : Allemand, 96; Hispanic : Espagnol, 96; Icelandic : Islandais, 96; Islamic Studies : Etudes islamiques, 97; Slavic Studies : Etudes slaves, 97
    History : Histoire, 98; Music : Musique, 101; Philosophy : Philosophie, 102; Religion, 104
  D Social Sciences : Sciences sociales   105
    General : Généralités, 105; Anthropology : Anthropologie, 106; Economics & Political Science : Economie et sciences politiques, 106; Geography : Géographie, 108; Psychology : Psychologie, 110; Sociology : Sociologie, 114
  E Mathematics and the Sciences : Mathematiques et les sciences   115
    General : Généralités, 115; Astronomy : Astronomie, 118; Biology : Biologie, 118; Chemistry : Chimie, 119; Geology : Géologie, 120; Mathematics : Mathématiques, 121; Physics : Physique, 122
  F Professional Education : Enseignement professionel   124
    Agriculture : Agriculture, 124; Architecture, Town Planning : Architecture, urbanisme, 125; Business Administration & Public Affairs : Commerce, finance et administration, 127; Dentistry : Art dentaire, 131; Engineering : Génie, 133; Forestry : Génie forestier, 137; Household Science : Sciences domestiques, 138; Journalism : Journalisme, 140; Law : Droit, 140; Library Science : Bibliothéconomie, 144; Medicine : Médecine, 148
      General : Généralités, 148; Historical Development : Développement historique, 152; The M.D. Programme : Doctorat en médecine, 157; Internship

& Residence : Internat et résidence, 164; Specialization : Spécialités, 165 Continuing Education : Education permanente, 167 Nursing : Nursing, 168; Pharmacy : Pharmacie, 174; Optometry : Optométrie, 177; Physical & Health Education : Education physique, 177; Physical & Occupational Therapy : Thérapeutique physique et professionnelle, 179; Public Health : Hygiéne publique, 181; Social Work : Sciences sociales, 183; Teacher Training & Education : Formation des enseignants et Enseignement, 185; Theology : Théologie, 191; Veterinary Medicine : Médecine vétérinaire, 194; Vocational Guidance : Orientation professionnelle, 195

G	Graduate Studies : Etudes post-universitaires	197
H	Adult Education : Education des adultes	200
I	Admissions : Inscriptions	205
J	Evaluation and Grading : Evaluation et classement	209
K	Instructional Aids : Aides didactiques	209
4	Research and Scholarship : Recherche et études	213
A	General : Généralités	213
B	Historical Development : Développement historique	216
C	In the Sciences : Sciences	217
D	In the Humanities and Social Sciences : Humanités et les sciences sociales	219
E	In Education : Enseignement	221
F	Libraries : Bibliothèques	223
G	Museums and Art Galleries : Galeries d'Art et les musées	230
H	Learned and Professional Societies : Sociétés savantes et professionnelles	231
I	Learned and Professional Journals : Revues professionnelles	234
5	The Student and Student Services : L'Etudiant et les services aux étudiants	236
A	General : Généralités	236
B	Political and Social Involvement : Engagement politique et sociale	238
C	Financial Aid : Aide financière	243
D	Housing : Logement	244
E	Counselling and Guidance : Orientation	245
F	Placement : Emploi	247
G	External Organizations : Organisation extérieures	248
6	The Professor and Conditions of Work : Le Professeur et les conditions de travail	250
A	General : Généralités	250
B	Professor as Teacher : Le Professeur comme enseignant	252
C	Academic Freedom : Libertés universitaires	253
D	Salary and Benefits : Salaires et bénéfices	255

II NON-DEGREE GRANTING INSTITUTIONS :
    ETABLISSEMENTS QUI NE CONFERENT PAS DE GRADE   259

    1 General : Généralités   261
    2 Newfoundland : Terre-Neuve   265
    3 Prince Edward Island : Ile-du-Prince-Edouard   265
    4 Nova Scotia : Nouvelle-Ecosse   265
    5 New Brunswick : Nouveau-Brunswick   265
    6 Quebec : Québec   266
    7 Ontario   269
    8 Manitoba   271
    9 Saskatchewan   271
   10 Alberta   272
   11 British Columbia : Colombie-Britannique   273

III AGENCIES AND GOVERNMENT DEPARTMENTS :
    ORGANISMES ET DEPARTEMENTS GOUVERNEMENTAUX   277

    Dominion Bureau of Statistics : Bureau fédéral de la statistique, 277; Economic Council of Canada : Conseil Economique du Canada, 277; Medical Research Council : Conseil des recherches médicales, 278; National Research Council of Canada : Conseil national des recherches du Canada, 279; Science Council of Canada, 280; Association of Atlantic Universities, 281; Prince Edward Island Commission of Post-Secondary Education, 281; University Grants Committee of Nova Scotia, 281; New Brunswick Higher Education Commission : Commission de l'Enseignement supérieur au Nouveau-Brunswick, 282; Centre d'animation, de développement et de recherche en éducation, 282; Conference of Rectors and Principals of Quebec Universities : Conférence des recteurs et des principaux des universités de Québec, 283; Superior Council of Education [of Quebec] : Conseil supérieur de l'éducation (Québec), 283; Committee of Presidents of Universities of Ontario : Comité des présidents des universités de l'Ontario, 284; Committee on University Affairs [of Ontario], 285; Department of University Affairs of Ontario, 285; University Grants Commission of Manitoba, 286; Alberta Colleges Commission, 286; Alberta Universities Commission, 287; Academic Board for Higher Education in British Columbia, 287

Index   289

Introduction

The 1971 *Supplement* to *A Bibliography of Higher Education in Canada* adds about 3,500 entries to the approximately 7,000 listed in the original volume and the 1965 *Supplement*. The original volume, published in 1960, included items published up to December 31, 1958. The 1965 *Supplement* was primarily designed to cover the five-year period 1959-63, but it included appropriate pre-1959 items which had been omitted from the first volume and such 1964 items as had been compiled by the editor at the time his final manuscript was submitted to the University of Toronto Press. The present volume is designed to extend the coverage forward an additional six years by providing as complete a listing as possible for the years 1964 to 1969. But once again there are additional pre-1959 (and pre-1964) items and a considerable number from 1970. It must be emphasized, however, that the 1970 coverage is incomplete, being drawn in the main from the literature which appeared during the first six months of the year. The searching of the journals listed on pages xxii-xxxii has in many cases extended into the first one or more issues of 1970 but it will be noted that the terminal date given, with the exception of one journal which began publication in 1970, is never later than 1969. A future supplement would contain many more 1970 entries.

One of the more striking features of the 1971 *Supplement* is the remarkable increase in the number of journals which it has been found appropriate to search for articles bearing on Canadian higher education. The number searched for the original volume was 157. This increased to 182 for the 1965 *Supplement*. For the 1971 *Supplement* the number has risen to 264. Of these over 70 are journals which have commenced publication since 1963. The original volume included a number of journals which had ceased publication before 1959, for example, *The Canadian Magazine of Politics, Science, Art and Literature* (1893-1939), and both the 1965 and 1971 *Supplements* record (by their omission from the list of journals searched) additional drop-outs. Nonetheless, the net increase in the number of learned and professional journals is impressive and reflects the increasing concern with matters related to the cultural, intellectual and professional life of Canada that has characterized the 1960's.

Like its predecessors the 1971 *Supplement* is essentially a listing of the secondary sources related to Canadian higher education – books, articles, theses, dissertations, reports. The rule adopted in the original volume of excluding journal articles of less than five pages has been relaxed, as it was in the 1965 *Supplement,* but 'short' articles have been included only if in the editor's judgment they are of more than passing interest.

While the same basic procedure has been followed with respect to the reporting and arrangement of entries, there have been substantial changes in the overall organization of the material. Two major sections have been eliminated, two new major divisions have been created, more than a dozen sections have been subdivided, and a substantial number of new sections has been added.

The sections eliminated, 'Canadian Culture' and 'Canadian Education,' constituted in the two earlier volumes one of the two main divisions: 'Part I: Background.' Their inclusion was explained on page x of the Introduction to *A Bibliography:*

> The Bibliography has two parts. Part I provides the context for the study of higher education in Canada. Our universities do not exist in a vacuum; they are conditioned by (and in turn condition) the economic, political, religious and social life of the country itself. It is impossible to study any aspect of Canadian higher education without taking into full account the basic forces which motivate Canadian life. Hence a section called 'Canadian Culture,' listing histories of Canada and its provinces, history of its religious and social institutions, histories of its art, its economy, its racial groups, its relations with other countries. But it is also impossible to study higher education in Canada without reference to other levels of Canadian education. Our universities are what they are partly because our elementary and secondary schools are what they are. Hence a section called 'Canadian Education,' soliciting works concerned with educational developments and problems at all levels.

This statement is as valid in 1971 as it was in 1959, and in the best of all possible worlds the sections would have been retained. But in the best of all possible worlds *A Bibliography of Higher Education in Canada* would be annotated, and this it is not. In the case of items related to Acadia University or to the teaching of Physics or of Law or to the subject of Academic Freedom the simple listing of author and title of the book, article, thesis or report, together with the information needed to locate it, is normally all that the researcher requires; he can tell from the title whether the item is of potential significance to him and from the bibliographical data how he can obtain it. But in the case of the type of item that has been listed under 'Canadian Culture' the title is not necessarily informative (John Porter's *The Vertical Mosaic* and Northrop Frye's *The Modern Century* are examples) and in the case of those listed under 'Canadian Education' a necessarily selective listing is of dubious value, being neither complete nor functionally focussed. Since annotation was not possible, it has been decided to eliminate these sections and refer the reader to such continuing bibliographies as 'Recent Publications Relating to Canada' (in each issue of *Canadian Historical Review*), 'Répertoire bibliographique' (in each issue of *Culture*), and the *Canadian Education Index*.

In 1960 the term *higher education* referred almost exclusively to work that was carried on at universities. By 1964 it was beginning to be apparent that the term also applied to work carried on at a variety of other institutions operating at the post-secondary level but not granting degrees; hence the inclusion in the 1965 *Supplement* of a section entitled 'Technical Institutes, Community Colleges, etc.' Since 1964 the development of post-secondary education in non-degree-granting institutions has expanded dramatically in Canada as elsewhere, and it is now necessary to recognize this formally. Part I of the 1971 *Supplement* is therefore entitled 'Degree-Granting Universities and Colleges,' and Part II is entitled 'Non-Degree-Granting Institutions.'

There is also a Part III entitled 'Agencies and Governmental Departments' in which the publications of some twenty non-teaching institutions that are active in the field of post-secondary education in Canada are listed separately. The majority of these agencies have been established since 1964 and their existence reflects both the increasing systematization and complexity of Canadian higher education.

The systematization of Canadian higher education has revealed itself particularly at the provincial level, and in all provinces where there is more than one degree-granting institution both Government and universities (and in some cases non-degree granting institutions as well) have developed organizations to deal with matters bearing on post-secondary education. In recognition of this, sections have been added under 'History and Organization' for the universities of seven of the ten provinces, and there has also been introduced a section headed 'Atlantic Provinces' for items bearing on the universities of the four eastern provinces as a group. There are new sections for the universities which have been granted degree-granting powers since 1963. Two older institutions, Collège Sainte-Anne and Mount Saint Vincent University, appear for the first time. The Collèges Classiques section has been retained in Part I despite the absorption of many of the *collèges* by the non-degree granting CEGEPs, but items concerning the latter will be found in the 'Quebec' section of Part II.

In the original volume, all items bearing on the history and organization of universities other than those dealing with particular institutions were listed under 'General.' The 1965 *Supplement* added separate categories for 'University Government' and 'University Finance.' In the present volume it has seemed desirable to add four additional categories – 'The University and the State,' 'The University and the Economy,' 'The University and the Church' and 'University Planning.'

The main changes under 'Curriculum and Teaching' are the introduction of separate sub-sections for 'Art,' 'Music' and 'Drama' (previously grouped together), for the various languages previously grouped under 'Modern Languages Other than English and French' and for six subdivisions under 'Medicine'; the addition of sub-sections for 'Languages and Linguistics,' 'The Problem of Admissions,' 'Evaluation and Grading,' and 'Instructional Aids'; and the separation of Graduate Studies from Research.

'Research and Scholarship' have been given a section of their own with nine sub-headings, four of which – 'Libraries,' 'Museums and Art Galleries,' 'Learned and Professional Societies,' 'Learned and Professional Journals' – pertain to what can be described as the conditions of scholarship and research. In the case of these latter, relevant items from earlier volumes (under 'Canadian Culture' and 'Graduate Studies and Research,' for example) have been relisted.

Aside from the increasing tendency towards systematization at provincial, regional and national levels and the expansion of post-secondary education in institutions other than degree-granting universities and colleges, the most remarkable development of the period since 1964, in Canada again as elsewhere, has been the steadily expanding role of student and professor in the determination of policy. It seems incredible now that only ten years ago it was possible to list on three pages all the items bearing on the problems and the role of the Canadian student that had been published over the course of a century, and that a page and a half could contain all those bearing on the problems and the role of the Canadian professor. Nor, as will be seen by glancing at the section devoted to 'The Student' and 'The Professor' in the 1965 *Supplement*, had the situation changed very much by the spring of 1964. But 1964 was, among other things, the year of the Free Speech Movement at Berkeley, and the world of the university has changed immeasurably, and one suspects permanently, since then. This is reflected both in the large number of entries and in the introduction of subheadings in those sections of the 1971 *Supplement* devoted to 'The Student and Student Services' and to 'The Professor and Conditions of Work.'

I wish to express my gratitude to the considerable number of people who have been involved in the preparation of this *Supplement*. These include the librarians of all the universities of Canada who have responded to my request to check the items proposed for inclusion under their institutions and to propose additions, the directors or secretaries of the various agencies included in Part III, and a substantial number of my professorial colleagues at the University of Toronto and elsewhere who have vetted the sections on individual disciplines and professional fields. For assistance in the matter of organization and nomenclature – and in other matters as well – I am indebted to Professor Claude Galarneau of Université Laval, Professors J. D. Hamilton and E. F. Sheffield of the University of Toronto, Mr. Richard Greene and Dr. Lucien Michaud of the Association of Universities and Colleges of Canada, Miss Shirley Wigmore of the Ontario Institute for Studies in Education, Miss Eileen Bradley, Miss Patricia Norman and Miss Katherine Wales of the University of Toronto Library, Messrs. Ian Montagnes, John Ecclestone and Ron Schoeffel of the University of Toronto Press and Patricia Harris. Mrs. Harris prepared the index.

My greatest debt, however, is to my three research assistants, Miss Arlene Tinkler, Mr. Michael Boyko and Mr. Richard Luckhurst – all of the University of Toronto – and to my secretary, Miss Beverley Carter. Mr. Luckhurst and Mr. Boyko bore major responsibility for identifying the items in French-language and English-language journals respectively. Miss Tinkler was involved in the searching of entries in both languages, typed most of the entry cards and was responsible for much of the correspondence that an undertaking of this type inevitably generates. And, as so often has been the case during the past few years with projects with which I have been involved, it has been Miss Carter who has dotted all the i's and crossed all the t's.

R.S.H.

Introduction

Le *Supplément* de 1971 à la *Bibliographie de l'enseignement supérieur au Canada* ajoute environ 3,500 mentions aux 7,000 titres présentés dans le premier volume et le *Supplément* de 1965. Le premier volume publié en 1960 comprenait des écrits qui avaient été publiés jusqu'au 31 décembre 1958. Le *Supplément* de 1965 était premièrement destiné à couvrir la période de cinq ans allant de 1959 à 1963, mais il renfermait les écrits appropriés qui dataient d'avant 1959 et qui avaient été omis dans le premier volume et les écrits de 1964 tels qu'ils avaient été compilés par le rédacteur au moment où il a présenté son manuscrit définitif à la University of Toronto Press. Le présent volume vise à couvrir six autres années en fournissant la liste aussi complète que possible pour les années 1964 à 1969. Mais on fait de nouveau mention d'autres ouvrages parus avant 1959 (et avant 1964) et d'un nombre considérable d'autres ouvrages parus en 1970. Il faut souligner, toutefois, que la liste des ouvrages parus en 1970 est incomplète vu qu'elle comprend principalement les écrits parus durant les six premiers mois de l'année. Le dépouillement des journaux énumérés dans les pages xxii-xxxii comprend en de nombreux cas le premier ou plusieurs autres numéros de 1970, mais il convient de signaler que la dernière date donnée, à l'exception d'un journal qui a commencé à paraître en 1970, n'est jamais postérieure à 1969. Le futur supplément contiendra sûrement un grand nombre d'autres mentions d'ouvrages parus en 1970.

L'une des caractéristiques les plus frappantes du *Supplément* de 1971 est l'augmentation remarquable du nombre de revues qu'on a jugé approprié de dépouiller pour examiner les articles portant sur l'enseignement supérieur au Canada. On en avait compulsé 157 pour le premier volume. Ce nombre a été porté à 182 pour le *Supplément* de 1965. Pour le *Supplément* de 1971, le nombre de revues dépouillées s'élève à 264. De ce nombre, 70 revues ont commencé à paraître depuis 1963. Le premier volume comprenait un certain nombre de périodiques qui avaient cessé de paraître avant 1959, par exemple, *The Canadian Magazine of Politics, Science, Art and Literature* (1893-1939) et les *Suppléments* de 1965 et 1971 en rapportent d'autres (en les omettant de la liste des périodiques dépouillés). L'augmentation totale du nombre des revues savantes et professionnelles est tout de même impressionnante et traduit l'intérêt croissant porté aux questions relatives à la vie culturelle, intellectuelle et professionnelle du Canada, caractéristique des années 60.

Comme les bibliographies précédentes, le *Supplément* de 1971 est essentiellement la liste des sources secondaires qui se rapportent à l'enseignement supérieur au Canada: livres, articles, thèses, dissertations, rapports. La règle adoptée dans le premier volume et qui consiste à exclure les articles de revues de moins de cinq pages n'a pas toujours été suivie, comme dans le *Supplément* de 1965, mais de 'courts' articles ont été inclus seulement si le rédacteur a jugé qu'ils présentaient un intérêt plus que passager.

Bien que la façon de procéder en ce qui a trait à l'indication et la disposition des mentions soit fondamentalement la même, il y a des changements importants dans l'organisation générale de la matière. Deux sections principales ont été éliminées, de nouvelles divisions importantes ont été créées, plus d'une douzaine de sections ont été subdivisées et un nombre important de nouvelles sections ont été ajoutées.

Les sections éliminées, 'Culture canadienne' et 'L'enseignement au Canada,' constituaient l'une des deux divisions principales dans les deux premiers volumes: 'Partie I: Contexte socio-culturel.' A la page xiv de l'Introduction à la *Bibliographie,* on explique la raison pour laquelle on les avait incluses:

> La bibliographie se divise en deux parties. La première partie, elle-même subdivisée en deux chapitres, se rapporte au contexte socio-culturel canadien. Nos universités n'existent pas dans le vide; elles subissent l'influence du milieu dont elles font partie et elles-mêmes, à leur tour, agissent sur ce milieu. Quel que soit l'aspect considéré, toute étude sur l'enseignement supérieur au Canada doit tenir compte des multiples forces qui animent et orientent la vie canadienne. C'est pourquoi l'on a consacré un chapitre de la bibliographie à la 'Culture canadienne'; ce chapitre contient des références se rapportant à l'histoire du Canada et de ses provinces, à l'histoire des institutions religieuses, politiques et sociales, à l'évolution des groupes ethniques au Canada et aux relations de notre pays avec l'étranger.
>
> Pour des raisons analogues, le deuxième chapitre de la bibliographie groupe des ouvrages traitant de l'évolution de l'enseignement et de ses problèmes à tous les niveaux. Nos universités, sous plusieurs rapports, dépendent intimement des systèmes scolaires dont elles font partie intégrante; dans une large mesure les traits qui les caractérisent proviennent de ce que nos écoles élémentaires et secondaires sont elles-mêmes d'un certain type.

Cette déclaration est aussi valable en 1971 qu'elle l'était en 1959 et l'idéal aurait été de conserver ces sections. Mais l'idéal serait d'annoter la *Bibliographie de l'enseignement supérieur au Canada* et tel n'est pas le cas. En ce qui a trait aux mentions relatives à l'Université Acadia ou à l'enseignement de la physique ou du droit ainsi qu'à la question de la liberté universitaire, la simple énumération de l'auteur et du titre du livre, de l'article, de la thèse ou du rapport ainsi que le renseignement nécessaire à sa localisation sont normalement tout ce que le chercheur demande. Il peut dire d'après le titre si l'ouvrage peut être important pour lui et d'après les données bibliographiques comment il peut l'obtenir. Mais dans le cas du genre d'ouvrage énuméré dans la section 'Culture canadienne' le titre ne renseigne pas beaucoup (*The Vertical Mosaic* de John Porter et *The Modern Century* de Northrop Frye en sont des exemples) et dans le cas des ouvrages énumérés dans la section 'L'enseignement au Canada' on doute de la valeur d'une liste nécessairement éclectique vu qu'elle n'est ni complète ni fonctionnelle. Etant donné que l'annotation n'était pas possible, on a décidé d'éliminer ces sections et de renvoyer le lecteur à des bibliographies suivies comme 'Recent Publications Relating to Canada' (dans chaque numéro de *Canadian Historical Review*), 'Répertoire bibliographique' (dans chaque numéro de *Culture*) et au *Répertoire canadien sur l'éducation*.

En 1960, le terme *enseignement supérieur* signifiait presque exclusivement le travail accompli dans les universités. En 1964, il commençait à être évident que le terme s'appliquait aussi au travail effectué dans une variété d'autres établissements du niveau post-secondaire, mais qui ne conféraient pas de grade; c'est pourquoi on a inclus dans le *Supplément* de 1965 la section intitulée 'Autres institutions d'enseignement supérieur.' Depuis 1964, le développement des études post-secondaires dans les établissements qui ne confèrent pas de grade a pris une expansion considérable au Canada comme ailleurs et il est maintenant nécessaire de le reconnaître d'une façon explicite. La Partie I du *Supplément* de 1971 est par conséquent intitulée 'Universités et collèges qui confèrent des grades' et la Partie II, 'Etablissements qui ne confèrent pas de grade.'

Il y a aussi la Partie III intitulée 'Organismes et ministères gouvernementaux' dans laquelle les publications de quelques vingt institutions qui ne sont pas des institutions d'enseignement mais s'occupent des études post-secondaires au Canada sont énumérées séparément. La majorité de ces organismes ont été établis depuis 1964 et leur existence traduit à la fois la systématisation et la complexité croissantes de l'enseignement supérieur au Canada.

La systématisation de l'enseignement supérieur au Canada s'est manifestée elle-même particulièrement au niveau provincial et dans toutes les provinces où il y a plus d'un établissement qui confèret des grades, tant le gouvernement que les universités (et dans certains cas des établissements qui ne confèrent pas de grade) ont établi des organisations destinées à s'occuper de questions qui touchent les études post-secondaires. On a tenu compte de cela et ajouté des sections sous la rubrique 'Histoire et organisation' pour les universités de sept des dix provinces et en a aussi ajouté une section intitulée 'Provinces atlantiques,' pour les ouvrages qui portent sur les universités des quatre provinces de l'est. Il y a de nouvelles sections pour les universités qui ont le pouvoir de conférer des grades depuis 1963. Deux vieux établissements, le Collège Sainte-Anne et l'Université Mount Saint Vincent, apparaissent pour la première fois. La section des collèges classiques a été conservée dans la Partie I malgré l'absorption d'un grand nombre des *collèges* par les CEGEP qui ne confèrent pas de grade, mais les titres des ouvrages qui se rapportent au CEGEP se trouvent dans la section de la Partie II intitulée 'Québec.'

Dans le premier volume, tous les ouvrages qui traitent de l'historique et de l'organisation des universités, autres que ceux qui portent sur des établissements particuliers, sont énumérés dans la section intitulée 'Généralités.' Le *Supplément* de 1965 a ajouté des catégories séparées, intitulées 'Gouvernement des Universités' et 'Finances universitaires.' Dans le présent volume, il a semblé souhaitable d'ajouter quatre autres catégories: 'L'Université et l'Etat,' 'L'Université et l'économie,' 'L'Université et l'Eglise' et 'Planification universitaire.'

Les principaux changements à la section intitulée 'Programmes d'études et méthodes d'enseignement' consiste dans l'établissement de sous-sections séparées pour les 'arts plastiques,' la 'musique' et le 'théâtre' (disciplines groupées ensemble auparavant), pour les diverses langues auparavant groupées ensemble sous la rubrique 'Langues modernes (à l'exception de l'anglais et du français)' et pour six subdivisions sous la rubrique 'Médecine'; l'addition de sous-sections aux rubriques intitulées 'Langues et linguistique,' 'Inscriptions,' 'Evaluation et classement,' 'Aides didactiques,' et la séparation des études supérieures de la recherche.

On a établi une section particulière pour 'La Recherche et les études,' qui comprend neuf sous-titres dont quatre d'entre eux – 'Bibliothèques,' 'Galeries d'art et musées' 'Sociétés savantes et professionnelles,' 'Revues professionnelles,' se rapportent à ce qui peut être décrit comme les conditions des études et de la recherche. Dans le cas de ces dernières, des titres pertinents, extraits des volumes précédents (contenus par exemple sous les rubriques 'Culture canadienne' et 'Etudes post-graduées et recherche') sont énumérés de nouveau.

En plus de la tendance accrue vers la systématisation aux niveaux provincial, régional et national et de l'expansion des études post-secondaires dans les établissements autres que les universités et collèges qui confèrent des grades, le développement le plus remarquable depuis 1964 au Canada comme ailleurs, a été le rôle, accru d'une façon régulière, qu'ont joué l'étudiant et le professeur dans la détermination des lignes de conduite. Il semble maintenant incroyable qu'il y a seulement dix ans il était impossible d'énumérer en trois pages tous les titres des ouvrages qui portaient sur les problèmes et le rôle de l'étudiant canadien, ouvrages qui avaient été publiés au cours d'un siècle, et qu'une page et demi pourrait contenir tous les titres d'ouvrages qui portaient sur les problèmes et le rôle du professeur canadien. Cette situation n'avait pas beaucoup changé au printemps de 1964 comme on peut le constater en jetant un coup d'oeil aux sections intitulées 'L'Etudiant' et 'Le Professeur' dans le *Supplément* de 1965. Mais 1964 a été entre autres choses l'année du mouvement vers la liberté de parole à l'Université de Californie; le monde universitaire a changé considérablement depuis ce temps et l'on s'attend à ce qu'il continue à changer. Cela se traduit à la fois par le grand nombre de mentions et les nouveaux sous-titres des sections du *Supplément* de 1971 intitulées 'L'étudiant et les services aux étudiants' et 'Le professeur et les conditions de travail.'

Je désire exprimer ma gratitude aux nombreuses personnes qui ont participé à la préparation du présent *Supplément*. Elles comprennent les bibliothécaires de toutes les universités du Canada qui ont répondu à la demande que je leur ai adressée de vérifier les titres qui devaient être insérés dans la section réservée à leurs établissements et de me proposer des additions, les directeurs ou secrétaires des divers organismes énumérés dans la Partie III et un nombre important de mes collègues de l'Université de Toronto et d'ailleurs qui ont examiné les sections sur les disciplines individuelles et les diverses professions. J'esprime aussi ma reconnaissance aux personnes suivantes qui m'ont aidé dans l'organisation et l'établissement de la nomenclature ainsi que dans d'autres domaines: le professeur Claude Galarneau de l'Université Laval, les professeurs J. D. Hamilton et E. F. Sheffield de l'Université de Toronto, M. Richard Greene et le R. P. Lucien Michaud de l'Association des Universités et Collèges du Canada, Mlle Shirley Wigmore du Ontario Institute for Studies in Education, Mlle Eileen Bradley, Mlle Patricia Norman et Mlle Katherine Wales de la University of Toronto Library, MM. Ian Montagnes, John Ecclestone et Ron Schoeffel de la University of Toronto Press et Mme Patricia Harris qui a preparé l'index.

    Je suis surtout reconnaissant à mes trois adjoints aux recherches, Mlle Arlene Tinkler, M. Michael Boyko et M. Richard Luckhurst, tous de l'Université de Toronto et à ma secrétaire, Mlle Beverley Carter. MM. Luckhurst et Boyko ont assumé l'importante responsabilité de dépouiller les revues françaises et anglaises respectivement. Mlle Tinkler a participé à la recherche des mentions dans les deux langues, dactylographié la plupart des fiches, et a été chargée d'une grande partie de la correspondance qu'entraîne inévitablement une tâche de ce genre. Enfin, comme c'est arrivé si souvent au cours des années passées dans les projets auxquels j'ai participé, c'est Mlle Carter qui s'est chargée de la révision finale.

R.S.H.

Sources

I: BIBLIOGRAPHIES

1958-69   'Letters in Canada: Education' in July issue of *University of Toronto Quarterly.*

1964-69   **Canadian Education Index.**
'Recent Publications Relating to Canada' in each issue of *Canadian Historical Review.*

1961   **Canadian Association for Adult Education.**
The Literature of Adult Education. Toronto: The Association. Pp. 75.

1964   **Canada, Bureau of Statistics.**
A Bibliographical Guide to Canadian Education. Ottawa: Queen's Printer.

1965   **Drolet, A.**
'Bibliographie' in *Les Bibliothéques Canadiennes.* (Ottawa: Cercle de Livre de France), 215-31.

1966   **Watters, R. E. and I. F. Bell.**
On Canadian Literature 1806-1960: a Check List of Articles, Books and Theses on English-Canadian Literature. Toronto: U. of T. Press. Pp. 184.

1968   **Canadian Association for Adult Education.**
'Non-Degree Research on Adult Education in Canada: an Annotated Bibliography.' Toronto: The Association and the Ontario Institute for Studies in Education. Pp. 76. Mimeographed.

1970   **Commission on the Relations between Universities and Governments.**
'Selected Bibliography' in *The University Society and Government* (Ottawa: Univ. of Ottawa), 233-52.

II: CANADIAN JOURNALS : PERIODIQUES CANADIENS

The journals have been searched for the years indicated. Journals not included in the *1965 Supplement to A Bibliography of Higher Education in Canada* are indicated by an asterisk. A dagger beside a date indicates the cessation of publication of the journal.

Abbreviation	Title	Dates
Act. Nat.	L'Action Nationale	1964-69
Act. Econ.	Actualité Economique	1964-69
Agr.	Agriculture	1964-69
ACFAS	Annales de l'A.C.F.A.S.	1964-66
Alta. Hist. Rev.	Alberta Historical Review	1964-69
Alta. Jour. Ed. Res.	Alberta Journal of Educational Research	1955-69
Alta. Law Rev.	Alberta Law Review	1964-68
Alta. Lib. Assoc. Bull.	Alberta Library Association Bulletin	1964-68†
	Superseded by Lib. Assoc. Alta. Bull.	
Alta. Med. Bull.	Alberta Medical Bulletin	1964-69
Anthrop. Jour. Can.*	Anthropological Journal of Canada	1963-67
App. Therapeutics	Applied Therapeutics	1964-69
Arch.	Architecture – Bâtiment – Construction	1965-68†
	Superseded by	
Arch. Concept*	Architecture Concept	1969
Arch. Can.*	Architecture Canada	1966-69
	Supersedes R. Arch. Inst. Can. Jour.	
Arts Canada*	Arts Canada	1967-69
	Supersedes Can. Art	
Atlan. Prov. Lib. Bull.*	Atlantic Provinces Library Association Bulletin	1954-69
A.U.C.C. Proc.*	Association of Universities and Colleges of Canada Proceedings	1965-69
	Supersedes N.C.C.U.C. Proc.	
Atlantic Advocate*	Atlantic Advocate	1956-69
Bien-être	Bien-être Social Canadien	1965-68
Bas. Teacher*	Basilian Teacher	1960-68†
Bibl. Med. Laval*	Bibliothèque Médicale Université Laval	1968-69
B.C. Lib. Q.	British Columbia Library Quarterly	1964-69
B.C. Med. Jour.*	British Columbia Medical Journal	1966-69

Abbreviation	Title	Dates
Bull. African Studies*	Bulletin of African Studies in Canada *Superseded by* Can. Jour. African Studies	1963-66
Bull. Bibl.	Bulletin de l'Association Canadienne des Bibliothèques de Langue Française	1964-69
Bull. Fed. Coll.	Bulletin des Fédération des Collèges Classiques *Superseded by* Prospectives	1964-65[†]
Bull. Inf. Cath.	Bulletin des Infirmières Catholiques du Canada	1964-68
Bull. Recherches Hist.*	Bulletin des Recherches Historiques	1966-68
Bus. Q.	Business Quarterly	1964-69
Cah. Acad. Can.-Fr.	Cahiers de l'Academie Canadienne-française	1964-68
Cah. Cité Libre*	Cahiers de Cité Libre *Supersedes* Cité Libre	1968-69
Cah. Dix	Cahiers des Dix	1964-68
Cah. Géog.	Cahiers de Géographie de Québec	1964-69
Cah. Hist.	Cahiers d'Histoire	1964-69
Cah. Nursing	Cahiers du Nursing Canadien	1964-69
Can. Mental Health	Canada's Mental Health	1964-69
Can. Admin.*	Canadian Administrator	1961-69
Can. Anaesth. Jour.*	Canadian Anaesthetists' Society Journal	1954-69
Can. Arch.	Canadian Architect	1964-69
Can. Army Jour.	Canadian Army Journal	1964-65[†]
Can. Art	Canadian Art *Superseded by* Arts Canada	1964-66[†]
Can. Audio-Visual Rev.*	Canadian Audio-Visual Review *Superseded by* Educational Media	1965-68[†]
Can. Med. Stud. Jour.*	Canadian Association of Medical Students and Internes Journal	1964-68
Can. H.P.E.R. Jour.*	Canadian Association for Health, Physical Education and Recreation Journal	1965-69
Can. Radiol. Jour.*	Canadian Association of Radiologists Journal	1950-69

Abbreviation	Title	Dates
C.A.U.T. Bull.	Canadian Association of University Teachers Bulletin	1964-69
Can. Bar Assoc. Papers	Canadian Bar Association Papers	1964-69
Can. Bar Jour.	Canadian Bar Journal	1964-69
Can. Bar Rev.	Canadian Bar Review	1964-69
Can. Bus.	Canadian Business	1959-69
Can. Cath. Hist. Report	Canadian Catholic Historical Association Report	1964-69
Can. Chart. Acc.	Canadian Chartered Accountant	1964-69
Can. Chem. Proc.*	Canadian Chemical Processing *Supersedes* Can. Chem & Process Ind.	1964-69
Can. Church Hist. Soc. Jour.	Canadian Church Historical Society Journal	1964-69
Can. Composer*	Canadian Composer	1965-69
Can. Consulting Eng.	Canadian Consulting Engineer	1964-69
Can. Counsellor*	Canadian Counsellor	1968-69
Can. Dent. Assoc. Jour.*	Canadian Dental Association Journal *Supersedes* Jour. Can. Dent. Assoc.	1964-69
Can. Dimension*	Canadian Dimension	1963-69
Can. Doctor	Canadian Doctor	1964-69
Can. Ed. Research Digest	Canadian Education Research Digest *Superseded by* Ed. Canada	1964-68[†]
Can. Econ. Outlook*	Canadian Economic Outlook	1963-69
Can. Ethnic Studies*	Canadian Ethnic Studies	1969
Can. Family Physician*	Canadian Family Physician *Supersedes* Coll. Gen. Practice Jour.	1967-69
Can. Forum	Canadian Forum	1964-69
Can. Geographer	Canadian Geographer	1964-69
Can. Geog. Jour.	Canadian Geographic Journal	1964-69
Can. Hist. Assoc. Report	Canadian Historical Association Annual Report *Superseded by* Hist. Papers	1964-65[†]
Can. Hist. Rev.	Canadian Historical Review	1964-69
Can. Home Econ. Jour.	Canadian Home Economics Journal	1964-69
Can. Hosp.	Canadian Hospital	1964-69
Can. Jewish Outlook*	Canadian Jewish Outlook	1963-69
Can. Jour. African Studies*	Canadian Journal of African Studies *Supersedes* Bull. African Studies	1967-69

Abbreviation	Title	Dates
Can. Jour. Agric. Econ.	Canadian Journal of Agricultural Economics	1964-69
Can. Jour. Behav. Science*	Canadian Journal of Behavioural Science	1969
Can. Jour. Bot.	Canadian Journal of Botany	1964-69
Can. Jour. Chem.	Canadian Journal of Chemistry	1964-69
Can. Jour. Chem. Eng.	Canadian Journal of Chemical Engineering	1964-69
Can. Jour. Comp. Med.	Canadian Journal of Comparative Medicine and Veterinary Science	1964-67
Can. Jour. Econ.*	Canadian Journal of Economics *Supersedes* (with Can. Jour. Pol. Sci.)	1968-69
Can. Jour. Econ. Pol. Sci.	Canadian Journal of Economics and Political Science	1964-67[†]
Can. Jour. Hist.*	Canadian Journal of History	1966-69
Can. Jour. Linguistics*	Canadian Journal of Linguistics	1954-69
Can. Jour. Math.	Canadian Journal of Mathematics	1964-69
Can. Jour. Occup. Therapy	Canadian Journal of Occupational Therapy	1964-69
Can. Jour. Phys.	Canadian Journal of Physics	1964-69
Can. Jour. Psych.	Canadian Journal of Psychology	1964-69
Can. Jour. Pol. Sci.*	Canadian Journal of Political Science *Supersedes* Can. Jour. Econ. Pol. Sci.	1968-69
Can. Jour. Public Health	Canadian Journal of Public Health	1964-69
Can. Jour. Surgery*	Canadian Journal of Surgery	1957-69
Can. Jour. Theology	Canadian Journal of Theology	1964-69
Can. Jour. Zoology	Canadian Journal of Zoology	1964-69
Can. Library*	Canadian Library *Superseded by*	1964-68[†]
Can. Library Jour.*	Canadian Library Jour.	1969
Can. Lit.*	Canadian Literature	1959-69
Can. Math. Bull.	Canadian Mathematics Bulletin	1964-69
Can. Med. Assoc. Jour.	Canadian Medical Association Journal	1964-69
Can. Mod. Lang. Rev.	Canadian Modern Language Review	1964-69
Can. Museum Assoc. Gaz.*	Canadian Museum Association Gazette	1966-69
Can. Music Newsletter*	Canadian Music Centre Newsletter *Superseded by* Musicanada	1964-65[†]

Abbreviation	Title	Dates
Can. Music Educator*	Canadian Music Educator	1959-69
Can. Nuclear Tech.	Canadian Nuclear Technology	1964-66†
	Superseded by Can. R. and D.	
Can. Nurse	Canadian Nurse	1964-69
Can. P. R. Jour.*	Canadian Personnel and Industrial Relations Journal	1959-69
Can. Pharm. Jour.	Canadian Pharmaceutical Journal	1964-69
Can. Physiotherapy Jour.	Canadian Physiotherapy Association Journal	1964-69
Can. Psych.	Canadian Psychologist	1964-69
Can. Public Admin.*	Canadian Public Administration Journal	1958-69
Can. Psych. Assoc. Jour.	Canadian Psychiatric Association Journal	1964-69
Can. R. and D.*	Canadian Research and Development	1968-69
	Supersedes Can. Nuclear Tech.	
Can. Rev. Amer. Studies*	Canadian Review of American Studies	1970
Can. Rev. Soc. Anthrop.*	Canadian Review of Sociology and Anthropology	1964-69
Can. Slav. Papers*	Canadian Slavonic Papers	1956-69
Can. Slav. Studies*	Canadian Slavic Studies	1967-69
Can. Speech Jour.*	Canadian Speech Communication Journal	1968-69
Can. Surveyor	Canadian Surveyor	1964-69
Can. Univ.*	Canadian University	1966-69†
	Superseded by	
Can. Univ. & Coll.*	Canadian University and College	1969
Can. Vet. Jour.*	Canadian Veterinary Journal	1960-69
Catalyst	Catalyst	1967-69
Chem. Can.	Chemistry in Canada	1964-69
Chitty's Law Jour.	Chitty's Law Journal	1964-69
Cité Libre	Cité Libre	1964-66†
	Superseded by Cah. Cité Libre	
Climatology Bull.*	Climatology Bulletin	1967-69
Coll. et Fam.	Collège et Famille	1964-68
Coll. Gen. Practice Jour.*	College of General Practice Journal	1964-67†
	Superseded by Can. Family Physician	
Comm. Jour.	Commerce Journal	1964-68
Comm. Planning Rev.*	Community Planning Review	1962-69
Comp. Inter. Ed. Soc.*	Comparative and International Education Society of Canada Papers	1967-69

Abbreviation	Title	Dates
Conj. Econ. Can.*	Conjuncture Economique Canadienne	1963-69
Continuous Learning	Continuous Learning	1964-69
Convergence*	Convergence	1968-69
Culture	Culture	1964-69
Dalhousie Med. Jour.	Dalhousie Medical Journal	1964-69
Dalhousie Rev.	Dalhousie Review	1964-69
Design Eng.	Design Engineering	1964-69
Dialogue	Dialogue	1964-69
Ed. Canada*	Education Canada	1969
	Supersedes Can. Ed. Research Digest	
Ed. Media*	Educational Media	1969
	Supersedes Can. Audio-Visual Rev.	
Ed. Record Prov. Quebec	Educational Record of the Province of Quebec	1964-65[†]
Eng. Jour.	Engineering Journal	1964-69
English Q.*	English Quarterly	1968-69
Etudes Lit.*	Etudes Littéraires	1968-69
	Supersedes Rev. Litt. Mod.	
Etudes Slav.	Etudes Slaves et Est-européenes	1964-69
Executive	Executive	1964-69
Food in Canada	Food in Canada	1964-69
For. Chron.	Forestry Chronicle	1964-69
For. et Cons.	Forêt et Conservation	1964-67
Hist. Bull. Calgary Clinic*	Historical Bulletin of the Calgary Associates Clinic	1936-58[†]
Hist. Papers*	Historical Papers Presented to the Annual Meeting of the Canadian Historical Society	1966-68
Industrial Can.	Industrial Canada	1964-69
Ing.	L'Ingénieur	1964-69
Inst. Publ.	Instruction Publique	1964-69
Inst. Prof. Lib. Ont.*	Institute of Professional Librarians of Ontario Newsletter	1959-69

Abbreviation	Title	Dates
Jour. Assoc. Student Services*	Journal of the Council of Association of University Student Personnel Services *Superseded by*	1966-67†
Jour. Council Student Services*	Journal of the Council of Associations of University Student Personnel Services	1968-69
Jour. Can. Studies*	Journal of Canadian Studies	1966-69
Jour. Ed.	Journal of Education of the Faculties and Colleges of Education: Vancouver and Victoria	1964-69
Jour. Ed. (N.S.)*	Journal of Education: Department of Education Halifax, Nova Scotia	1943-69
Jour. Ed. Thought*	Journal of Educational Thought	1967-69
Jour. Musicales	Journal des Jeunesses Musicales du Canada	1964-69
Laënnec Méd.	Laënnec Médicale	1964-69
Lakehead Univ. Rev.	Lakehead University Review	1968-69
Laval Méd.	Laval Médicale	1964-69
Laval Théol. Philos.	Laval Théologique et Philosophique	1964-69
Liberté	Liberté	1964-69
Lib. Assoc. Alta. Bull.*	Library Association of Alberta Bulletin *Supersedes* Alta. Lib. Assoc. Bull.	1969
McGill Jour. Bus.*	McGill Journal of Business	1964-65†
McGill Jour. Ed.*	McGill Journal of Education	1966-69
McGill Law Jour.	McGill Law Journal	1964-67
McMaster Lib. News*	McMaster University Library Research News	1968-69
Maclean's*	Maclean's Magazine	1938-69
Mag. Maclean*	Le Magazine Maclean	1962-69
Maintenant	Maintenant	1964-69
Man. Bar News	Manitoba Bar News	1964-69
Man. Jour. Ed. Res.*	Manitoba Journal of Educational Research *Superseded by*	1965-68†
Man. Jour. Ed.*	Manitoba Journal of Education	1968-69
Man. Law Jour.*	Manitoba Law Journal	1962-69
Man. Med. Rev.	Manitoba Medical Review	1964-69

Abbreviation	Title	Dates
Med. Grad.	Medical Graduate	1964-69
Med. Services Jour.	Medical Services Journal	1964-67
Mém. S.R.C.	Mémoires de la Societè Royale du Canada	1964-69
Mod. Med. Canada*	Modern Medicine of Canada	1946-69
Monday Morning*	Monday Morning	1967-69
Musicanada*	Musicanada *Supersedes* Can. Music Newsletter	1967-68
Mysterious East*	Mysterious East	1969
Nat. Can.	Le Naturaliste Canadien	1964-69
New Rev.*	New Review	1961-67
Nouv.-France	Nouvelle France	1964
N.S. Med. Bull.	Nova Scotia Medical Bulletin	1964-69
N.C.C.U.C. Proc.	Proceedings of the National Conference of Canadian Universities and Colleges *Superseded by* A.U.C.C. Proc.	1964[†]
Ont. Coll. Pharm. Bull.	Ontario College of Pharmacy Bulletin	1964-69
OCUFA Newsletter*	Ontario Confederation of University Faculty Associations Newsletter	1969
Ont. Math. Gaz.*	Ontario Mathematics Gazette	1962-69
Ont. Hist.	Ontario History	1964-69
Ont. Jour. Ed. Res.	Ontario Journal of Educational Research	1964-68
Ont. Lib. Rev.	Ontario Library Review	1964-69
Ont. Med. Rev.	Ontario Medical Review	1964-69
Ont. Psych.	Ontario Psychologist	1969
Orbit	Orbit	1969
Orient. Prof.	Orientation Professionnelle	1964-69
Osgoode Law Jour.	Osgoode Hall Law Journal	1964-69
Our Generation	Our Generation	1961-69
Perf. Arts Can.	Performing Arts in Canada	1961-69
Pharm.	Le Pharmacien	1964-69
Phoenix	Phoenix	1964-69
Physics in Canada	Physics in Canada	1964-69
Plant Admin. Engin.	Plant Administration and Engineering	1964-68
Prêtre	Prêtre Aujourd'hui	1964-68

Abbreviation	Title	Dates
Proc. Assoc. Stud. Services	Proceedings of the Canadian Association of Student Personnel Services	1965-68
Proc. Inst. Pub. Admin.*	Proceedings of the Institute of Public Administration of Canada	1949-59[†]
Proc. R.S.C.	Proceedings of the Royal Society of Canada	1964-69
Proc. Schools Bus.*	Proceedings of the Annual Conference of Canadian Schools of Business	1960-68
Proc. Geol. Assoc. Can.	Proceedings of the Geological Association of Canada	1964-69
Profile Ed. N.B.*	Profile of Education in New Brunswick	1962-69
Prospectives	Prospectives *Supersedes* Bull. Fed. Coll.	1965-69
Queen's Q.	Queen's Quarterly	1964-69
Recherches Soc.*	Récherches Sociographiques	1960-69
Relations	Relations	1964-69
Relations Ind.	Relations Industrielles	1964-69
Rev. Barr.	Revue du Barreau	1964-69
Rev. Can. Biol.	Revue Canadienne de Biologie	1964-69
Rev. Can. Urb.	Revue Canadienne d'Urbanisme	1964-69
Rev. Desjardins	Revue Desjardins	1964-69
Rev. Géog. Montréal*	Revue de Géographie de Montréal	1964-69
Rev. Hist.	Revue d'Histoire de L'Amérique Française	1964-69
Rev. Hist. Gaspésie*	Revue d'Histoire de la Gaspésie	1963-69
Rev. Lég.	Revue Légale	1964-69
Rev. Lit. Moderne*	Revue de la Littératue Moderne *Superseded by* Etudes Lit.	1967[†]
Rev. Notariat	Revue du Notariat	1964-69
Rev. Pharm.	Revue de Pharmacie: Prefessionnelle et Pratique	1964-66
Rev. Scolaire*	Revue Scolaire	1963-69
Rev. Univ. Laur.*	Revue de l'Université Laurentienne	1968-69
Rev. Univ. Laval	Revue de l'Université Laval	1964-66[†]
Rev. Univ. Moncton*	Revue de l'Université de Moncton	1968-69
Rev. Univ. Ottawa	Revue de l'Université d'Ottawa	1964-69

Abbreviation	Title	Dates
Rev. Univ. Sherbrooke*	Revue de l'Université de Sherbrooke	1964[†]
R. Arch. Inst. Can. Jour.	Royal Architecture Institute of Canada Journal *Superseded by* Arch. Can.	1964-66[†]
R. Astron. Soc. Jour.	Royal Astronomical Society of Canada Journal	1964-69
Sask. Bar Rev.	Saskatchewan Bar Review	1964-66
Sask. Hist.	Saskatchewan History	1964-69
Sask. Lib. Assoc. Bull.*	Saskatchewan Library Association Bulletin *Superseded by*	1962-65[†]
Sask. Lib.*	Saskatchewan Library	1966-69
Scholarly Publishing*	Scholarly Publishing	1969
Sch. Prog.	School Progress	1964-69
Sci. Eccl.	Sciences Ecclésiastiques *Superseded by*	1964-67[†]
Science et Esprit*	Science et Esprit	1968-69
Science Forum*	Science Forum	1968-69
Sem. Rel. Québec	Semaine Religieuse de Québec	1964-66
Semaines Sociales	Semaines Sociales du Canada	1964
Séminaire	Séminaire	1965-69
Service Social	Service Social	1964-68
Soc. Worker	The Social Worker	1964-69
Technique*	Technique	1967-69
Thémis	Thémis	1965-68
This Magazine*	This Magazine is About Schools	1966-69
Tor. Ed. Q.	Toronto Education Quarterly	1964-69
Trans. R.S.C.	Transactions of the Royal Society of Canada	1964-69
Union Méd.	Union Médicale du Canada	1964-69
Univ. Affairs*	University Affairs	1959-69
U.B.C. Law Rev.	University of British Columbia Law Review	1964-69
U.N.B. Law Rev.	University of New Brunswick Law Review	1964-68
Univ. Tor. Law Jour.	University of Toronto Law Journal	1964-69

Abbreviation	Title	Dates
Univ. Tor. Q.	University of Toronto Quarterly	1964-69
Univ. Windsor Rev.*	University of Windsor Review	1965-69
West. Can. Jour. Anthrop.*	Western Canadian Journal of Anthropology	1969

I Degree-granting universities and colleges
   Universités et collèges qui confèrent des grades

History and organization
Histoire et organization

A. GENERAL : GÉNÉRALITÉS

1890 **DeCourbertin, P.**
Universites Transatlantiques. Paris: Hachette. Pp. 380.

1914 **Wesbrook, F. F.**
'The Provincial University in Canadian Development,' *Science* [U.S.] XXXIX, 407-17.

1923 **Brett, G. S.**
'Higher Education,' *Annals of American Academy of Political and Social Science* CVII, 126-33.

1952 **Moir, J. S.**
'Methodism and Higher Education, 1843-1849: a Qualification,' *Ont. Hist.* XLIV, 109-28.

1959 **Hutton, E.**
'The Hectic Scramble for the Class of '59,' *Maclean's* LXXII (9), 22-23, 46-50.

1960 **Brunet, M.**
'The University as a Public Institution in French Canada from Louis XIII to the Electoral Campaign of 1960,' *Can. Public Admin.* III, 344-49.

1963 **Stackpole, S. H.**
Carnegie Corporation Commonwealth Program 1911-1961. New York: Carnegie Corporation of New York. Pp. 67.

1966 **Harris, R. S.**
'English Influence in Canadian Education,' *Can. Forum* XLVI, 289-91.
Sullivan, A. D.
'Patterns of Interinstitutional Cooperation in Canadian Catholic Higher Education.' Unpublished doct. dissertation, Catholic Univ. of America.
Thistle, M.
The Inner Ring: the Early History of the National Research Council of Canada. Toronto: U. of T. Press. Pp. 435.
Toombs, W. N.
'An Analysis of Parliamentary Debates on Federal Financial Participation in Education in Canada, 1960-67.' Unpublished doct. dissertation, Univ. of Alberta.

1968 **Hyman, C.**
'Federal Aid to Higher Education with Particular Reference to Universities in the Period 1951 to 1967.' Unpublished M.A. thesis, McGill Univ.
Mitchener, R. D.
'The Pattern of University-Government Relationships in Canada,' *C.A.U.T. Bull.* XVII (2), 12-18.

1969 **Bissell, C. T.**
'Institutions of Higher Education in Canada: Some Recent Developments' in W. R. Niblett, ed., *Higher Education: Demand and Response* (London: Tavistock), 139-51
Firestone, O. J.
Industry and Education: a Century of Canadian Development.
Ottawa: Univ. of Ottawa Press. Pp. 295.
Harris, R. S.
'On Higher Education in Australia and Canada,' *Australian Univ.* VII (3), 190-203.
Munroe, D., A.-M. Parent and R. Guindon.
All Eyes Towards the Future: Report of the Tribunal on Bilingual Higher Education/Les Yeux vers l'avenir ... Halifax: Govt. of Nova Scotia. Pp. 95 (English) and 103 (français).

1970 **Commission of Inquiry on Forty Catholic Church-Related Colleges and Universities.**
Report of ... : a Commitment to Higher Education in Canada. Ottawa: National Education Office. Pp. 272.
Zsigmond, Z. E. and C. J. Wenaes.
Enrolment in Educational Institutions by Province, 1951-52 to 1980-81. Ottawa: Queen's Printer. Pp. 306.

B. THE ATLANTIC PROVINCES :
LES PROVINCES ATLANTIQUES

1958 **Kirkconnell, W.**
'Maritime University Problems,' *Atlantic Advocate* XLVIII (9), 21-24.
1965 **Association of Atlantic Universities.**
Education in the Atlantic Provinces: a Report to the Commission on the Financing of Higher Education in Canada. Halifax: The Association. Pp. 77.

Graham, J. F.
'The Bladen Report and the Universities of the Atlantic Provinces: Two Plus Two Equal Three,' *C.A.U.T. Bull.* XIV (2), 87-92.
1966 Rimmington, G. T.
'The Universities of the Atlantic Provinces,' *Can. Geog. Jour.* LXXIII, 38-49.
Somers, H. J.
'The Atlantic Universities' in R. S. Harris, ed., *Changing Patterns in Higher Education in Canada* (Toronto: U. of T. Press), 17-37.
1967 Stewart, C. B.
'How Many Medical Schools are Needed in the Atlantic Provinces?' *N.S. Med. Bull.* XLVI, 41-44, 65-68, 85-89.
1969 Crean, J. G., M. F. Ferguson and H. J. Somers.
Higher Education in the Atlantic Provinces for the 1970's: a Study Prepared under the Auspices of the Association of Atlantic Universities for the Maritime Union Study. Halifax: Assoc. of Atlantic Univs. Pp. 121.
Gillis, A. A.
'The University of Halifax, 1876-1881.' Unpublished M.A. thesis, Dalhousie Univ.
1970 Arnold, M. H.
'Interprovincial Grants and Payments in Support of Post-Secondary Education in the Atlantic Region (with special reference to Prince Edward Island).' Charlottetown: Prince Edward Island Commission on Post-Secondary Education. Pp. 28. Mimeo.

MEMORIAL UNIVERSITY OF NEWFOUNDLAND

1958 West, P.
'Newfoundland's University: its Promising Problems,' *Atlantic Advocate* XLVIII (9), 19-20.
1961 Harrington, M. F.
'A Century-Old Dream Realized in Newfoundland,' *Atlantic Advocate* LI (9), 21-31.
'Memorial University March Past,' *Atlantic Advocate* LII (12), 65-72.
Pushie, G.
'Memorial University,' *Atlantic Advocate* LI (9), 17-20.
Robinson, C. and B. Beaver.
'St. John's Salutes its New Campus,' *Weekend Magazine* Dec. 2, 1961.
1964 Rowe, F. W.
The Development of Education in Newfoundland. Toronto: Ryerson. Pp. 225.

1965 **Coleman, S. J.**
'Memorial University in Relation to Industry and Commerce,'
Newfoundland Journal of Commerce XXXII (Feb.), 25-26.
1967 **MacLeod, S.**
'Newfoundland's Controversial "Free" University,' *Weekend Magazine* Feb. 11, 1967, 2-6.
Royal Commission on Education and Youth.
Report of... St. John's, Newfoundland: Province of Newfoundland and Labrador. 2 vols.
1968 **Taylor, Lord.**
'Memorial Moves Up,' *Atlantic Advocate* LVIII (9), 13-19.
1969 **Ryan, D. and M. Williams.**
'Memorial University of Newfoundland and its Library,' *Can. Lib. Jour.* XXVI, 202-03.

UNIVERSITY OF PRINCE EDWARD ISLAND

1964 **McKinna, Sister M. O.**
'The Impact of Religion and Politics on the Structure of Higher Education in the Province of Prince Edward Island.' Unpublished doct. dissertation, Boston College.
1965 **Royal Commission on Higher Education for Prince Edward Island.**
Report of... Charlottetown: The Commission. Pp. 64.
1966 **Campbell, A. B.**
Policy Statement on Post-Secondary Education [in Prince Edward Island]. Charlottetown: Office of the Premier. Pp. 39.
1970 **Prince Edward Island Commission on Post-Secondary Education.**
First Annual Report covering the period to December 31, 1969. Charlottetown: The Commission. Pp. 28.

THE UNIVERSITIES OF NOVA SCOTIA :
LES UNIVERSITES DE LA NOUVELLE-ECOSSE

1964 **University Grants Committee of Nova Scotia.**
Higher Education in Nova Scotia: A Survey Report with Recommendations. Halifax: The Committee. Pp. 106.
1965 **University Grants Committee of Nova Scotia.**
Higher Education in Nova Scotia. Annual Report of the University Grants Committee for the Calendar Year 1964. Halifax: The Committee. Pp. 153.

1966 **Elliott, S.**
'The Higher Learning a Century Ago,' *Jour. Ed. (N.S.)* XV (3), 38-45.
Rimmington, G. T.
'The Founding of Universities in Nova Scotia,' *Dalhousie Rev.* XLVI, 319-37.
Rimmington, G. T.
'The Protestant Colleges of Nova Scotia in the Early Nineteenth Century,' *Jour. Ed. (N.S.)* XVI (1), 31-39.
University Grants Committee of Nova Scotia.
Higher Education in Nova Scotia: Annual Report of the University Grants Committee for the Calendar Year 1965. Halifax: The Committee. Pp. 81.
1969 **Vagianos, L.**
'New Look for Library Cooperation in Nova Scotia,' *Can. Univ.* IV (1), 21-23.

ACADIA UNIVERSITY

1950 **Redmond, D. A.**
'Some College Libraries of Canada's Maritime Provinces: Selected Aspects.' Unpublished M.L.S. thesis, Univ. of Illinois. (Abridgement published in *College and Research Libraries* [U.S.] XI, 355-62.)
1953 **Way, H. H.**
'An Experiment in Teacher Education,' *Jour. Ed. (N.S.)* II (3), 34-37.
1964 **Fraser, D. G. L.**
'Acadia University and West Indian Studies,' *Acadia Bulletin* L (1), 14-16.
Kirkconnell, J. W.
'Watson Kirkconnell: a Scholarly Volcano,' *Acadia Bulletin* L (1), 19-22.
1965 **Fiander, R. W.**
'Forty-Six Years of the A.D.S.,' [Acadia Dramatic Society] *Acadia Bulletin* LI (3), 9-11.
1966 **Franklin, S.**
'Acadia: The Baptists and the Battle for Academic Freedom,' *Weekend Magazine* June 11, 1966, 12-19.
1967 **Kirkconnell, W.**
A Slice of Canada: Memoirs. Toronto: U. of T. Press. Pp. 393. [Especially 148-71.]

1967 **Rimmington, G. T.**
'Twelve Years of Progress,' [Report of the Acadia University Institute] *Acadia Bulletin* LIII (2), 7-8.
1968 **Kirkconnell, W.**
The Fifth Quarter-Century: Acadia University, 1938-1963. Wolfville: Acadia Univ. Pp. 141.

COLLÈGE SAINTE-ANNE

1901 **Boulay, D.**
Le R. P. Cochet, prêtre-eudiste. Paris. Surtout 291-316.
1905 **Dagnaud, P.-M.**
Les Français du Sud-Ouest de la Nouvelle-Ecosse. Besançon. Surtout 213-38.
1921 **Georges, E.**
Le Révérend Père Prosper Lebastard, eudiste. Bathurst: Collège du Sacré Coeur. Surtout 15-19.
1923 **Georges, E.**
Mgr Gustave Blanche, c.j.m. Bathurst: Collège du Sacré Coeur. Surtout 39-66.
1925 **Lauvrière, E.**
La Tragédie d'un peuple. Paris: H. Goulet. 2 vols. Surtout Ch. XXVII.
1926 **LeGresley, O.**
L'Enseignement du Français en Acadie. Mamers: G. Enault. Surtout 183-92.
1931 **Gauthier, Y.**
Le Père Pierre-Marie Dagneau, prêtre-eudiste. Québec: Action Social. Surtout 49-53.
1935 **Bernard, A.**
Histoire de la Survivance Acadienne. Montréal: Clercs de Sainte-Viateur. Surtout 258-69.
1940 **Collège Sainte-Anne.**
Album Souvenir: Les Cinquante Ans du Collège Sainte-Anne. Church Point: Le Collège. Pp. 34.
1955 **Rumilly, R.**
Histoire des Acadiens. Montréal: Imprimière Saint-Joseph. 2 vols. Surtout Ch. LIII.
1968 **Deveau, A.**
La Ville Française. Québec: Ferland. Surtout 167-79.

1969 Munroe, D., A.-M. Parent and R. Guindon.
All Eyes Towards the Future: Report of the Tribunal on Bilingual Higher Education/Les Yeux vers l'avenir ... Halifax: Govt. of Nova Scotia. Pp. 95 (English) and 103 (français).

DALHOUSIE UNIVERSITY: UNIVERSITY OF KING'S COLLEGE

1908 Burpee, L. C.
'Canadian Libraries of Long Ago,' *American Library Association Bulletin* II, 136-43.
1931 'The Inauguration of Carleton W. Stanley as President of Dalhousie University,' *Dalhousie Univ. Bulletin* No. 4 (Oct.). Pp. 19.
1946 Falconer, J. W. and W. G. Watson.
A Brief History of Pine Hill Divinity Hall and the Theological Department at Mount Allison University. Halifax: privately published. Pp. 55.
1946 McKenzie, K. A.
'The Dalhousie Medical School,' *Hist. Bull. Calgary Clinic* XI, 78-81.
1950 Redmond, D. A.
'Some College Libraries of Canada's Maritime Provinces: Selected Aspects.' Unpublished M.L.S. thesis, Univ. of Illinois. (Abridgement published in *College and Research Libraries* [U.S.] XI, 355-62.)
1956 MacKenzie, K. A. and C. B. Stewart.
'Canadian Medical Faculties through the Years: Dalhousie University,' *Can. Med. Stud. Jour.* XI, 78-81.
1962 Blakeley, P.
'Dalhousie: A Challenge for the Future,' *Atlantic Advocate* LII (9), 48-55.
1964 Stewart, C. B.
'The Finances of Dalhousie Medical School,' *Dalhousie Med. Jour.* XVIII (1), 10-21.
Thomas, C. E.
'The Early Days of King's College, Windsor, Nova Scotia,' *Can. Church Hist. Soc. Jour.* VI, 30-45.
1965 McLean, J. D.
'Faculty of Dentistry, Dalhousie University,' *Can. Dent. Assoc. Jour.* XXXI, 298-302.
1966 Wilkinson, J. P.
'A History of the Dalhousie University Main Library, 1867-1931.' Unpublished doct. dissertation, Univ. of Chicago.

1967 **Cameron, I.**
'One Hundred Years of Dalhousie,' *Dalhousie Med. Jour.* XXI (1), 5-9.
1968 **Gibson, D. A.**
'The Audio-Visual Division of Dalhousie Medical School,' *N.S. Med. Bull.* XLVII (3), 91-93.
MacLeod, D. E.
'A Critical Biography of James De Mille.' Unpublished M.A. thesis, Dalhousie Univ.
Robinson, S. C.
'Medical Education at Dalhousie,' *Dalhousie Med. Jour.* XXI (4), 107-113.
Stewart, C. B.
'One Hundred Years of Medical Education at Dalhousie,' *N.S. Med. Bull.* XLVII (5), 149-52.
1969 **Bisakowski, K.**
'A Summary of the History of Athletics and Physical Education at Dalhousie University,' *Can. H.P.E.R. Jour.* XXXV (6), 26-28.
Garrard, R.
'Dalhousie University Master Plan,' *Arch. Can.* XLVI, 44-45.
Whiteside, S.
'Review, Change and Implementation: Library Education at Dalhousie,' *Atlan. Prov. Lib. Bull.* XXXIII, 23-25. See also R. Krzys, 'Thoughts on Library Education and the Dalhousie Plan,' 28-30.
1970 **McBrine, R. W.**
'Archibald MacMechan, Canadian Essayist,' *Dalhousie Rev.* L, 23-33.

MOUNT SAINT VINCENT

1956 **Maura, Sister.**
'Mount Saint Vincent College' in *The Sisters of Charity* (Toronto: Ryerson), 252-63.
1966 **Mackenzie, N. A. M.**
'View of Education with Reference to the Atlantic Region,' *Atlantic Advocate* LVI, 13-14, 16.
Michael, Sister Alice.
'The Education of Women.' Halifax: Mount Saint Vincent Univ. (Inaugural Address as President.)

NOVA SCOTIA COLLEGE OF ART AND DESIGN

1967 **Blakeley, P.**
'Key Roles Played by the Nova Scotia College of Art' *Atlantic Advocate* LVII (May), 33-39

1968 **Kennedy, G.**
'Nova Scotia College of Art and Design,' *Arts Canada* XXV (5), 30-32.
1970 **Ferguson, G.**
'A Professional Lithography Workshop,' *Arts Canada* XXVII (2), 59-61.
Rombout, L.
'Un Nouveau Décor dans un école ancienne,' *Vie des Artes* LVIII (Spring), 104-05.

NOVA SCOTIA TECHNICAL COLLEGE

1950 **Cochrane, H. G.**
'Postwar Engineering Education for Ex-Servicemen,' *Eng. Jour.* XXXIII, 461-70.
1953 **Ball, S.**
'Civil Engineering,' *Jour. Ed. (N.S.)* II (4), 55-58.
1957 **Cameron, E. L.**
'Metallurgical Engineering,' *Jour. Ed. (N.S.)* VI (2), 24-28.

ST. FRANCIS XAVIER UNIVERSITY

1953 **Saint Miriam, Sister.**
'The Congregation of Notre Dame in Early Nova Scotia,' *Can. Cath. Hist. Report* 67-80. [re Mount Saint Bernard College.]
1965 **Anselm, Sister.**
Antigonish Idea and Social Welfare. Antigonish: St. Francis Xavier Univ. Pp. 16.
1969 **Lynch, M.**
'A Canadian Record?' [re teaching of public speaking] *Can. Speech Commun. Jour.* II (1), 13-17.
MacDonald, A. A.
Extension Philosophy and Operation: The Antigonish Concept. Antigonish: St. Francis Xavier Univ. Pp. 13.
Smyth, F.
'The Development of the Antigonish Movement,' *Convergence* II (1), 61-65.

ST. MARY'S UNIVERSITY

1959 **Matlik, C.**
The University and the Crisis; an Address Delivered at Saint Mary's University Convocation Exercises, May 12, 1959. Halifax: Saint Mary's Univ. Pp. 8.

1959 'Saint Mary's University – A Study in Growth,' *Monthly Bulletin* LII, 119-21.
1969 **Fogarty, D.**
A Proposed Inner College for Saint Mary's University. Halifax: Saint Mary's Univ. Pp. 40.

THE UNIVERSITIES OF NEW BRUNSWICK : LES UNIVERSITÉS DU NOUVEAU-BRUNSWICK

1966 **Ali, A. H.**
'Federal Aid to Education in New Brunswick: the Effects of Federal Aid on the Development of Technical and Vocational Education in New Brunswick.' Unpublished M.A. thesis, Univ. of New Brunswick.
1967 **Committee on the Financing of Higher Education in New Brunswick.**
Report of... Fredericton: Queen's Printer. Pp. 72.
1969 **New Brunswick Higher Education Commission.**
Investing in the Future: a Programme for Government Assistance to Universities, Technical Schools and their Students. Fredericton: The Commission. Pp. 67.
See also Publications of New Brunswick Higher Education Commission.

UNIVERSITÉ DE MONCTON

1965 **LeBlanc, R.**
'La Bibliothèque de l'Université de Moncton,' *Atlan. Prov. Lib. Bull.* XXIX, 10-11.
1968 **Marcotte, N.**
'L'Enseignement de génie à l'Université de Moncton,' *Rev. Univ. Moncton* I (2), 53-56.
Savoie, A.
'Mission de l'Université,' *Rev. Univ. Moncton* I (1), 6-10.
Université de Moncton.
Brief to the New Brunswick Higher Education Commission... Moncton: The University. Pp. 72.
1969 **Even, A.**
'Une Université sous-développée dans une région défavorisée,' *Rev. Univ. Moncton* II, 60-62.
Munroe, D., A.-M. Parent and R. Guindon.
All Eyes Towards the Future: Report of the Tribunal on Bilingual Higher Education/Les Yeux vers l'avenir... Halifax: Govt. of Nova Scotia. Pp. 95 (English) and 103 (français).

1970 **Malloch, A. and L. P. Taschereau.**
'Le Cas de sociologie à l'Université de Moncton,' *C.A.U.T. Bull.* XVIII (3), 43-46.
Newbold, B. T.
'La Recherche à l'Université de Moncton,' *Rev. Univ. Moncton* III, 113-15.

MOUNT ALLISON UNIVERSITY

1946 **Falconer, J. W. and W. G. Watson.**
A Brief History of Pine Hill Divinity Hall and the Theological Department at Mount Allison University. Halifax: privately published. Pp. 55.
1950 **Redmond, D. A.**
'Some College Libraries of Canada's Maritime Provinces: Selected Aspects.' Unpublished M.L.S. thesis, Univ. of Illinois. (Abridgement published in *College and Research Libraries* [U.S.] XI, 355-62.)
1958 **Ross, V. B.**
Moments Make a Year. Sackville: Tribune Press. Pp. 216.
1960 **Allison, L. M.**
'Library Expansion at Mount Allison, New Brunswick,' *Atlan. Prov. Lib. Bull.* XXIV, 31-32.
1963 **Cragg, L. H.**
An Installation Address. Sackville: Mount Allison Univ. Pp. 38.
1964 **Dow, H. J.**
'Mount Allison's Owens Museum: a Look at 19th Century Values,' *Can. Art* XXI (2), 76-79.
1969 **Nichol, J.**
'Why Mount Allison Plans to Stay Small,' *Can. Univ. & Coll.* XII (12), 22-23.

UNIVERSITY OF NEW BRUNSWICK

1925 **University of New Brunswick.**
A Retrospect and a Prospect. Fredericton: Half Million Dollar Endowment Fund Committee. Pp. 32.
1930 **Prince, G. H.**
'The New Provincial Government Forestry and Geology Building at University of New Brunswick,' *For. Chron.* VI (4), 8-13.
1945 **Bailey, A. G., ed.**
Messages to the University of New Brunswick from Sir Frederick Williams-Taylor, Kt., LL.D. Fredericton: Univ. of New Brunswick. Pp. 34.

1950 **Redmond, D. A.**
'Some College Libraries of Canada's Maritime Provinces: Selected Aspects.' Unpublished M.L.S. thesis, Univ. of Illinois. (Abridgement published in *College and Research Libraries* [U.S.] XI, 355-62.)

1952 **Coughey, D. J.**
'The U.N.B. Beaverbrook Scholarships.' Unpublished B.Ed. thesis, Univ. of New Brunswick.

1961 **University of New Brunswick.**
Brief to the Royal Commission on Higher Education in New Brunswick. Fredericton: Univ. of New Brunswick. Pp. 30.

1962 **Pacey, W. D.**
'Sir Charles G. D. Roberts' in R. L. McDougall, ed., *Our Living Tradition Fourth Series* (Toronto: U. of T. Press), 31-56.

1963 **Chapman, J. K.**
'Dr. Edwin Jacob: a Biography,' *Encaenia 1963*. (Fredericton; Univ. of New Brunswick), 23-25.

1965 **Condon, T. J.**
'Similar Origins: Effects of Isolation on the Early Development of the University of New Brunswick and Harvard University,' *Atlantic Advocate* LV (May), 34-41.

1965 **Pidhany, O. S.**
'East-European History at St. Thomas University,' *New Rev.* V (2-3), 63-64.

1967 'The Development of Physical Education – University of New Brunswick,' *Can. H.P.E.R. Jour.* XXXIII (4), 36-40.
Ryan, W. F.
'The University of New Brunswick Law Faculty,' *Can. Bar Jour.* X, 43-49.

1969 **Berland, A.**
'A Report on the Strax Case at the University of New Brunswick,' *C.A.U.T. Bull.* XVII (4), 20-64.
Milner, J. B.
'The Strax Affair,' *C.A.U.T. Bull.* XVII (3), 36-42.

C. THE UNIVERSITIES OF QUEBEC :
LES UNIVERSITÉS DU QUÉBEC

1962 **Brazeau, J.** *et al.*
Les Resultats d'une enquête auprès des étudiants dans les universités de langue française du Québec. Montréal: Univ. de Montréal, Dept. de Sociologie. Pp. 80.

1964 *Collège et Famille* XXI (2-3) Numéro spécial, 'La Jeunesse étudiante du Québec en 1964,' inclut: P. Mondon, 'Leur Engagement politique?' 90-100; G. Gaudreau, 'Leur Avenir professionnel?' 111-16; J. Genest, 'Que pensent-ils de leurs études?' 143-56.

1965 **Holt, H. E.**
'Quebec's New Ministry of Education.' Unpublished M.A. thesis, Carleton Univ.
Paquet, J.-C.
'Attention: le Québec ne produit pas assez de savants,' *Mag. Maclean* V (5), 32, 70, 72-74, 76-77.

1966 **Lebel, Maurice.**
'Les Universités du Québec,' *Can. Geog. Jour.* LXXIII, 111-27.
Martin, J.-M.
'Quebec' in R. S. Harris, ed., *Changing Patterns of Higher Education in Canada* (Toronto: U. of T. Press), 63-84.
Parent, A.-M.
'L'Enseignement supérieur dans la Province de Quebec' in J. E. Hodgetts, ed., *Higher Education in a Changing Canada* (Toronto: U. of T. Press), 14-24.

1968 **Brunet, M.**
'Quebec's French-Speaking Universities and the Law of Double Imbalance,' *Queen's Q.* LXXV, 613-31.
Cinq-Mars, E.
'L'Année noire du conseil supérieur de l'éducation,' *Act. Nat.* LVII, 513-23.
Cinq-Mars, E.
'Le Conseil supérieur de l'éducation et ses avis,' *Act. Nat.* LVIII, 316-32.
Rocher, G.
'Pour une politique de financement de l'enseignement supérieur au Québec,' *Orient. Prof.* IV, 177-83.

1969 'Bilan d'une réforme,' *Mag. Maclean* VIII (10), 13-19.
Bratley, P.
'Elaboration d'un système informatique de gestion pour les universités du Québec,' *ACFAS* XXXVI, 27.
Dion, G.
'L'Orientation dans un Québec qui cherche à se définir,' *Orient. Prof.* V, 330-38.
Lacombe, T.
'A Study of University Government in the Province of Quebec.' Unpublished M.A. thesis, Carleton Univ.

1970 **Pétolas, J. P.**
'Structures and Procedures for the Determination of Grants to the Universities of the Province of Quebec' in *Studies in the University, Society and Government...* (Ottawa: Univ. of Ottawa Press. 2 vols.), II, 103-36.

BISHOP'S UNIVERSITY

1857 **Bishop's University.**
Historical Sketch of the University of Bishop's College, Established at Lennoxville C. E., Showing its Origin, Progress and Present Condition with a List of Officers, Course of Reading, Terms, etc. Montreal. Pp. 26.

1898 **Adams, T.**
'On the Duties of Universities towards the Community and towards other Educational Institutions,' *Proc. Dominion Educational Assoc.* 1898. 259-72.

1967 **Sheldon, M.**
'Management Training on the Campus,' *Can. Bus.* XL, no. 12, 85-88.

COLLÈGES CLASSIQUES

1903 **Prince, J.-E.**
Le Séminaire de Nicolet, Souvenir des fêtes du centenaire, 1803-1903: recets des fêtes, adresses, discours, poesie, etc. Québec. Pp. 248.

1905 **Roy, J.-E.**
Souvenirs d'une classe au Séminaire de Québec (1867-1877). Lévis. Pp. 41.

1907 **Chapais, T.**
'Souvenirs de Séminaire,' *Nouv.-France* XII, 549-54.

1920 **Auclair, E.-J.**
Un Educateur d'il y a cent ans: M. le curé Charles-Joseph Ducharme, fondateur du Séminaire de Sainte Thérèse. Montréal: Arbour et Dupont. Pp. 30.

Lecompte, E.
Les Jésuites au Canada au XIXe Siécle. I: 1842-1872. Montréal: Pp. 333.

1939 **Caron, I.**
'Collège Classique de St. Roch de Québec,' *Bull. Recherches Hist.* XLV, 97-100.

1942 **Sanssoucy, L.**
'Le Séminaire de St.-Hyacinthe et le renaissance religieuse de 1840 à 1855,' *Can. Cath. Hist. Report* 123-29.

1953 **Letendre, A.**
Album-souvenir du 150ᵉ Anniversaire de fondation de Séminaire de Nicolet. Arthabaska: Imprimerie d'Arthabaska. Pp. 213.
1962 **Levasseur, J. H.**
'The Classical College in Quebec, Canada, 1961.' Unpublished M.A. thesis, Catholic Univ. of America.
1963 **Hurtubise, R.**
'D'une Evolution nécessaire: les collèges classiques et leur intégration,' *Cite Libre* XIV (Mai), 20-24.
1964 **Lebel, Marc**
'Enseignement de la philosophie au Petit Séminaire de Québec (1765-1880),' *Rev. Hist.* XVIII, 405-24, 462-73, 582-93.
Provost, H.
'Le Petit Séminaire de Québec devenu Collège,' *Rev. Univ. Laval* XVIII, 787-80.
1965 **Aganier, H.**
'L'Eglise diocésaine laisse graduellement la direction de l'enseignement classique,' *Prospectives* I (6), 21-23.
Angers, P.
'Les Tâches de l'Eglise dans l'enseignement,' *Prospectives* I (4), 21-61.
Beauchemin, J.-M.
'Le Financement des collèges classiques: un problème immédiat à résoudre,' *Prospectives* I (3), 43-48.
Beauregard, C.
'La Fonction administrative dans les collèges classiques,' *Prospectives* I (6), 34-47.
Doyon, J.
'Pourquoi des institutions privées de l'enseignement?' *Rev. Univ. Sherbrooke* V, 161-66.
'La Fédération des collèges classiques face à l'évolution de notre système d'éducation,' *Prospectives* I (6), 24-33.
'Financing Classical Colleges,'/'Le Financement des collèges classiques,' *Education Weekly* [*Hebdo-éducation*] II, 101-13.
Levesque, U.
'Les Eleves du Collège Ste.-Anne-de-la Pocatière (1829-1842).' Thèse de license, Univ. Laval.
Simard, J. V.
'Les Debuts de Petit Séminaire de Chicoutimi (1871-1875).' Thèse de license, Univ. Laval.

1965 **Vezina, R.**
'La Musique au Petit Séminaire de Québec: la Société Ste-Cecile.'
Thèse de license, Univ. Laval.

1966 **Alexander, W.**
'Les Options et leur choix au cours classiques,' *Orient. Prof.* II, 282-305.
Corbett, R.
'The Classical College of Quebec.' Unpublished M.A. thesis, McGill Univ.
Cousineau, R.
'Effectifs étudiants au cours classiques pour l'année scolaire 1965-66,' *Prospectives* II, 65-69.
'Une Enquête sur la conception de la philosophie dans les collèges classiques,' *Prospectives* II, 129-33.
Galarneau, C.
'Recherches sur l'histoire de l'enseignement secondaire classique au Canada français,' *Rev. Hist.* XX (1), 18-27.
Hervieux, G.
'Les Opérations financières courantes des collèges classiques de 1960 à 1966,' *Prospectives* II, 254-57.
Rogers, G. W.
'The Classical College in Quebec.' Unpublished M.Ed. thesis, Univ. of Toronto.

1967 **Martineau, A.**
'Programme des études au Canada durant la période de 1760-1790,' *Rev. Univ. Ottawa* XXXVII, 206-30.
Plante, Sister L.
'La Fondation de l'enseignement classique féminin au Québec 1908-1926.' Thèse de license en lettres, Univ. Laval.
Provost, H.
'Le Collège' in *Saint-Marie de la Nouvelle Beauce: histoire religieuse* (Québec: Société Historique de la Chaudière), 427-91.

1968 **Levesque, U.**
'Les Elèves du Collège de Sainte-Anne-de-la-Pocatière 1825-1842,' *Rev. Hist.* XXI, 774-91.

UNIVERSITÉ LAVAL

1908 **Burpee, L. C.**
'Canadian Libraries of Long Ago,' *American Library Association Bulletin* II, 136-43.

1941 Maheux, A.
Propos sur l'education. Quebec: Libraire de l'Action Catholique. Pp. 259.

1942 **Université Laval, Faculté des Sciences.**
Liste des Gradués 1907-1942. Québec: L'Université. Pp. 32.

1949 Parent, A.-M.
'Laval Medical School – Quebec,' *Hist. Bull. Calgary Clinic* XIV, 1-5.

1952 Drolet, A.
'La Bibliothèque de l'Université Laval,' *Rev. Univ. Laval* VII, 34-41.
Lemelin, R.
'The Silent Struggle at Laval,' *Maclean's* LXV (15), 10-11, 36-38.

1960 Lafrenière, A.
'Project de réforme des programmes à la faculté des arts de l'Université Laval,' *Univ. Affairs* II (2), 1-2.

1963 Campeau, L.
'Le Séminaire de Québec dans le plan de Monseigneur de Laval,' *Rev. Hist.* XVII, 315-24.
Provost, H.
'Le Séminaire de Québec – premièr logiment, premièr esprit,' *Rev. Univ. Laval* XVII, 787-97.
Vachon, L.-A.
Mémorial de l'histoire du Séminaire de Québec depuis sa fondation en 1663. Quebec: Presses Univ. Laval. Pp. 165.

1964 **Lebel, Marc.**
'Enseignement de la philosophie au Petit Séminaire de Quebec (1765-1880),' *Rev. Hist.* XVIII, 405-24, 582-93; XIX 106-25, 238-54.
Provost, H.
'Le Petit Séminaire de Québec devenu collège,' *Rev. Univ. Laval* XVIII, 787-800.
Provost, H.
Le Séminaire de Québec: documents et biographies. Québec: Archives du Séminaire de Québec. Pp. 542.

1965 Lachance, D.
'Etude sur le journal 'L'Abeille'.' Thèse de license, Univ. Laval.
Lavallée, J.-G.
'Mgr. Antoine Racine, premier évêque de Sherbrooke en 1874, et la question universitaire canadienne,' *Can. Cath. Hist. Report* 43-54.
Pratte, Y.
'The Faculty of Law at Laval University,' *Univ. Tor. Law Jour.* XVI (1), 175-76.

1965 **Provost, H.**
'Le Séminaire de Québec; terrains et construction (1663-1700),'
Rev. Univ. Laval XX, 3-23.
Savard, P.
'Le Journal de l'abbé Benjamine Paquet, étudiant à Rome 1863-1866,'
Culture XXVI, 64-83.
1966 **Bonneau, L.-P.**
'Internal University Government,' *A.U.C.C. Proc.* 74-77.
Université Laval.
Rapport du Comité de Planification. Québec: L'Université. Pp. 250.
1967 **Mackey, W.**
'The International Center for Research on Bilingualism,' *Univ. Affairs*
VIII (4), 1-3.
Provost, H.
'Les Premières Constructions du Séminaire de Québec (1663-1700),'
ACFAS XXX, 101-02 (Resumé).
'Struggle for Progress in the Faculty of Medicine at Laval University/
L'Histoire de l'Université de Laval,' *Can. Med. Stud. Jour.* New Series
I (1), 44-46.
Université Laval.
*Rapport du Comité d'étude des relations entre l'Université Laval, la
Faculté de Médecine, et les hôpitaux d'enseignement.* Quebec:
L'Université. Pp. 245.
1968 **Hamelin, L.-E. and A. Cailleux.**
'"L'Hudsonie," programme de recherches au Centre d'Etudes nordiques
de l'Université Laval,' *Cah. Géog.* XXVI, 277-82.
1969 **Brunet, J.**
'Les Sciences de la santé et le nouveau programme des études à la
Faculté de Médecine de l'Université Laval,' *Can. Med. Assoc. Jour.* C,
653-56.

McGILL UNIVERSITY

1929 **Hussey, C.**
Tait McKenzie: A Sculptor of Youth. London: Country Life Ltd.
Pp. 107.
1930 **Lomer, G. R.**
The University Library: 1920-30. McGill University Publications, Series
VII, no. 24.

1930 **Lomer, G. R.**
The University Library: 1920-30. McGill University Publications, Series VII, no. 24.

1933 **McKenzie, R. T.**
'Reminiscences of James Naismith,' *Journal of Health, Physical Education and Recreation* [U.S.] IV (1), 21, 55.

1938 **McGill University.**
The Installation of Lewis William Douglas as the Principal and Vice-Chancellor of McGill University. Montreal: The University. Pp. 22.

1942 **Lomer, G. R.**
'The Redpath Library: Half a Century, 1892-1942,' *McGill News* XXIV, 9-13.

1944 **Lamb, A. S.**
'Tait McKenzie in Canada,' *Journal of Health, Physical Education and Recreation* [U.S.] XV, 69-70, 85.

1947 **Pearce, C. A.**
'The Development of Special Libraries in Montreal and Toronto.' Unpublished M.L.S. thesis, Univ. of Illinois.

1948 **Berton, P.**
'New Crop on the Campus,' *Maclean's* LXI (22), 8, 60-63.

1949 **Johnson, G. R.**
'McGill University – Medical Faculty,' *Hist. Bull. Calgary Clinic* XIV, 41-47; XV, 1-7.

1956 **Meagher, J. W.**
'Physical Education Teacher Training at McGill: an Historical, Interpretative and Evaluative Study.' Unpublished doct. dissertation, Pennsylvania State Univ.
Peterson, P. L.
'My Heart Belongs to Old McGill,' *Maclean's* LXIX (2), 19, 27-31.
Scarlett, E. P.
'Eastern Gate and Western Cavalcade: Being a Commentary on the Part Played by Men of the Montreal General Hospital and McGill Medical School in the Early Medical History of Western Canada,' *Hist. Bull. Calgary Clinic* XXI, 8-24.

1958 **Penfield, W. G.**
'History of Canadian Surgery: Edward Archibald, 1872-1945,' *Can. Jour. Surgery* I, 167-72.

1961 **Hanson, F.**
'Music at Macdonald,' *Can. Music Educator* II (4), 21-22.

1963 **Bindra, D.**
'Exploring the Newer Technological Aids to Instruction at McGill,' *Univ. Affairs* IV (4), 3-4.
Fenton, A.
'McGill's Graduate School of Business; a Late Starter with a New Idea,' *Can. Bus.* XXXVI (9), 44-47, 52, 54, 57-58, 60.

1964 **Chiffins, R. I.**
'Legal Education at McGill: Some Problems and Proposals,' *McGill Law Jour.* X, 126-57.
Hébert, G.
'L'Université McGill et le Canada français,' *Relations* no. 277, 24-25.
Lee, R. S.
'Legal Implications of McGill's High Altitude Research Project,' *McGill Law Jour.* X, 158-70.

1965 **Nicol, E.**
'Stephen Butler Leacock' in P. Berton, ed., *Great Canadians* (Toronto: McClelland & Stewart), 79-82.
Penfield, W. G.
'Sir William Osler' in P. Berton, ed., *Great Canadians* (Toronto: McClelland & Stewart), 87-90.
Rogers, M. A. *et al.*
'Faculty of Dentistry, McGill University,' *Can. Dent. Assoc. Jour.* XXXI, 311-16.
Worthington, F. F.
'Sir Arthur Currie' in P. Berton, ed., *Great Canadians* (Toronto: McClelland & Stewart), 47-50.

1966 **Tunis, B. L.**
In Caps and Gowns: The Story of the School for Graduate Nurses. McGill University 1920-1964. Montreal: McGill Univ. Press. Pp. 154.

1967 **Garnier, B. J.**
'Climatology at McGill University,' *Climatology Bull.* no. 1, 1-6.
Martin, L.
'Québec est-il injuste pour McGill?' *Mag. Maclean* VII (7), 13, 32-34, 36.
Ridge, A. D.
'The McGill University Archives,' *Archives* [U.K.] VIII (37), 16-23.

1968 **Maas, C. E.**
The Story of the Women's Association of McGill. Montreal: The Association. Pp. 36.

1969 **Buller, H.**
'McGill University and an Aroused Quebec,' *Can. Jewish Outlook* VII (4), 8-11.

1969 **Grey, J.**
'The Paradox of Stanley Gray,' *Can. Dimension* VI (5), 6-9.
Spinks, S.
'Notes on McGill and Sir George,' *This Magazine* III (2), 135-44.
1970 **Morrison, R. N.**
'Back to School: Preparation for Higher Management,' *Can. Bus.* XLIII (5), 48-52.

UNIVERSITÉ DE MONTRÉAL

1885 **Colin, M. L.**
Oraison funèbre de Monsieur Ignace Bourget; prononcée dans l'Eglise de Notre Dame de Montréal, le 12 juin 1885. Montréal. Pp. 26.
1906 **Monier, F.**
Les Origines du Séminaire de St-Sulpice (Conférences données à l'Institut Catholique de Paris en Décembre 1905 et en Janvier 1906). Limoges. Pp. 31.
1922 **Université de Montréal.**
Montreal University; General View. Montréal: L'Université. Pp. 49.
1924 **L'Association des Anciens Elèves de l'Ecole Polytechnique.**
L'Ecole Polytechnique de Montréal; cinquantième anniversaire de fondation, 1873-1923. Montréal. Revue Trimestrielle Canadienne. Pp. 54.
1925 **Maurault, O.**
A Mari Usque ad Mare: Voyage de l'Université de Montréal à Travers le Canada sous la conduite du Pacifique Canadien. Montréal: Univ. de Montréal. Pp. 55.
1933 **Beaugrand-Champagne, R.-P.**
Album-souvenir de l'Université de Montréal. Montréal: Thérien Frères. Pp. 145.
Université de Montréal.
L'Université de Montréal; son oeuvre, son problème financier. Montréal: L'Université. Pp. 15.
1934 **Villeneuve, Cardinal et Monseigneur Gauthier.**
L'Université, ecole de haut savoir et source de directives sociales. Montréal: L'Imprimerie Populaire, collection 'Le Document.' Pp. 24.
1939 **Baudoin, J. A.**
'L'Ecole d'Hygiène sociale appliquée de l'Université de Montréal,' *Rev. Trim. Can.* XXV, 198-216.

1940 **Gowan, Sister M. O.**
'Report of a Survey of L'Ecole d'Hygiene Socíale Appliquée, Université de Montréal, Montreal, Canada, August 19, 20, 21, 1940.' Typewritten manuscript, Catholic University of America, Washington, D.C.

1941 **Baril, G.**
La Faculté des Sciences: vingtième anniversaire de sa fondation (20 avril 1941). *ACFAS* VII, 179-220.

1942 **Université de Montréal.**
'L'Inauguration de l'Université,' *Act. Univ.* IX (1). Pp. 92.

1944 **Université de Montréal.**
'L'Université et le monde de demain,' *Act. Univ.* XI (2). Pp. 68.

1945 **Brunet, J.** *et al.*
'Hommage à l'oeuvre du Frère Marie-Victoria,' *Act. Univ.* XI (6), 2-19.
'Hommage à l'Université de Montréal à l'occasion de son vingt-cinquième anniversaire d'autonomie,' *Act. Univ.* XI (10). Pp. 132.

1947 **Pearce, C. A.**
'The Development of Special Libraries in Montreal and Toronto.' Unpublished M.L.S. thesis, Univ. of Illinois.

1952 **Groulx, L.**
'Henri Bourassa et la Chaire d'histoire du Canada à l'Université de Montréal,' *Rev. Hist.* III, 430-39.

1956 **Lussier, I.**
L'Université de Montréal, votre affaire. Montréal: Pierre DesMarais. Pp. 21.

1957 **Dufresne, R. R.**
'La Faculté de Médecine de l'Université de Montréal,' *Médecine de France* LXXXVII, 3-6. Voir aussi 7-8 (W. Bonn, 'L'Enseignement') et 9-11 (E. Desjardines, 'Deux Personalités de la Médecine à Montréal: Joseph-Edmund Dubé [1868-1939] et Albert LeSage [1869-1954]').

1959 **Lefoli, K.**
'The College Where Joe College Wouldn't Fit,' *Maclean's* LXXII (20), 26-27, 60-64.

1962 **Association des Professeurs de l'Université de Montréal.**
'Mémoire à la Commission Royale d'enquête sur l'enseignement.' Unpublished typescript. L'Association. Pp. 176.
Université de Montréal.
Réponses au questionnaire de la Sacrée Congrégation des Séminaires et études universitaires; dans les cadres d'une étude statistico-historique sur toutes les universités dépendant du St-Siège. Montréal: L'Université. Pp. 16.

1964　**Desrochers, R. D.**
'Laboratoire de physique nucléaire à l'Université de Montréal,' *Ing.* L (201), 58-64.
Gagnon, C.
'L'Université, milieu bourgeois,' *Cité Libre* LXV, 12-19.
Langis, J.
'Les Debuts de St-Sulpice à Montréal (1657-1688),' *Can. Cath. Hist. Report* 15-22.
Meyer, J.
'L'Ecole [des Hautes Etudes Commerciales]: An Academic Answer to Quebec's Needs,' *Executive* VI (11), 50-55.

1965　**Audet, L.-P.**
'La Fondation de l'Ecole Polytechnique de Montréal,' *Cah. Dix.* 149-91.
Lavallée, J.-G.
'Mgr Antoine Racine, premier évêque de Sherbrooke en 1874, et la question universitaire canadienne,' *Can. Cath. Hist. Report* 43-54.
Lussier, J.-P.
'La Faculté de chirurgie dentaire de l'Université de Montréal,' *Can. Dent. Assoc. Jour.* XXXI, 317-23. Also in English 324-29.
Rioux, B.
'Déconfessionnalisation et démocratisation de l'Université de Montréal,' *Cité Libre* LXXIV, 21-25.

1966　'A l'Ecole de bibliothéconomie de l'Université de Montréal,' *Bull. Bibl.* XII, 72-76.
Association Générale des Étudiants de l'Université de Montréal [AGEUM].
Votre Avenir commence à l'université. Montreal: Editions du Jour. Pp. 191.
Gagnon, L.
'L'Université de Montréal de demain,' *Le Magazine de 'La Presse'* 12 février, 14-17.
Université de Montréal.
Discours pronouncé par Monsieur Roger Gaudry, Recteur de l'Université de Montreal à l'occasion de son investiture solennelle et allocution de chancellier son Eminence le cardinal Paul-Emile Leger. Montréal: Presses Univ. Montréal. Pp. 27.

1967　**Durand, M.**
Bibliothèque de la Faculté des Sciences de l'Education. Montréal: Université de Montréal. Pp. 61.

1967 **Messier, J. A.**
'Ecole d'Optométrie, Université de Montréal,' *Can. Jour. Optometry* XXIX, 99-105.
Rumilly, R.
Histoire de l'Ecole des Hautes Etudes Commerciales de Montréal. Montréal: Beauchemin. Pp. 215.

1968 'Campagne de cinquantenaire de l'Université de Montréal,' *Ing.* LIV (236), 29-30.
Denis, L.-G.
'A l'Ecole de bibliothéconomie. Le nouveau programme ... deux ans après son instauration,' *Bull. Bibl.* XIV, 139-41.
Denis, L.-G.
'La Formation des bibliothécaires de langue française du Quêbec' in B. Peel, ed., *Librarianship in Canada, 1946-1967* (Victoria, B.C.: Can. Library Assoc.), 149-62.
Diplômés de l'Université de Montréal.
Les Investissements universitaires; planification et coordination. Montréal: Editions du Jour. Pp. 155.
Lapointe, S.
'Recherche post-gradué à l'Université de Montréal,' *Physics in Canada* XXIV (2), 18-24.
Van der Bellen, L.
'Nouvelles des Ecoles de bibliothéconomie, Université de Montreal: quelques statistiques,' *Bull. Bibl.* XIV, 133-36; XV, 180-84.

1969 **Lanctôt, B.**
'Ecole Polytechnique, Operation "Choix de Matières,"' *Ing.* LV (247), 20-25.
Lauzon, A.
'L'Université remise en question,' *Mag. Maclean* VIII (10), 21, 63-66, 69.

1970 **Université de Montréal.**
Les Etudiants et leurs préoccupations: annexes au Rapport de la Commission Conjointe du Conseil et de l'Assemblée Universitaire, Université de Montréal. Montréal: Presses Univ. Montréal. Pp. 334.

UNIVERSITÉ DU QUÉBEC

1967 **Gingras, R.-E.**
'A Quand la deuxième Université?' *Relations* no. 321, 286-88.

1969 **Dorais, L.**
'Universités nouvelles, nouvelle Université,' *Forces* IX (Automne), 17-27.
Lamarche, S.
L'Université du Québec. Montreal: Collection du CEP. Pp. 174.
Pierre, G. E.
'L'Université du Québec,' *Can. Univ. and Coll.* IV (6), 26-29, 43.
'L'Université du Québec; une proposition de la Société Générale des Systèmes Urbains,' *Architecture* XXIII (271), 12-18.
1970 **Dumas, M.**
'L'Université du Québec, une université pas comme les autres,' *Actualité* Mai 1970, 22-25.

UNIVERSITÉ DE SHERBROOKE

1955 'L'Université de Sherbrooke' in *Annaire Général* I (1955), 11-26.
1964 **Crepeau, R.**
'La Faculté de Droit de l'Université de Sherbrooke,' *Univ. Tor. Law Jour.* XV, 436-37.
1967 **Beauregard, M.**
'A New School of Medicine is Born in Quebec,' *Can. Med. Assoc. Jour.* XCVI, 1031-35.
'Co-operative Education – How Good Is It?' *Can. Bus.* XL (10), 52-58.
1968 **Lapalme, M.**
'Sherbrooke sort de l'ombre,' *Mag. Maclean* VIII (5), 20-23, 69-72, 74.
1969 **LeClair, M. A., A. Trias and M. L. Munam.**
'The Medical School of Sherbrooke and the Undergraduate Education,' *Can. Med. Assoc. Jour.* C, 657-58.

SIR GEORGE WILLIAMS UNIVERSITY

1956 **Stephenson, B.**
'The College that's for Everyone,' *Maclean's* LXIX (10), 34-40.
1967 **Hall, H.**
The Georgian Spirit: The Story of Sir George William University. Montreal: Sir George William Univ. Pp. 138.
'One Building Campus,' *Can. Univ.* II (1), 38-42.
1969 **Compton, N.**
'Sir George Williams Loses its Innocence,' *Can. Forum* XLIX, 2-4.

1969 **Desbarets, P.**
'Sir George Williams: A Dossier,' *Mon. Morn.* III (7), 17-19.
Eber, D.
The Computer Centre Party ... Part I. Montreal: Tundra Books. Pp. 318.
McIntyre, H. C.
'The Sir George Williams Story,' *Can. Univ. and Coll.* IV (4), 48-53.
Sheps, G. D.
'The Apocalyptic Fires at Sir George Williams University,' *Can. Dimension* V (8), 6-7, 52-53.
Spinks, S.
'Notes on McGill and Sir George,' *This Magazine* III (2), 135-44.

D. THE UNIVERSITIES OF ONTARIO :
LES UNIVERSITÉS DE L'ONTARIO

1869 The College Question; being the Debate of the Legislative Assembly of Ontario, on December 2, 1868, on the Outlying Colleges and Sectarian Grants. Reported by J. K. Edwards. Toronto. Pp. 84.
1964 **Ontario Council of University Faculty Associations.**
'University Education in Ontario: A Brief Prepared for Presentation to the Prime Minister of Ontario,' *C.A.U.T. Bull.* XII (3), 10-41.
Smith, D.
'Current Comment: University Grants,' *Can. Forum* XLIII, 268-70.
1965 **Drummond, I. M.**
'Current Comment: On University Federation,' *Can. Forum* XLIV, 219-20.
Harris, R. S.
'The Universities of Ontario,' *Can. Geog. Jour.* LXX, 2-19.
1966 **Bissell, C. T.**
'Ontario' in R. S. Harris, ed., *Changing Patterns of Higher Education in Canada* (Toronto: U. of T. Press), 87-106.
Committee of Presidents of Universities of Ontario.
From the Sixties to the Seventies: an Appraisal of Higher Education in Ontario by the Presidents' Research Committee. Toronto: The Committee. Pp. 101.
Committee of Presidents of Universities of Ontario. Presidents' Research Committee.
The Health Sciences in Ontario Universities: Recent Experience and Prospects for the Next Decade. Toronto: The Committee. Pp. 26.

1966 **Dadson, D. F., ed.**
On Higher Education: Five Lectures. Toronto: U. of T. Press. Pp. 149. Includes R. S. Harris, 'The Establishment of a Provincial University in Ontario' (3-35) and 'The Evolution of a Provincial System of Higher Education in Ontario' (36-62); F. C. A. Jeanneret, 'The Contribution of Sir Robert Falconer to Higher Education' (63-85).
Harris, R. S., C. Allen and M. Lewis.
A List of Reports to the Legislature of Ontario Bearing on Higher Education in the Province. Toronto: Innis College. Pp. 17.
Harris, R. S., C. Allen and M. Lewis.
An Annotated List of the Legislative Acts Concerning Higher Education in Ontario. Toronto: Innis College. Pp. 79.
Watson, C. and S. Quazi.
Ontario School and University Enrolment Projections to 1981-82. Toronto: Ontario Institute for Studies in Education. Pp. 68. (Projection Series no. 1, 1966.)

1967 **Committee of Presidents of Universities of Ontario.**
System Emerging: First Annual Review (1966-67). Toronto: The Committee. Pp. 59.
Watson, C., S. Quazi and S. Burnham.
Ontario Secondary School Enrolment Projections to 1981-82. Toronto: Ontario Institute for Studies in Education. Pp. 117. (O.I.S.E. Projections Series, no. 2.)

1968 **Committee of Presidents of Universities of Ontario.**
Collective Autonomy: Second Annual Review (1967-68). Toronto: The Committee. Pp. 68.

1969 **Committee of Presidents of Universities of Ontario.**
Campus and Forum: Third Annual Review, 1968-69. Toronto: The Committee. Pp. 75.

1970 **Stewart, E. E.**
'The Role of the Provincial Government in the Development of Universities in Ontario 1791-1964.' Unpublished doct. dissertation, Univ. of Toronto.

BROCK UNIVERSITY

1964 **Hart, J.**
'Brock University,' *Sch. Prog.* XXXIII (7), 41-43.

1965 **Gibson, J. A.**
Springtime for Universities. Address at Annual Education Night ... Niagara Falls, April 26, 1965. St. Catharines: Brock Univ. Pp. 10.

1969 'Brock Stresses Interdisciplinary Relationships,' *Chem. Can.* XXI (6), 37-38.
Carroll, J.
'What a Way to Study,' *Weekend Magazine* XIX (30), 10-11.

CARLETON UNIVERSITY

1953 **Pickersgill, J. W.**
Address at the Official Opening of the School of Public Administration, Carleton College, Ottawa, October 23, 1953. Ottawa: Carleton College. Pp. 17

1954 **Carleton College.**
A Summary Report on Graduates of Carleton College, 1946-53. Ottawa: Carleton College. Pp. 61.
MacFarlane, R. O.
'Specialized Education for Public Administration,' *Proc. Inst. Pub. Admin.* 301-06.

1958 **Dunton, A. D.**
Knowledge and Freedom. Address at his Installation as Fourth President of Carleton University. Ottawa: Carleton Univ. Pp. 13.

1963 **Gifford, H.**
'The MacOdrum Library of Carleton University,' *College and Research Libraries* [U.S.] XXIV, 43-46.

1964 **Abbott, R. D.**
'Legal Studies at Carleton University,' *Canadian Legal Studies* I (2), 71-74.

1969 **Carleton University.**
Goals and Requirements to 1975. Ottawa: The University. Pp. 82. Also *October 1969 Revisions*, pp. 42.
Carleton University.
Commission on Undergraduate Teaching and Learning in the Faculty of Arts. Chairman: M. Frumhartz. *Preliminary Report.* Ottawa: The University. Pp. 60.
Robbins, J. E.
Convocation Address [on the 25th anniversary of the first Carleton convocation] *Carleton University, Nov. 7, 1969.* Ottawa: The University. Pp. 8.

UNIVERSITY OF GUELPH

1949 *Ontario Agricultural College 1874-1949: Proceedings of the Celebration of the Seventy-Fifth Anniversary June 18, 1949.* Guelph: The College. Pp. 27.

1964 **Shaw, E. C.**
'An Analytical Study of the Correspondence Courses Conducted by the Ontario Agricultural College, Guelph, Ontario.' Unpublished M.Sc. thesis, Univ. of Toronto.
1965 **University of Guelph.**
Arts 1. Building Program and Brief to the Architect. Guelph: The University. Pp. 62.
University of Guelph.
Space Utilization and Programming. Toronto: Project Planning Associates. Pp. 102.
'University of Guelph.' Special Issue, *The Guelph Daily Mercury*, Tuesday, November 30, 1965. Pp. 32.
1966 **Ontario Institute for Studies in Education and The University of Guelph.**
The Students of the 1966 Spring Admission Programme at the University of Guelph: Who are They? Why did They Come? The Guelph Spring Admission Research Project: Study no. 1. Guelph: Univ. of Guelph. Pp. 81.
1969 'Guelph's "New Look" in Chemistry,' *Chem. Can.* XXI (2), 27-28.

LAKEHEAD UNIVERSITY

1966 **Ballantyne, P. M.**
'A History of Lakehead University: Lakehead Technical Institute 1947-1956, Lakehead College of Arts, Science and Technology, 1957-1965, Lakehead University 1966.' Mimeographed. [Only copies available at Lakehead University Library.]
'Part-time Faculties for Smaller Colleges?' *Can. Univ.* I (2), 37-38.

LAURENTIAN UNIVERSITY OF SUDBURY :
UNIVERSITÉ LAURENTIENNE DE SUDBURY

1938 **Plante, A.**
Vingt-cinq ans de vie française: Le Collège de Sudbury. Montréal: Imprimerie du Messager. Pp. 151.
1968 **Farrant, R. H. and G. Thibaudeau.**
'L'Enseignement de la psychologie [à l'Université Laurentienne]' *Can. Psych.* IX (1), 1-5.
1969 **Black, J. L.**
'Slavic Studies at Laurentian University,' *New Rev.* IX, 301-05.

McMASTER UNIVERSITY

1927 **Van Pratten, N.**
'College and University Libraries of Ontario,' *Library Jour.* [U.S.] LII, 457-61.

1959 **Hale, C.**
'Keep Your Eye on McMaster,' *Can. Bus.* XXXII (8), 50-52.

1964 **Siddall, J. N.**
'McMaster Course Faces Design's Future,' *Design Eng.* X (3), 40-41.

1967 **Kirkconnell, W.**
A Slice of Canada: Memoirs. Toronto: U. of T. Press. Pp. 393.

1969 'New Biochemistry Department Expands at McMaster,' *Chem. Can.* XXI (1), 8-9.
Ready, W.
'McMaster's Acquisition of the Russell Papers,' *Can. Lib. Jour.* XXVI, 136-39.
Spaulding, W. B.
'The Undergraduate Medical Curriculum (1969 Model): McMaster University.' *Can. Med. Assoc. Jour.* C, 659-64.

1970 'McMaster Health Sciences Center,' *Hosp. Admin. in Canada* XII (2), 26-30.

UNIVERSITY OF OTTAWA : UNIVERSITÉ D'OTTAWA

1927 **Van Pratten, N.**
'College and University Libraries of Ontario,' *Library Jour.* [U.S.] LII, 457-61.

1949 **La Framboise, J.-C.**
'A l'Aube d'un second siècle,' *Rev. Univ. Ottawa* XIX, 19-45.

1957 **Carrière, G.**
Histoire documentaire de la Congrégation des Missionaires Oblats de Marie-Immacultée dans l'Est du Canada. Ottawa: Editions Univ. d'Ottawa. 8 vols. (to 1969).

1964 **Carrière, G.**
'Trois Quarts de siècle au service des sciences sacrées (1889-1964),' *Rev. Univ. Ottawa* XXXIV, 234-38.

1965 **Guindon, R.**
'L'Université d'Ottawa (une nouvelle charte),' *Relations* no. 296, 224-25.

1965 Paul VI (S. S.)
'Lettre au chancelier de l'Université d'Ottawa,' *Rev. Univ. Ottawa* xxxv, 133-35.
1966 **Carrière, G.**
'En Marge d'un centenaire: la charte de l'Université d'Ottawa (15 Août, 1866.),' *Rev. Univ. Ottawa* xxxvi, 393-407.
1967 **Carrière, G.**
'A la Mémoire d'un grand educateur: le père Phillipe Cornellier,' *Rev. Univ. Ottawa* xxxvii, 5-10.
1968 **Isabelle, L.**
'La Psychologie à l'Université d'Ottawa,' *Can. Psych.* ix (1), 6-12.
Morisset, A.-M.
'Nouvelles des Ecoles de bibliothéconomie, Université d'Ottawa: quelques statistiques,' *Bull. Bibl.* xiv, 137-18; xv, 185-86.
'Physics at the University of Ottawa,' *Physics in Canada* xxiv (4), 13-17.

QUEEN'S UNIVERSITY

1841 **Mowat, J.**
Queen's University. Incidents Related by John Mowat, One of the Founders, in Reference to its Early History. Kingston. Pp. 6.
1845 *Report of the Discussion of the Disruption ... Which Took Place in St. Andrew's Church, Galt, May 27, 1845, Between Rev. Princ. Liddell, of Queen's College, Kingston, and the Rev. John Bayne.* Galt. Pp. 60.
Thoughts on the University Question, Respectfully Submitted to the Members of Both Houses of the Legislature of Canada, by a Master of Arts. Kingston. Pp. 36.
The University Question Considered: by a Graduate. Toronto. Pp. 67.
1892 **Grant, G. M.**
Speech by Rev. Principal Grant to the General Assembly on the Relation of Queen's University to the Church. Toronto. Pp. 16.
1896 **Bell, J. J.**
'Queen's University and its Founders,' *The Canadian Magazine* vii, 19-27.
1901 **Glover, T. R.**
'Symposium on the "University Question,"' *Queen's Q.* viii, 257-68.
Grant, G. M.
'The University Question,' *Queen's Q.* viii, 211-20.

1902   **Chown, A. A.**
'The Women's Residence,' *Queen's Q.* x, 80-83.
Macdonald, J. A.
The Message of a Strenuous Life: In Memoriam the Very Rev. George Munro Grant. A Sermon Preached at the Memorial Service in St. Andrew's Church, Toronto, May 18, 1902. Toronto. Pp. 16.
Queen's Journal.
Queen's University Journal Memorial Number, [*for Principal Grant*] November 6, 1902. Kingston. Pp. 74.

1903   **Gordon, D. M.**
'The Functions of a Modern University (An Address by Principal Gordon to the University Council of Queen's),' *Queen's Q.* x, 487-97.

1904   **Gordon, D. M.**
'The Installation Address of Principal Gordon,' *Queen's Q.* xi, 318-25.

1908   **Cappon, J.**
'The Case of Queen's Before the Assembly,' *Queen's Q.* xvi, 98-115.

1910   **Cappon, J.**
'The Situation in Queen's,' *Queen's Q.* xvii, 193-211.

1916   **Shortt, E. S.**
Historical Sketch of Medical Education of Women in Kingston. Ottawa. Pp. 13.

1919   **Taylor, R. B.**
'Inaugural Address' (as Principal of Queen's University), *Queen's Q.* xxvii, 125-46.

1927   **Van Pratten, N.**
'College and University Libraries of Ontario,' *Library Jour.* [U.S.] lii, 457-61.

1928   **Gibson, T.**
'Notes on the Medical History of Kingston,' *Can. Med. Assoc. Jour.* xviii, 331-34, 446-51.

1930   **Fyfe, W. H.**
Inaugural Address of William Hamilton Fyfe on the Occasion of his Installation as Principal and Vice-Chancellor of Queen's University: Grant Hall, Queen's University, Friday, October 24th, 1930. Kingston: Queen's Univ. Pp. 4.

1936   **Wallace, R. C.**
Inaugural Address of Robert Charles Wallace on the Occasion of his Installation as Principal and Vice-Chancellor of Queen's University: Grant Hall, Queen's University, Friday, October 9th, 1936. Kingston: Queen's Univ. Pp. 8.

1941 **McNeill, W. E.**
The Story of Queen's; an Address Delivered on Student and Alumni Day, Queen's University Centenary Celebration, Oct. 16-18, 1941. Kingston: Queen's Univ. Pp. 16.

1948 **Connell, W. T.**
'The Medical Faculty, Queen's University,' *Hist. Bull. Calgary Clinic* XIII, 45-50.

1950 'Queen's University: 110 Years of Service to Canada Through Education,' Special Supplement of *The Whig-Standard.* October 6, 1950. Pp. 38.

1951 **Queen's University.**
The Proceedings on the Occasion of the Installation of William Archibald Mackintosh as Twelfth Principal of Queen's University, Kingston, Ontario, Friday, October 19th, 1951. Kingston: Queen's Univ. Pp. 50.

1954 **Robertson, J. K.**
'An Experiment in Medical Education [at Queen's Univ.]' *British Jour. Radiology* XXVII, 593-603.

1961 **Millett, F. B.**
Professor. New York: Macmillan. Pp. 189.

1964 'Kingston and Its Universities,' *Chem. Can.* XVI (2), 41-44.
'Queen's University Century II,' *Kingston Whig-Standard* (Souvenir Edition), October 16, 1964. Pp. 48.

1965 **Davies, R.**
'George Monro Grant' in P. Berton, ed., *Great Canadians* (Toronto: McClelland & Stewart), 71-74.
MacKintosh, W. A.
'O. D. Skelton' in R. L. McDougall, ed., *Canada's Past and Present: a Dialogue* [Our Living Tradition: Fifth Series] (Toronto: U. of T. Press), 59-77.
Queen's University, Alumnae Association.
Queen's University Alumnae Association, 1900-1961 and Women's Residences at Queen's. Edited by Mary McPhail Chown. Kingston: Queen's Univ. Pp. 73.

1966 **Beschel, R. E.**
A History of the Biology Department and the Fowler Herbarium of Queen's University. Summarized for the Opening of Earl Hall on May 19, 1966. Kingston: Queen's Univ. Pp. 14.
Beschel, R. E.
'Some Early History of the Biology Department,' *Queen's Review* XL (4), 92-99.

1966 **Ferguson, K.**
'George Dalrymple Ferguson: First Professor of History at Queen's University,' *Historic Kingston* XIV, 51-66.
Thistle, M.
The Inner Ring: The Early History of the National Research Council of Canada. Toronto: U. of T. Press. Pp. 435. [Particularly 45-74.]

1967 **Conkie, W. R. and J. H. Montague.**
'Research in Physics at Queen's University,' *Physics in Canada* XXIV (6), 17-22.
Gundy, H. P.
Queen's University. Kingston: Queen's Univ. Alumni Office. Pp. 87.
Kirkconnell, W.
A Slice of Canada: Memoirs. Toronto: U. of T. Press. Pp. 393. [Particularly 148-71.]
Lower, A. R. M.
My First Seventy-Five Years. Toronto: Macmillan. Pp. 384. [Particularly 312-29.]
'Sir John A. Macdonald and Queen's,' *Queen's Univ. Alumni Review* XLI (5), 110-20.

1968 **Downee, J.**
'Chemical Engineering Developments at Queen's,' *Chem. Can.* XX (2), 30-31.
Henderson, G. F.
'The Royal Commission Collection at Queen's University Library,' *Douglas Library Notes* XVI (3), 20-23.
Trotter, B.
Queen's University, 1963-1968: Some Facts and Figures. Kingston: Queen's Univ., Office of Academic Planning. Pp. 45.

1969 **Deutsch, J. J.**
'The Role of a Changing University in a Changing Society,' *Queen's Q.* LXXVI, 392-400.
Queen's University.
University Government at Queen's: Report of the Committee on Structure of the Senate. Kingston: Queen's Univ. Pp. 28.
Soberman, D. A.
'The Faculty of Law of Queen's University,' *Univ. Tor. Law Jour.* XIX, 420-23.

1970 **Corry, J. A.**
Farewell the Ivory Tower: Universities in Transition. Montreal: McGill-Queen's Univ. Press. Pp. 121.

1970 **Queen's University, Principal's Committee on Teaching and Learning**
(G. A. Harrower, Chairman).
Report of... Kingston: Queen's Univ. Pp. 83.

ROYAL MILITARY COLLEGE

1964 'Kingston and Its Universities,' *Chem. Can.* XVI (2), 41-44.
1966 **Ferguson, K.**
'George Dalrymple Ferguson: First Professor of History at Queen's University,' *Historic Kingston* XIV, 51-66.
1967 **Preston, R. A.**
Canada and Imperial Defence. Toronto: U. of T. Press. Pp. 576.
Preston, Adrian.
'The Founding of the Royal Military College,' *Queen's Q.* LXXIV, 398-412.
1968 **McArthur, N. M.**
'The Canadian Military Colleges,' *Can. Geog. Jour.* LXXVIII, 95-107.
Preston, R. A.
'R.M.C. and Kingston: The Effect of Imperial and Military Influences on a Canadian Community,' *Ont. Hist.* LX, 105-23.
1969 **Preston, R. A.**
Canada's R.M.C.: the History of the Royal Military College. Toronto: U. of T. Press. Pp. 415.

UNIVERSITY OF TORONTO

1891 **Wilson, D.**
Address at the Convocation of Faculties of the University of Toronto and University College, October 5th, 1891. Toronto. Pp. 20.
1892 **Fraser, W. H.**
Pass French and German in the University of Toronto. Paper read before Modern Language Assoc. of Toronto, April 20, 1892. Toronto. Pp. 15.
1897 **Ross, G. W.**
Speech by the Hon. G. W. Ross LL.D., Minister of Education on the Policy of the Education Department Delivered in the Legislative Assembly March 4, 1897. Toronto. Pp. 27.
1906 **Whitney, J. P.**
Speech Delivered on Moving the Legislative Assembly into Committee on the Bill Respecting the University of Toronto and University College on the second of May, 1906. Toronto. Pp. 34.

1909 **Stock, V.**
A Review of the Whitney Government's Educational Policy: Speech of Valentine Stock, M.P.P. for South Perth Delivered March 10, 1909 in the Ontario Legislature. Toronto. Pp. 15.

1927 **Van Pratten, N.**
'College and University Libraries of Ontario,' *Library Jour.* [U.S.] LII, 457-61.

1943 **Dibrick, H.**
'The Old Days at Toronto: Further Reminiscences concerning Faculty Members of the Medical School of the University of Toronto at the Turn of the Century,' *Hist. Bull. Calgary Clinic* VII (4), 6-9.

1948 **Anglin, G.**
'Lifesaver in a Lab Coat,' [C. H. Best] *Maclean's* LXI (11), 17-18, 38, 41-42.

Clarkson, F. A.
'The Medical Faculty of the University of Toronto,' *Hist. Bull. Calgary Clinic* XIII, 21-30.

1952 **Callwood, J.**
'Biggest Man on the Biggest Campus,' [Sidney E. Smith] *Maclean's* LXV (9), 7-9, 52-55.

Cameron, M. H. V.
'Medical Education in Toronto,' *Hist. Bull. Calgary Clinic* XVII, 71-74.

1953 **Foster, M.**
The First Fifty Years: A History of the University Women's Club of Toronto, 1903-1953. Toronto: Hunter Rose. Pp. 50.

1955 **Ferns, H. S. and B. Ostrey.**
The Age of MacKenzie King: The Rise of the Leader. London: Heinemann. Pp. 356. [Particularly 7-29.]

1959 **Moon, B.**
'The University of Toronto: Can It Survive Sheer Size?' *Maclean's* LXXII (9), 18-20, 55-58.

1960 **McCorkell, E. J.**
'The Spirit of the Pontifical Institute,' *Bas. Teacher* V, 37-40.

1962 **Hamilton, J. D.**
'The Future of Medical Education at the University of Toronto,' *Med. Grad.* VIII (1), 2-9.

Harris, C. W.
'William Thomas Atkins, Professor of Surgery, Toronto School of Medicine; First Dean, Faculty of Medicine, University of Toronto,' *Can. Jour. Surgery* V, 131-37.

1962 'Porte Dauphine: Great Lakes Investigator,' *Can. Geog. Jour.* LXV, 170-73.
1963 **Samuel, S.**
In Return: the Autobiography of Sigmund Samuel. Toronto: U. of T. Press. Pp. 166.
Williams, E. E.
'The Significance of a Millionth Item,' *Can. Library* XIX, 364-69.
1964 **Frye, H. N. and R. Daniells.**
'Recollections of E. J. Pratt,' *Can. Lit.* No. 21, 6-12.
McCorkell, E. J.
'Federation: The Legacy of Father Carr,' *Bas. Teacher* VIII, 301-07.
McIlwraith, T. F.
'Sir Daniel Wilson: A Canadian Anthropologist of One Hundred Years Ago,' *Trans. R.S.C. Sect.* II, 129-36.
Shook, L. K.
'Father Carr: Educator, Superior, Friend,' *Bas. Teacher* VIII, 291-300.
Walker, G. C.
'The Faculty of Pharmacy, University of Toronto,' *Amer. Jour. Pharm. Ed.* XXVIII, 360-77.
Williams, D. C. *et al.*
'University of Toronto – Scarborough College,' *R. Arch. Inst. Can. Jour.* XLI (7), 61-66.
1965 **Bertin, L.**
'Sir Frederick Banting' in P. Berton, ed., *Great Canadians* (Toronto: McClelland & Stewart), 23-26.
Creighton, D. G.
'Harold Adams Innis' in P. Berton, ed., *Great Canadians* (Toronto: McClelland & Stewart), 75-78.
Ellis, R. G.
'Faculty of Dentistry, University of Toronto,' *Can. Dent. Assoc. Jour.* XXXI, 330-37.
Hanley, C.
'The Toronto Teach-In,' *Can. Forum* XLV, 130-31.
Pape, A.
'Teach-In as Institution,' *Can. Forum* XLV, 178.
Pilisuk, M.
'The Evolution of the Teach-In,' *Can. Forum* XLV, 176-77.
Reaney, J.
'E. J. "Ned" Pratt' in P. Berton, ed., *Great Canadians* (Toronto: McClelland & Stewart), 91-94.

1965 Wickens, G. M.
'Islamic Studies at the University of Toronto,' *Modern Lang. Jour.* [U.S.] XLIX, 312-13.

1966 Bissell, C. T.
'A Proposal for University Government at the University of Toronto,' *C.A.U.T. Bulletin* XV (2), 42-46.

Bissell, C. T.
'Internal University Government,' *A.U.C.C. Proc.* 67-73.

Clarkson, S. and A. Rotstein.
'China Teach-In: The Ivory Microphone,' *Can. Forum* XLVI, 176-78.

Cohen, R.
'H. M. McLuhan's Centre for Culture and Technology,' *Can. Univ.* I (2), 33-34, 46.

Craigie, E. H.
A History of the Department of Zoology of the University of Toronto up to 1912. Toronto: U. of T. Press. Pp. 108.

Godfrey, C. M.
'Trinity Medical School,' *App. Therapeutics* VIII, 1024-28.

Jeanneret, F. C. A.
'The Contribution of Sir Robert Falconer to Higher Education' in D. F. Dadson, ed., *On Higher Education: Five Lectures* (Toronto: U. of T. Press), 63-85.

Land, R. B.
'University of Toronto School of Library Science,' *Can. Library* XXII, 223-25.

Spragge, G. W.
'The Trinity Medical College,' *Ont. Hist.* LVIII (2), 63-98.

Trigger, B. G.
'Sir Daniel Wilson: Canada's First Anthropologist,' *Anthropologica* (New Series) VII (1), 3-28.

Wasteneys, H.
'A Brief History of the Faculty of Medicine,' *Med. Grad.* XII (3), 6-7, 13.

1967 Godfrey, C. M.
'King's College: Upper Canada's First Medical School,' *Ont. Med. Rev.* XXXIV, 19-22, 26.

Heard, J. F. and H. S. Hogg.
'Astronomy at the David Dunlop Observatory,' *R. Astron. Soc. Jour.* LXI, 257-76.

1967 **Humphries, C. W.**
'James P. Whitney and the University of Toronto' in M. Zaslow, ed., *Profiles of a Province* (Toronto: Ontario Historical Society), 118-25.
Lower, A. R. M.
'My Winter Education' in *My First Seventy-Five Years* (Toronto: Macmillan), 41-60.
Snowland, C. P.
'A Day in the Life of a University,' *Maclean's* LXXX (11), 11-13, 44-48.
'University of Toronto Humanities and Social Sciences Research Library,' *Can. Library* XXIV, 25-28.

1968 **James, L.**
'Will Scarborough College "Flunk Out?"' [re Adult Education] *Continuous Learning* VII (5), 198-202.
Rotstein, A.
'The Makings of a President,' *Can. Forum* XLVIII, 124-27.
Ruth, Sister.
'Henry Carr, C.S.B., 1880-1963, Canadian Educator.' Unpublished M.Ed. thesis, Univ. of Saskatchewan.

1969 **Chipman, M. L., G. G. Clarke and J. W. Steiner.**
'Career Choice Within Medicine: A Study of One Graduating Class at the University of Toronto,' *Can. Med. Assoc. Jour.* CI, 646-51.
Defries, R. D.
The First Forty Years, 1914-1955: Connaught Medical Research Laboratories, University of Toronto. Toronto: U. of T. Press. Pp. 342.
Marshall, J.
'Major Issues in Library Education: Toronto's Approach to its New Program,' *Sask. Lib.* XXIII (1), 3-15.
McCorkell, E. J.
Henry Carr, Revolutionary. Toronto: Griffin Press. Pp. 161.
Montagnes, I.
An Uncommon Fellowship: the Story of Hart House. Toronto: U. of T. Press. Pp. 203.

1970 **Beatty, J. D.**
'History of Medical Education in Toronto,' *Univ. of Toronto Med. Jour.* XLVII, 152-57.
Carpenter, H. M.
'The University of Toronto School of Nursing: an Agent of Change' in M. Q. Innis, ed., *Nursing Education in a Changing Society* (Toronto: U. of T. Press), 86-108.

1970 **How, H. R.**
'Ferment and Transition at U. of T.,' *Can. Bus.* XLIII (3), 60-66.
Milnes, H.
'University College, Toronto, as an Art Gallery,' *Univ. Windsor Rev.* V (2), 11-26.
University of Toronto Commission on the Government of the University of Toronto.
Toward Community in University Government. Toronto: U. of T. Press. Pp. 240.

TRENT UNIVERSITY

1964 **Smith, D.**
'Trent University Prepares for First Classes,' *Sch. Prog.* XXXIII (7), 39-40.
1965 **Trent University.**
Official Opening Ceremonies. 17-18 October, 1964. Peterborough: Trent Univ. Pp. 23.
1966 **Symons, T. H. B.**
'Trent University' in R. Borg, *Peterborough, Land of Shining Waters: an Anthology* (Peterborough: Centennial Committee for the City and County of Peterborough), 493-509.
1967 **Thom, R. J. and M. Yolles.**
'Champlain College, Trent University,' *Can. Arch.* XLIV (12), 26-38.
1969 **Erickson, A., R. J. Thom and D. Piper.**
'Idyllic University – Trent,' *Canadian Interiors* VI (6), 29-40.

UNIVERSITY OF WATERLOO

1962 **Stevens, M. S.**
'Co-operative Education in Engineering at the University of Waterloo,' *Canadian Mining Journal* LXXXIII (12), 54-57.
1966 **Grayhurst, D.**
'Funding Squeeze at Waterloo U.,' *Can. Univ.* I (2), 32.
1967 **Mungall, C.**
'Co-operative Education – How Good Is It?' *Can. Bus.* XL (10), 52-58.
Scott, J.
Of Mud and Dreams: University of Waterloo, 1957-1967. Toronto: Ryerson. Pp. 194.

1967 **University of Waterloo, Senate Committee on Optometric Education in the University.**
'Report of ... ,' *Can. Jour. Optometry* XXIX, 107-36.
'Waterloo School of Architecture,' *Arch. Can.* XLIV (5), 57-59.
1969 'How University of Waterloo Teaches Creative Engineering,' *Can. Consulting Eng.* II (2), 49-50, 68.
1970 **Watt, L. A. K.**
'The Choosing of a University President,' *OCUFA Newsletter* III (5), 13-14.

UNIVERSITY OF WESTERN ONTARIO

1927 **Hague, D.**
Bishop Baldwin. A Brief Sketch of one of Canada's Greatest Preachers and Noblest Church Leaders. Toronto: Evangelical Publishers. Pp. 63.
Van Pratten, N.
'College and University Libraries of Ontario,' *Library Jour.* [U.S.] LII, 457-61.
1948 **Crane, J. W.**
'The University of Western Ontario Medical School,' *Hist. Bull. Calgary Clinic* XII, 1-3.
1952 **Gray, W. A.**
'Early Years in our Medical School,' *Univ. Western Ont. Med. Jour.* XXII, 106-12.
1961 **Lusztig, P. A. and J. Haskett.**
'A Look at Two Canadian Business Schools,' *Can. Bus.* XXXIV (4), 96-102.
1964 **Cartwright, J. R.**
'A Tribute to Ivan Cleveland Rand,' *Can. Bar Jour.* VII, 372-75, 382.
Fox, W. S.
Sherwood Fox of Western: Reminiscences. Toronto: Burns and MacEachern. Pp. 250.
1965 **Dunn, W. J.**
'Canada's Eighth Dental School is Born,' *Can. Dent. Assoc. Jour.* XXXI, 693-99.

1966 **Bulani, W.**
'Chemical Engineering at Western,' *Chem. Can.* XVIII (1), 52-56.
Keyes, M. E.
'John Howard Crocker LL.D. 1870-1959,' *Western Ontario History Nuggets* No. 32. Pp. 96.
1968 'Developments at Western,' *Can. Fam. Physician* II (9), 71-74.
University of Western Ontario.
President's Committee of Inquiry into Social Behaviour (A. W. R. Carrothers, Chairman), *Report of ... : Let Right Be Done.* London: The University. Pp. 55.

UNIVERSITY OF WINDSOR

1964 **Ruth, N. J.**
'Assumption University and the University of Windsor,' *Bas. Teacher* VIII, 154-68.
1967 **Cerwin, V. B. and W. Grewe.**
'Psychology of Individual and Social Human Learning at the University of Windsor,' *Can. Psych.* VIIa (3), 193-201.
Ruth, N. J.
'The University of Windsor: an Example of Ecumenical Cooperation,' *Jour. Higher Ed.* [U.S.] XXXVIII, 90-95.
1969 **Bringmann, W. G., R. C. Fehr and R. H. Mueller.**
'Psychology at Windsor,' *Can. Psych.* X, 371-82.
Tarnopolsky, W. S.
'The New Law School at the University of Windsor,' *Univ. Tor. Law Jour.* XIX, 622-26.

YORK UNIVERSITY

1962 **Moon, B.**
'The Perils and Pleasure of a Brand-New University,' *Maclean's* LXXV (7), 12-13, 52-54.
1964 **Corbett, E. A.**
'Atkinson College,' *Continuous Learning* III, 22-25.
Johnson, A. C.
'York's Plans Crystallizing,' *Sch. Prog.* XXXIII (7), 36-38.
'York University, Toronto,' *R. Arch. Inst. Can. Jour.* XLI (7), 56-60.
1965 **York University.**
These Five Years ... 1960-65. Toronto: York Univ. Pp. 126.

1966 **Ross, M. G.**
'York University' in M. G. Ross, ed., *New Universities in the Modern World* (Toronto: Macmillan), 69-86.
York University.
The Opening of Glendon College, York University by the Right Honourable L. B. Pearson, Prime Minister of Canada. Toronto: York University. Pp. 28. Includes the Glendon College Experiment – an address to the Rotary Club of Toronto on October 21, 1966 by Principal Escott Reid.

1969 **Innanen, K. A. and R. W. Nicholls.**
'Astronomy and Astrophysics at York University,' *R. Astron. Soc. Jour.* LXIII, 87-89.
O'Connell, T. F.
'The Creation of a Canadian Research Library,' *Can. Library Jour.* XXVI, 132-35.
Verney, D. V.
'The Government and Politics of a Developing University: A Canadian Experience,' *Review of Politics* [U.S.] XXXI, 291-311.

1970 **Presidential Committee on Rights and Responsibilities of Members of York University (B. Laskin, Chairman).**
Report of... Toronto: U. of T. Press. Pp. 64.
Ross, M. G.
Those Ten Years 1960-70: The President's Report on the First Decade of York University. Toronto: York Univ. Pp. 62.

E. THE UNIVERSITIES OF MANITOBA :
LES UNIVERSITÉS DU MANITOBA

1955 **Driedger, L.**
'Developments in Higher Education among Mennonites in Manitoba,' *Man. Jour. Ed. Res.* III, 24-34.

1965 **Gordon, J. M.**
'The Prairie Universities,' *Can. Geog. Jour.* LXXV, 112-25.

1966 **Macdonald, J. B.**
'The West' in R. S. Harris, ed., *Changing Patterns of Higher Education in Canada* (Toronto: U. of T. Press), 41-60.

1968 **Manitoba, Universities Grants Commission.**
Annual Report ... for the Year Ending March 31, 1968.

1969 **Manitoba, Universities Grants Commission.**
      Annual Report ... for the Year Ending March 31, 1969. Winnipeg: The Commission. Pp. 17 + appendices.

BRANDON UNIVERSITY

1969 **Stone, C. G. and F. J. Garnett.**
      Brandon College: A History, 1899-1967. Brandon: Brandon Univ. Pp. 217.

UNIVERSITY OF MANITOBA

1905 **Hart, T.**
      'The Educational System of Manitoba,' *Queen's Q.* XII, 240-51.
1917 **Smith, G. W.**
      'A Canadian Provincial University,' *Aberdeen University Review* V, 240-46.
1921 **Rumball, W. G. and D. A. MacLennan, eds.**
      Manitoba College: Published on the Occasion of the Fiftieth Anniversary of the Founding of Manitoba College being an Account of her Achievements, Past and Present and of her Contribution to the Development of Western Canada and to the Progress of Presbyterianism; Including a Report of the Proceedings and Addresses of the Jubilee Celebrations November 14 to 20, 1921. Winnipeg: Manitoba College. Pp. 86.
1938 **Reid, E. H.**
      'A Comparative Study of Secondary and Higher Educational Interests among the Different Racial Groups of Manitoba.' Unpublished M.Ed. thesis, Univ. of Manitoba.
1949 **Bernier, A.**
      'Les Pionniers du Collège de Saint-Boniface,' *Can. Cath. Hist. Report* 71-79.
1955 **Mitchell, R.**
      'Manitoba's Medical School' in *Medicine in Manitoba: the Story of its Beginnings* (Winnipeg: Stovel-Advocate Press), 84-91.
1962 **McCormack, P. D.**
      'Psychology at Manitoba,' *Can. Psych.* IIIa, 38-42.
1964 'The Faculty of Architecture – University of Manitoba,' *R. Arch. Inst. Can. Jour.* XLI (3), 57-68.

1964 **Régnier, P. R.**
'A History of St. Boniface College.' Unpublished M.Ed. thesis, Univ. of Manitoba.
1966 **Frazer, W. J.**
'A History of St. John's College, Winnipeg.' Unpublished M.A. thesis, Univ. of Manitoba.
Mitchell, R. and T. K. Thorlakson.
'James Kerr, 1848-1911 and Harry Hyland Kerr, 1881-1963: Pioneer Canadian American Surgeon,' *Can. Jour. Surgery* IX, 213-20.
1967 **Kirkconnell, W.**
A Slice of Canada: Memoirs. Toronto: U. of T. Press. Pp. 393.
[Particularly 135-37.]
Lindal, W. J.
'The Department of Icelandic in the University of Manitoba' in *The Icelanders in Canada* (Winnipeg: Canada Ethnic Press Fed.), 330-65.
Lower, A. R. M.
My First Seventy-Five Years. Toronto: Macmillan. Pp. 384.
[Particularly 159-74.]
1968 **Brown, W. J.**
'Retrospect and Prospect; a Decade of Geography at the University of Manitoba,' *Manitoba Geography Teacher* I (3), 15-20.
1969 **Fyles, T. W.**
'A Good Place to Carry Out Medical Life,' *Man. Med. Rev.* XLIX (8), 12-14.
1970 **Wilt, J. C.**
'The History of Medical Microbiology at the University of Manitoba,' *Man. Med. Rev.* L (3), 16-21.

UNIVERSITY OF WINNIPEG

1921 **Rumball, W. G. and D. A. MacLennan, eds.**
Manitoba College: Published on the Occasion of the Fiftieth Anniversary of the Founding of Manitoba College, Being an Account of her Achievements, Past and Present and of her Contribution to the Development of Western Canada and to the Progress of Presbyterianism; Including a Report of the Proceedings and Addresses of the Jubilee Celebrations November 14 to 20, 1921. Winnipeg: Manitoba College. Pp. 86.

1967 **Kirkconnell, W.**
A Slice of Canada: Memoirs. Toronto: U. of T. Press. Pp. 393.
[Particularly 135-37.]
Lower, A. R. M.
My First Seventy-Five Years. Toronto: Macmillan. Pp. 384.
[Particularly 159-74.]

F. THE UNIVERSITY OF SASKATCHEWAN

1952 **Anderson, A. L.**
'The School of Medical Sciences and the Medical College of the University of Saskatchewan,' *Hist. Bull. Calgary Clinic* XVII, 1-9.
1964 **Kaller, C. L.**
'The Status of the University Computer Centre,' *Computer Science Association Newsletter* I (2), 6-8.
Leddy, J. F.
'Father Carr in Saskatoon,' *Bas. Teacher* VIII, 308-14.
1965 **Gordon, J. M.**
'The Prairie Universities,' *Can. Geog. Jour.* LXXV, 112-25.
1966 **Begg, R. W. et al.**
University of Saskatchewan: Organization and Structure – Report of a Committee on the Organization and Structure of the University as Amended and Adopted by the Senate of the University of Saskatchewan, November 4, 1966. Saskatoon: The University. Pp. 35.
Billinton, R. and R. J. Fleming.
'Electric Power System Studies at the University of Saskatchewan,' *Eng. Jour.* XLIX (6), 22-25.
Macdonald, J. B.
'The West' in R. S. Harris, ed., *Changing Patterns of Higher Education in Canada* (Toronto: U. of T. Press), 41-60.
1967 **Fiddes, J. and L. B. Jacques.**
Reminiscences. Saskatoon: Department of Physiology and Pharmacology, Univ. of Saskatchewan. Pp. 70.
King, C.
Extending the Boundaries. Saskatoon: Univ. of Saskatchewan. Pp. 161.
Simpson, E. R.
'College of Home Economics – University of Saskatchewan,' *Can. Home Econ. Jour.* XVII (3), 64-65.

1967 **Wood, J. A.**
'New Pharmacy Facilities at University of Saskatchewan,' *Can. Pharm. Jour.* C, 23-29.
1968 **Courtney, J. C.**
'The Government-University Controversy in Saskatchewan, 1967-68,' *C.A.U.T. Bull.* XVII (2), 19-33.
'Developments at University of Saskatchewan,' *Can. Family Physician* XIV (10), 79-81.
Spinks, J. W.
University of Saskatchewan in Transition. Regina: Univ. of Saskatchewan. Pp. 24.
1969 **McCorkell, E. J.**
Henry Carr, Revolutionary. Toronto: Griffin Press. Pp. 161.
Thomson, J. S.
Yesteryears at the University of Saskatchewan 1937-1949. Saskatoon: Modern Press. Pp. 91.
1970 **Thompson, W. P.**
The University of Saskatchewan: A Personal History. Toronto: U. of T. Press. Pp. 233.

G. THE UNIVERSITIES OF ALBERTA :
   LES UNIVERSITÉS DE L'ALBERTA

1955 **Roberts, W. G. and A. O. Ackroyd.**
'Post-School Occupations of Alberta 1949 High School Graduates with University Entrance Standards,' *Alta. Jour. Ed. Res.* I (3), 43-53.
1965 **Gordon, J. M.**
'The Prairie Universities,' *Can. Geog. Jour.* LXXV (4), 112-25.
1966 **Macdonald, J. B.**
'The West' in R. S. Harris, ed., *Changing Patterns of Higher Education in Canada* (Toronto: U. of T. Press), 41-60.
1967 **Chalmers, J. W.**
Schools of the Foothills Province; the Story of Public Education in Alberta. Toronto: U. of T. Press for Alberta Teachers' Assoc. Pp. 489.
Macintosh, D. F. and J. G. Nelson.
'The New Universities Act in the Province of Alberta,' *C.A.U.T. Bull.* XVI (1), 83-95.
1969 **Tod, A. J.**
'A Survey of Staff Characteristics in Post-Secondary Institutions in Alberta.' Unpublished M.Ed. thesis, Univ. of Alberta.

1970 **Alberta, Department of Education.**
Post-Secondary Education until 1972: an Alberta Policy Statement.
Edmonton: The Department. Pp. 17.

UNIVERSITY OF ALBERTA

1939 **Tory, H. M.**
'Intellectual Co-operation between Canada and the United States' in A. B. Corey, R. G. Trotter, W. M. McLaren, eds., *Proceedings of the Conference on Canadian-American Affairs* (Boston: Ginn), 165-72.

1942 **University of Alberta, Survey Committee.**
Interim Report to the Lieutenant Governor in Council, Province of Alberta. Tabled in Alberta Legislative Assembly February 25, 1942. [Sessional Paper No. 50 of 1942.] Edmonton: King's Printer. Pp. 81.

1948 **Revell, D. G.**
'The Medical Faculty: University of Alberta,' *Hist. Bull. Calgary Clinic* XIII, 65-75.

1952 'The Acid-Minded Professor,' [Prof. William Rowan] *Maclean's* LXV (10), 20-21, 56-59.

1956 **Collins, R.**
'The Campus that Covers a Province,' *Maclean's* LXIX (4), 26-32.
Dunlop, G. M.
'A Challenge to the Faculty of Education,' *Alta. Jour. Ed. Res.* II (2), 71-78.

1958 **Evenson, A. B. and D. E. Smith.**
'A Study of Matriculation in Alberta,' *Alta. Jour. Ed. Res.* IV (2), 67-83.
Rawlinson, H. E.
'History of Canadian Surgery: Frank Hamilton Mewburn,' *Can. Jour. Surgery* II, 1-5.
Wilson, L.
'How Many Alberta Matriculants Register as Freshmen at the University of Alberta,' *Alta. Jour. Ed. Res.* IV (2), 108-13.

1962 **Coutts, H. T. and D. B. Black.**
'The Carnegie – University of Alberta Joint Project on Educational Research: A Report After Five Years,' *Alta. Jour. Ed. Res.* VIII (3), 133-46.

1963 **Scott, J. W.**
The History of the Faculty of Medicine of the University of Alberta 1913-1963. Edmonton: Univ. of Alberta. Pp. 43.

1964 **Coutts, H. T. and B. E. Walker.**
'The Faculty of Education at the University of Alberta,' *Sch. Prog.*
XXXIII (9), 31-37, 50.
Johnson, L. P. V.
'The First Fifty Years as Five Deans Found Them,' *New Trail* XXII (2),
5-12.
Paulson, B. D.
'An Analysis of the University of Alberta Reading and Language Centre
Clinical Cases.' Unpublished M.Ed. thesis, Univ. of Alberta.

1965 **Knowles, D. W.**
'Problems of Admission to the University of Alberta,' *Alta. Jour. Ed.
Res.* XI (1), 3-16.
MacLean, H. R.
'Faculty of Dentistry, University of Alberta,' *Can. Dent. Assoc. Jour.*
XXXI, 285-92.
Peel, B. B.
History of the Library, University of Alberta. Edmonton: Univ. of
Alberta. Pp. 18.

1966 **Hertzman, L.**
'Alberta and the Intellectuals,' *Culture* XXVII, 163-75. See also
H. Beissel, 'Letter to the Editor,' 457-59.
Smith, W. A. S.
'Academic Planning at the U. of A.,' *New Trail* XXIV (1), 16-20.
Wilkinson, W. K.
'Residence Culture: A Descriptive Study of the Culture of the Lister
Hall Residence Complex, University of Alberta, Edmonton.'
Unpublished M.Ed. thesis, Univ. of Alberta.

1967 **Canadian Association of University Teachers, Academic Freedom and**
Tenure Committee.
'Statement on the Williamson-Murray Case/Declaration ... Affaire
Williamson-Murray,' *C.A.U.T. Bull.* XV (3), 32-43.

1968 **Arvidson, R. M. and T. M. Nelson.**
'Sixty Years of Psychology at the University of Alberta,' *Can. Psych.*
IX, 500-04.
Johns, W. H.
These Sixty Years: An Address to the Diamond Jubilee Convocation.
Edmonton: Univ. of Alberta. Pp. 7.

1969 **Diamond, A. J. and B. Myers.**
'University of Alberta Long Range Development Plan,' *Arch. Can.* LXVI
(4), 37-39.

1969 **Johns, W. H.**
'Reminiscences,' *New Trail* XXVI (3), 6-11.
'The University and the North,' *New Trail* XXVI (1), 13-43.

UNIVERSITY OF CALGARY

1961 **Simon, F. A.**
'A Brief History of the Alberta Institute of Technology and Art.' Unpublished M.A. thesis, Univ. of Alberta.
1964 **Ryder, D.**
'The Library of the University of Alberta in Calgary,' *Alta. Lib. Assoc. Bull.* XI, 6-10.
1966 **Brown, D. W. R.**
'An Analysis of the Achievements of Junior College Students at the University of Calgary.' Unpublished M.A. thesis, Univ. of Calgary.
1968 'Medical Education: The Revolution Has Already Begun,' *Can. Doctor* XXXIV (6), 44-47.
1969 **Dickson, A. D.** *et al.*
'Planning for Medical Education at the University of Calgary,' *Can. Med. Assoc. Jour.* C, 665-69.

UNIVERSITY OF LETHBRIDGE

1965 **Harries, H. and Associates Ltd.**
A Study to Examine and Report on the Feasibility of Developing University Facilities in Lethbridge; a Study for the City of Lethbridge. Lethbridge. Pp. 59.
Lethbridge Junior College.
Past, Present and Future of the Lethbridge Junior College. Lethbridge: The College. Pp. 37.
Markle, A. G.
'Genesis of the Lethbridge Public Junior College.' Unpublished M.Ed. thesis, Univ. of Alberta.
1966 **Lethbridge Junior College.**
Historical Survey of the Lethbridge Junior College. Lethbridge: The College. Pp. 25.
1967 **Maisey, D. P.**
'A Study of Students Enrolled in the Adult Education Evening Program of the Lethbridge Junior College.' Unpublished M.Ed. thesis, Univ. of Alberta.

1968 'Crisis that Created a Real University at Lethbridge,' *Maclean's* LXXXI (9), 2-3.
Mardon, E. G.
The Founding Faculty. Lethbridge: University of Lethbridge. Pp. 108.
Oldman River Regional Planning Commission.
Future City of Lethbridge Expansion and University Location. Lethbridge: The Commission. Pp. 12.
Perkins, S. A.
An Examination of Five Different Groups of First-Year Students at the University of Lethbridge on the College Qualification Test and Grade Point Average, 1967-68. Lethbridge: University of Lethbridge. Pp. 30.
University of Lethbridge.
The University of Lethbridge Academic Plan and User's Report. Lethbridge: The University. Pp. 156.

1969 **Smith, W. A. S.**
'There is No Joy in Mudville; Remarks to the Annual Meeting of the Association of Universities and Colleges of Canada, November 6, 1969,' *A.U.C.C. Proc.* 97-104.

H. THE UNIVERSITIES OF BRITISH COLUMBIA :
LES UNIVERSITÉS DE LA COLOMBIE-BRITANNIQUE

1966 **Johnson, F. H.**
'The Universities of British Columbia,' *Can. Geog. Jour.* LXXIII, 182-93.
Macdonald, J. B.
'The West' in R. S. Harris, ed., *Changing Patterns of Higher Education in Canada* (Toronto: U. of T. Press), 41-60.

UNIVERSITY OF BRITISH COLUMBIA

1946 **Gilmour, C.**
'Big Larry of U.B.C.,' [N. A. M. MacKenzie] *Maclean's* LIX (21), 9, 57-60.

1951 **Ranta, L. E.**
'The Medical School of British Columbia,' *Hist. Bull. Calgary Clinic* XVI, 1-9.

1954 'Vancouver: Developments in Medical Education,' *Mod. Med. Canada* IX (5), 31-33.
1961 **Lusztig, P. A. and J. Haskett.**
'A Look at Two Canadian Business Schools,' *Can. Bus.* XXXIV (4), 96-100, 102.
Yi-t'ung Wang.
'The P'u-pan Chinese Library at the University of British Columbia,' *Pacific Affairs* [U.S.] XXXIV, 101-11.
1962 'The School of Librarianship; The University of British Columbia,' *Alta. Lib. Assoc. Bull.* IX (2), 16-19.
1964 **Nicholls, W.**
'The Role of a Department of Religion in a Canadian University' in K. R. Bridston and D. W. Calver, eds., *The Making of Ministers: Essays on Clergy Training Today* (Minneapolis: Augsburg Publishing House), 72-90.
Oliver, M. J.
'The Vancouver Story,' [Father Henry Carr] *Bas. Teacher* VIII, 315-22.
Selman, G.
'University Extension 1915-1963,' *Jour. Ed. (B.C.)* No. 10, 17-25.
1965 **Eliot, C. W. J.** *et al.*
Discipline and Discovery: A Proposal to the Faculty of Arts of the University of British Columbia. Vancouver: Univ. of British Columbia. Pp. 43.
Leung, S. W.
'Faculty of Dentistry, University of British Columbia,' *Can. Dent. Assoc. Jour.* XXXI, 293-97.
Marquis, G. W.
'Canadian Music at the University of British Columbia,' *Can. Composer* No. 2, 10, 42-43.
1966 **Bredin, G.**
'The Child Study Centre of the U.B.C.: Its History and Development,' *Jour. Ed. (B.C.)* No. 12, 39-47.
Gibson, W. C.
'The University of British Columbia and the City of Vancouver,' *Canadian Federation News* VIII (January), 3-8.
Golden Anniversary Alumni Association of the University of British Columbia.
Being the Autumn 1966 (Vol. XX, No. 3) issue of the *UBC Alumni Chronicle* and devoted almost entirely to reminiscence of the University from 1915 on.

1966 **McGechaen, J. and P. G. Penner.**
Teacher Education at the University of British Columbia 1956-1966.
Vancouver: Faculty of Education, Univ. of British Columbia. Pp. 99.
Rose, W. J.
'The School of Slavonic and East European Studies, 1937-1947,'
Slavonic and East European Review XLIV, 8-17.
Rothstein, S.
'Historical Notes: University of British Columbia School of Librarianship,' *Can. Library* XXII, 226-28.
Selman, G.
A History of Fifty Years of Extension Service by the University of British Columbia 1915-1965. Toronto: Can. Assoc. for Adult Ed. Pp. 60.
Shorthouse, T. ed. *et al.*
'Scrapbook for a Golden Anniversary: The University Library 1915-1965,' *B.C. Lib. Q.* XXIX (3), 2-80.
Tucker, F.
The Alumni Association of the University of British Columbia: The First Fifty Years 1916-1966. Vancouver: Univ. of British Columbia. Pp. 24.

1967 **Bullman, M.**
'Concepts behind U.B.C.'s New Medical Complex, and the Role of Rehabilitation Medicine in Such a Complex,' *Can. Physiotherapy Jour.* XIX, 16-19.
Gibson, W. C.
'Frank Fairchild Wesbrook (1868-1918), A Pioneer Educator in Minnesota and British Columbia,' *Journal of the History of Medicine and Allied Sciences* [U.S.] XXII, 357-79.
Gibson, W. C.
'President Wesbrook – His University, His Profession and the Community,' *B.C. Med. Jour.* IX (1), 10-20.
Mathews, W. H.
'Geological Engineering at the University of B.C.,' *B.C. Professional Engineer* XVIII (5), 11-16.
Ng, T. K.
'The Birth and Growth of an East Asian Vernacular Library: Being the Asian Studies Division of the University of British Columbia Library,' *Canadian Library Association Occasional Paper* LIII, 1-5.
Pickard, G. L.
'Physical Oceanography at the University of British Columbia,' *Physics in Canada* XXIII (1), 7-11.

1968 **Dennison, J. D. and G. Jones.**
A Study of the Characteristics and Subsequent Performance of Vancouver City College Students Who Transferred to The University of British Columbia in September 1967. Vancouver: U.B.C. and Vancouver City College. Pp. 77. [Also available as ERIC Document No. D26061.]
Walters, J.
An Annotated Bibliography of Reports, Theses, and Publications Pertaining to the Campus and Research Forests of The University of British Columbia. Vancouver: Faculty of Forestry, U.B.C. Pp. 71.

1969 **Chronister, G. M. and K. M. Ahrendt.**
'Development of a Reading-Study Skills Centre at the University of British Columbia,' *Journal of the Reading Specialist* VIII (4), 174-75, 198.
McCorkell, E. J.
Henry Carr, Revolutionary. Toronto: Griffin Press. Pp. 161.
McCreary, J. F.
'The Concepts behind the Health Sciences Centre,' *Can. Jour. Occup. Therapy* XXXVI (2), 49-55.
University of British Columbia, Commission on the Future of the Faculty of Education.
The COFFE Report. Vancouver: The University. Pp. 125.

1970 **Rodenhizer, J.**
'The Student Campaign of 1922 to "Build the University" of British Columbia,' *B.C. Studies* No. 4, 21-37.

NOTRE DAME UNIVERSITY OF NELSON

1965 'Notre Dame University of Nelson,' *Nelson Daily News.* Special Supplement, November 10, 1965. Pp. 12.

1966 **Nagle, P.**
'One University's Plan to Build Intelligent Champions,' *Weekend Magazine* XVI (10), 2-7.

SIMON FRASER UNIVERSITY

1964 **Baker, R. J.**
'B.C.'s New Simon Fraser University,' *Sch. Prog.* XXXIII (7), 34-35.
Baker, R. J.
'Simon Fraser University, Burnaby, B.C.,' *R. Arch. Inst. Can. Jour.* XLI (7), 51-55.

1965 **McKinnon, A. R.**
'Notes on Teacher Education at Simon Fraser University,' *B.C. School Trustee* XXI (Winter-Spring), 16-18.
Reder, F. M.
'S.F.U. Plan: Let's Think about It!' *B.C. School Trustee* XXI (Winter-Spring), 18-19.
1966 **Ruddy, J.**
'The Mountain-Top Radical,' *Maclean's* LXXIX (11), 12, 39-41.
Thom, R. J. and L. Tiger.
'Academe on a Mountain Top: Two Comments,' *Can. Forum* XLV, 224-26.
1968 **Milner, J. B., A. Berland and J. P. Smith.**
'Report on Simon Fraser University by the Investigating Committee of the Canadian Association of University Teachers,' *C.A.U.T. Bull.* XVII (4), 4-28.
Smith, J. P.
'Developments at Simon Fraser University,' *C.A.U.T. Bull.* XVII (1), 23-33.
Smith, J. P.
'Faculty Power and Simon Fraser,' *Can. Forum* XLVIII, 122-24.
1969 **Harding, J.**
'What's Happening at Simon Fraser University?' *Our Generation* VI (3), 52-64.
1970 **Briemberg, M.**
'A Taste of Better Things – P.S.A. at S.F.U.,' *This Magazine* IV (1), 32-55.

UNIVERSITY OF VICTORIA

1967 **Jackman, S. W. and R. R. Jeffel.**
Joseph Badinock Clerihue. Victoria: Univ. of Victoria. Pp. 48.
1968 **Eshleman, W.**
'Mini-tape Gives Maxi-boost to UVIC Teacher Education Program,' *B.C. Teacher* XLVII, 246-49.
1969 **University of Victoria, Faculty of Education.**
Learning: Proceedings of Conference for District Superintendents Held at Harrison Springs, January 1969. Victoria: Univ. of Victoria. Pp. 65.

Current trends and problems
Orientation et problèmes présents

A. GENERAL : GÉNÉRALITÉS

1948 **Lower, A. R. M.**
'Does Our Education Educate?' *Maclean's* LXI (22), 9, 72-76.

1958 **Bissell, C. T.**
'Universities Must Answer Sputnik with Higher Standards,' *Maclean's* LXX (1), 8, 23, 48-50.
Major, M.
'Letting Out the Seams in Our Universities,' *Atlantic Advocate* XLVIII (9), 25-29.

1959 'A Special Report On: Our Booming Campuses,' *Can. Bus.* XXII (3), 26-35.
'Here's the Growth Picture of Our Big Universities,' *Can. Bus.* XXXII (4), 110-15.

1960 **Kerr, A. E.**
'The Importance of the Imponderables in University Education,' *Atlantic Advocate* L (9), 75-78.
MacKinnon, F.
'The University: Community or Utility?' *Can. Pub. Admin.* III, 337-43.
McEown, A. C.
'The University as a Public Institution: Its Relationships with the Community,' *Can. Pub. Admin.* III, 350-53.

1962 **De Chantal, R. and D. Edmonds, eds.**
The University in Canadian Life/L'Université dans la vie canadienne.
Ottawa: National Federation of Canadian University Students. Pp. 89.
Includes: J. H. S. Reid, 'Development of Canadian Universities,' 10-16;
L. Lortie, 'Les Universités canadiennes de langue française et de langue anglaise,' 17-27; R. Jones, 'Aims of University Education: A Realistic Appraisal from the Industrial Point of View,' 28-31 and (en français) 32-36; H. Hicks, 'A Realistic Appraisal from the Academic Point of View,' 37-41; D. Johnston, 'The Role of the University,' 50-53;
B. Ostry, 'Problems of Priorities: Teaching and Research Facilities and Students,' 54-63; J. G. Kaplan, 'Problems of Freedom in the University,' 64-70; J. F. Leddy, 'The Future of the University,' 71-77 and 78-86.

1964 **Andrew, G. C.**
'Canadian Universities Face the Future,' *Sch. Prog.* XXXIII (7), 27-28, 52.
Drummond, I. M.
'The Robbins Commission and the Canadian Scene,' *Can. Forum* XLIII, 265-68.
Gagnon, C.
'L'Université, milieu bourgeois,' *Cité Libre* LXV, 12-19.
Gill, C., ed.
Year-Round Operation of the University/Fonctionnement de l'université à l'année longue. (Supplement to the Proceedings of the 1964 annual meeting of the NCCUC/Supplement aux délibérations de la réunion annuelle de la CNUCC, 1964.) Ottawa: Canadian Universities Foundation/Fondation des Universités Canadiennes. Pp. 181.
Hertzman, L.
'Challenges to the Modern University,' *Culture* XXV, 223-32.
Jackson, B. W. et al.
'Committee on Year-Round Operation of Universities,' *C.A.U.T. Bull.* XIII, September (Special Issue), 3-26.
Jackson, R. W. B.
'The Crisis of Numbers,' *Tor. Ed. Q.* III (2), 18-22.
Scarfe, N. V.
'The Modern University,' *Can. Ed. Research Digest* IV, 102-05.
Schurman, D. M.
'The Robbins Report and Canada,' *Queen's Q.* LXXI, 214-25.
Vachon, L.-A.
Progrès de l'université et consentement populaire. Québec: Presses Univ. Laval. Pp. 190.

1965 **Bissell, C. T.**
'The Importance of Greatness,' *C.A.U.T. Bull.* XIII (4), 3-9.
Corry, J. A.
'The University and the Canadian Community,' *A.U.C.C. Proc.* 40-48.
Gibson, J. A.
Springtime for Universities. Address at Annual Education Night ... Niagara Falls, April 26, 1965. St. Catharines: Brock Univ. Pp. 10.
Harris, R. S.
'Horizons in Professional Education,' *Amer. Jour. Pharm. Ed.* XXIX, 669-74.
Lorrain, P.
'L'Université en 1965,' *Physics in Canada* XXI (5), 9-15.

1965 **Martin, Y.**
'L'Education et la société de demain,' *Rev. Scolaire* XV, 297-301.
Mathews, R. D.
'University Crisis and the Common Weal,' *Can. Forum* XLV, 32-34.
Miller, R. S.
'The Multiversity – Education or Training,' *Proc. Assoc. Stud. Services* 32-35.
Nursall, J. R.
'Pattern of a University,' *Univ. Tor. Q.* XXXIV, 332-48.
Sirluck, E.
'A No-Title Address,' *Amer. Jour. Pharm. Ed.* XXIX, 781-84.
Sirluck, E.
'Universities in Crisis,' *University of Manitoba Alumni Journal* XXV (2), 7-13.
Whitworth, F. E.
'Random Thoughts on Producing a Surplus of University Graduates,' *Ont. Jour. Ed. Res.* VIII (2), 133-48.

1966 **Allen, R. T.**
'Let's Quit Worshipping the Kid with a B.A.,' *Maclean's* LXXIX (18), 21, 42-43.
Corry, J. A.
'Higher Education in Canada: Trends and Prospects' in J. E. Hodgetts, ed., *Higher Education in a Changing Canada* (Toronto: U. of T. Press), 3-13.
Dhalla, N. K.
'The College Growth Market,' *Can. Bus.* XXXIX (7), 74-83.
MacKenzie, N. A. M.
'A View on Education,' *Atlantic Advocate* LVI (9), 13-16.
Mathews, R.
'The Higher Learning,' *Can. Dimension* III (6), 16-17.
S[mith] D.
'Higher Education: The Problems of Change,' *Can. Forum* XLV, 217-18.

1967 **Corry, J. A.**
'University Education: Prospect and Priorities,' *Queen's Q.* LXXIV, 561-72.
Grant, G.
'Wisdom in the Universities,' *This Magazine* I (4), 71-85; I (5), 52-57. Also in H. Adelman and D. Lee, eds., *The University Game* (Toronto: Anansi), 47-68.

1967 **Guindon, R.**
'National Unity and Universities,' *Proc. Assoc. Stud. Services* 24-30.
Howlett, L. E.
'The Role of Universities in Education for the Professions,'
Can. Surveyor XXI, 13-28.
Leddy, J. F.
'A Question of Priorities,' *Can. Ed. Research Digest* VII, 19-23.
LePan, D. V.
'Responsibility and Revolt,' *Queen's Q.* LXXIV, 201-21.
Marshall, D.
'Campus '67,' *Maclean's* LXXX (11), 11-13 and 44-48. See also Webb, C. W., 'A Consumer's Report on Canada's Top Universities,' 14-15, 88, 90-91; Snowland, C. P., 'A Day in the Life of a University,' [U. of T.] 16-19, 57-60 ...
Martin, L.
'Polyvalence mon amour ... ' *Mag. Maclean* VII (9), 13-15, 60.
Petitpas, H.
'Newman's Universe of Knowledge: Science, Literature, Theology,'
Dalhousie Rev. XLVI, 494-507.
Smith, J. P.
'Questions Old and New,' *C.A.U.T. Bull.* XV (4), 9-14.
1968 **Adelman, H. and D. Lee**
The University Game. Toronto: Anansi. Pp. 178. See also V. DiNorcia, 'Games Universities Play,' *Laur. Univ. Rev.* II (4), 84-91.
Association Canadienne de Professeurs d'université.
'Mémoire à la Commission d'Etude Munroe sur les statistiques d'éducation du Bureau fédéral de la statistique,' *C.A.U.T. Bull.* XVI (4), 87-113.
Association of Universities and Colleges of Canada.
Proceedings Annual Meeting 1967 (Ottawa: The Association), Vol. II includes: R. S. Harris, 'A Matter of Balance,' 7-32; W. Beckel, 'The University as Educator: It's got to be the Real Old Lady,' 41-55; M. Ross, 'The University and Community Service,' 62-97.
Bissell, C. T.
The Strength of the University. Toronto: U. of T. Press. Pp. 248.
Duceppe, G.
'La Nature de l'université contemporaine,' *A.U.C.C. Proc.* 84-86.

1968 Erickson, A.
'The New Visual Environment' in M. Ross, ed., *The University and the New Intellectual Environment* (Toronto: Macmillan), 49-65.
Hennuy, G.
'Contestation Universitaire et morale humaine,' *Rev. Univ. Moncton* I (2), 6-13.
Lacoste, P.
'Les Problèmes de la communauté universitaire,' *A.U.C.C. Proc.* 87-96.
Lee, D.
'Getting to Rochdale,' *This Magazine* II (5), 72-96. Also in H. Adelman and D. Lee, eds., *The University Game* (Toronto: Anansi), 69-94.
Lotz, J.
'University in the North,' *Can. Forum* XLVIII, 110-11.
Macpherson, C. B., P. Warrian and D. C. Williams.
'The Nature of the Contemporary University,' *A.U.C.C. Proc.* 97-100, 101-03, 104-11.
Pelletier, G.
'Réflexions sur l'Université,' *A.U.C.C. Proc.* 112-18.
Sparshott, F. E.
'Four Views of a University,' *Can. Forum* XLVIII, 80-81.

1969 Burgess, J. P.
'Canadianizing the University,' *Can. Forum* XLIX, 77-79.
Calam, J.
'The Pleasures and Perils of University Publishing,' *McGill Jour. Ed.* IV (1), 31-39.
Cook, G. R.
'Letter from Cambridge, Mass.,' *Can. Forum* XLIX, 80-81.
Deutsch, J. J.
'The Role of a Changing University in a Changing Society,' *Queen's Q.* LXXVI, 392-400.
Frye, H. N.
'The University and Personal Life: Student Anarchism and the Educational Contract' in W. R. Niblett, ed., *Higher Education: Demand and Response* (London: Tavistock), 35-51.
Hertzman, L. and J. L. Black.
'Americans in Canadian Universities,' *Laur. Univ. Rev.* II (4), 107-08, 109-12.
Hodgetts, J. E. and R. Rae.
'The Contemporary University: Ideology and Commitments,' *A.U.C.C. Proc.* 77-81, 82-88.

1969 **Lamontagne, L.**
'La Technologie et l'accés aux études post-secondaires,' *Mém. S.R.C.* sect. 1, 87-92.
Lamontagne, M.
'Crisis in Higher Education,' *A.U.C.C. Proc.* 105-10.
Macpherson, C. B.
'Forces Relating University and Community,' *C.A.U.T. Bull.* XVII (3), 2-5.
Macpherson, C. B.
'The Violent Society and the Liberal,' *C.A.U.T. Bull.* XVIII (1), 7-15.
Mathews, R.
'The Americanization of Canadian Universities,' *Can. Dimension* V (8), 15-16, 53.
Mathews, R. and J. Steele.
The Struggle for Canadian Universities: A Dossier. Toronto: New Press. Pp. 184.
McCarter, J. A.
'Why Not Nationalize the Universities? A Researcher's View,' *Sci. Forum* II (1), 21-23.
Rocher, G.
'Idéologies et engagements de l'université d'aujourd'hui et de demain,' *A.U.C.C. Proc.* 89-96.
Smith, W. A. S.
'There Is No Joy in Mudville,' *A.U.C.C. Proc.* 97-104.
Theall, D. F.
'Universities: Traditions and Change,' *Univ. Laur. Rev.* II (4), 64-74.

1970 **Carrier, H.**
'L'Université dans une société nouvelle,' *Relations* XXX, 55-57.
Corry, J. A.
Farewell the Ivory Tower: Universities in Transition. Montreal: McGill-Queen's Univ. Press. Pp. 121.
Cruikshank, G.
'It's High Time We Did Away with Universities,' *Atlantic Advocate* LX (9), 19-21.
Hughes, P.
'Native Fathers, Alien Sons,' *Can. Forum* L, 96-97.
Jowett, G.
'The Dossier as Hornet's Nest,' [Three Reviews of Mathews and Steele] *Can. Rev. Amer. Studies* I, 1, 48-56. See also J. Gold, 'We Stand on Guard for Thee?,' 56-62 and R. Bates, 'Who's Afraid of Cultural Identity? or, Stand Up and Be Counted Down,' 62-68.

1970 **Lotz, J.**
'The Idea of a Northern University,' in *Northern Realities: The Future of Northern Development in Canada* (Toronto: New Press), 239-49.
Lumsden, I.
'American Imperialism and Canadian Intellectuals' in I. Lumsden, ed., *Close the 49th Parallel etc.: The Americanization of Canada* (Toronto: U. of T. Press), 321-36.
McGuigan, G. F.
'Reform of the University,' *Can. Forum* L, 100-02.
Porter, J.
'The Democratization of the Canadian Universities and the Need for a National System,' *Minerva* [U.K.] VIII, 325-56.
Robson, J. M.
'One If by Land,' [re Americanization of Canadian universities] *Can. Forum* XLIX, 256-57.
Rocher, G.
'Idéologies et engagements de l'Université d'aujourd'hui et de demain,' *Rev. Univ. Moncton* III, 66-73.
Spinks, S.
'Dreaming in the Beds of Academe,' *This Magazine* IV (1), 80-108.
Steele, J. and R. Mathews.
'The Universities: Takeover of the Mind' in I. Lumsden, ed., *Close the 49th Parallel etc.: The Americanization of Canada* (Toronto: U. of T. Press), 169-78.
Sutherland, W. H.
'The New Revolution,' *B.C. Med. Jour.* XII, 89-92.
'Winstanley'
'What Sort of University?' *Can. Forum* L, 98-99.

B. UNIVERSITY GOVERNMENT :
ADMINISTRATION UNIVERSITAIRE

1951 **Sheffield, E. F.**
'The Allocation of Administrative Responsibilities in the Liberal Arts College,' *College and University* [U.S.] XXVI (2), 236-46.
1955 *Comparison of Governing Bodies of Canadian Universities.* Ottawa: School of Public Administration, Carleton College. Pp. 10.
1957 **Rowat, D. C.**
'Faculty Participation in Canadian University Government,' *Bull. of the American Association of University Professors* XLIII (3), 462-76.

1964   Freedman, S.
'University Government,' *C.A.U.T. Bull.* XIII (1), 14-26.
Hart, J.
'A Science Chairman's Lament,' *C.A.U.T. Bull.* XII (3), 42-47.
1965   **Cyert, R. M.**
'The Role of Leadership in Academic Organizations,' *Proc. Schools Bus.* Pp. 11.
Huntingford, A.
'Discipline,' *Proc. Assoc. Stud. Services* 24-28.
Mayo, H. B.
'University Government – Trends and a New Model,' *C.A.U.T. Bull.* XIII (4), 10-24.
Ross, M. G.
'In the Public Domain,' *Univ. Affairs* VI (4), 1-3.
1966   **Adelman, H.**
'Tokenism: A Report on the Duff-Berdahl Report,' *Can. Forum* XLVI, 34-37.
Begg, R. W. et al.
University of Saskatchewan: Organization and Structure – Report of a Committee on the Organization and Structure of the University, as Amended and Adopted by the Senate of the University of Saskatchewan, November 4, 1966. Saskatoon: The University. Pp. 35.
Bissell, C. T.
'A Proposal for University Government at the University of Toronto,' *C.A.U.T. Bull.* XV (2), 42-46.
Bissell, C. T., L.-P. Bonneau, J. B. Macdonald and J. St. Pierre.
'Internal University Government,' *A.U.C.C. Proc.* 67-85; 'Structures Administratives des Universités,' 193-213.
Cameron, P.
'The Duff-Berdahl Report: Will the Patient Live?' *C.A.U.T. Bull.* XV (2), 47-52.
D[rummond], I. M.
'The Duff-Berdahl Report,' *Can. Forum* XLVI, 34.
Duff, J. and R. O. Berdahl.
University Government in Canada: Report of a Commission Sponsored by the Canadian Association of University Teachers and the Association of Universities and Colleges of Canada. Toronto: U. of T. Press. Pp. 97.
Gonick, C. W.
'Self-Government in the Multiversity,' *Can. Dimension* III (3-4), 18-19.

1966   **Monahan, E. J.** *et al.*
'The North Hatley Conference on the Future of the C.A.U.T.,'
C.A.U.T. Bull. XV (2), 4-41.
Rowat, D. C.
'Democracy in the University Community: C.U.S. Eighth Seminar,'
C.A.U.T. Bull. XIV (4), 36-42.
Rowat, D. C.
'The Duff-Berdahl Report on University Government: A Summary and Critique of Its Findings and Main Recommendations,' *C.A.U.T. Bull.* XIV (4), 23-30.
Smith, J. P.
'The Duff/Berdahl Report on University Government,' *Univ. Affairs* VII (4), 1-3.

1967   **Flynn, M.**
'A Survey of Student Involvement in the Decision-Making Process at Canadian Universities,' *Jour. Assoc. Student Services* II (1), 12-14.
LePan, D. V.
'Responsibility and Revolt,' *Queen's Q.* LXXIV, 201-21.
Monahan, E. J.
'The Inevitability of Gradualness: A Report on Changes in University Government in Canada,' *C.A.U.T. Bull.* XVI (2), 33-41.

1968   **Adams, P. R.**
'Needed: More Effectively Trained Administrators for Post-secondary Education,' *Educational Administration Reporter* [U.S.] II (4), 2-3.
Committee of Presidents of Universities of Ontario, Subcommittee on Research and Planning.
Student Participation in University Government. Toronto: The Committee. Pp. 21.
Corry, J. A.
'Student Involvement is Better Than Student Indifference' (Convocation Address, University of Manitoba), *Queen's Univ. Alumni Review* XLII (1), 6-10.
Courtney, J. C.
'Within or Without: The Location of the Faculty Association,' *C.A.U.T. Bull.* XVII (2), 34-35.
Fowke, D. V.
'The Ottawa Plan,' *Can. Univ.* III (2), 40-43.
Gordon, P. J.
'Objectifs d'une formation à l'administration,' *Rev. Univ. Moncton* I (2), 40-45.

1968 Hare, F. K.
On University Freedom in the Canadian Context. Toronto: U. of T. Press. Pp. 80.
Milner, J. B., A. Berland and J. P. Smith.
'Report on Simon Fraser University by the Invertigating Committee of the Canadian Association of University Teachers,' *C.A.U.T. Bull.* XVII (4), 4-28.
Monahan, E. J.
'Consultation and Participation: A Report on the Ontario College of Art,' *C.A.U.T. Bull.* XVII (2), 46-52.
Monahan, E. J.
'Duff-Berdahl Conference on University Government,' *C.A.U.T. Bull.* XVI (3), 54-62.
Rotstein, A.
'The Makings of a President,' *Can. Forum* XLVIII, 124-27.
Sparshott, F. E.
'Four Views of a University,' *Can. Forum* XLVIII, 80-81.
Webster, S.
'Student Discipline: Are Universities Using a Double Standard?' *Proc. Assoc. Stud. Services* 23-27.
Young, P.
'The O.C.A. [Ontario College of Art] Affair: Getting the Stiffs off the Property,' *This Magazine* II (2), 62-71.

1969 Carleton University, Students' Council. New University Government Study Committee.
Report of ... Ottawa: The University. Pp. 74.
Corry, J. A.
Universities and Governments. Toronto: Gage. Pp. 61.
Corry, J. A.
'University Government,' *Queen's Q.* LXXVI, 567-76.
Fisher, G. L.
'An Analysis of the Decision-making Process in a College Advisory Committee.' Unpublished doct. dissertation, Univ. of Calgary.
Lacombe, T.
'A Study of University Government in the Province of Quebec.' Unpublished M.A. thesis, Carleton Univ.
Lauzon, A.
'L'Université [de Montréal] remise en question,' *Mag. Maclean* VIII (10), 21, 63-66, 69.

1969 **Queen's University.**
University Government at Queen's: Report of the Committee on Structure of the Senate. Kingston: Queen's Univ. Pp. 28.
Université de Montréal, Commission Conjoint du Conseil et de l'Assemblée Universitaire.
L'Université: son rôle, le rôle de ses composantes, la relation entre ses composantes. Montréal: Presses Univ. Montréal. Pp. 333.
Williams, D. C.
'Who Shall Govern?' *Can. Univ.* IV (5), 17-20, 30.

1970 **Association of Universities and Colleges of Canada.**
Guidelines on University Organization/Directives... Ottawa: The Association. Pp. 14.
Briemberg, M.
'A Taste of Better Things – P.S.A. at S.F.U.,' *This Magazine* IV (1), 32-55.
Commission of Inquiry on Forty Catholic Church-Related Colleges and Universities.
Report of... : A Commitment to Higher Education in Canada. Ottawa: National Education Office. Pp. 272.
Gilmor, R. P. and W. G. Scott.
'University Government and Student Organization,' *Jour. Council Student Services* V (1), 23-30.
How, H. R.
'Ferment and Transition at U. of T.,' *Can. Bus.* XLIII (3), 60-66.
Presidential Committee on Rights and Responsibilities of Members of York University (B. Laskin, Chairman).
Report of... Toronto: U. of T. Press. Pp. 64.
University of Toronto Commission on the Government of the University of Toronto.
Toward Community in University Government. Toronto: U. of T. Press. Pp. 240.
Watt, L. A. K.
'The Choosing of a University President,' *OCUFA Newsletter* III (5), 13-14.
Winter, F. E.
'Reform of University Government at the University of Toronto,' *C.A.U.T. Bull.* XVIII (3), 16-24.

C. UNIVERSITY FINANCE : FINANCES UNIVERSITAIRES

1959 **MacLean, J. F.**
'Unions on the University Campus,' *Can. P. R. Jour.* VI (2), 39-45.

1961 **Stewart, F. K.**
'Government Aid and Control of Education in Canada,' *Current History* [U.S.] XL, 353-60.
Willis, R. B. and F. R. Stone.
'Money Management in the Universities,' *Univ. Affairs* II (3), 1-2.

1963 **Smiley, D. V.**
'Conditional Grants and Canadian Federalism.' Toronto: Canadian Tax Foundation. Pp. 72.
Whitworth, F. E.
'Student Investment in Higher Education,' *Ont. Jour. Ed. Res.* VI, 173-85.

1964 **Canadian Association of University Teachers.**
'Brief to the Minister of Finance on the Financing of Universities,' *C.A.U.T. Bull.* XII (4), 25-35.
Glendenning, D. E. M.
'Impact of Federal Financial Support on Vocational Education in Canada.' Unpublished doct. dissertation, Indiana Univ.
Moffatt, H. P.
'Some Principles of Educational Finance – a New Look,' *Can. Ed. Research Digest* IV, 193-207.

1965 **Andrew, G. C.**
'Church-State Relationships and Federal Aid to Higher Education in Canada,' *Liberal Education* [U.S.] LI, 1-7.
Association of Atlantic Universities.
Education in the Atlantic Provinces: A Report submitted to the Commission on The Financing of Higher Education. Halifax: Assoc. of Atlantic Univs. Pp. 77.
Beauchemin, J.-M.
'Le Financement des collèges classiques: un problème immédiat à résoudre,' *Prospectives* I (3), 43-48.
Bladen, V. W.
'Address to the Association of Universities and Colleges of Canada,' *A.U.C.C. Proc.* 57-61.
Bladen, V. W.
'The Bladen Commission Recommends ... ' *Univ. Affairs* VII (1), 1-3.

1965 **Canadian Association of University Teachers, Committee on University Financing.**
The Financing of Universities. Ottawa: The Association. Pp. 10.
Canadian Teachers' Federation. Research Division.
Financing Education in Canada. Ottawa: The Federation. Pp. 107.
Commission of the Financing of Higher Education (V. W. Bladen, Chairman).
Financing Higher Education in Canada: Being the Report of a Commission to the Association of Universities and Colleges of Canada ...
Ottawa: Assoc. of Univs. and Colleges of Canada. Pp. 104.
Gill, C., ed.
'Proceedings of 2nd Joint Meeting on Corporate Aid to Higher Education, Seignory Club, Montebello, Feb. 22-23, 1965.' Ottawa. Pp. 36.
Issued by the Steering Committee on Corporate Aid to Higher Education 'for restricted distribution'; copies obtainable upon request from two organizations represented on the Committee: Assoc. of Univs. and Colleges of Canada, 151 Slater Street, Ottawa; National Industrial Conference Board, 615 Dorchester Blvd. W., Montreal. Includes:
W. J. Waines, 'Comments on Report of the Bladen Comm.,' 15-18;
Y. Dube, 'Comments on the Report of the Parent ... Comm.,' 19-20;
E. F. Sheffield, 'Timing of University Fund-Raising Campaigns,' 21-25;
R. J. Albrant, 'The Case for Fund Raisers in the University,' 27-30;
A. R. Maybee, 'The Role of Professional Fund Raisers,' 31-33;
W. B. MacKinnon, 'Professional Fund Raisers from the Corporate Point of View,' 35-36.
Graham, J. F.
'The Bladen Report and the Universities of the Atlantic Provinces: Two Plus Two Equal Three,' *C.A.U.T. Bull.* XIV (2), 87-92.
Judy, R. W. and J. B. Levine.
A New Tool for Educational Administrators. A Report to the Commission on the Financing of Higher Education. Toronto: U. of T. Press. Pp. 33.
Laskin, B. and H. E. English.
'The Financing of Universities,' *C.A.U.T. Bull.* XIV (2), 75-86.
Mackay, C. B.
'The Pressing Need for Additional Federal Assistance for Education,' *Atlantic Advocate* LV (9), 18-20.
Rosenbluth, G.
'Reflections on the Bladen Commission Report,' *C.A.U.T. Bull.* XIV (2), 93-103.

1966 **Adam, W. G.**
'Financial Aid to New Brunswick High School Graduates for University Education.' Unpublished M.Ed. thesis, Univ. of New Brunswick.
Andrew, G. C.
'The Bladen Report: Its Impact on Governments,' *Can. Univ.* I (1), 24-26.
Bennett, P. H.
'Problems of Corporate Aid to Higher Education,' *Industrial Can.* LXVI (11), 43-48.
Byleveld, H.
Corporate Aid to Higher Education in Canada. National Industrial Conference Board; Canadian Studies No. 11. Montreal: The Board. Pp. 94.
Canadian Association of University Teachers.
'The Public Financing of Universities: A Brief Presented to the Governments of Canada and of the Provinces/'Le Mode de financement des universités par les deniers publics: mémoire soumis aux gouvernements du Canada et des provinces,' *C.A.U.T. Bull.* XIV Special Issue (Feb. '66). Pp. 51.
Drummond, I. M.
'Financing University Growth: The Bladen Report,' *Can. Forum* XLV, 220-22.
Gill, C., ed.
'Proceedings of 3rd Joint Meeting on Corporate Aid to Higher Education, Chateau Frontenac, Quebec, March 6-8, 1966.' Ottawa. Pp. 52. Issued by the Steering Committee on Corporate Aid to Higher Education 'for restricted distribution'; copies obtainable upon request from two organizations represented on the Committee: Assoc. of Univs. and Colleges of Canada, 151 Slater Street, Ottawa; National Industrial Conference Board, 615 Dorchester Blvd. W., Montreal. Includes: Papers by L. Brown, P. H. Bennett, E. L. Nelson on 'Industry's Role and Problems in Supporting Higher Education,' 13-27; Papers by J. A. Corry, C. B. MacKay, L.-P. Bonneau, J. B. Macdonald on 'Accounting for Universities' Needs,' 29-45; E. F. Sheffield, 'The Timing of University Fund-Raising Campaigns,' 47-52.
Hanson, E. J.
Financing Education in Alberta. Edmonton: Alberta Teachers' Association. Pp. 81.
Lougheed, W. C.
'The Widow's Cruse,' [review article on Bladen Report] *Queen's Q.* LXXIII, 119-29.

1966 **Moore, A. M., A. I. Gullman and P. H. White.**
Financing Education in British Columbia. Vancouver: British Columbia School Trustees Assoc. Pp. 81.
Peel, B.
'Problems of Canadian Academic Libraries,' *C.A.U.T. Bull.* XIV (4), 7-14.
Robinson, A. J.
'The Bladen Commission and Graduate Education,' *Can. Jour. Econ. Pol. Sci.* XXXII, 520-25.
Toombs, W. M. P.
'An Analysis of Parliamentary Debates on Federal Financial Participation in Education in Canada (1867-1960).' Unpublished doct. dissertation, Univ. of Alberta.
'Venture Capital and Academic Freedom,' *Can. Univ.* I (3), 21-25.

1967 **Byleveld, H.**
'Business Aid to Universities – A Margin of Freedom,' *Can. Bus.* XL (1), 26-30.
Canada, Department of National Health and Welfare.
The Economics and Costs of Medical Care. Ottawa: The Department. Pp. 192.
Gautier, G.
'Quatrième réunion conjointe sur l'aide des sociétés à l'enseignement supérieur,' *Univ. Affairs* VIII (4), 6-8.
Hemphill, H. D.
'Trends in Educational Finance and the Public Sector: 1946-60,' *Can. Ed. Research Digest* VII, 334-48.
Paterson, I. W.
'Determinants of Expenditures for Education,' *Can. Ed. Research Digest* VII, 155-69.
Rosenbluth, G.
'The Structure of Academic Salaries in Canada,' *C.A.U.T. Bull.* XV (4), 19-27.
Stager, D. A.
'Your Financial Fate in '67: New Guessing Game for University Administrators,' *Can. Univ.* II (1), 32-34.
Wright, D. T.
'A Provincial View of the Roles of the Federal Government, the Provincial Government and Industry,' *Univ. Affairs* VIII (4), 3-6.

1968 **Canada, Dept. of the Secretary of State, Education Support Branch.**
Federal Expenditures on Research in the Academic Community 1966-67, 1967-68. Ottawa: Queen's Printer. Pp. 113.

1968 **de Grandpré, J.**
'Le Financement des universités: question de participation,'
Univ. Affairs IX (3), 4-5.
Les Diplômés de l'Université de Montréal.
Les Investissements Universitaires: Planification et coordination.
Montréal: Editions du Jour. Pp. 155. Inclut:
M. Brunet, 'Les Subventions de rattrapage,' 83-100; J. de Grandpré, 'La Participation des diplômés, de l'industrie, des étudiants et du public au financement des universités,' 101-09; J. Tremblay, 'L'Effort budgétaire comparàtif au Québec,' 111-33; G. Boucher, 'Pour une politique du financement de l'enseignement supérieur au Québec,' 135-55.
Hyman, C.
'Federal Aid to Higher Education with Particular Reference to Universities in the Period 1951 to 1967.' Unpublished M.A. thesis, McGill Univ.
Liswood, S.
'Who Should Pay for Medical Education in the Hospital?' *Can. Hosp.* XLV (11), 49-52.
MacKay, C. B.
'Are We Really Willing to Pay for Higher Education?' *Atlantic Advocate* LVIII (9), 25-28.
Rideout, E. B.
'The Financial Support of Education,' *Can. Ed. Research Digest* VII, 85-103.
Rocher, G.
'Pour une politique de financement de l'enseignement supérieur au Québec,' *Orient. Prof.* IV, 177-83.

1969 **Cameron, D. M.**
'The Politics of Education in Ontario, with Special Reference to the Financial Structure.' Unpublished doct. dissertation, Univ. of Toronto.
Canada, Dept. of the Secretary of State, Education Support Branch.
Federal Expenditures on Post-Secondary Education 1966-67, 1967-68.
Ottawa: Queen's Printer. Pp. 34.
Clark, E., D. Cook, G. Fallis and M. Kent.
'Student Aid and Access to Higher Education in Ontario.' Mimeograph report issued by Professor R. W. Judy, Univ. of Toronto. Pp. 259.
Macdonald, J. B.
'The Macdonald Report: The Federal Role in University Research,' *Sci. Forum* II (3), 3-6. See also L.-P. Dugal, 'The Minority Report:

Too Little Attention to Quebec's Problems,' 6-7; H. G. Thode, 'A Courageous Report which Will Spark Both Discussion and Dissent,' 8-12; J. Brazeau, 'A Social Scientist's View: Much Useful Information but Too-Radical Advice.'

1969 **New Brunswick Higher Education Commission.**
Investing in the Future: Programme for Government Assistance to Universities, Technical Schools and their Students. Fredericton: The Commission. Pp. 67.
Scott, D. H.
'Dissent from Formula Financing,' *Can. Univ.* IV (1), 24-27, 44.
Selby-Smith, C. and M. Skolnik.
Concerning the Growth of Provincial Expenditures on Education in Ontario, 1938-1966. Toronto: Ontario Institute for Studies in Education. Pp. 36.

1970 **Commission of Inquiry on Forty Catholic Church-Related Colleges and Universities.**
Report of ... : a Commitment to Higher Education in Canada. Ottawa: National Education Office. Pp. 272.
Kockebakker, J.
'Are We Wasting Money on Higher Education?' *Can. R. and D.* III (1), 35-36.
Michaud, L.
'Government Policies of Financial Support of Church-Related Colleges and Universities in Canada.' Unpublished doct. dissertation, Columbia Univ.
Primeau, W. J.
'Public Financial Aid to Undergraduates in Canadian Universities for the Year 1970-71 / Aides financières des gouvernements ... '
Univ. Aff. XI (6), 1-6; 11-16.
Queen's University, Institute of Intergovernmental Relationships.
'The Functional Spending Priorities of Canadian Governments, with Particular Reference to Education' in *Studies on the University, Society and Government ...* (Ottawa: U. of Ottawa Press. 2 vols.), II, 1-102.

D. THE UNIVERSITY AND THE STATE :
L'UNIVERSITÉ ET L'ETAT

1959 **Martin, J.-M.**
The Role of the University in Quebec (Third J. J. Morrison Memorial Lecture). Guelph: Ontario Agricultural College. Pp. 8.

1964 **Anderson, R. N.**
'The Role of Government in Canadian Education: An Analysis of Bureaucratic Structure.' Unpublished doct. dissertation, Univ. of Minnesota.
Drummond, I. M.
'The Robbins Commission and the Canadian Scene,' *Can. Forum* XLIII, 265-68.
Laskin, B. and J. H. S. Reid.
'Memorandum Concerning R.C.M.P. Activities on University Campuses,' *C.A.U.T. Bull.* XII (3), 36-41; XIII (1), 54-60.
Morin, J.-Y.
'L'Université, conscience du peuple,' *Maintenant* XXXVI, 410-11.
Pelletier, D.
'Université, personne canonique, personne civile,' *Maintenant* XXXIV, 298-300.
Symposium on 'Organization and Support of Basic Scientific Research in Canada,' *Tr. R.S.C.* Includes:
J. W. T. Spinks, 'The National Research Council Forecast of Support Needed for Basic Research in Canadian Universities,' 327-38;
H. G. Thode, 'Basic Scientific Research – Its Importance and Support,' 339-48; F. R. Hayes, 'Co-Operation between Universities and Government,' 349-54; C. M. Drury, 'A Partnership in Science between Government, Industry, and the Universities,' 355-61.
Vachon, L.-A.
Progrès de l'université et consemtement populaire. Quebec: Presses Univ. Laval. Pp. 190.

1965 **Carrothers, F.**
'R.C.M.P. Activities on University Campuses,' *C.A.U.T. Bull.* XIII (2), 41-44.
Mathews, R. D.
'University Crisis and the Common-Weal,' *Can. Forum* XLV, 32-34.
Scott, P. D.
'America's "Knowledge Industry"; what Protection for a Smaller Power?' *Tamarack Review* (Winter, 1965), 65-77.
Sheffield, E. F.
'Emerging Provincial Systems of Higher Education,' *School Administration* II (5), 31-34.

1966 **Cooper, W. M., W. G. Davis, A.-M. Parent and T. R. McConnell.**
Governments and the University. The Frank Gerstein Lectures, York University, 1966. Toronto: Macmillan. Pp. 108.

1966 **Harris, R. S.**
'The Evolution of a Provincial System of Higher Education in Ontario' in D. F. Dadson, ed., *On Higher Education: Five Lectures* (Toronto: U. of T. Press), 36-62.
Hosken, F.
'The Urban University and the Urban Environment,' *Arch. Can.* XLIII (10), 48-50.
McCarthy, J. R.
'The Department of University Affairs [of Ontario] and How It Developed,' *Can. Univ.* I (4), 36-37.
Porter, J.
'Social Change and the Aims and Problems of Education in Canada,' *McGill Jour. Ed.* I, 125-30.
Smith, J. P.
'Universities and Governments,' *Can. Forum* XLV, 218-19.
Somers, H. J., J. A. Corry, R. Gaudry and W. Swift.
'University-Provincial Government Relations,' *A.U.C.C. Proc.* 115-33; 'Rapports entre les universités et les gouvernements provinciaux,' 243-61.

1967 **Cardinal, J.-G.**
'Ce que la Société attend de l'université,' *Univ. Affairs* IX (2), 4-6.
Committee of Presidents of Universities of Ontario.
System Emerging: First Annual Review (1966-67). Toronto: The Committee. Pp. 59.
Gunn, C. R.
'The Role of the Atlantic Provincial Governments in Adult Education.' Unpublished doct. dissertation, Univ. of Toronto. Summary in *Jour. Ed. (N.S.)* XVII (1), 16-24.
Ross, M. G.
'The University and Community Service,' *A.U.C.C. Proc.* 62-76.
Wright, D. T.
'A Provincial View of the Roles of the Federal Government, the Provincial Government and Industry,' *Univ. Affairs* VIII (4), 3-6.

1968 **Andrew, G. C.**
'Institutional Identity and Public Systems of Higher Education,' *Western College Association Addresses and Proceedings* ... 1968, 7-13.
Begg, R. W.
'The Freedom and Autonomy of Universities,' *Univ. Affairs* IX (3), 9-10.

1968 **Brunet, M.**
'Quebec's French-Speaking Universities,' *Queen's Q.* LXXV, 613-31.
Cardinal, J.-G.
'Le Pari de l'éducation,' *Maintenant* No. 76, 115-20.
Chapman, J. H.
'Joint Research in Canada,' *Trans. R.S.C.* 77-83.
Committee of Presidents of Universities of Ontario.
Collective Autonomy: Second Annual Review (1967-68). Toronto: The Committee. Pp. 68.
Corry, J. A.
'Universities, Government and the Public,' *Queen's Q.* LXXV, 424-31.
Courtney, J. C.
'The Government-University Controversy in Saskatchewan, 1967-68,' *C.A.U.T. Bull.* XVII (2), 19-33.
Duckworth, H. E.
'University Research and Governments,' *Trans. R.S.C.* 43-52.
Grand'maison, J.
'Un Rôle nouveau pour les campus,' *Maintenant* No. 81, 267-70.
Hare, F. K.
On University Freedom in the Canadian Context. Toronto: U. of T. Press. Pp. 80.
Mitchener, R. D.
'The Pattern of University-Government Relationships in Canada,' *C.A.U.T. Bull.* XVII (2), 12-18.
Saucier, P. and Y. Gosselin.
'Pour une Université rénovée,' *Maintenant* No. 80, 227-29.

1969 **Academic Board for Higher Education in British Columbia.**
College-University Articulation. Vancouver: The Board. Pp. 51.
Deutsch, J.
'The Role of a Changing University in a Changing Society,' *Queen's Q.* LXXVI, 392-400.
Macdonald, J. B. *et al.*
The Role of the Federal Government in Support of Research in Canadian Universities. Special Study No. 7 of the Science Council of Canada. Ottawa: Queen's Printer. Pp. 361.
Schneider, W. G.
'Science, Technology and the Federal Government,' *Trans. R.S.C.* Sect. 3, 263-70.
Seville, B.
'Current Trends in Canadian University-Government Relationships,' *Man. Jour. Ed.* IV (2), 83-93.

1970 **Commission on the Relations between Universities and Governments.**
Studies on the University, Society and Government Prepared for the Commission. Ottawa: Univ. of Ottawa Press. 2 vols.
Harvey, J.
'L'Université, service à la société – le Rapport Deschênes,' *Relations* XXX, 36-37.
Hurtubise, R. and D. C. Rowat.
The University, Society and Government: The Report of the Commission on the Relations between Universities and Governments. Ottawa: Univ. of Ottawa Press. Pp. 252.
Macdonald, J. B.
'Change and the Universities: University-Government Relationships,' *Can. Pub. Admin.* XIII, 6-18.
Porter, J.
'The Democratization of the Canadian Universities and the Need for a National System,' *Minerva* [U.K.] VIII, 325-56.
Stewart, E. E.
'The Role of the Provincial Government in the Development of Universities in Ontario 1791-1964.' Unpublished doct. dissertation, Univ. of Toronto.

E. THE UNIVERSITY AND THE CHURCH :
L'UNIVERSITE ET L'EGLISE

1961 **LeBel, E. C.**
'The Catholic University and the Dialogue,' *Bas. Teacher* V, 199-205.
1963 **Lupul, M. R.**
'Relations in Education between the State and the Roman Catholic Church in the Canadian North-West with Special Reference to the Provisional District of Alberta from 1880 to 1905.' Unpublished doct. dissertation, Harvard Univ.
1964 **Theall, D. F.**
'The Church's Role in the University,' *Bas. Teacher* IX, 79-87.
1965 **Andrew, G. C.**
'Church-State Relationships and Federal Aid to Higher Education in Canada,' *Liberal Education* [U.S.] LI (May 1965), 1-7.
Kennedy, L. A.
'The Catholic University and Freedom,' *Culture* XXVI, 135-40.

1965 **Rioux, B.**
'Déconfessionnalisation et démocratisation de l'Université de Montréal,' *Cité Libre* LXXIV, 21-25.
Sarrazin, G.
'Les Chrétiens à l'université,' *Maintenant* XLI, 171-72.
Skora, S. J.
'Notes on the Freedom of the Scholar and the Authority of the Church,' *Rev. Univ. Ottawa* XXXV, 198-206.
Vachon, L.-A.
'Nouveau Type d'université catholique,' *Rev. Univ. Laval* XIX, 795-800.
1966 **Angers, F.-A.**
'Les Trois Libertés à sauver à l'heure actuelle' Part III: 'L'Université,' *Act. Nat.* LV, 1046-56.
Drummond, I. M.
Costs and Benefits in Anglican Higher Educational Efforts. Toronto: Anglican Church of Canada. Pp. 35.
Hewson, J.
'Secular and Denominational Institutions: The Separation of Church and State,' *Culture* XXVII, 146-50.
McKinna, Sister M. O.
The Impact of Religion and Politics on the Structure of Higher Education in the Province of Prince Edward Island. Halifax: Mount St. Vincent Univ.
Sullivan, A. D.
'Patterns of Interinstitutional Co-operation in Canadian Catholic Higher Education.' Unpublished doct. dissertation, Catholic Univ. of America.
1967 'Can the Church University Compete in Today's World?' *Can. Univ.* II (5), 56-58.
Greco, J.
'Les Enseignements missionaires du II concile oecuménique du Vatican et les universités,' *Rev. Univ. Ottawa* XXXVII, 719-48.
Nicholls, C. G. W. and W. B. Heeney.
University and Church: Two Points of View. Toronto: Anglican Church of Canada. Pp. 39.
1969 **Magnuson, R.**
'The Decline of Roman Catholic Education in Quebec: Some Interpretations and Explanations,' *Culture* XXX, 193-98.
1970 **Commission of Inquiry on Forty Catholic Church-Related Colleges and Universities.**

Report of ... : A Commitment to Higher Education in Canada.
Ottawa: National Education Office. Pp. 272.

1970 **Croteau, J.**
'L'Université chrétienne,' *Act. Nat.* LIX, 966-87.
Harvey, J.
'L'Université nouvelle et la théologie engagée,' *Relations* XXX, 80-82.
Michaud, L.
'Government Policies of Financial Support of Church-Related Colleges and Universities in Canada.' Unpublished doct. dissertation, Columbia Univ.

F. THE UNIVERSITY AND THE ECONOMY :
   L'UNIVERSITE ET L'ECONOMIE

1965 **Drummond, I.**
'Some Economic Issues in Educational Expansion' in A. Rotstein, ed., *The Prospect of Change* (Toronto: McGraw Hill), 267-85.
Johnson, H. G.
'The Economics of the "Brain Drain": The Canadian Case,' *Minerva* [U.K.] III (3), 299-311.
Lorimer, J.
'Economists and Educational Planning − A Critical Discussion,' *Can. Ed. Research Digest* V, 210-18.
Meltz, N. M.
The Applications and Limitations of Manpower Forecasting. Ottawa: Privy Council Office Special Planning Secretariat. Pp. 19.
Meltz, N. M.
Changes in the Occupational Composition of the Canadian Labour Force 1931-61. Ottawa: Queen's Printer. Pp. 136.
Parai, L.
Immigration and Emigration of Professional Skilled Manpower During the Post-War Period. Ottawa: Economic Council of Canada. Pp. 248.
Taylor, K. W.
'Some Aspects of Canada's Economic Prospects,' *Queen's Q.* LXXII, 466-79.
Verrier, W. L.
'Investment in Technical and Vocational Education in Canada.' Unpublished M.A. thesis, McGill Univ.

1965 **Whitworth, F. E.**
'Random Thoughts on the Possibility of Surplus of University Graduates,' *Ont. Jour. Ed. Res.* VIII, 133-48.
Wilkinson, B. W.
Studies in the Economics of Education. Ottawa: Department of Labour, Economics and Research Branch. Pp. 148.
Wilson, G. W., S. Gordon and S. Judek.
Canada: An Appraisal of Its Needs and Resources. Toronto: U. of T. Press. Pp. 528.

1966 **Bertram, G. W.**
The Contribution of Education to Economic Growth. Ottawa: Queen's Printer. Pp. 150.
Duclos, G. C.
'Role of Universities in Canada's Manpower Development,' *Proc. Assoc. Student Services* 9-14.
Hartle, D. G.
The Employment Forecast Survey. Toronto: U. of T. Press. Pp. 156.
Organization for Economic Cooperation and Development.
Training of and Demand for High-Level Scientific and Technical Personnel in Canada. Paris: The Organization. Pp. 136.
Shrum, G. M.
'A Critique on Education and Economic Growth,' *Proc. Schools Bus.* Pp. 12.
Twaits, W. O.
'Education and Economic Growth,' *Dalhousie Rev.* XLVI, 79-87.

1967 **Cockburn, P. and Y. Raymond.**
Women University Graduates in Continuing Education and Employment/La Femme diplômee face à l'education permanente et au monde du travail. Toronto: Canadian Federation of University Women. Pp. 196.
Mengall, C.
'Industry and the University,' *Executive* IX (7), 32-35.
Peitchinis, S. G.
'The Economic Value of Education,' *Bus. Q.* XXXII, 59-67.

1968 **Kruger, A. and N. M. Meltz, eds.**
The Canadian Labour Market: Readings in Manpower Economics. Toronto: Univ. of Toronto, Centre for Industrial Relations. Pp. 312.
Orr, J. L.
'A Pragmatic View of University-Industry Relationships,' *Eng. Jour.* LI (8), 8-10.

1968 **Ross, M. G.**
'The Universities and Big Business,' *Can. Dimension* V (2-3), 39-41.
Smith, A. J. R.
'The Social Sciences and the "Economics of Research,"' *Trans. R.S.C.*
21-33.

1969 **Belanger, G.**
'L'Université, une perspective économique,' *Act. Econ.* XLV, 488-98.
Fisher, E. A.
International Market for Graduates. Ottawa: Canadian Council for Research in Education. Pp. 8.
Lithwick, N. H.
Canada's Science Policy and the Economy. Toronto: Methuen. Pp. 176. Includes:
'The University,' 25-36.
Meltz, N. M.
'Manpower Policy: Nature, Objectives, Perspectives,' *Relations Ind.* XXIV, 33-54.
Neher, P. A. and K. A. J. Hay.
'Education and Capital Misallocation in a Growing Economy,'
Can. Jour. Econ. I, 609-18.
Stager, D. A.
Some Economic Aspects of Alternative Systems of Post-Secondary Education. Ottawa: Canadian Council for Research in Education. Pp. 35.
Watkins, M. H.
'Education in the Branch Plant Economy,' *Can. Dimension* VI (5), 37-39. Also in *This Magazine* IV (1), 121-28.

1970 **France, N.**
'Teachers in Canada: Supply and Demand for the '70's,' *Ed. Canada* X (1), 3-7.

G. UNIVERSITY PLANNING :
   LA PLANIFICATION UNIVERSITAIRE

1961 **Sheffield, E. F.**
'Population Projection and the Provision of Community Facilities: Projecting University Enrolment,' *Can. Pub. Admin.* IV, 113-16.

1965 **Judy, R. W. and J. B. Levine.**
A New Tool for Educational Administrators: A Report to the Commission on the Financing of Higher Education. Toronto: U. of T. Press. Pp. 33.
Lorimer, J.
'Economists and Educational Planning – A Critical Discussion,' *Can. Ed. Research Digest* V, 210-18.
Meltz, N. M.
The Applications and Limitations of Manpower Forecasting. Ottawa: Privy Council Office Special Planning Secretariat. Pp. 19.

1966 **Berlyne, D. E.**
'The Relationship of the Social Sciences to Educational Planning, Research and Development' in *Emerging Strategies and Structures for Educational Change: Proceedings of the Anniversary International Conference June 12-15, 1966.* (Toronto: Ontario Institute for Studies in Education), 109-21. Comments by C. Watson, 122-26 and P. C. Dodwell, 126-29.
Munroe, D.
'Educational Planning as an Aspect of Social Change in Quebec' in *Emerging Strategies and Structures for Educational Change: Proceedings of the Anniversary International Conference June 12-15, 1966* (Toronto: Ontario Institute for Studies in Education), 84-93.
Organization for Economic Cooperation and Development.
Training and Demand for High-Level Scientific and Technical Personnel in Canada. Paris: The Organization. Pp. 136.
Smith, W. A. S.
'Academic Planning at the U. of A.,' *New Trail* XXIV (1), 16-20.
'Total Planning for Tomorrow's Campus,' *Can. Univ.* I (1), 27-31.
Vaughan, W. N.
'Space Planning and Space Utilization,' *Can. Univ.* I (2), 22-25.

1967 'Interior Design: Architectural Necessity and Emotional Stimulus,' *Can. Univ.* II (3), 36-37, 73-74.
Rosenbluth, G.
'Regional Academic Planning,' *C.A.U.T. Bull.* XV (4), 3-8.
Watson, C.
'Educational Planning,' *Can. Ed. Research Digest* VII, 24-28.
Watson, C.
'The Training and Use of Educational Planners' in C. Watson, ed., *Educational Planning: Papers of the International Conference March 20-22, 1967* (Toronto: Ontario Institute for Studies in Education), 73-76.

1968 **Black, D. B. and W. D. Dannenmaier.**
'Institutional Research and the Canadian University Registrar' in *Proc. Can. Conference on Educational Research* (Ottawa: Council for Research in Education), 36-44.

1969 **Bakan, D. R.**
'A Plan for a College,' *Can. Univ. & Coll.* IV (6), 30-34, 42-43.
Levine, J.
'Campus,' *Arch. Can.* XLVI (6), 42-43.
Wilson, R. *et al.*
'Systems Analysis in Health Sciences Educational Planning,' *Can. Med. Assoc. Jour.* C, 715-23.

1970 **Anden, T. M.**
'Let's Pull Planning out of the Amateur Class ... [Report on Conference at Lakehead University, May 1970],' *Can. Univ.* V (6), 22-23, 43.
Judy, R. W.
A Research Progress Report on Systems Analysis for Efficient Resource Allocation in Higher Education. Toronto: Univ. of Toronto: Institute for the Quantitative Analysis of Social and Economic Policy. Pp. 24.
Scott, D. H.
'Campus Planning at the University of Oz,' *Can. Univ. & Coll.* V (1), 22-25.

Curriculum and teaching
Programme d'étude et méthodes d'enseignement

A. THE FACULTY OF ARTS AND SCIENCE

1961 **Murphy, J. F.**
'Science and the Liberal Arts in Catholic Colleges,' *Bas. Teacher* V, 281-84.

1964 **Gunn, K. L. S.**
'Class Size: Is There an Optimum Number?' [McGill Univ.] *Bulletin of Educational Procedures* no. 1. Pp. 4.

1965 **Eliot, C. W. J.** *et al.*
Discipline and Discovery: A Proposal to the Faculty of Arts of the University of British Columbia. Vancouver: Univ. of British Columbia. Pp. 43.
Sullivan, J. R.
'Articulation of Curricula,' *Univ. Windsor Rev.* I, 160-72.

1967 **Beckel, W.**
'The University as Educator: It's Got to Be the Real Old Lady,' *A.U.C.C. Proc.* II, 41-53.
Guindon, R.
'Surgery Suggested for Arts and Science,' *Univ. Affairs* IX (2), 12-13.
University of Toronto, Presidential Advisory Committee on Under- graduate Instruction in the Faculty of Arts and Science (C. B. Macpherson, Chairman).
Undergraduate Instruction in Arts and Science. Toronto: U. of T. Press. Pp. 150.

1968 **MacDonald, D.**
'Liberal Education: The Crisis Compounded,' *Culture* XXIX, 219-29.
Waterton, P. and J. P. Blaney.
A Diploma Program in Liberal Studies: Report on a Preliminary Investigation. Vancouver: Univ. of British Columbia, Department of University Extension. Pp. 17. Occasional Papers in Continuing Education, No. 1.

1969 **Carleton University. Commission on Undergraduate Teaching and** Learning in the Faculty of Arts (M. Frumhartz, Chairman).
Preliminary Report. Ottawa: The University. Pp. 60.

1969 **Fogarty, D.**
A Proposed Inner College for Saint Mary's University. Halifax: Saint Mary's Univ. Pp. 40.
Gordon, C. B.
'A Modest Proposal for Modernizing Academe,' *Queen's Q.* LXXXVI, 503-10.
1970 **Queen's University, Principal's Committee on Teaching and Learning** (G. A. Harrower, Chairman).
Report of ... Kingston: Queen's Univ. Pp. 83.
Sheffield, E. F., ed.
'Curriculum Innovations in Arts and Science: Report of a Canadian Universities Workshop.' Toronto: Higher Education Group, Univ. of Toronto. Pp.

B. FACULTÉ DES ARTS

1880 **Provencher, L.**
'L'Histoire naturelle dans les collèges classiques,' *Nat. Can.* No. 136, 123-25. Voir aussi 118-23.
1898 'L'Enseignement universitaire,' *Rev. Notariat* I, 77-90.
1911 'Les Etudes classiques,' *Rev. Notariat* XIV, 132-39.
1930 'L'Enseignement des Science Naturelles,' *Rev. Trim. Can.* II, 177-89.
1938 **Plante, A.**
Vingt-cinq ans de vie française: Le Collège de Sudbury. Montréal: Imprimerie du Messager. Pp. 151.
1941 **Maheux, A.**
Propôs sur l'éducation. Québec: Libraire de l'Action Catholique. Pp. 259.
1946 **Roy, P.-G.**
'Les Premiers Manuels scolaires canadiens,' *Bull. Recherches Hist.* LII, 287-303; 319-41.
1947 **Charland, T.-M.**
'Un Gaumist canadien: l'abbé Alexis Pelletier,' *Rev. Hist.* I, 195-236.
1960 **Bourgault, R.**
'Propositions sur l'essence du cours classique,' *Coll. et Fam.* IV, 180-85.
Lafrenière, A.
'Project de réforme des programmes à la faculté des arts de l'Université Laval,' *Univ. Affairs* II (2), 1-2.

1964 Angers, P.
'Un Enseignement secondaire pour notre temps,' *Québec '64* [France]
I (2), 55-63.
Blain, M.
'L'Ecole laïque, école de démocratie,' *Cité Libre* XVI (70), 17-20.
Savard, M.
Paradoxes ... et Réalités de notre Enseignement secondaire. Montréal:
Centre de Psychologie et de Pédagogie. Pp. 145.
Tremblay, J.
'Le Collège privé: notre deuxième ministère de l'éducation,'
Cité Libre XVI (71), 6-11.

1965 **Lebel, M.**
'Le Rôle du maître de l'enseignement secondaire,' *Act. Nat.* LIV,
439-63.

1966 **Alexander, W.**
'Les Options et leur choix au cours classiques,' *Orient. Prof.* II,
282-305.
Desjarlais, L. et L.-M. Richer.
'Commentaire sur la fonction éducative,' *Rev. Univ. Ottawa* XXXVI,
608-12.
Galarneau, C.
'Recherches sur l'histoire de l'enseignement secondaire classique au
Canada français,' *Rev. Hist.* XX, 18-27.

1967 **Duval, l'Archevêque et B. Richard.**
'Une Experience de non-directroisme didactique à l'université,'
ACFAS XXXIV, 176-77 (Resumé).
Plante, Sister L.
'La Fondation de l'enseignement classique féminin au Québec
1908-1926.' Thèse de licence en lettres, Univ. Laval.

1969 **Gregoire, G.-A.**
'Et les facultés des Arts ...' *Prospectives* V, 142-45.
Lortie, L.
'Grandeur et servitude des arts et des sciences,' *Mém. S.R.C.* 3-16.

C. THE HUMANITIES : LES HUMANITÉS

GENERAL : GÉNÉRALITÉS

1964 **Lebel, M.**
'L'Avenir des humanités,' *Rev. Univ. Laval* XIX, 246-53.

1965 **Daniells, R.**
'A Humanist Talks to the Scientists,' *Univ. of British Columbia Alumni Chronicle* XIX (Autumn), 5-8.
Fancott, E.
'Culture and Communication,' *Continuous Learning* IV, 9-15.

1966 **Gaudron, E.**
'Civilisation scientifique ou humanisme nouveau,' *Culture* XXVII, 58-73.
Leddy, J. F.
The Humanities in Modern Education. Toronto: Gage. Pp. 68.
Medeiros-Gutierrez, M. A.
'Humanisme et Formation Technique,' *Can. Ed. Research Digest* VII, 26-33.
Medeiros-Gutierrez, M. A. *et al.*
'Humanisme et formation technique,' *ACFAS* XXXII, 137-38 (Resumé).
Vachon, L.-A.
Les Humanités aujourd'hui. Quebec: Presses Univ. Laval. Pp. 92.
Vachon, L.-A.
'The Humanities and the Modern World,' *A.U.C.C. Proc.* 34-44.
Wiles, R. M.
The Humanities in Canada, Supplement to December 31, 1964. Toronto: U. of T. Press. Pp. 236.

1967 **Kirkconnell, W.**
'Organizing the Humanities' in *A Slice of Canada: Memoirs* (Toronto: U. of T. Press), 233-48.
Lebel, M.
Les Humanités classiques au Québec. Québec: Editions de l'Acropole et du Forum. Pp. 152.

1968 **Daniells, R.**
'Literary Studies in Canada' in R. H. Hubbard, ed., *Scholarship in Canada, 1967* (Toronto: U. of T. Press), 29-39.
Lebel, M.
'Les Humanités et les sciences,' *Culture* XXIX, 313-21.
Pacey, W. D.
'Research in the Humanities,' *A.U.C.C. Proc.* 1967, II, 133-50; commentaries by A. Decarie, 151-54 and M. B. Smith, 155-61.
Poole, C. F.
'A Misconception in the Humanities,' *Dalhousie Rev.* XLVII, 5-12.

1968 **Priestley, F. E. L.**
'The Future of the Humanities in Ontario Universities,' *Humanities Association Bull.* XIX (1), 3-13.
Priestley, F. E. L.
'The Humanities: Specific Needs' in R. H. Hubbard, ed., *Scholarship in Canada, 1967* (Toronto: U. of T. Press), 11-16.

1969 **Lebel, M.**
'Le Rôle des humanités dans un ère technologique,' *Mém. S.R.C.* 17-38.
Murray, W. J.
'Scientific and Humanistic Education and the Notion of Paidea,' *Culture* XXX, 208-16.
Smith, J. P.
'Teach – or Get Lost,' *C.A.U.T. Bull.* XVII (4), 2-19.

1970 **Bono, J. D.**
'Languages, Humanities and the Teaching of Values,' *Mod. Lang. Jour.* LIV, 335-47.
Humphreys, E. H.
Focus on Canadian Studies. Toronto: Ontario Institute for Studies in Education. Pp. 125.
Priest, R. R.
'The Humanities in the Nursing Curriculum' in M. Q. Innis, ed., *Nursing Education in a Changing Society* (Toronto: U. of T. Press), 184-92.

ARCHAEOLOGY : ARCHÉOLOGIE

1952 **Kidd, K. E.**
'Sixty Years of Ontario Archaeology' in J. B. Griffin, ed., *Archaeology of the Eastern United States* (Chicago: Univ. of Chicago Press), 71-82.

ART : ARTS PLASTIQUES

1963 **Groome, L. J.**
'Art Education Today for Tomorrow,' *Can. Ed. Research Digest* III, 304-15.

1964 **Colton, A. S.**
A Survey on Educational Resources in the Visual Arts in British Columbia. Vancouver: British Columbia Art Teachers' Federation. Pp. 91.

1965 **Cutler, M. I.**
'Crisis in Canada's Art Schools,' *Can. Art* XXII,(5), 14-26.
'The Education of 12 Practising Artists,' *Can. Art* XXII (5), 27-29, 46.
Savard, M.
'Les Arts plastiques dans l'enseignement: une longue et curieuse randonnée,' *Prospectives* I (3), 32-36.
1966 **Rockman, A.**
'Visual Arts in a University Setting,' *Can. Art* XXIII (2), 11-13, 52.
Young, P.
'Don't Ship Them Off to Art School,' *This Magazine* I (2), 43-50.
1967 **Lavallee, J.-G.**
'L'Enseignement des arts plastiques dans les nouveaux collèges,' *Prospectives* III, 325-34.
1968 **Bayefsky, A.**
'Renewal at the Ontario College of Art,' *Arts Canada* XXV (4), 25-27.
Boggs, J. S.
'The History of Art in Canada' in R. H. Hubbard, ed., *Scholarship in Canada, 1967* (Toronto: U. of T. Press), 40-50.
Doray, V.
'The Future of Education in the Arts,' *Arts Can.* XXV (4), 31-34.
Frenkel, V.
'The New School of Art: Insight Explosions,' *Arts Can.* XXV (4), 13-16.
Schafer, R. M.
'Cleaning the Lenses of Perception,' *Arts Canada* XXV (4), 10-12.
Von Meier, K.
'On Teaching 20th Century Art,' *Arts Can.* XXV (4), 23-24.
Young, P.
'The O.C.A. [Ontario College of Art] Affair: Getting the Stiffs off the Property,' *This Magazine* II (2), 62-71.
1970 **Ferguson, G.**
'A Professional Lithography Workshop,' *Arts Canada* XXVII (2), 59-61.

DRAMA : THÉÂTRE

1966 **Chusid, H.**
'University Theatres in Canada, their Influence on Future Audiences,' *Perf. Arts Can.* IV (4), 22-26.
1968 **Bilsland, J. W.**
'On the Teaching of Drama,' *English Q.* I, 41-51.

1968 **Courtney, R.**
'Drama Now – Why Wait?' *B.C. Teacher* XLVII, 346-47.
Peacock, G.
'Theatre has a Place in Higher Learning,' *Perf. Arts Can.* VI (1), 42-43, 45.
Spensley, P. J.
'Drama at the University of Guelph: Establishing an Ideal" *Can. Speech Commun. Jour.* I (1), 40-44.

LANGUAGE AND LINGUISTICS : LANGUES ET LINGUISTIQUE

1954 **McDavid, R. I.**
'Linguistic Geography in Canada: An Introduction,' *Can. Jour. Linguistics* I (1), 3-8.
Vinay, J.-P.
'Linguistics at the University of Montreal,' *Can. Jour. Linguistics* I (1), 20-21.
1955 **Seary, E. R.**
'The Place of Linguistics in English Studies,' *Can. Jour. Linguistics* I (2), 9-13.
1964 **Ontario Curriculum Institute, Modern Languages Committee.**
Interim Report Number 2. Toronto: The Institute. Pp. 80.
St.-Pierre, G.
'Réflections sur l'enseignement des langues vivantes,' *Bull. Fed. Coll.* IX (3), 4-11.
1965 **Dembowski, P. and D. G. Mowatt.**
'Literary Study and Linguistics,' *Can. Jour. Linguistics* XI, 40-62.
1966 **Jeanes, R. W. and D. A. Massey.**
'Language Labs – a New Look,' *Can. Mod. Lang. Rev.* XXII (2), 40-50.
1967 **Gagne, G.**
'Théories de la communication et critères d'évaluation des méthodes d'enseignement de langues secondes,' *ACFAS* XXXIV, 110 (Resumé).
1968 **Biname, J.-J.**
'Message de la linguistique appliquée à l'enseignement des langues: des réformes s'imposent,' *Rev. Univ. Laur.* I (2), 16-24.
Leon, P.
'Les Recherches en phonétique à l'Université de Toronto,' *Can. Mod. Lang. Rev.* XXIV (2), 24-30.
1969 **Backman, L. B.**
'Some Psychological Perspective on Bilingualism and Second Language Teaching,' *McGill Jour. Ed.* IV (1), 48-58.

1969 **Steinhauer, D.**
'The Professional Training of Teachers of Modern Languages at the Elementary Level,' *Can. Mod. Lang. Rev.* XXV (2), 22-30.
Stern, H. H.
'Language Centers Today and a New Modern Language Center at OISE,' *Can. Mod. Lang. Rev.* XXV (2), 9-21.
1970 **Bono, J. D.**
'Languages, Humanities and the Teaching of Values,' *Mod. Lang. Jour.* LIV, 335-47.
Horner, L. T.
'Broader Participation in Foreign Language Teacher Training,' *Mod. Lang. Jour.* LIV, 250-52.
Leon, P.
'Reflexions sur le laboratoire de langues et le linguistique appliquée,' *Can. Mod. Lang. Rev.* XXVI (2), 20-26; (3), 16-23.
Valdman, A.
'Toward a Better Implementation of the Audio-Lingual Approach,' *Mod. Lang. Jour.* LIV, 309-19.

African Studies : Etudes Africaines

1963 **Cohen, R.**
'Les Etudes afro-asiatiques au Canada/Afro-Asian Studies in Canada,' *Bull. African Studies* I (1), 4-29.
1964 **Dobson, W. A. C. H., ed.**
The Contribution of Canadian Universities to an Understanding of Asia and Africa/Contribution des universités canadiennes à la connaissance de l'Asie et de l'Afrique. Ottawa: Canadian National Commission for UNESCO, 1964. Pp. 70.
1965 **Weidner, D. L.**
'African Studies in Canada,' *African Studies Bulletin* [U.S.] VIII (3), 71-75.
1967 **Savage, D. C.**
'African Studies in Canada,' *Can. Jour. African Studies* I, 5-11.

Byzantine Studies : Etudes Byzantines

1965 **Schlieper, H. C.**
'Byzantine Studies in Canada,' *New Rev.* V (1), 54-56.
1966 **Wolock, M.**
'The Present State of Byzantine Studies in Canada,' *New Rev.* VI (2-3), 57-59.

1968 **Woloch, M.**
'Byzantine Studies in Canada, 1967-68,' *New Rev.* VIII, 75-79.

Classics : Langues anciennes

1892 **Fraser, W. H.**
Pass French and German in the University of Toronto. Paper read before Modern Language Assoc. of Toronto April 20, 1892. Toronto: Pp. 15.

1898 **Reynar, A. H.**
'The Ancient Classics and the Modern Classics in our Schools,' *Proc. Dominion Educational Assoc.* 1898. 179-91.

1962 **McKay, A. G.**
'Latin Studies in Canada,' *Romanitas* [Brazil] V, 323-31.

1964 **Krésic, S.**
'L'Enseignement des ≪ Classiques en traduction ≫ ,' *Rev. Univ. Ottawa* XXXIV, 153-68.

1965 **Heyen, J.**
'Le Latin selon le rapport Parent,' *Enseignement Secondaire* XLIV, 161-72.

1967 **Gareau, E.** *et al.*
'Colloque sur les humanités gréco-latines à l'heure du Rapport Parent,' *ACFAS* XXX, 83-84.

White, M.
'Phoenix: the First Twenty Years,' *Phoenix* XX, 273-84.

East Asian Studies : Etudes sur l'Asie de l'Est

1961 **Yi-t'ung Wang.**
'The P'u-pan Chinese Library at the University of British Columbia,' *Pacific Affairs,* Spring 1951, 101-11.

1963 **Cohen, R.**
'Les Etudes afro-asiatiques au Canada'/'Afro-Asian Studies in Canada,' *Bull. African Studies* I (1), 4-29.

1964 **Dobson, W. A. C. H.,** ed.
The Contribution of Canadian Universities to an Understanding of Asia and Africa/Contribution des universités canadiennes à la connaissance de l'Asie et de l'Afrique. Ottawa: Canadian National Commission for UNESCO, 1964. Pp. 70.

1970 **Ng, T. K.**
'Librarianship in East Asian Studies,' *Can. Library Jour.* XXVII, 102-14.

English : Anglais

1955 **Seary, E. R.**
'The Place of Linguistics in English Studies,' *Can. Jour. Linguistics* I (2), 9-13.

1958 **Elder, A. T.**
'The Teaching of English to Science Students at the University of Alberta,' *Bull. of the Canadian Conference of Pharmaceutical Faculties* XI (5), 98-102.

1960 **Scargill, M. H.**
'Linguistics and the Teaching of English in Schools,' *Can. Jour. Linguistics* VI (2), 136-38.

1966 **Gajadharsingh, J.**
'An Evaluation of the Pre-Service Education Programs Provided by Western Canadian Universities for High School Teachers of English.' Unpublished M.Ed. thesis, Univ. of Saskatchewan.

1967 **Mickleburgh, B.**
'We Teach English Like a Foreign Language,' *Mon. Morn.* II (1), 22-33.

1968 **Bilsland, J. W.**
'On the Teaching of Drama,' *English Q.* I, 41-51.
Livesay, D.
'A Creative Climate for English Teaching,' *English Q.* I, 31-38.
MacLennan, H.
'The Author as Teacher,' *McGill Jour. Ed.* III, 3-11.
Ontario Institute for Studies in Education.
English: Four Essays; the Aims and Problems of English in School, Community Colleges and Universities of Ontario. Toronto: The Institute. Pp. 47.

1969 **Lynch, M.**
'A Canadian Record?' [re teaching of public speaking] *Can. Speech Jour.* II (1), 13-17.
Mandel, E.
'Revolution and Reaction: Direction in English Studies,' *English Q.* II, 7-15.
Mayne, B.
'English Studies in an Experimental Arts Programme,' *English Q.* II, 31-39.
Thomas, W. K.
'The Medium Helps the Message,' *English Q.* II, 57-62.

1970 **Cole, W., V. Rock and R. L. White.**
'A Tentative Report on "American" and "Canadian" Courses in Canadian University Curricula,' *Can. Rev. Amer. Studies* I (1), 39-47.

1970 **Gutteridge, D.**
'Teaching Structure in English,' *English Q.* III (2), 35-49.
King, D. B. and E. Cotter.
'An Experiment in Writing Instruction [Innis College Writing Laboratory],' *English Q.* III (2), 50-56.
Wayman, T.
'English: Art or Science?' *U.B.C. Alumni Chronicle* Summer 1970, 9-12.

French : Français

1892 **Fraser, W. H.**
Pass French and German in the University of Toronto. Paper Read before the Modern Language Assoc. of Toronto, April 20, 1892. Toronto. Pp. 15.
1963 **Hayne, D. M.** *et al.*
'L'Enseignement de la littérature canadienne-française au Canada,' *Culture* XXIV, 325-42.
1964 **Arès, R.**
'Situation de l'enseignement français au Canada,' *Rev. Scolaire* XIV, 262-68.
Ontario Curriculum Institute, Modern Languages Committee.
Interim Report Number 2. Toronto: The Institute. Pp. 80.
Therio, A.
'Une Enquête manquée ou le français dans nos collèges,' *Rev. Univ. Laval* XIX, 37-45.
1965 **Ontario Curriculum Institute.**
French as a Second Language; an Interim Report of the Second Language Committee. Toronto: The Institute. Pp. 35.
1966 **Hawkins, S. C.**
New Trends in the Teaching of a Modern Second Language (French). Montreal: Faculty of Education, McGill Univ. Pp. 7.
1967 **Creighton, R. A.**
'An Enquiry into the Qualifications of Teachers of French in the Secondary Schools of Nova Scotia.' Unpublished M.A. thesis, Dalhousie Univ.
1968 **Aylwin, U.**
'La Pédagogie du français au CEGEP,' *Prospectives* IV (3), 182-97.
Léon, P.
'Les Recherches en Phonétique à l'Université de Toronto,' *Can. Mod. Lang. Rev.* XXIV, 24-31.

1968 **Menard, J., ed.**
Recherche et littérature canadienne-français. Ottawa: Presses Univ. d'Ottawa. Pp. 297.
Richer, E.
'L'Enseignement de Français à l'heure de la science linguistique,' *Rev. Univ. Laur.* I (2), 25-40.
Seguinot, A.
'La Conversation au niveau du collège,' *Can. Mod. Lang. Rev.* XXIV (4), 29-39.

1970 **Léon, P.**
'Réflexions sur le laboratoire de langues et le linguistique appliquée,' *Can. Mod. Lang. Rev.* XXVI (2), 20-26; (3), 16-23.

German : Allemand

1892 **Fraser, W. H.**
Pass French and German in the University of Toronto. Paper Read before Modern Language Assoc. of Toronto, April 20, 1892. Toronto. Pp. 15.

Hispanic : Espagnol

1963 **Levy, K. L.**
'Literature in our Classrooms – Quixotic Whim or Realistic Vision?' *Can. Mod. Lang. Rev.* XIX (2), 28, 30.

1965 **Mollica, A.**
'Italian in Ontario,' *Can. Mod. Lang. Rev.* XXII, 19-23.

1966 **Jackson, R. L.**
'Beginning Spanish Study at Carleton University: an Effective Solution to the Methods Controversy?' *Can. Mod. Lang. Rev.* XXII (2), 24-35.
Oglesby, J. C. M.
'Latin American Studies in Canada,' *Latin American Research Review* [U.S.] II (1), 80-88.

1967 **Brecher, I. and R. A. Brecher.**
'Canada and Latin America,' *Queen's Q.* LXXIV, 462-71.
Parker, J. H.
'Hispanic Studies in Canada 1917-1967,' *Hispanics* [U.S.] L, 836-40.

Icelandic : Islandais

1967 **Lindal, W. J.**
'The Department of Icelandic in the University of Manitoba' in *The Icelanders in Canada* (Winnipeg: Canada Ethnic Press Fed.), 330-65.

Islamic Studies : Etudes Islamiques

1965 **Wickens, G. M.**
'Islamic Studies at the University of Toronto,' *Mod. Lang. Jour.* [U.S.] XLIX, 312-13.

Slavic Studies : Etudes Slaves

1949 **Jurkszus, J.**
'L'Institut sud et est-europ´een d'Ottawa,' *Rev. Univ. Ottawa* XIX, 484-87.

1954 **St. Clair-Sobell, J.**
'Slavonic Studies in Canadian Universities,' *External Affairs* VI, 365-66.

1955 **Rose, W. J.**
'Cradle Days of Slavic Studies: Some Reflections,' *Slavistica* XXIII (Winnipeg: Ukrainian Free Academy of Sciences), 13.

1956 **Domaradzki, T. F.**
'Etudes Soviétologiques,' *Etudes Slav.* I, 132-38.
Liewinowicz, V.
'Some Aspects of Russian Studies in Canada,' *Etudes Slav.* I, 81-86.

1957 **Kirkconnell, W.**
'The Place of Slavic Studies in Canada,' *Slavistica* XXXI (Winnipeg: Ukrainian Free Academy of Sciences), 14.
Vinay, J.-P.
'Les Tâches de la linguistique slave,' *Etudes Slav.* II, 232-37.

1958 **Maurault, O.**
'Slavic Studies in the Light of the University's Mission,' *Etudes Slav.* III, 14-24.
Rose, W. J.
'Slavonic Studies in the University of British Columbia,' *Slavonic and East European Review* [U.K.] XXXVII, 246-53.

1959 **Zolobka, V.**
'The Semi-Centenary of Slavics in Canadian Learned Institutions, 1900-1950.' Unpublished M.A. thesis, Univ. of Ottawa.

1960 **Strakhovsky, L. I.**
'The Department of Slavonic Studies at the University of Toronto,' [in Russian] *Sovremennik* I, 45-47.

1961 **Grebenschikov, W.**
'Quelques Problèmes méthodologiques de l'enseignement de russe en rapport avec d'autres langues étrangères,' *Etudes Slav.* VI, 76-79.

1961 **Zyla, W. T.**
Contribution to the History of Ukrainian and Other Slavic Studies in Canada: Department of Slavic Studies, University of Manitoba, 1949-1959. Winnipeg: Ukrainian Free Academy of Sciences. Pp. 96.

1963 **Garrard, J. G.**
'Russian Studies in Canada: an Educational Gap,' *Queen's Q.* LXX, 12-21.

Radwanski, P. A.
'Psychological Method in Teaching of Slavonic Languages,' *Etudes Slav.* VIII, 232-37.

1965 **Black, J. L.**
'Eastern European Historical Studies in Canadian Universities since 1945,' *New Rev.* V (4), 46-58.

Buyniak, V. O.
'Ukrainian language in the University of Saskatchewan,' *Northern Lights* XI, 176-81.

Pidhainy, O. S.
'East-European History at St. Thomas University,' *New Rev.* V, 63-64.

1966 **Rose, W. J.**
'The School of Slavonic and East European Studies, 1937-1947,' *Slavonic and East European Review* [U.K.] XLIV, 8-17.

1967 **Buyniak, V. O.**
'Slavic Studies in Canada: An Historical Survey,' *Can. Slav. Papers* IX, 3-23.

Shein, L. J.
'Slavistic Studies in Canada,' *Can. Slav. Papers* IX, 37-40.

1968 **Folejewski, Z.**
'William John Rose, A Tribute,' *Can. Slav. Papers* X, 111-13.

Orchard, G. E.
'Slavic Studies in Alberta Universities,' *New Rev.* VIII, 136-38.

1969 **Black, J. L.**
'Slavic Studies at Laurentian University,' *New Rev.* IX, 301-05.

1970 **Hotimsky, C. M.**
'Slavic Studies and Libraries,' *Can. Library Jour.* XXVII (2), 119-23.

History : Histoire

1883 **Le Moine, J. M.**
'Nos Quatre Historiens Modernes: Bibaud, Garneau, Ferland, Faillon,' *Mém. S.R.C.* sect. 1, 1-13.

1887 **Lesperance, J.**
'The Analytical Study of Canadian History,' *Trans. R.S.C.* sect. 2, 55-61.
1952 **Groulx, L.**
'Henri Bourassa et la Chaire d'histoire du Canada à l'Université de Montréal,' *Rev. Hist.* III, 430-39.
1954 **Saint-Martin, L. P.**
'L'Histoire du Canada de F. X. Garneau et la critique,' *Rev. Hist.* VIII, 380-94.
1962 *Recherches Sociographiques* III, Numéro Spécial, inclut:
Vachon, A. 'Etat des recherches sur le régime français (1632-1760),' 11-24; Ouellet, F. 'L'Etude du XIXe siècle canadien-français,' 27-42.
1963 **Burchill, C. S.**
'History as Prophecy,' *Dalhousie Rev.* XLIV, 333-42.
Hanrahan, T. J.
'History Looks at Teaching,' *Bas. Teacher* VIII (Supplement), 6-19.
Hertzmann, L.
'The Sad Demise of History: Social Studies in the Alberta Schools,' *Dalhousie Rev.* XLIII, 512-31.
Nadel, G. H.
'The Uses of History,' *Dalhousie Rev.* XLIII, 155-61.
1964 **Barbeau, V.**
L'Oeuvre du chamoine Lionel Groulx. Montréal: Académie canadienne-française. Pp. 197.
Brunet, M.
'French-Canadian Interpretations of Canadian History,' *Can. Forum* XLIV, 5-7.
Rule, J. C.
'L'Historiographie du Canada français,' *Mém. S.R.C.* sect. 1, 97-103.
1965 **Black, J. L.**
'Eastern European Historical Studies in Canadian Universities since 1945,' *New Rev.* V (4), 46-58.
Boissonault, C.-M.
'Historiens canadiens anglais de le Confédération,' *Mém. S.R.C.* sect. 1, 29-39.
Pidhany, O. S.
'East-European History at St. Thomas University,' *New Rev.* V (2-3), 63-64.
Schlieper, H. C.
'Byzantine Studies in Canada,' *New Rev.* V (1), 54-56.

1965 **Windsor, K. N.**
'Historical Writing in Canada' in C. F. Klink, ed., *Literary History of Canada* ... (Toronto: U. of T. Press), 208-50. See also W. M. Kilbourn, 'The Writing of Canadian History [since 1920],' 496-518.

1966 **Ferguson, K.**
'George Dalrymple Ferguson: First Professor of History at Queen's University,' *Historic Kingston* xiv, 51-66.
Ouellet, F.
'Histoire et Sociologie: le point de vue d'un historien,' *Hist. Papers* 166-77.
Stanley, G. F. G.
'Lionel-Adolphe Groulx: Historian and Prophet of French Canada' in L. LaPierre, ed., *Four O'Clock Lectures: French-Canadian Thinkers of the Nineteenth and Twentieth Centuries* (Montreal: McGill Univ. Press), 97-114.

1967 **Cook, G. R.**
'French Canadian Interpretations of Canadian History,' *Jour. Can. Studies* II (2), 3-17.
Giguere, G.-E.
'Le Professeur d'histoire: un idéal et la réalité,' *ACFAS* xxiv, 105 (Resumé).
Hodgetts, A. B.
'The Teaching of Canadian History and Civics,' *Can. Ed. Research Digest* vii, 305-11.
Humphries, C. W.
'A Cure for Dullness,' *Mon. Morn.* I (1), 11-15.
Lower, A. R. M.
My First Seventy-Five Years. Toronto: Macmillan. Pp. 384.
Preston, R. A.
'Two-Way Traffic in Canadian History,' *Queen's Q.* LXXIV, 380-91.
Saunders, R. M.
'The Historians and the Nation,' *Hist. Papers* 1-9.
Upton, L. F. S.
'In Search of Canadian History,' *Queen's Q.* LXXIV, 674-83.

1968 **Angers, F.-A.** *et al.*
'Lionel Groulx, ptre: l'homme, l'oeuvre,' *Act. Nat.* LVII, 831-1115.
Bliss, J. M.
'Searching for Canadian History,' *Queen's Q.* LXXV, 496-508.
Careless, J. M. S.
'Somewhat Narrow Horizons,' *Hist. Papers* 1-10.

1968 **Cook, G. R.**
'Canadian Historical Writing' in R. H. Hubbard, ed., *Scholarship in Canada, 1967* (Toronto: U. of T. Press), 71-81.
Hodgetts, A. B.
What Culture? What Heritage? a Study of Civic Education in Canada. Report of the National History Project. Toronto: Ontario Institute for Studies in Education. Pp. 122; *Quelle Culture? Quel heritage ...* Pp. 139.

1969 **Careless, J. M. S.**
'"Limited Identities" in Canada,' *Can. Hist. Rev.* L, 1-10.
Careless, J. M. S.
'Nationalism, Pluralism, and Canadian History,' *Culture* XXX, 19-26.
Copp, T.
'The Whig Interpretation of Canadian History,' *Can. Dimension* VI (1), 23-24, 33.
Thomas, L. H.
'Documentary Sources for Teaching Western Canadian History,' *Alta. Hist. Rev.* XVII (4), 23-25.
Tomkins, G.
'The Scandal in Canadian Studies,' *Mon. Morn.* III (5), 23-26.

1970 **Cole, W., V. Rock and R. L. White.**
'A Tentative Report on "American" and "Canadian" Courses in Canadian University Curricula,' *Can. Rev. Amer. Studies* I (1), 39-47.
Sinclair, G.
'Canadian History and Political Science Source Materials at McMaster University,' *McMaster Lib. News* I (3), 1-16.

Music : Musique

1961 **Hanson, F.**
'Music at Macdonald,' *Can. Music Educator* II (4), 21-22.

1962 **Marquis, G. W.**
'The Summer Music Program at U.B.C.,' *Can. Music Educator* III (4), 23-24.
Normann, T. F.
'The Central Purpose of Music Education,' *Can. Music Educator* IV (2), 35-40.

1963 **Kaplan, M.**
'Reflections on Music Education in the United States and Canada,' *Can. Music Educator* V (1), 37-50.

1963 **Rodwell, L.**
'The Saskatchewan Association of Music Festivals,' *Sask. Hist.* XVI, 1-21.
1964 **Lasalle-Leduc, A.**
La Vie musicale au Canada. Québec: Ministère des Affaires Culturelles. Pp. 99.
1965 **Marquis, G. W.**
'Canadian Music at the University of British Columbia,' *Can. Composer* no. 2, 10, 42-43.
1966 **Adaskin, M.**
'The University and Audience Training,' *Can. Composer* no. 11, 6, 38.
Adeney, M.
'The One World of Musicians and Music Editors,' *Queen's Q.* LXXIII, 35-47.
Procter, G. A.
'The Bachelor of Music Degree in Canada and the United States,' *Can. Music Educator* VII (2), 27-33.
1967 **Churchley, F.**
'Contemporary Approaches in Music Education,' *McGill Jour. Ed.* II, 45-48.
1968 **Chartier, Y.**
'La Musicologie à l'Université; méthodes et expériences,' *Rev. Univ. Ottawa* XXXVIII, 403-30.
Sampson, G.
'Music on Campus,' *Perf. Arts Can.* V (3-4), 52-54.
Walter, A.
'The Growth of Music Education' in his *Aspects of Music in Canada* (Toronto: U. of T. Press), 247-87.
1969 **Brown, A. M.**
A Study of Music Curriculum in Degree and Diploma Programs offered at Canadian Institutions of Higher Learning, 1968-1969. Calgary: Canadian Association of University Schools of Music. Pp. 34.
Kaplan, D. L.
'New Needs for Future Teachers of Music,' *Ed. Canada* IX (3), 37-42.

Philosophy : Philosophie

1890 **Baldwin, J. M.**
Philosophy; its Relation to Life and Education. Toronto. Pp. 20.
1935 **Roy, M.**
'Pour l'Histoire du Thomism au Canada,' *Can. Franç.* XXIII, 161-71.

1942 **Beauregard, L.**
'Le Part de M. Desaulniers à l'introduction du Thomisme au Canada, vers l'époque de la renaissance religieuse,' *Can. Cath. Hist. Report* 77-88.

1963 **Lockquell, C.**
'Quelle a été l'influence de notre enseignement de la philosophie sur notre littérature,' *Mém. S.R.C.* sect. 1, 25-30.

1964 **Lebel, Marc.**
'Enseignement de la philosophie au Petit Séminaire de Québec,' *Rev. Hist.* XVIII, 405-24, 582-93; XIX, 106-25, 238-54.

1966 **Houde, R.** *et al.*
'Une Enquête sur la conception de la philosophie dans les collèges classiques,' *Prospectives* II, 129-33.

1967 **Brehaut, W., ed.**
Philosophy and Education: Proceedings of the International Seminar March 23-25, 1966. Toronto: Ontario Institute for Studies in Education. Pp. 157.
Goudge, T. A.
'A Century of Philosophy in English-Speaking Canada,' *Dalhousie Rev.* XLVII, 537-49.
Hennuy, G. J. G.
'Le Philosophe et son enseignement dans le cadre du pluralisme scolaire,' *ACFAS* XXXIV, 138 (Resumé).
Racette, J.
'La Philosophie dans les collèges autrefois dits classiques,' *Relations* no. 314, 66-69.

1968 **Cauchy, V.**
'Philosophy in French Canada: Its Past and Its Future,' *Dalhousie Rev.* XLVIII, 384-401.
Hennuy, G.
'Pluralisme pédagogique et l'enseignement historique de la philosophie,' *Rev. Univ. Moncton* I (1), 16-21.

1969 **Blackwell, K. M.**
'The Importance to Philosophers of the Bertrand Russell Archive,' *Dialogue* VII, 608-15.
Fournier, J.-L. *et al.*
'L'Enseignement de la philosophie dans les collèges,' *Prospectives* V, 51-54, 213-15.
'La Philosophie pour tous au CEGEP; nécessité ou perte de temps?' *Maintenant* no. 89, 239-55.

Religion : Religion

1959 **Conway, J. S.**
'The Universities and Religious Studies,' *Can. Jour. Theology* v, 269-72.

1960 **Carr, H.**
'Teaching the Catholic Religion in a Secular University,' *Bas. Teacher* v, 3-12.

1961 **Barrosse, T.**
'Aims and Methods in Teaching Scripture in the High School and College,' *Bas. Teacher* v, 171-81.

1962 **Falardeau, J.-C.**
'Les Recherches religieuses au Canada français,' *Recherches Soc.* III, 209-28.
Hughes, D.
'Theology: Core and Catalytic of Intellectual Integration,' *Bas. Teacher* VII, 100-08.

1964 **Breton, A.**
'L'Enseignement de la religion dans les écoles du Québec,' *Mag. Maclean* IV (9), 13-15.
Nicholls, W.
'The Role of a Department of Religion in a Canadian University' in K. R. Bridston and D. W. Calver, eds., *The Making of Ministers: Essays on Clergy Training Today* (Minneapolis: Augsburg Publishing House), 72-90.

1965 **Bouchard, R.**
'Au Niveau collégial: catéchèse ou sciences religieuses?' *Prospectives* I (5), 40-43.
Fortier, E.
'L'Enseignement religieux au niveau collégial: sciences religieuses ou catéchèse?' *Prospectives* I (3), 22-32.

1966 **Barbin, R.**
'Sciences religieuses ou catéchèse: une distinction à préciser et à maintenir,' *Prospectives* II, 6-7.
Despland, M.
'Religion à l'université: Objet de musée?' *Maintenant* XLIX, 20-23.
Hamelin, J.-M. *et al.*
'Recherche sur l'enseignement religieux à l'université,' *ACFAS* XXXII, 142 (Resumé).

1967 **Anderson, C. P. and T. A. Nosanchuk.**
The 1967 Guide to Religious Studies in Canada. Vancouver: Dept. of Religious Studies, Univ. of British Columbia. Pp. 78.

1968 **Grant, G. P.**
'The Academic Study of Religion in Canada' in R. H. Hubbard, ed., *Scholarship in Canada, 1967* (Toronto: U. of T. Press), 59-68.

D. SOCIAL SCIENCES : SCIENCES SOCIALES

GENERAL : GÉNÉRALITÉS

1965 **Binhammer, H. H. and M. Booth.**
'Research Assistance in the Humanities and Social Sciences,' *C.A.U.T. Bull.* XIII (2), 23-26.

1966 **Berlyne, D. E.**
'The Relationship of the Social Sciences to Educational Planning, Research and Development' in *Emerging Strategies and Structures for Educational Change: Proceedings of the Anniversary International Conference June 12-15, 1966* (Toronto: Ontario Institute for Studies in Education), 109-21. Comments by C. Watson, 122-26, and P. C. Dodwell, 126-29.
Hanley, C.
'Developments in Peace Research,' *Can. Forum* XLVI, 196-97.
Johnson, H. G.
'The Social Sciences in the Age of Opulence,' *Can. Jour. Econ. Pol. Sci.* XXXII, 423-42.

1967 **Ross, M. G.**
'Medicine and the Social Sciences,' *Can. Med. Assoc. Jour.* XCVII, 965-69.
Scott, A.
'The Recruitment and Migration of Canadian Social Scientists,' *Can. Jour. Econ. Pol. Sci.* XXXIII, 495-508.

1968 **Boucher, J.**
'Les Sciences sociales, préparatifs de décollage,' *Trans. R.S.C.* 9-20.
Graham, J. F.
'The Social Sciences: Specific Needs' in R. H. Hubbard, ed., *Scholarship in Canada, 1967* (Toronto: U. of T. Press), 17-25.
Mohr, J.
'La Science sociale et le traitment social,' *Bien-être* XX, 42-46.
Oliver, M.
'Research in the Social Sciences,' *A.U.C.C. Proc. 1967* II, 113-22; commentaries by P. Garigue, 123-29 and H. C. Eastman, 130-32.
Sutherland, N.
'The "New" Social Studies and Teacher Education,' *McGill Jour. Ed.* III (2), 168-80.

1968 Timlin, M. F. and A. Faucher.
The Social Sciences in Canada: two studies/Les Sciences sociales au Canada: deux études. Ottawa: Social Science Research Council. Pp. 136.
1969 Anderson, D. O.
'The Social Sciences and Public Health – An Epidemiologist's View,' *Can. Jour. Public Health* LX, 1-6.
Lewis, J., ed.
Teaching for Tomorrow: A Symposium on the Social Studies in Canada. Toronto: Nelson. Pp. 251.
Schindeler, F. and C. M. Lanphier.
'Social Science Research and Participating Democracy in Canada,' *Can. Public Admin.* XII (4), 481-98.

ANTHROPOLOGY : ANTHROPOLOGIE

1964 Belshaw, C. S.
'Anthropology and Public Administration,' *Can. Public Admin.* VIII, 189-96.
McIlwraith, T. F.
'Sir Daniel Wilson: A Canadian Anthropologist of One Hundred Years Ago,' *Trans. R.S.C.* sect. II, 129-36.
1966 Trigger, B. G.
'Sir Daniel Wilson: Canada's First Anthropologist,' *Anthropologica* (New Series) VIII (1), 3-28.

ECONOMICS AND POLITICAL SCIENCE :
ECONOMIE ET SCIENCES POLITIQUES

1929 MacKintosh, W. A.
'The Use of Case Material in Economics' in *Contributions to Canadian Economics* II (Toronto: U. of T. Press), 34-44.
1962 *Recherches Sociographiques* III, Numéro Spécial, inclut;
Faucher, A. 'Le Histoire économique de la province de Québec jusqu'à la fin du XIXe siècle,' 45-53; Raynauld, A. 'Recherches économiques récentes sur la province de Québec,' 55-64; Bonenfant, J.-C. 'Les Etudes Politiques,' 75-82; Henripin, J. 'Les Etudes demographiques,' 133-41.
1965 Kerr, D.
'Some Aspects of the Geography of Finance in Canada,' *Can. Geog.* IX, 175-92.

1965 **MacKintosh, W. A.**
'O. D. Skelton' in R. L. McDougall, ed., *Canada's Past and Present: a Dialogue* (Toronto: U. of T. Press – Our Living Traditions Fifth Series), 59-77.
Painchaud, P.
'L'Enseignement de la science politique: une formule riche de possibilités,' *Prospectives* I (3), 39-42.

1966 **Faucher, A.**
'Edouard Montpetit' in L. LaPierre, ed., *Four O'Clock Lecture: French-Canadian Thinkers of the Nineteenth and Twentieth Century* (Montreal: McGill Univ. Press), 77-95.
Jones, B. M.
'A Descriptive Survey of the Amount of Economics Education in the Social Studies in the Senior High Schools of Alberta.' Unpublished M.Ed. thesis, Univ. of Alberta.

1967 **Hodgetts, J. E.**
'Canadian Political Science: a Hybrid with a Future' in R. H. Hubbard, ed., *Scholarship in Canada, 1967* (Toronto: U. of T. Press), 94-104.
Smiley, D. V.
'Contributions to Canadian Political Science since the Second World War,' *Can. Jour. Econ. Pol. Sci.* XXXIII, 569-80.
Taylor, K. W.
'The Founding of the Canadian Political Science Association,' *Can. Jour. Econ. Pol. Sci.* XXXIII, 581-85.

1968 **Dales, J. H.**
'Canadian Scholarship in Economics' in R. H. Hubbard, ed., *Scholarship in Canada, 1967* (Toronto: U. of T. Press), 82-93.
Johnson, H.
'Canadian Contributions to the Discipline of Economics since 1945,' *Can. Jour. Econ.* I, 129-46.

1970 **Cole, W., V. Rock and R. L. White.**
'A Tentative Report on "American" and "Canadian" Courses in Canadian University Curricula,' *Can. Rev. Amer. Studies* I (1), 39-47.
Sinclair, G.
'Canadian History and Political Science Source Materials at McMaster University,' *McMaster Lib. News* I (3), 1-16.
Watkins, M. H.
'The Dismal State of Economics in Canada' in I. Lumsden, ed., *Close the 49th Parallel etc.: The Americanization of Canada* (Toronto: U. of T. Press), 197-208.

GEOGRAPHY : GEOGRAPHIE

1945 **Kimble, G. H. T.**
'The Craft of the Geographer' in *Two Inaugural Addresses* (Montreal: McGill Univ.), 1-19.

1957 **Camu, P.**
'La Quatre-vingtième Anniversaire de la Société de Géographie de Québec,' *Cah. Géog.* III, 135-41.
Laverdière, C.
'La Géographie à l'ACFAS,' *Rev. Can. Géog.* XI, 237-43.

1961 **Hamelin, L.-E.**
'Une Association canadienne des géographes ou plusieurs groupements des géographes au Canada?' *Cah. Géog.* V, 289-92.

1962 **Grenier, F.**
'Un Centre d'études nordiques à l'Université Laval,' *Cah. Géog.* V, 124.

1963 **Burton, I.**
'The Quantitative Revolution and Theoretical Geography,' *Can. Geographer* VII, 151-62.

1964 **Beauregard, L.**
'Géographie télévisé,' *Cah. Géog.* XVI, 297-303.
Clibon, P., M. Saint-Yves and L. Trotier.
'Nouveau Programme de licence en géographie à l'Université Laval,' *Rev. Géog. Montréal* XVIII, 296-301.
Girand, J.
'La Technique au service de la recherche,' *Can. Geographer* VIII, 22-26.
Hamell, L.
'The Training of Geographers for Business,' *Can. Geographer* VIII, 42-45.
Hare, F. K.
'A Policy for Geographical Research in Canada,' *Can. Geographer* VIII, 113-16. See also 203-04.
Lukermann, F.
'Geography as a Formal Intellectual Discipline and the Way in which it Contributes to Human Knowledge,' *Can. Geographer* VIII, 167-72.
Raveneau, J.
'Caractères de la cartographie géographique; Objectives de son enseignement à l'Université Laval,' *Cah. Géog.* XVI, 259-63.
Reeds, L. G.
'Agricultural Geography: Progress and Prospects,' *Can. Geographer* VIII, 51-63.

1965 **Hills, T. L.**
'Savannas: A Review of a Major Research Problem in Tropical Geography,' *Can. Geog.* IX, 216-25.
Hodge, G.
'The New Vista for Regional Planning: What Role for the Geographer,' *Can. Geog.* IX, 122-27.
Saint-Yves, M. et L. Trotier.
'Perspectives nouvelles de l'enseignement de la géographie au Québec,' *Cah. Géog.* XVII, 141-53.
Wolfe, R. I.
'Economic Non-geography of Canada,' *Can. Geographer* IX, 41-49.

1966 **Chapman, J. D.**
'The Status of Geography,' *Can. Geographer* X, 133-43.
Grenier, F.
'Le Nouveau Programme de géographie de la Faculté des Arts de Laval,' *Cah. Géog.* XX, 383-94.

1967 **Garnier, B. J.**
'Climatology at McGill University,' *Climatology Bull.* no. 1, 1-16.
Greer-Wooton, B.
'Geography and the New Educational Technology,' *Can. Geographer* XI, 133-42.
Nicholson, N. L., A. M. Blair and A. DeVos.
'The Geographer's Role in Contemporary Society: a Symposium,' *Can. Geographer* XI, 157-65.
Quick, E.
'The Development of Geography and History Curricula in the Elementary Schools of Ontario, 1846-1966.' Unpublished doct. dissertation, Univ. of Toronto.
Robinson, J. L.
'Growth and Trends in Geography in Canadian Universities,' *Can. Geographer* XI, 216-30.
Winter, E.
'Towards the New Geography,' *McGill Jour. Ed.* II, 74-80.

1968 **Brown, W. J.**
'Retrospect and Prospect; a Decade of Geography at the University of Manitoba,' *Manitoba Geography Teacher* I (3), 15-20.
Grime, A. R.
'Geography in the Secondary Schools of Ontario, 1800-1900.' Unpublished M.Ed. thesis, Univ. of Toronto.

1968 **Hamelin, L.-E. and A. Cailleux.**
'"L'Hudsonie," programme de recherches au Centre d'Etudes nordiques de l'Université Laval,' *Cah. Géog.* XXVI, 277-82.
1969 **Foster, H.**
'Geomorphology: Academic Exercise or Social Necessity,'
Can. Geographer XIII, 283-89.
Gill, D. and R. G. Ironside.
'The Role of Field Training in Canadian Geography,' *Can. Geographer* XIII, 373-81.
1970 **Cole, W., V. Rock and R. L. White.**
'A Tentative Report on "American" and "Canadian" Courses in Canadian University Curricula,' *Can. Rev. Amer. Studies* I (1), 39-47.

PSYCHOLOGY : PSYCHOLOGIE

1890 **Baldwin, J. M.**
Philosophy; its Relation to Life and Education. Toronto. Pp. 20.
1960 **Gaddes, W. H.**
'What do Canadians Think of Psychology,' *Can. Psych.* Ia, 50-58, and 'Are Public Relations Necessary,' *ibid.*, 118-22. See also D. Schonfield, 'Public Relations as a Defence Mechanism,' *ibid.*, IIa (1961), 38-41 and W. H. Gaddes, 'Reply to Prof. Schonfield,' 42-44.
1961 **Douglas, V. I.**
'Student Attitudes toward Formal Requirements in Graduate Training,' *Can. Psych.* IIa, 14-19.
Poser, E. G.
'The Case for Psychological Technicians,' *Can. Psych.* IIa, 2-5.
1962 **Ferguson, G. A.**
'Financial Aspects of Psychological Research in Canada,' *Can. Psych.* IIIa, 82-87.
Mailhiot, B.
'Les Recherches en psychologie sociale au Canada français (1946-62),' *Recherches Soc.* III, 189-204.
McCormack, P. D.
'Psychology at Manitoba,' *Can. Psych.* IIIa, 38-42.
1963 **Coons, W. H.** *et al.*
'Report of C.P.A. Committee on Professional Problems,' *Can. Psych.* IVa, 110-19.
1964 **Berry, D. G.**
'Legislation,' [re: certification] *Can. Psych.* Va, 43-45.

1964 **Boyd, J. B.**
'Some Comments on Professional Being and Becoming,' *Can. Psych.* va, 46-49.
Cervin, V. B.
'Comparison of Psychological Curricula at French, Russian, Czech and Canadian Universities,' *Can. Psych.* va, 75-86.
Inglis, J., *et al.*
'The Training of Psychologists,' *Can. Psych.* va, 88-102.
Pinard, A.
'Le Modèle scientiste-professionnel: synthèse ou prothèse,' *Can. Psych.* va, 187-208. Voir aussi 251-57.
Sutherland, J. S.
'The Case History of a Profession,' *Can. Psych.* va, 209-24.

1965 **Gibson, D.**
'Applied Psychology Training in Canada,' *Can. Psych.* vIa, 43-60. See also comments of D. G. Berry, *ibid.,* 61-63.
Hamilton, J.
'The Orientation of Applied Psychology,' *Can. Psych.* vIa, 253-58.
Heise, D. H.
'The Status and Role of the School Psychologist in Canada.' Unpublished M.A. thesis, Univ. of British Columbia.
Klonoff, H.
'Psychology in Medical Schools and Teaching Hospitals: a Survey,' *Can. Psych.* vIa, 259-65.
Myers, C. R.
'Notes in the History of Psychology in Canada,' *Can. Psych.* vIa, 4-17.
Sydiaha, D.
A Survey of Psychologists in Canada: Background Information for the Conference on the Training of Professional Psychologists. Saskatoon: Univ. of Saskatchewan. Pp. 90.

1966 **Barry, W. F.**
'Psychophysiology,' *Rev. Univ. Ottawa* XXXVI, 587-98.
Brison, D. W. and J. Hill, eds.
Psychology and Early Childhood Education: Papers Presented at the OISE Conference on Pre-School Education November 15-17, 1966. Toronto: Ontario Institute for Studies in Education. Pp. 107.
Hoyt, R.
'Financial Assistance Available in Canada for Students in Psychology,' *Can. Psych.* vIIa, 26-40.

1966 **Marineau, R. et L. Isabelle.**
'L'Etat actuel de la psychométrie au Québec,' *Rev. Univ. Ottawa* XXXVI, 655-67.
Smart, R. G.
'Subject Selection Bias in Psychological Research,' *Can. Psych.* VIIa, 115-21.
Steffy, R. A. and D. L. Watson.
'Suggestions for the Training of Clinical Psychologists,' *Can. Psych.* VIIa, 17-25.
Sydiaha, D.
'A Survey of Psychologists in Canada' (an Abridged Version of a Report Prepared as Background Information for the Conference on the Training of Professional Psychologists Held at the Couchiching Conference Centre, Geneva Park, Ontario, May 22-29, 1965). *Can. Psych.* VIIa, 413-85.

1967 **Appley, M. H. and J. Rickwood.**
Psychology in Canada. Ottawa: Science Council of Canada. Pp. 131. Special Study no. 3.
Cerwin, V. B. and W. Grewe.
'Psychology of Individual and Social Human Learning at the University of Windsor,' *Can. Psych.* VIIIa, 193-201.

1968 **Arvidson, R. M.**
'The Registration of Psychologists in Canada,' *Can. Psych.* IX, 40-41.
Arvidson, R. M. and T. M. Nelson.
'Sixty Years of Psychology at the University of Alberta,' *Can. Psych.* IX, 500-04.
Blum, F.
'A Note on the Neglected Middle in Teaching Under-Graduate Psychology,' *Can. Psych.* IX, 20-21.
Coons, W. H.
'Psychology and Society/Le Psycholoque dans la société,' *Can. Psych.* IX, 307-36.
Farrant, R. H. and G. Thibaudeau.
'L'Enseignement de la psychologie (à l'Université Laurentienne),' *Can. Psych.* IX, 1-5.
Hoyt, R.
'Financial Assistance Available in Canada for Students in Psychology,' *Can. Psych.* IX, 46-66.
Isabelle, L.
'La Psychologie à l'Université d'Ottawa,' *Can. Psych.* IX, 6-12.

1968 **Myers, C. R.**
'Departments of Psychology in Canada – 1967,' *Can. Psych.* IX, 42-45.
Pylyshyn, Z. W.
'Computer Science and the Enrichment of Psychological Research,'
Can. Psych. IX, 337-43.
1969 **Arthur, A. Z.**
'Clinical Training Programs in Ontario: A Survey Report,' *Ont. Psych.*
I, 65-110.
Bakan, D.
'Psychology, Student Unrest, and the Psychology of Learning,'
Ont. Psych. I, 12-22.
Bringmann, W. G., R. C. Fehr and R. H. Mueller.
'Psychology at Windsor,' *Can. Psych.* X, 371-83.
Day, H. I.
'Psychology in Community Colleges,' *Ont. Psych.* I, 146-49.
Gaddes, W. H.
'Can Educational Psychology Be Neurologized?' *Can. Jour. Behav. Science* I (1), 38-49.
Herbert, J. and D. P. Ausubel, eds.
Psychology in Teacher Preparation. Toronto: Ontario Institute for Studies in Education. Pp. 128.
Jung, J.
'Current Practices and Problems in the Use of College Students for Psychological Research,' *Can. Psych.* X, 280-90.
Quarrington, B. J.
'Doctoral Training in Clinical Psychology – Some Comments Concerning the Letter and the Spirit,' *Ont. Psych.* I, 3-11.
Wright, M. J.
'Canadian Psychology Comes of Age'/'L'Emancipation de la psychologie canadienne,' *Can. Psych.* X, 229-53.
1970 **Davidson, P. O.**
'Graduate Training and Research Funding for Clinical Psychology in Canada,' *Can. Psych.* XI, 101-27.
Goddard, G. V.
'Ph.D. Training: The End of an Era,' *Can. Psych.* XI, 133-36.
Gordon, G.
'Canadian Graduate Training in Psychology,' *Can. Psych.* XI, 137-45.

SOCIOLOGY : SOCIOLOGIE

1942 **Magnan, C. J.**
'Les Etudes sociales de Léon Gérin,' *Can. Français* XXIX, 454-58.

1962 *Recherches Sociographiques* III, Numéro Spécial, inclut:
Grenier, F. 'L'Etat présent des études régionales sur le Québec,' 89-101; Fortin, G. 'L'Etude du milieu rural,' 105-16; Martin, Y. 'Les Etudes urbaines,' 119-28; Rocher, G. 'Les Recherches sur les occupations et la stratification sociale,' 173-84; Rioux, M. 'L'Etude de la culture canadienne-française; aspects microsociologiques,' 267-72; Dumont, F. 'L'Etude systematique de la société globale canadienne-française,' 277-92.

1964 **Hall, O.**
'Carl A. Dawson, 1887-1964,' *Can. Rev. Soc. Anthrop.* I, 115-17.

1965 **LeFrançois, J.-J.**
'Sociologie: le processus de l'urbanisation de la communauté québécois,' *Rev. Desjardins* XXXI, 84-88.

1966 **Falardeau, J.-C.**
'Léon Gérin: His Life and Work' in L. LaPierre, ed., *Four O'Clock Lectures: French-Canadian Thinkers of the Nineteenth and Twentieth Centuries* (Montreal: McGill Univ. Press), 59-75.

Ouellet, F.
'Histoire et Sociologie: le point de vue d'un historien,' *Hist. Papers* 166-77.

Tilly, C.
'In Defense of Jargon,' *Hist. Papers* 178-86.

1967 **Card, B. Y.**
Possibilities and Problems of Research Collaboration by Educators and Sociologists in Canada. Ottawa: Canadian Council for Research in Education. Pp. 9.

Michelson, W.
'Urban Sociology as an Aid to Urban Physical Development: Some Research Strategies,' *Arch. Can.* XLIV (3), 69-71.

Thibault, A.
'L'Intégration du jeune sociologue dans le monde de l'entreprise,' *Relations Ind.* XXII, 263-71.

1968 **St.-Arnaud, P.**
'Pour une sociologie de la pratique médicale au Québec,' *Recherches Soc.* IX (3), 281-97.

1969 **Winthrop, H.**
'Does Sociology Have to be Polarized Into "Pure" and "Applied?"' *Can. Rev. Soc. Anthrop.* VI (1), 54-57.

1970 **Layne, N.**
'Can Sociology Be Made a Science?' *Sci. Forum* III (1), 27.

E. MATHEMATICS AND THE SCIENCES :
MATHEMATIQUES ET LES SCIENCES

GENERAL : GÉNÉRALITÉS

1854 **Langton, J.**
'The Importance of Scientific Studies to Practical Men,' *Can. Jour.* II, 201-04.
1887 **Laflamme, J. C. K.**
'Michel Sarrazin: Matériaux pour servir à l'histoire de la science en Canada,' *Mém. S.R.C.* sect. 4, 1-23.
1930 **Dalbis, L. J.**
'L'Enseignement des Science Naturelles,' *Rev. Trim. Can.* II, 177-89.
1963 **Trost, W. R.**
'Atlantic Provinces Inter-University Committee on the Sciences,' *Univ. Affairs* IV (3), 1-3.
1964 **Hart, J.**
'A Science Chairman's Lament,' *C.A.U.T. Bull.* XII (3), 42-47.
Mackenzie, C. J.
Report to Prime Minister on Government Science. Ottawa: Queen's Printer. Pp. 36.
Symposium on 'Organization and Support of Basic Scientific Research in Canada,' *Trans. R.S.C. 1964* includes:
J. W. T. Spinks, 'The National Research Council Forecast of Support Needed for Basic Research in Canadian Universities,' 327-28;
H. G. Thode, 'Basic Scientific Research – Its Importance and Support,' 339-48; F. R. Hayes, 'Co-operation Between Universities and Government,' 349-54; C. M. Drury, 'A Partnership in Science Between Government, Industry and the Universities,' 355-61.
1965 **Babbitt, J. D., ed.**
Science in Canada: Selections from the Speeches of E. W. R. Steacie. Toronto: U. of T. Press. Pp. 198.
Canadian Association of Graduate Schools.
'Forecasts of the Cost of Research and Graduate Studies in the Natural Sciences and Engineering in Canada.' Ottawa: The Association. Pp. 10. Mimeo.
Daniells, R.
'A Humanist Talks to the Scientists,' *Univ. of British Columbia Alumni Chronicle* XIX (Autumn), 5-8.

1965 **Marion, L.**
'Science Policy and the Universities,' *Trans. R.S.C.* 3-10.
National Research Council of Canada.
Sigma; International Co-operation and Science. Ottawa: The Council. Pp. 36.

1966 **Blake, V. R.**
New Trends in the Teaching of Science. Halifax: Dalhousie Univ. Pp. 6.
Bonn, G. S.
Science-Technology Literature Resources in Canada: Report of a Survey for the Associate Committee on Scientific Information. Ottawa: National Research Council. Pp. 80.
Gaudron, E.
'Civilisation scientifique ou Humanisme Nouveau,' *Culture* XXVII, 58-73.
'Science Education in Canada' in J. E. Hodgetts, ed., *Higher Education in a Changing Canada: Symposium Presented to the Royal Society of Canada in 1965* (Toronto: U. of T. Press), contains C. C. Dolman, 'The Catablepha's Glance and the Coil of Ouroboros,' 55-65; J. B. Macdonald, 'Science Education: Problems and Prospects,' 66-75; F. A. Forward, 'The Role of Governments in Science Education,' 76-81; R. Daniells, 'The Music of the Spheres,' 82-90.
Thistle, M.
The Inner Ring: The Early History of the National Research Council of Canada. Toronto: U. of T. Press. Pp. 435.

1967 **Van Cleave, A. B.**
'Science Education in Canada,' *Chem. Can.* XIX (10), 14-22.

1968 **Elliott, L. G., W. B. Lewis and A. G. Ward.**
'ING: A Vehicle to New Frontiers,' *Sci. Forum* I, 3-7. Also 8-13 for three other articles on ING [Intense Neutron Generator] by J. G. Parr, K. G. McNeill, J. D. Prentice.
Gaudry, R.
'Les Problèmes en Sciences naturelles,' *A.U.C.C. Proc. 1967* II, 98-100; commentaries by H. E. Petch, 105-09 and J. D. Hamilton, 110-12.
Holmes, E. L.
'Wanted: A New Unit on a Canadian Campus to Study Science Policy,' *Sci. Forum* I (4), 23-25. See also J. W. Grove, 'Now in Operation: An Experiment at Queen's University,' 25.
Lebel, M.
'Les Humanités et les sciences,' *Culture* XXIX, 313-21.
Macdonald, J. B.
'Science Education: Backdrop for Discovery,' *Jour. Dental Research* [U.S.] XLVII, 855-59.

1968 **McTaggart-Cowan I.**
'Problems of Research in the Natural Sciences,' *A.U.C.C. Proc. 1967*
II, 101-04.
Orr, J. L. et al.
'Science and Technology: the University's Dominant Role,' *Can. Univ.*
III (6), 25-29.
Solandt, O. M.
'National Science and Engineering Critique,' *Trans. R.S.C.* 35-42.
Van Cleave, A. B.
'Science Education Policy? That's Not Our Business. We're Scientists,'
Chem. Can. XX (11), 41-43.

1969 **Engineering Institute of Canada.**
'National Objectives for Canadian Science and Technology'/'Orientation de la politique scientifique du Canada,' *Eng. Jour.* LII (6), 4-14.
(Brief presented to Senate Special Committee on Science Policy,
June 6, 1969.)
Field, J., S. Langdon and B. Keith.
'Why Are Many Students So Hostile to Science? Three Give Their
Reasons,' *Sci. Forum* II (4), 11-15.
Murray, W. J.
'Scientific and Humanistic Education and the Notion of Paidea,'
Culture XXX, 208-16.
Transactions of the Royal Society of Canada section 3, includes:
W. G. Schneider, 'Science, Technology and the Federal Government,'
263-70; H. E. Gunning, 'Towards a Constructive National Science
Policy for Canada,' 289-96; A. E. Douglas, 'Towards a National
Science Policy, or Away,' 297-302; H. R. Wynne-Edwards, 'A Review
of the Current Status of Science Policy in Canada,' 303-12.

1970 **Hart, J.**
'For Science Technicians at University, an Attempt to Find Order in
Confusion,' *Can. Univ. & Coll.* V (5), 28-29, 34-37.
Kikauka, T.
'Today's Labs: Long on Tradition, Short on Science?' *Can. Univ. & Coll.*
V (6), 15-17.
Mathews, R.
'Science Policy, Teaching, and the Non-Canadian,' *Sci. Forum* III (1),
24-25.
McIntosh, R. L.
'Attacking the Problem of Over-Specialization,' *Sci. Forum* III (2),
14-15.

1970 **Trainor, L.**
'Science in Canada – American Style' in I. Lumsden, ed., *Close the 49th Parallel etc.: The Americanization of Canada* (Toronto: U. of T. Press), 241-56.

ASTRONOMY : ASTRONOMIE

1967 **Heard, J. F. and H. S. Hogg.**
'Astronomy at the David Dunlop Observatory,' *R. Astron. Soc. Jour.* LXI, 257-76.
Northcott, Ruth J., ed.
Astronomy in Canada: Yesterday, Today and Tomorrow. Toronto: Royal Astron. Soc. of Canada. Pp. 127. (Reprint from *R. Astron. Soc. Jour.* LXI, 211-338.)
1969 **Innanen, K. A. and R. W. Nicholls.**
'Astronomy and Astrophysics at York University,' *R. Astron. Soc. Jour.* LXIII, 87-89.

BIOLOGY : BIOLOGIE

1860 **Lawson, G.**
'Remarks on the Present State of Botany in Canada and the Objects to be Attained by the Establishment of a Botanical Society,' *Botanical Society of Canada* I, 4-9.
1880 **Provencher, L.**
'L'Histoire naturelle dans les collèges classiques,' *Nat. Can.* no. 136, 123-25. See also 118-23.
1917 **McMurrich, J. P.**
'Fifty Years of Canadian Zoology,' *Trans. R.S.C.* sect. 4, 1-14.
1945 **Brunet, J.** *et al.*
'Hommage à l'oeuvre du Frère Marie-Victoria,' *Act. Univ.* XI (6), 2-19.
1952 **Moon, B.**
'The Acid-Minded Professor,' [Prof. William Rowan] *Maclean's* LXV (10), 20-21, 56-59.
1958 **Rigby, M. S. and A. G. Huntsman.**
'Materials Relating to the History of the Fisheries Research Board of Canada (formerly the Biological Board of Canada) for the Period 1898-1924.' Manuscript Report Series (Biological) no. 660. Ottawa: Fisheries Research Board of Canada. Pp. 272. Typescript.

1965 **Hachey, H. B.**
'History of the Fisheries Research Board of Canada.' Manuscript Report Series (Biological) no. 843. Ottawa: Fisheries Research Board of Canada. Pp. 499. Typescript.

1966 **Beschel, R. E.**
'Some Early History of the Biology Department,' *Queen's Review* XL (4), 92-99.
Craigie, E. H.
A History of the Department of Zoology of the University of Toronto up to 1912. Toronto: U. of T. Press. Pp. 108.
Savile, D. B. O.
'Unity for Diversity in Biological Research,' *Trans. R.S.C.* sect. 4, 245-51.

1967 **Selye, H.**
'Réflexions sur la recherche et l'enseignement postgradué dans les sciences de la vie,' *Rev. Can. Biol.* XXVI, 83-93.
Uffen, R. J.
'Mathematics, Biology and Engineers,' *Bus. Q.* XXXII (2), 5, 79, 83.

1968 **Desmarais, A.**
'The Future of Biological Education and Research,' *Can. Univ.* III (2), 53-54.

1970 **Chant, D. A.**
'Pollution Probe: Fighting the Pollutors with Their Own Weapons,' *Sci. Forum* III (2), 19-22.

CHEMISTRY : CHIMIE

1932 **Flahault, J.**
'Science et Enseignement: Perplexités et doléances d'un professeur de chimie,' *Rev. Trim. Can.* XVIII, 83-91.

1964 *Chemistry in Canada* XVI (12), Special section entitled 'Chemical Education' includes:
M. Adelman, 'Chemical Engineering at the University of Windsor,' 38;
O. C. W. Allenby, 'Reassess the Teaching vs. Research Role,' 24-25;
R. M. Butler, 'Chemistry Grows in Importance in Chemical Engineering,' 26-27; H. H. J. Nesbitt, *et al.*, 'Is There a Shortage of University Chemistry Teachers?' 24-25, 58.
Newbold, B. T.
'Qualifications of High School Chemistry Teachers in the Atlantic Provinces,' *Chem. Can.* XVI (8), 3-4, 36.

1965 **Allen, A. D. and R. G. Barradas.**
'The Department of Chemistry, University of Toronto,' *Education in Chemistry* [U.K.] II (1), 3-6.
Riedel, B. E.
'Biochemistry in a Pharmaceutical Chemistry Course,' *American Journal Pharmaceutical Education* XXIX, 743-57.

1967 **Gingras, B. A. and T. W. West.**
'Fifty Years of Scholarships,' *Chem. Can.* XIX (11), 58-63.

1968 **Beamish, F. E.**
'Analytical Chemistry and the University,' *Chem. Can.* XX (10), 28-30.
Chemistry in Canada XX includes reports on Chemistry at Mount Allison (no. 1, 14-16), British Columbia (no. 4, 16, 18-19) and Simon Fraser (no. 4, 17-18).
Gnyp, A. W. et al.
'Experiences in Continuing Education: the University Viewpoint,' *Chem. Can.* XX (9), 34, 36.

1969 **Baurno, A. N.**
'Canadian Chemistry at a Crossroads,' *Chem. Can.* XXI (5), 21-23; (6), 32-34.
'Brock Stresses Interdisciplinary Relationships,' *Chem. Can.* XXI (6), 37-38.
'Guelph's "New Look" in Chemistry,' *Chem. Can.* XXI (2), 27-28.
'New Biochemistry Department Expands at McMaster,' *Chem. Can.* XXI (1), 8-9.
Westman, A. E. R.
Chemistry and Chemical Engineering: a Survey of Research and Development in Canada. Ottawa: Science Council of Canada. Pp. 102. Special Study no. 9.

1970 'Fifty Years of Chemistry at the University of Montreal,' *Chem. Can.* XXII (3), 21-24.

GEOLOGY : GEOLOGIE

1930 **Prince, G. H.**
'The New Provincial Government Forestry and Geology Building at University of New Brunswick,' *For. Chron.* VI (4), 8-13.

1966 **Nowlan, J. P.**
'Presidential Address: Geologists in Our Present Economy,' *Proc. Geol. Assoc. Can.* XVII, 13-19.

1970 **Jones, J. R.**
'Geology of Canada: An Outdoor Approach to University Education at the Adult Level,' *Continuous Learning* IX, 134-36.

MATHEMATICS : MATHÉMATIQUES

1929 **Coats, R. H.**
'The Place of Statistics in National Administration – Function and Organization of Statistics – Scope and Method of the Dominion Bureau of Statistics,' *Trans. R.S.C.* sect. II, 81-93.

1946 **Jeffrey, R. L.**
'The Future of Mathematics in Canada,' *Queen's Q.* LIII, 304-12.

1957 **Kartzke, P., A. W. Tucker and I. Niven.**
'Panel Discussion on Mathematics in the University and in Industry' in *Proceedings of the Fourth Canadian Mathematical Congress, Banff, 1957* (Toronto: U. of T. Press), 56-72.

Zassenhaus, H.
'The Education of Graduate Students of Mathematics' in *Proceedings of the Fourth Canadian Mathematical Congress, Banff, 1957* (Toronto: U. of T. Press), 73-78.

1964 **Crawford, D. H.**
'Developments in School Mathematics in Canada – A Survey,' *Can. Ed. Research Digest* IV, 306-19.

Cross, G.
'On University Education,' *Ont. Math. Gaz.* III (3), 29-30, 33.

Northover, F. H.
'University Training in Applied Mathematics,' *Can. Math. Bull.* VII, 463-66.

Schiff, H. I. *et al.*
'Report on Mathematical Instruction in Canadian Universities,' *Can. Math. Bull.* VII, 173-76.

1965 **Anctil, P.**
'Ces Mathématiques qui nous gouvernent,' *Mag. Maclean* V (11), 20-21, 50, 52-55.

Sawyer, W. W.
'Problems in Teaching Mathematics in Schools and Universities,' *Bull. of the Institute of Mathematics and Its Applications* [U.K.] I (4), 59-63.

1966 **Horne, E. B.**
'A Comparative Study of College Preparatory Mathematics Curricula in Canada 1964-1965.' Unpublished doct. dissertation, Univ. of Illinois.

1967 Uffen, R. J.
'Mathematics, Biology and Engineers,' *Bus. Q.* XXXII (2), 5, 79, 83.
1968 Keeping, E. S.
Twenty-One Years of the Canadian Mathematical Congress. Montreal: Can. Math Congress. Pp. 22.
May, K. O.
'Undergraduate Research: Some Conclusions,' *American Math. Monthly* LXXV (1), 70-74.
1969 Althouse College of Education.
'The Education of Mathematics Teachers: A Survey of Teacher Attitudes,' *Ont. Math. Gaz.* VII (3), 191-210.
Brossard, R.
'Voies nouvelles dans l'enseignement de la géometrie,' *ACFAS* XXXVI, 2.
Gotlieb, C. C.
'Computers and Society,' *Trans. R.S.C.* sect. 3, 271-78.
1970 Coleman, A. J.
'Mathematics in the Second Half of the Twentieth Century,' *Ont. Math. Gaz.* VIII (2), 75-88.

PHYSICS : PHYSIQUE

1964 Desrochers, R. D.
'Laboratoire de physique nucléaire à l'Université de Montréal,' *Ing.* L (201), 58-64.
Hart, J. and P. Kelly.
'The P.S.S.C. Course in a University Curriculum,' *Physics in Canada* XX (3), 13-16.
1965 Breton, A.
'Le Nouveau Laboratoire de physique de l'état solide de l'Ecole Polytechnique,' *Ing.* LI (206), 42-44.
Brewer, A. W.
'Meteorology at the University of Toronto: I. The Past,' *Atmosphere* III (1), 4-8.
Murty, R. C.
'Another Approach to the First-Year Physics Laboratory Course,' *American Journal of Physics,* XXXIII (3), 205-07.
Vogt, E. W., L. Katz and P. A. Forsythe.
'A Statistical Report on Canadian Physicists – Education, Employment Characteristics, Financial Support,' *Can. Assoc. Physicists Bull.* XXI (3), 5-55.

1966 **Johns, M.**
'The Elementary Undergraduate Teaching Problem,' *Physics in Canada* XXII (5), 6-13.
1967 **Breckon, S. W.**
'Research in Physics at Memorial University,' *Physics in Canada* XXIII (3), 22-25.
Conkie, W. R. and J. H. Montague.
'Research in Physics at Queen's University,' *Physics in Canada* XXIV (6), 17-22.
Robson, J.
'Challenge of the Future/Le Defi de l'avenir,' *Physics in Canada* XXIII (4), 12-19.
Rose, D. C. et al.
Physics in Canada. Ottawa: Science Council of Canada. Pp. 385. Special Study no. 2.
Tremblay, L. M.
'Six Étages de Physique à l'Université Laval,' *Physics in Canada* XXIII (5), 22-27.
1968 **Côté, F.**
'Une Nouvelle Discipline au CEGEP: La méteorologie,' *Technique* XLII (7), 8-10.
Lapointe, S.
'Recherche post-gradué à l'Université de Montréal,' *Physics in Canada* XXIV (2), 18-24.
'Physics at the University of Ottawa,' *Physics in Canada* XXIV (4), 13-17.
'Research in Physics at McGill,' *Physics in Canada* XXIV (1), 12-18.
Robson, J. M.
'The Future of the Rose Report,' *Trans. R.S.C.* 73-76.
Sullivan, H. M.
'Space Research and the Emerging University,' *Physics in Canada* XXIV (2), 6-12.
Thumm, W.
'Physics in Institutes of Technology,' *Physics in Canada* XXIV (2), 13-17.
1969 **Boivin, A. et R. Trembley.**
'Vers une école d'optique nationale à l'Université Laval,' *ACFAS* XXXVI, 75-76.
Innanen, K. A. and R. W. Nicholls.
'Astronomy and Astrophysics at York University,' *R. Astron. Soc. Jour.* LXIII, 87-89.

F. PROFESSIONAL EDUCATION : ENSEIGNEMENT-PROFESSIONEL

AGRICULTURE : AGRICULTURE

1923 **Hopkins, E. S.**
'Agricultural Research in Canada: its Origin and Development,' *Annals of American Academy of Political and Social Science* CVII (May), 82-87.

1945 **Maxwell, R. W.**
'The Need for Vocational Agricultural Education,' *Jour. Ed. (N.S.)* XVI, 819-22.

1955 **Perron, M. A.**
Un Grand Educateur agricole: Edouard-A. Barnard. Montréal: 51 Station Youville. Pp. 355.

1963 **Jasmin, J.-J.**
'Où en est rendu l'Institut de Technologie Agricole de St.-Hyacinthe?' *Agr.* XX, 100-02.

1964 **Lettre, J.-P.**
'Enseignement agricole et relations agronomes-techniciens,' *Agr.* XXI, 90-95.

Yeh, M. H.
'The Role of Econometrics in Agricultural Research,' *Can. Jour. Agric. Econ.* XII, 54-61.

1965 **Bowser, W. E. ed.**
The Faculty of Agriculture, University of Alberta, 1915-1965. Edmonton: Univ. of Alberta.

1966 **Lacourcière, H.**
'L'Enseignement de l'agriculture au Québec,' *Agr.* XXIII (3), 29-31.

Manning, T. W.
'Graduate Education in Agricultural Economics,' *Can. Jour. Agr. Econ.* XIV (2), 1-14.

1968 **Austman, H. H.**
'An Experiment in Agricultural Vocational Education,' *Continuous Learning* VII, 67-70.

Garrow, P.
Agricultural Education in Canada: A Survey of Opportunities for Agricultural Education in the Canadian Provinces. Calgary: The Department of Educational Administration, Univ. of Calgary. Pp. 135.

1968 **Hoichberg, S. W.**
'A Study of Relationships Between a Student's Ontario High School Background and Performance in the Diploma Course in Agriculture at the Ontario Agricultural College.' Unpublished M.Sc. thesis, Univ. of Guelph.
Nikolaiczuk, N.
'Agricultural Education in Quebec,' *Agr.* XXV (4), 26-28.

1969 **Gilson, J. C.**
'The Demand for Agricultural Economists by Canadian Universities and Governments,' *Can. Jour. Agric. Econ.* XVII (3), 124-32.
Ouellette, G.-J.
'La Recherche agricole à l'université,' *Agr.* XXVI (4), 3-8.
Robertson, C. S.
'Olds Agricultural and Vocational College: Enrolment, Graduation and Employment Patterns.' Unpublished M.Ed. thesis, Univ. of Calgary.
Shuh, J. E.
'A College with a Difference,' [Nova Scotia Agricultural College] *Atlantic Advocate* LIX (9), 45-49.

1970 **Matthews, B. C.**
'Memo to Colleges of Agriculture,' *Agriculture Institute of Canada Rev.* XXV (1), 7-8.
Reaman, G. E.
A History of Agriculture in Ontario. Toronto: Saunders. 2 vols.

ARCHITECTURE, TOWN PLANNING : ARCHITECTURE, URBANISME

1948 **Russell, J. A., L. E. Shore and J. Bland.**
'Vocational Opportunities for the Architectural Graduate,' *R. Arch. Inst. Can. Jour.* XXV, 139-43.

1960 **Laserre, R.**
'A Major Change of Program: UBC School of Architecture,' *R. Arch. Inst. Can. Jour.* XXXVIII, 107-08.
Russell, J. A.
'Programming a School of Architecture Building,' *R. Arch. Inst. Can. Jour.* XXXVIII, 325-28.
Smith, E. J.
'School of Architecture, University of Manitoba, Winnipeg,' *R. Arch. Inst. Can. Jour.* XXXVIII, 317-24.

1964 *Community Planning Review* (*Revue Canadienne d'Urbanisme*) XIV (2), devoted to 'History of CPAC [Community Planning Association of Canada].'

1964 'The Faculty of Architecture-University of Manitoba,' *R. Arch. Inst. Can. Jour.* XLI (3), 57-68.
Willis, J.
'Education for Town Planning in Canada,' *Plan Canada* Special Supplement (April 1964) for The Town Planning Institute of Canada.
1966 **Hosken, F.**
'The Urban University and the Urban Environment,' *Arch. Can.* XLIII (10), 48-50.
'Maîtrise en architecture; programme d'études de l'Ecole d'Architecture de l'Université de Montréal,' *Arch.* XXI (244), 46-49.
Ontario Association of Architects.
'Architectural Education Expansion in Ontario: Report of the O.A.A. Study Committee,' *Arch. Can.* XLIII (10), 5-9.
Raymore, W. G.
Survey of the Profession. Ottawa: Royal Architectural Institute of Canada. Pp. 147.
Styliarios, D.
'Education for Planning, Urban Design and Architecture,' *Arch. Can.* XLIII (10), 91-93.
1967 **Acland, J. H.**
'Architectural Education: the Search for Change,' *Can. Arch.* XII (7), 37-40.
Hoffart, R., D. A. Foreman and T. B. Watt.
'Architectural Education: Student's View,' *Can. Arch.* XII (9), 88-90, 94.
Jackson, A.
'Curriculum,' *Arch. Can.* XLIV (7), 61-62.
Michelson, W.
'Urban Sociology as an Aid to Urban Physical Development: Some Research Strategies,' *Arch. Can.* XLIV (3), 69-71.
Page, J. E.
'Address to the Graduating Seniors of the University of Manitoba Faculty of Architecture,' *Arch. Can.* XLIV (4), 59-60.
'Waterloo School of Architecture,' *Arch. Can.* XLIV (5), 57-59.
1968 **Benjamin, S.**
'Operational Gaming in Architecture,' *Arch. Can.* XLV (2), 57-59.
Greer, W. N.
'Education and Communication: the Stanley House Architect-Education Conference'/'Education et Communication: la Conférence à Stanley House,' *Arch. Can.* XLV (12), 47-70.

1968 **Howarth, T.**
'A Recent Development: Architectural History in Canada' in R. H. Hubbard, ed., *Scholarship in Canada, 1967* (Toronto: U. of T. Press), 51-58.
Lehrman, J. and C. Nelson, Jr.
'Architectural Education: the Search for Change,' *Can. Arch.* XIII (3), 53-54.
McCue, G.
'The Critical Consequences of Tradition on Architectural Education,' *Arch. Can.* XLV (7), 65-66.
1969 'Architectural Education and the Humanities,' *Arch. Can.* XLVI (2), 56-57.
'Les Ecoles d'architecture,' *Architecture* XXIV (276), 24-33.
Grelton, R. et al.
'The Winds of Change: an Examination of the New Curriculum of the Toronto School of Architecture,' *Can. Arch.* XIV (2), 29-44.
Harper, W. D.
'L'Etudiante paysagiste,' *Architecture* XXIV (272), 36-37.
'University of Toronto Department of Architecture,' *Arch. Can.* XLVI (4), 47-50.

BUSINESS ADMINISTRATION AND PUBLIC AFFAIRS :
COMMERCE, FINANCE ET ADMINISTRATION

1949 **Gathercole, G. E.**
'The Role of the Institute of Public Administration of Canada,' *Proc. Inst. Pub. Admin.* 183-99.
Gulick, L.
'Public Administration as a Profession,' *Proc. Inst. Pub. Admin.* 112-27.
Mackintosh, W. A.
'Should We Have Specialized Degrees in Public Administration Given by Universities?' *Proc. Inst. Pub. Admin.* 27-34.
Martin, J.-M.
'Education for Public Service in French Canada,' *Proc. Inst. Pub. Admin.* 34-44.
1950 **Callard, K. B.**
'Graduate Studies in Public Administration,' *Proc. Inst. Pub. Admin.* 25-31.
Gilley, J. R.
'Extension Courses for Public Administration,' *Proc. Inst. Pub. Admin.* 19-23.

1950 **Laframboise, J.-C.**
'Trends in Teaching Public Administration in French Canada,' *Proc. Inst. Pub. Admin.* 9-18.

1952 **Brady, A.**
'The Training and Development of Administrators,' *Proc. Inst. Pub. Admin.* 319-31.

1953 **Pickersgill, J. W.**
Address at the Official Opening of the School of Public Administration, Carleton College, Ottawa, October 23, 1953. Ottawa: Carleton College. Pp. 17.

1954 **MacFarlane, R. O.**
'Specialized Education for Public Administration,' *Proc. Inst. Pub. Admin.* 301-06.

1959 **Hale, C.**
'Keep your Eye on McMaster,' *Can. Bus.* XXXII (8), 50-52.
Heasman, D. J.
'Public Administration: the Focus of Academic Interest,' *Can. Public Admin.* II, 242-54.

1960 **Fuller, J. A.**
'The Qualities Which Industry Seeks in Graduates of Schools of Commerce and Business Administration,' *Proc. Schools Bus.* 6-12.

1961 **Harris, R. F.**
'Prospects for Business Research in Canadian Universities,' *Proc. Schools Bus.* 103-07.
Juvet, C. S.
'Training in Public Administration at Carleton University under Canada's External Aid Program,' *Can. Public Admin.* IV, 396-405.
Lusztig, P. A. and J. Haskett.
'A Look at Two Canadian Business Schools,' [U.B.C., U.W.O.] *Can. Bus.* XXXIV (4), 96-102.
Smiley, D. V.
'The Research Program of the Institute of Public Administration of Canada,' *Can. Public Admin.* IV, 41-43.

1962 **Rowat, D. C.**
'The Study of Public Administration in Canada,' *Public Administration* [U.K.] XL, 319-24.

1963 **Fenton, A.**
'McGill's Graduate School of Business; a Late Starter with a New Idea,' *Can. Bus.* XXXVI (9), 44-47, 52, 54, 57-58, 60.

1963 **Sandiford, P. J.**
'Education for Operations Research,' *Proc. Schools Bus.* 1-10.

1964 **Armstrong, D. E.**
'The Changing World of Business and of Business Education,' *McGill Jour. Bus.* I (1), 9-11.

Belshaw, C. S.
'Anthropology and Public Administration,' *Can. Public Admin.* VII, 189-96.

Blanar, J. A.
'Why Not a School for Export Trade?,' *Can. Bus.* XXXVII (5), 62-65.

Byrd, K. F.
'The University's Contribution to the Education of C.A.'s,' *Can. Chart. Acc.* LXXXIV, 41-48.

Coté, R.
L'Homme d'affaires canadien-français d'aujourd'hui et de demain,' *Rev. Desjardins* XXX, 190-93.

Meyer, J.
'L'Ecole [des Hautes Etudes Commerciales] : An Academic Answer to Quebec's Needs,' *Executive* VI (11), 50-55.

O'Neill, I.
'Computer Schools for Managers,' *Can. Bus.* XXXVII (8), 30-38.

Ready, R. K.
'The Behavioral Science of Management,' *Bus. Q.* XXIX (2), 46-53.

Woods, H. D.
'Reflections on the Labour College of Canada,' *Continuous Learning* III, 91-97.

1965 **Cameron, J. W., R. M. Ayert and W. O. Twaits.**
'Panel on Business Education,' *Proc. Schools Bus.* Pp. 42.

Chartier, R.
'Planification par l'entreprise du recrutement des diplômés universitaires,' *Relations Ind.* XX, 637-58.

Moore, R. K.
'Education and the Future of the Profession,' *Can. Chart. Acc.* LXXXVI, 358-62.

Mulcahy, G.
'Canadian Accounting Education Planning,' *Can. Chart. Acc.* LXXXVI, 439-45.

Sinclair, S.
'School for Women Executives,' *Can. Bus.* XXXVIII (7), 71.

1966 **Armstrong, D. E.**
'Creating an Integrated Programme,' *McGill University Bulletin of Educational Procedures No. 9.* Pp. 4.
Coutts, W. B.
'The Profession's Need for Teachers,' *Can. Chart. Acc.* LXXXVIII, 432-32.
Harbron, J. D.
'Learning the New Thinking on International Business,' *Executive* VIII (8), 29-31.
Muir, J. D.
'Why the Big Turnover in Business Graduates?' *Can. Bus.* XXXIX (12), 32-37.
Muir, J. D. and N. Ruzesky.
'Job Placement in Canadian Business Schools,' *Can. P. R. Jour.* XIII (3), 41-50.
Preshing, W. A.
'The Commerce Undergrad Program – the Rock of Sisyphus,' *Can. P. R. Jour.* XIII (3), 35-37.

1967 **Muir, J. D.**
'How to Recruit Business Graduates,' *Can. Bus.* XL (9), 42-51.
Proceedings Annual Conference Association of Canadian Schools of Business 1967 includes:
W. R. Blackmore, 'Comments Related to Business Game Utilization in Canadian Universities' (pp. 6) and L. Moore, 'A Study of Business Game Utilization in Canadian Universities' (pp. 28).
Rumilly, R.
Histoire de l'Ecole des Hautes Etudes Commerciales de Montréal. Montréal: Beauchemin. Pp. 215.
Sheldon, M.
'Management Training on the Campus,' *Can. Bus.* XL (12), 85-88.

1968 **Burton, G. F. A.**
'Industry and Education: Investment in the Future – Part I,' *Industrial Can.* LXVIII (12), 17-21.
Collette, J.
'Peut-on améliorer l'enseignement de la comptabilité?' *Rev. Univ. Moncton* I (1), 35-37.
Isbister, F. and W. J. Medec.
'Hiring an M.B.A.,' *Can. P. R. Jour.* XV (2), 21-28.
Kernaghan, D. K.
'An Overview of Public Administration in Canada Today,' *Can. Public Admin.* XI, 291-308.

1968 **Maxwell, S. R.**
'The Postgraduate Business School and the Corporation,' *Industrial Can.* LXIX (8), 18-22.
Proceedings Annual Conference Association of Canadian Schools of Business 1968 includes:
W. G. Bolstad, 'A New Approach to Administrative Studies at the Undergraduate Level,' 52-66; R. Mattessich, 'Graduate Studies in Business Administration – A Comparative Analysis,' 126-42; P. C. Parr, 'The Position and Role of Management Education in Canadian Universities,' 11-23.
Sinclair, S.
'How Does Business Stack Up on Campus?' *Can. Bus.* XLI (5), 32-42.
Timmis, W. G.
'The Utilization of the M.B.A.,' *Proc. Assoc. Stud. Services* 37-39.

1969 **Dickinson, J. R.**
'Introduction to the Science of Decision Making,' *Eng. Jour.* LII (3), 18-19.
Ford, J. E.
'The Accountancy Profession: a Forward-Looking Programme,' *Can. Chart. Acc.* XCIV (2), 108-12.
Hartung, H.
'La Formation des Administrateurs,' *Can. Chart. Acc.* XCV (2), 107-12.
Wood, A. R. and J. R. M. Gordon.
Management Development in Management Science,' *Bus. Q.* XXXIV (3), 47-56.

1970 **Morrison, R. N.**
'Back to School: Preparation for Higher Management,' *Can. Bus.* XLIII (5), 48-52.

DENTISTRY : ART DENTAIRE

1964 **Davey, K. W.**
'Paedodontics as a Specialty,' *Can. Dent. Assoc. Jour.* XXX, 776-80.

1965 **Dunn, W. J.**
'Canada's Eighth Dental School is Born,' [Univ. of Western Ontario] *Can. Dent. Assoc. Jour.* XXXI, 693-99.
Leung, S. W.
'Objectives of the U.B.C. Dental School,' *Univ. of British Columbia Medical Journal* IV (2), 10-11.

1965 May issue of *Can. Dent. Assoc. Jour.* XXXI (5), contains articles on seven Faculties of Dentistry:
H. R. MacLean, Alberta, 289-92; S. W. Leung, British Columbia, 293-97; J. D. McLean, Dalhousie, 298-302; J. W. Neilson, Manitoba, 303-10; M. A. Rogers, McGill, 311-16; J.-P. Lussier, Montréal, 317-29; R. G. Ellis, Toronto, 330-37.
Paynter, K. J.
Dental Education in Canada. Ottawa: Queen's Printer. Pp. 109. [Study prepared for Royal Commission on Health Sciences.]
Paynter, K. J.
'How to Continue to Learn Even Though Graduated,' *U. of T. Undergraduate Dental Journal* II (1), 12-13, 16.

1966 **Committee of Presidents of Universities of Ontario, Presidents'** Research Committee.
The Health Sciences in Ontario Universities: Recent Experience and Prospects for the Next Decade. Toronto: The Committee. Pp. 26.
Fish, D. G. and B. I. Brown.
'A Comparison of Applicants and Applications to Canadian Medical and Dental Schools, 1965-66,' *Can. Med. Assoc. Jour.* XCV, 68-71.

1967 **Harrop, T. J. and D. G. Middaugh.**
'A New Approach to Clinical Teaching in Dentistry,' *Can. Dent. Assoc. Jour.* XXXIII, 258-64.
Kenyon, R.
The Ontario Dental Association: A Profile, The First One Hundred Years. Toronto: Ontario Dental Assoc. Pp. 32.
Purdy, C. E.
'Student Training in the Utilization of Dental Assistants at the University of Toronto,' *Can. Dent. Assoc. Jour.* XXXIII, 137-40.

1968 'The Role of the University in Training of Personnel in the Health Sciences,' *N. S. Med. Bull.* XLVII (2), 29-31.

1969 **Brown, H. K., D. J. Yeo and K. F. Pownall.**
'Attitudinal Roadblocks and Dental Programs: Opinions of Dental Students, Dentists, and Ten Other Health Disciplines,' *Can. Jour. Pub. Health* LX, 442-46.
Dunn, W. J., G. Albert and G. Zarb.
C[anadian] F[ederation of] D[ental] E[ducation] : What Has It Done for Dentistry?' *Can. Dent. Assoc. Jour.* XXXV, 436-40.
More, A.
'The Relation of High School Grades, Achievement and Intelligence Test Scores to Success in Dental School,' *Can. Counsellor* III (1), 56-58.

1969 **Young, W. G.**
'An Environment for Intellectual Development of the Dental Student,' *Can. Dent. Assoc. Jour.* XXXV, 487-91.

1970 **House, R. K.**
Dentistry in Ontario: a Study for the Committee on Healing Arts. Toronto: Queen's Printer. Pp. 274.
MacLean, M. B.
'Employment Expectancy of the Dental Hygienist,' *Can. Dent. Assoc. Jour.* XXXVI, 115-19.
Thomson, A. H.
'Eudodontics: Where do We Go from Here?' *Oral Health* LX (3), 7-9.

ENGINEERING : GÉNIE

1920 **Ruttan, R. F.**
'The Training of the Chemical Engineer,' *Eng. Jour.* III, 123-27.

1938 **Wendling, A.-V.**
'L'Ingénieur et l'enseignement technique français,' *Rev. Trim. Can.* XXIV, 124-43.

1945 **Bladon, L. W.**
'Thoughts on Mining Engineering' in *Two Inaugural Addresses* (Montreal: McGill Univ.), 20-32.

1952 **Fogarty, W. P.**
'Pre-Professional Training for Engineering,' *Jour. Ed. (N.S.)* II (1), 33-37.

1953 **Ball, S.**
'Civil Engineering,' [at Nova Scotia Technical College] *Jour. Ed. (N.S.)* II (4), 55-58.
Foran, M. R.
'What About Chemical Engineering?' *Jour. Ed. (N.S.)* II (2), 13-16.
Nichol, D. S.
'What is Electrical Engineering?' *Jour. Ed. (N.S.)* II (3), 45-49.

1954 **Flynn, A. E.**
'The Education of Mining Engineers,' *Jour. Ed. (N.S.)* III (3), 40-44.
Montgomery, S. J.
'What is Mechanical Engineering?' *Jour. Ed. (N.S.)* III (2), 50-57.

1955 **Redmond, D. A.**
'Engineering Students and Their College Libraries,' *Atlan. Prov. Lib. Bull.* XX, 6-8.

1957 **Cameron, E. L.**
'Metallurgical Engineering,' [at Nova Scotia Technical College]
Jour. Ed. (N.S.) VI (2), 24-28.
1964 **Holbrook, G. W.**
'The Educator's Dilemma,' *Eng. Jour.* XLVII (12), 23-24.
'How to Teach Engineering Design,' *Design Eng.* (Jan.), 32-34.
Konecny, G.
'Survey of Educational Facilities for Photogrammetry in Canada,'
Can. Surveyor XVIII, 320-25.
Neville, A. M.
'Civil Engineering Education in the University,' *Eng. Jour.* XLVII (1), 29-31.
Porter, A.
'Why No Challenge for Canada's Industrial Engineers?' *Plant Admin. Engin.* XXIV (1), 34-36.
Scott, D. S.
'Objectives in Continuing Education for the Engineer,' *Eng. Jour.* XLVII (9), 31-34.
Soudack, A. C.
'Utopia U,' *Eng. Jour.* XLVII (11), 21-23.
Twaits, W. O.
'Management – a New Dimension in Engineering,' *Can. Consulting Eng.* VI (12), 48-51.
Walters, S. Z.
'The New Look in Engineering Education,' *Can. Consulting Eng.* VI (7), 55-60.
Williamson, D.
'Graduate Industrial Engineers are at a Premium; Here's Why,'
Plant Admin. Engin. XXIV (8), 50-51, 68.
1965 **Audet, L.-P.**
'La Fondation de l'École Polytechnique de Montréal,' *Cah. Dix.* XXX, 149-91.
Booth, A. D.
'Biomedical Engineering at the University of Saskatchewan,'
Jour. Engineering Institute of Canada XLVIII (April), 23-25.
Canadian Association of Graduate Schools.
'Forecasts of the Cost of Research and Graduate Studies in the Natural Sciences and Engineering in Canada.' Ottawa: The Association. Pp. 10. Mimeo.

1965 **Cragg, L. H.**
Educating Tomorrow's Professional Chemists and Chemical Engineers.
Montreal: Chemical Institute of Canada. Pp. 12.
Hatfield, S.
'Meeting the Manpower Shortage,' *Can. Consulting Eng.* VII (2), 44-48.
1966 **Brandenberger, A. J.**
'The Educational Status of Surveying and Photogrammetry in North America,' *Can. Surveyor* XX, 121-29.
Buckley, P.
'Teaching Engineering How to Program,' *Can. Consulting Eng.* VIII (1), 33-34.
Bulani, W.
'Chemical Engineering at Western,' *Chem. Can.* XVIII (1), 52-56.
Dickinson, G.
'A Survey of Continuing Education for British Columbia Engineers,' *Continuous Learning* V, 276-78.
Ham, J. M.
'University – Industry Interaction in Engineering,' *Can. Univ.* I (1), 36-39.
Shortreed, J. H.
'Transportation Education and Research at Waterloo,' *Eng. Jour.* XLIX (7), 19-22.
Swartman, R. K.
'More Impetus is Needed to Reach the Goal of Continuing Education,' *Can. Consulting Eng.* VIII (Dec.), 35-38.
Wright, D. T.
'Changing Patterns in Engineering Education,' *Univ. Affairs* VII (3), 3-5.
1967 **Blackie, W. V.**
'Control Surveys and Mapping – What is Done, What Should be Done in the Next Decade and the Optimum Education for the Survey Engineers and Technicians to do it,' *Can. Surveyor* XXI, 55-66.
Dineen, J. O.
'Education for the Professional Surveyor in Canadian Universities,' *Can. Surveyor* XXI, 93-114.
Dineen, J. O.
'A Review of the Requirements for Surveyors and Survey Technicians in Canada,' *Can. Surveyor* XXI, 5-12.
Fahidy, T. Z.
'Proposes New Chemical Engineering Program,' *Chem. Can.* XIX (Feb.), 26-28.

1967 **MacLean, W. J.**
'A Profile of Land Surveying – What is Done, What Should be Done and the Optimum Education for Land Surveyors and Their Technical Assistants,' *Can. Surveyor* XXI, 40-54.
Mathews, W. H.
'Geological Engineering at the University of B.C.,' *B.C. Professional Engineer* XVIII (5), 11-16.
Uffen, R. J.
'Mathematics, Biology and Engineers,' *Bus. Q.* XXXII (2), 5, 79, 83.

1968 **Bordan, J.**
'Engineering at S.G.W.U.,' *Postgrad* [Assoc. of Alumni of Sir George William's University] 5, 15, 20.
Downee, J.
'Chemical Engineering Curricula in Ontario,' *Chem. Can.* XX (6), 22-23.
Downee, J.
'Chemical Engineering Developments at Queen's,' *Chem. Can.* XX (2), 30-31.
Genest, B.-A.
'Une Decision importante: la poursuite d'études post-universitaires,' *Ing.* LIV (235), 22-25.
Marcotte, N.
'L'Enseignement de Génie à l'Université de Moncton,' *Rev. Univ. Moncton* I (2), 53-56.
'What's the Role of University Research in Chemical Engineering?' *Chem. Can.* XX (11), 26-27.

1969 **Anger, P. E.**
'Les Besoins d'ingénieurs pour les années "70,"' *Eng. Jour.* LII (4), 23-28.
Gignac, J.-P.
'Engineering Managers in Tomorrow's Society,' *Eng. Jour.* LII (12), 9-11.
Gross, A. C.
'Education, Employment and Utilization Patterns of French-Canadian and English-Canadian Engineering Graduates,' *Relations Ind.* XXIV, 559-78.
Handa, V. K. and P. H. O. Roe.
'A New Plan for Engineering Education,' *Eng. Jour.* LII (7), 9-13.
'How University of Waterloo Teaches Creative Engineering,' *Can. Consulting Eng.* II (2), 49-50, 68.

1969 **Lanctôt, B.**
'Ecole Polytechnique, Operation "Choix de Matières,"' *Ing.* LV (247), 20-25.
Pinder, K. L.
'More Maturity Noted in Chemical Engineering Research,' *Chem. Can.* XXI (4), 12-13.

1970 **Crowley, C. P.**
'Credibility Gap: Threat or Portent for Discovery,' *Can. Consulting Eng.* XII (2), 20-23.
Hershfield, C. and G. W. Heinke.
'Civil Engineering Education in Canada, Present and Future,' *Eng. Jour.* LIII (1), 7-11.

FORESTRY : GÉNIE FORESTIER

1903 **Goodwin, W. L. et al.**
'Forest Education for Canada' in *Report of the Fourth Annual Meeting of the Canadian Forestry Association* (Ottawa), 87-95.

1904 **Loudon, J. et al.**
'Education in Forestry' in *Report of Fifth Annual Meeting of the Canadian Forestry Association* (Ottawa), 42-59.

1920 **Howe, C. D.**
'A Canadian Forester's Training,' 'Practical Training for Foresters,' 'Rewards for Trained Foresters in Canada,' *Can. Forestry Magazine* XVI, 408-09, 471-72, 526-28.

1930 **Prince, G. H.**
'The New Provincial Government Forestry and Geology Building at University of New Brunswick,' *For. Chron.* VI (4), 8-13.

1947 **Sisam, J. W. B.**
'Forestry Department of the University of Toronto,' *Woodlands Review* June '47, 85-90.

1964 **Sisam, J. W. B.**
'Teaching Forestry and Utilization,' *Unasylva* [Italy] XVIII (4), 14-21.

1966 **Smith, J. H. G.**
'Are Canadian Financial Incentives for Graduate Study in Forestry Adequate?' *For. Chron.* XLII, 467-68.
Weetman, G. F.
'Problems in Research Communication,' *For. Chron.* XLII, 51-58.

1967 **Gacratt, G. A.**
'Technical Training Programs and Undergraduate Professional Forestry Education in Canada,' *For. Chron.* XLIII, 338-52.

1967 **Lortie, M.**
'The Training and Qualifications of the Forest Engineer in Quebec,' *For. Chron.* XLIII, 269-77.
1968 **Knight, V.**
'Tomorrow's Forester – What Will He be Like?' *For. Chron.* XLIV, 33-34.
Walters, J.
An Annotated Bibliography of Reports, Theses, and Publications Pertaining to the Campus and Research Forests of The University of British Columbia. Vancouver: Faculty of Forestry, U.B.C. Pp. 71.
1969 **Day, R. H.**
Sources of Advanced Education in Forestry and Allied Fields. Halifax: Nova Scotia Department of Lands and Forests. Pp. 4.
Haddock, P. G.
'Whither Forestry?' *For. Chron.* XLV, 298-99.
Sinclair, S.
'Graduate Education in Natural Resource Management,' *For. Chron.* XLV, 296-97.

HOUSEHOLD SCIENCE : SCIENCES DOMESTIQUES

1954 **Ritchie, E. M.**
'Some Historical Aspects in the Growth of Home Economics in the Province of Alberta.' Unpublished M.Ed. thesis, Univ. of Alberta.
1964 **Kernaliguen, A.**
'Principles Approach to the Teaching of Beginning Clothing Construction,' *Can. Home Econ. Jour.* XIV, 8-9, 31.
LeBaron, H. R.
'An Education for Women,' *Can. Home Econ. Jour.* XIV, 3-6, 30-31.
Simpson, E. C.
Home Economics in Canada. Saskatoon: Modern Press. Pp. 129.
1965 **Borror, M. J.**
'A Report of a Clothing Workshop at the University of British Columbia,' *Can. Home Econ. Jour.* XVI, 91-94, 103.
Hiltz, M. C.
'Research in Home Economics at Canadian Universities,' *Can. Home Econ. Jour.* XV, 41-42.
Stensland, P. G.
'The Need for Education in Home Economics,' *Can. Home Econ. Jour.* XV, 3-8.

1966 **Case, P.**
'Food Technology Education Lacks Clarity and Direction,' *Food in Canada* XXVI (8), 23-25.
Empey, E.
'University Education for Prospective Dieticians,' *Can. Hosp.* XLIII (9), 60-61.

1967 **Black, C.**
'Graduate Work ... What? Where?' *Can. Home Econ. Jour.* XVIII, 102-03.
Carmichael, M. M.
'Some Recent Research and Writing Related to the Teaching of Food and Nutrition,' *Can. Home Econ. Jour.* XVII, 18-21.
Neilson, H. R.
'Changing Philosophy of Education,' *Jour. Can. Dietetic Assoc.* XXVIII (1), 18-23. See also *ibid.*, 23-27.
Simpson, E. R.
'College of Home Economics – University of Saskatchewan,' *Can. Home Econ. Jour.* XVII, 64-65.
Vaines, E.
'The Same Subject Matter ... Two Approaches,' *Can. Home Econ. Jour.* XVIII, 95-96, 120.
Wardlaw, J. M.
'Contribution of Home Economics Research to the Improvement of Human Nutrition,' *Med. Services Jour.* XXIII, 942-50.
Wilson, J. H.
'A History of Home Economics in Manitoba, 1826-1966.' Unpublished M.Ed. thesis, Univ. of Manitoba.

1968 'Food Technology Education,' *Food in Canada* XXVII (1), 44-45, 53-55.
Lloyd, L. E.
'Why Home Economics?' *Can. Home Econ. Jour.* XVIII (2), 24-27.

1969 **Lloyd, L. E.**
'The Direction of Home Economics in Canada,' *Can. Home Econ. Jour.* XIX (3), 15-18, 31.
Sangster, M.
'What is a Dietary Technician?' *Can. Hosp.* XLVI (8), 44, 53.
Smith, R.
'Three Year College Courses Planned to Meet Food Technician Shortage,' *Food in Canada* XXIX (8), 42-43.

1970 **Lloyd, L. E.**
'Nutrition Education as Presently Offered,' *Jour. Can. Dietetic Assoc.* XXXI (1), 32-39.

JOURNALISM : JOURNALISME

1962 de Belleval, D.
'Portrait du journalisme étudiant au Canada,' *Univ. Affairs* III (4), 1-2.
1967 Kesterton, W. H.
A History of Journalism in Canada. Toronto: McClelland & Stewart. Pp. 307.
1968 Sauvageau, F.
'Les Journalistes, ces témoins de notre temps,' *Technique* XLII (4), 18-23.
Scanlon, T. J.
'Journalism Education: A Carleton Viewpoint,' *Can. Univ.* IV (3), 35-37.
Scanlon, T. J.
'Revolution in Journalism Education,' *Can. Univ.* III (4), 23-24.

LAW : DROIT

1880 Archambault, J.-L.
Etude Légale, ou Réponse à certain questions concernant les succursales de l'Université Laval à Montréal, avec commentaires. Montréal. Pp. 52.
1898 'L'Enseignement universitaire,' *Rev. Notariat* I, 77-90.
1900 Belanger, L.
'Les Dangers de l'instruction classique à outrance,' *Rev. Notariat* II, 235-39.
1905 Johnson, W. S.
'Legal Education in Quebec,' *Can. Law Review* IV, 451-57.
1911 'Les Etudes Classiques,' *Rev. Notariat* XIV, 132-39.
1916 Lee, R. W.
Legal Education, Uniformity of Law in the British Empire: Two Addresses. Toronto: Carswell Co. Pp. 44.
1923 Canadian Bar Association.
'Legal Education in Canada: Report of the Committee,' *Can. Bar Rev.* I, 671-84.
Denison, S.
'Legal Education in Ontario,' *Can. Bar Rev.* II, 85-92.
1930 Turgeon, H.
'Etudes sur la profession de notaire,' *Rev. Notariat* XXXIII, 112.
1931 Commission Spéciale des Interêts Professionnels.
'Rapport de ...' *Rev. Notariat* XXXIV, 72-78, 134-37.

1950 **McInerney, H. O.**
'The Development of the Law School' in A. G. Bailey, ed., *University of New Brunswick Memorial Volume* (Fredericton: Univ. of New Brunswick), 98-101.
Rand, I. C.
The Student at Law School. Fredericton: Univ. of New Brunswick. Pp. 9.

1952 **Fabre-Surveyer, E.**
'Louis-Guillaume Verrier (1690-1758),' *Rev. Hist.* VI, 159-76.

1964 **Abbott, R. D.**
'Legal Studies at Carleton University,' *Canadian Legal Studies* I (2), 71-74.
Association des Professeurs de Droit du Québec.
'Barreau – et l'enseignement universitaire du droit,' *Thémis* XIV, 179-95.
Beeson, E. W.
'An Introduction to Law Librarianship in Canada,' *Can. Bar Assoc. Papers* 132-38.
Cheffins, R. I.
'Legal Education at McGill: Some Problems and Proposals,' *McGill Law Jour.* X, 126-57.
Cohen, M.
'Legal Education in Canada – Fifteen Years Later, 1949-1964,' *Can. Bar Assoc. Papers* 116-31.
Côté, J. E.
'The Introduction of English Law into Alberta,' *Alta. Law Rev.* III, 262-77.
Crepeau, R.
'La Faculté de Droit de l'Université de Sherbrooke,' *Univ. Tor. Law Jour.* XV, 436-37.
Freedman, S.
'The Right to Practise One's Profession,' *Can. Med. Assoc. Jour.* XCI, 862-68.
Lee, R. S.
'Legal Implications of McGill's High Altitude Research Project,' *McGill Law Jour.* X, 158-70.
Scott, M.
'What Next for Canadian Law Libraries?' *Can. Bar Assoc. Papers,* 139-41.
Strayer, B. L.
'Tutorials in Legal Writing at Saskatchewan,' *Univ. Tor. Law Jour.* XV, 438-39.

1964 **Tallen, G. P. R.**
'Legal Education in Manitoba,' *Univ. Tor. Law Jour.* XV, 432-36.
Thompson, A. R.
'The Course in Land Titles at the University of Alberta,' *Alta. Law Rev.* III, 117-23.

1965 **Beeson, E. W.**
'Law Librarianship in Canada: An Introduction,' *Atlan. Prov. Lib. Bull.* XXIX, 125-30.
Beeson, E. W.
'A Survey of Library Resources Supporting Legal Education and Research in Canada,' *Can. Bar Assoc. Papers* 135-39.
Carrothers, A. B. B.
'Survey of Continuing Legal Education in Canada,' *Can. Bar Assoc. Papers* 141-60.
Carrothers, A. W. R.
'Legal Education at Western,' *Western Law Review* IV, 1-6.
Fairbairn, L. S.
'Legal Aid Clinics for Ontario Law Schools,' *Osgoode Law Jour.* III, 316-30.
Higenbottom, G. A.
'Manitoba Law Society – 50th Anniversary,' *Can. Bar Jour.* VIII, 38-43.
Lederman, W. R.
'Law Schools and Legal Ethics,' *Can. Bar Jour.* VIII, 212-20.
McClean, A. J.
'The Seminar Programme at U.B.C.,' *Univ. Tor. Law Jour.* XV, 439-42.
Morton, J. D.
'Legal Profession Owes Society Research and Scholarship,' *Can. Bar Jour.* VIII, 395-99, 412.
Newman, W. C.
'Bar Admission,' *Man. Bar News* XXXV, 407-09.
Pratte, Y.
'The Faculty of Law at Laval University,' *Univ. Tor. Law Jour.* XVI, 175-76.
Ryan, W. F.
'The University of New Brunswick Faculty of Law,' *Univ. Tor. Law Jour.* XVI, 172-75.

1966 **Baudoin, L.**
'Les Cadres juridiques' in G. Sylvestre, ed., *Structures sociales du Canada français* (Toronto: U. of T. Press), 84-97.

1966 **Curtis, G. F.**
'Methods of Law Reform: The Need for Expanded Research Facilities,' *U.B.C. Law Review* II, 307-15.
Edwards, C. H. C.
'Legal Education in Manitoba,' *Man. Law Jour.* II, 1-3. Also in *Univ. Tor. Law Jour.* XVI (2), 404-06.

1967 **Azard, P.**
'Vers une Normalisation souhaitable des rapports entre la profession et la faculte dans le domaine de l'enseignement du droit,' *McGill Law Jour.* XIII, 152-60.
Belleau, H.-G.
'Le Practicien du droit au Québec et en Ontario: une étude des professions informelles au sein de la profession et leurs effets,' *ACFAS* XXX, 188 (Résumé).
Cardinal, J.-G.
'La Faculté de Droit et le Notariat,' *Thémis* XVII, 151-60.
Prober, J. et al.
'Manitoba Bar Admissions Course,' *Man. Bar News* XXXVI, 61-74.
Ryan, W. F.
'The University of New Brunswick Law Faculty,' *Can. Bar Jour.* X, 43-49.

1968 **Bucknall, B. D., C. H. Baldwin and J. D. Lakin.**
'Pedants, Practitioners and Prophets: Legal Education at Osgoode Hall to 1957,' *Osgoode Law Jour.* VI, 137-229.
Lajoie, F.
'Entraînement professionnel,' *Rev. Barr.* XXVIII, 387-94.
Ryan, E. F.
'Television and the Law Schools - a Preliminary Appraisal,' *Chitty's Law Jour.* XVI, 293-98.
Woodsworth, K. C.
'Continuing Legal Education in British Columbia,' *Can. Bar Jour.* XI, 604-10.

1969 **Charles, W. H.**
'The Problem Method and Canadian Legal Education,' *U.B.C. Law Rev.* IV, 130-46.
Friedman, H. M.
'The American Federal System - An Introduction for Canadian Law Students,' *Man. Law Jour.* III (2), 19-26.
Iacobucci, N. E.
'Legal Research and Writing: A Proposed Programme,' *Univ. Tor. Law Jour.* XIX, 401-20.

1969 **Laskin, B.**
The British Tradition in Canadian Law (The Hamlyn Lectures, Twenty-First Series). London: Stevens. Pp. 138.
Parker, G.
'The Inhibitions of the Criminal Law Teacher,' *U.B.C. Law Rev.* IV, 29-55.
Soberman, D. A.
'The Faculty of Law of Queen's University,' *Univ. Tor. Law Jour.* XIX, 420-23.
Tarnopolsky, W. S.
'The New Law School at the University of Windsor,' *Univ. Tor. Law Jour.* XIX, 622-26.
1970 **Turner, K.**
'University Law Students and Exposure to Private Practice,' *Man. Bar News* XXXVIII, 75-81.

LIBRARY SCIENCE : BIBLIOTHÉCONOMIE

1956 **Dolores, Sister F.**
'What Library Schools Expect of the Employer,' *Atlan. Prov. Lib. Bull.* XX, 68-71.
1957 **Arnison, D.**
'Librarianship as a Profession,' *Atlan. Prov. Lib. Bull.* XXI, 87-90.
British Columbia, Public Library Commission, Special Committee on Library Education (E. S. Robinson, Chairman).
Training Professional Librarians for Western Canada; a Report. Victoria: The Commission. Pp. 24.
1962 **Desrochers, E.**
While Reading about a Philosophy of Librarianship. Ottawa: Canadian Library Association. Pp. 12. (Occasional Paper no. 35.)
'The School of Librarianship; The University of British Columbia,' *Alta. Lib. Assoc. Bull.* IX(2), 16-19.
1963 **Murray, F. B.**
'The Teaching of Bibliography in English-speaking Canada,' *Bibliographical Society of Canada Papers* II, 46-56.
Rothstein, S.
'New School, Old Problem: Admissions Policy and Procedure at the University of B.C. School of Librarianship,' *B.C. Lib. Q.* XXVII (1), 3-8.
1964 **Boylan, D. B.**
'Archives Course, Carleton University,' *Atlan. Prov. Lib. Bull.* XXVIII (3), 7-9.

1964 **Henderson, B.**
'Library Education in Canada,' *Can. Library* XXI, 176-77.
McPherson, A.
'Professional Library Training: McGill Revamps Course, U.B.C. offers B.L.S. and Toronto Expands,' *Sask. Lib. Assoc. Bull.* XVIII (1), 16-20.
Morisset, A.-M.
'Les Vingt-cinq ans de l'Ecole de Bibliothéconomie d'Ottawa,' *Bull. Bibl.* X, 112-15.

1965 **Association Canadienne des Bibliothèques de Collège et d'Université.**
'Prévision du coût des services des bibliothèques académiques au Canada, 1965-1975,' *Can. Library* XXII, 73-75.
Beeson, E. W.
'Law Librarianship in Canada: An Introduction,' *Atlan. Prov. Lib. Bull.* XXIX, 125-30.
Bishop, O. B.
'Notes on Library Education as Seen by a Perusal of Accredited Library School Announcements,' *Inst. Prof. Lib. Ont.* VI (6), 2-4.
Canadian Association of College and University Libraries.
Guide to Canadian University Library Standards: Report of the University Library Standards Committee. Ottawa: The Association. Pp. 53.
Harlow, N.
'The Education Problem,' *Can. Lib. Assoc. Bull.* XXII, 84-89.
Hart, P. W.
'Library Education and the Reference Librarian,' *Ont. Lib. Rev.* XLIX, 178-81.
'A Library School in the Prairie Provinces,' *Sask. Lib. Assoc. Bull.* XVIII (May), 13-14.
Marshall, J.
'Education for Librarianship; Challenge and Response,' *Ont. Lib. Rev.* XLIX, 186-88.
Rothstein, S.
'Nobody's Baby: Continuing Professional Education in Librarianship,' *Sask. Lib. Assoc. Bull.* XVIII (2), 15-17.
Swanson, D. R. *et al.*
Education for Library Planning. Ottawa: Canadian Library Association. Pp. 19.

1966 'A l'Ecole de Bibliothéconomie de l'Université de Montréal,' *Bull. Bibl.* XII, 72-76.

1966 Henderson, M. E.
'Library Manpower,' *Can. Library* XXIII, 162-65.
Land, R. B.
'School of Library Science Plans for the Future,' *Ont. Lib. Rev.* L (2), 72-73.
Land, R. B.
'University of Toronto School of Library Science,' *Can. Library* XXII, 223-25.
Rothstein, S.
'Historical Notes: University of British Columbia School of Librarianship,' *Can. Library* XXII, 226-28.
Rothstein, S.
'Placement at the University of British Columbia School of Librarianship,' *Can. Library* XXII, 278-79.
'The University of British Columbia Library 1915-65,' *B.C. Lib. Q.* XXIX (3), 1-84.
Wiedrick, S. G.
'The Role of the University of Alberta in Preparing School Librarians,' *Alberta School Library Review* III (2), 8-13.
1967 Bosa, R.
'La Formation professionnelle des bibliothécaires au Canada,' *Can. Library* XXIV (3), 215-17.
Gattinger, F. E.
'An Atlantic Provinces Library School,' *Atlan. Prov. Lib. Bull.* XXXI, 42-43.
Zielinska, M. F.
'"Library College": Une Nouvelle méthode d'enseignement,' *Bull. Bibl.* XIII, 35-41.
1968 Denis, L.-G.
'A l'Ecole de bibliothéconomie. Le nouveau programme ... deux ans après son instauration,' *Bull. Bibl.* XIV, 139-41.
Denis, L.-G.
'La Formation des bibliothécaires de langue française du Québec' in B. Peel, ed., *Librarianship in Canada 1946-67* (Victoria, B.C.: Can. Library Assoc.), 149-62.
Desrochers, E.
'The Canadian Association of Library Schools,' *Can. Library* XXIV, 518-19.
Henne, F.
'School Librarianship,' *Can. Library* XXV, 222-26.

1968 **Morisset, A.-M.**
'Nouvelles des Ecoles de bibliothéconomie, Université d'Ottawa: quelques statistiques,' *Bull. Bibl.* XIV, 137-38; XV, 185-86.
Peel, B., ed.
Librarianship in Canada, 1946-1967: Essays in Honour of Elizabeth Homer Morton. Victoria, B.C.: Can. Library Assoc. Pp. 205.
Penland, P. R.
'Librarianship in Canada-Impressions,' *Inst. Prof. Lib. Ont.* IX, 62-67.
Van der Bellen, L.
'Nouvelles des Ecoles de bibliothéconomie, Université de Montréal: quelques statistiques,' *Bull. Bibl.* XIV, 133-36; XV, 180-84.
Whiteside, S.
'Library Education: An Approach for Tomorrow,' *Atlan. Prov. Lib. Bull.* XXXII, 72-75.

1969 **Bates, I.**
'Continuing Education, the Student and the Library Association,' *Lib. Assoc. of Alta. Bull.* I (2), 10-17.
Bewley, L. M.
'To Educate Ourselves Continuously,' *B.C. Lib. Q.* XXXIII (1), 23-25.
Bosa, R.
'Considerations sur le programme de bibliotechnique offert dans les CEGEP,' *Bull. Bibl.* XV, 177-79.
Harris, M.
'Achievement of Professionalism,' *Can. Library Jour.* XXVI, 280-83.
Kelley, M. I.
'Knowledge and Professional Skill; Or is There a Place for Field Work in Library Education for Tomorrow?' *Atlan. Prov. Lib. Bull.* XXXIII (2), 13-15.
Land, B.
'The Master's Curriculum and the Library Profession,' *Inst. Prof. Lib. Ont.* X, 92-97.
Land, B.
'New Directions in Education for Librarianship in Canada,' *Can. Library Jour.* XXVI, 36-40.
Marshall, J.
'Major Issues in Library Education: Toronto's Approach to Its New Program,' *Sask. Lib.* XXIII (1), 3-15.
'Medical Record Librarians: Training to Fill a Void,' *Can. Doctor* XXXV (4), 60-61.

1969 **Pannu, G. S.**
'Admissions Dilemma,' *Sask. Lib.* XXIII (1), 19-24. Also in *Alta. Lib. Assoc. Bull.* II (2), 9-13 and *Manitoba Library Assoc. Bull.* XVI (4), 13-16.
Paradis, J.
'Quelques publications en bibliothéconomie au cours de 1968,' *Bull. Bibl.* XV, 67-72.
Shaw, R. F.
'Crisis at the University,' *Lib. Assoc. of Alta. Bull.* I (2), 18-26.
Spicer, E. J.
'The Case Against a Two-Year First Degree Course for Librarians in Canada,' *Can. Library Jour.* XXVI, 292-94.

1970 **Land, B.**
'Recent Developments in Education for Librarianship in Canada,' *Library Association Record* [U.S.] LXXII (4), 142-46.
Ng, T. K.
'Librarianship in East Asian Studies,' *Can. Library Jour.* XXVII (2), 102-14.
Reed, S.
'The Decade Ahead,' *Lib. Assoc. of Alta. Bull.* I (3), 27-30.
Wenckler, P. A.
'The Need for the Study of Library History,' *Atlan. Prov. Lib. Assoc. Bull.* XXXIV (2), 43-46.

MEDICINE : MÉDECINE

General : Generalités

1960 **Taylor, M. G.**
'The Role of the Medical Profession in the Formulation and Execution of Public Policy,' *Can. Jour. Econ. Pol. Sci.* XXVI, 108-27.
1962 **Royal College of Physicians and Surgeons of Canada.**
'Summary and Recommendations of Brief to the Royal Commission on Health Services,' *Can. Jour. Surgery* V, 237-40.
1964 **Canadian Medical Association, Special Committee on Policy**
(K. R. Trueman, Chairman).
'Statement on Medical Care with Conclusions and Recommendations,' *Can. Med. Assoc. Jour.* XCI (12) (Special Supplement), 1-15; 'Expose sur le sujet de soins medicaux ...' 17-33.

1964 'Educational Issue,' *Can. Med. Assoc. Jour.* XCI, includes:
J. T. Law, 'Hospital-Medical School Relationships,' 819-23;
H. S. Armstrong, 'The Medical Faculty and the Community,' 830-34.
Freedman, S.
'The Right to Practise One's Profession,' *Can. Med. Assoc. Jour.* XCI, 862-68.
Hamilton, J. D.
'L'Université et la pratique médicale,' *Union Méd.* XCIII, 869-74.
Hosking, D. J.
'An Experience in Medical Education,' *Coll. Gen. Practice Jour.* XI (2), 22-24.
Stewart, C. B.
'The Finances of Dalhousie Medical School,' *Dalhousie Med. Jour.* XVIII (1), 10-21.
Thompson, W. P.
Medical Care. Toronto: Clarke, Irwin. Pp. 178.

1965 **Penfield, W.**
'A Philosophy for Doctors,' *Can. Med. Stud. Jour.* XXIV (1), 20-29.
Slater, R. J.
'The University, the Health Professions and Patient Care,' *Queen's Q.* LXXII, 604-13.
Tollefson, E. A.
'The Aftermath of the Medicare Dispute in Saskatchewan,' *Queen's Q.* LXXII, 452-65.

1966 **deHesse, C. and D. G. Fish.**
'Canadian-Trained Medical Scientists View Canadian Academia from their American Laboratories,' *Can. Med. Assoc. Jour.* XCV, 970-73.
'Educational Issue' Part II, *Can. Med. Assoc. Jour.* XCV includes:
J. F. Mustard, J. C. Laidlaw and J. O. Godden, 'Medical Education and Research: the Foundation of Quality Health Care,' 795-99;
E. L. Thomas, 'The Physician of the Future,' 808-11.
Kerr, R. B.
'The Challenges to and the Challenges of Medicine,' *B.C. Med. Jour.* VIII, 140-47.
Pichette, L.-P.
'Education médicale: quelques réflections,' *Union Méd.* XCV, 453-63.

1967 **Blain, G.**
'L'Education permanente et le domaine paramédical,' *Union Méd.* XCVI, 312-17.

1967 **Canada, Department of National Health and Welfare.**
The Economics and Costs of Medical Care. Ottawa: The Department (Research and Statistics Memorandum). Pp. 192.
Canadian Medical Association.
'Conference on Medical Manpower,' *Can. Med. Assoc. Jour.* XCVII, 1555-1609.
Canadian Medical Association.
'Second Western Conference on Medical Education,' *Can. Med. Assoc. Jour.* XCVII, 705-51.
'Educational Issues,' *Can. Med. Assoc. Jour.* XCVI, include:
D. O. Anderson, E. Riches and J. F. McCreary, 'Medicine or Science: a Study of Career Decisions,' 1009-18; J. E. Flowers, 'Research in Medical Education: Some Methodological Considerations,' 942-46.
Evans, J.
'Les Problèmes actuels et l'orientation future de l'enseignement de la médecine,' *Laval Med.* XXXVIII, 272-81. Voir aussi *Union Med.* XCVI, 300-07.
Hamilton, J. D.
'Les responsabilités d'une faculté de médecine envers la société,' *Laval Méd.* XXXVIII, 249-51.
Jobin, F.
'Réflexions sur l'enseignement médical universitaire,' *Can. Med. Assoc. Jour.* XCVII, 402-11.
Kohn, R.
The Health of the Canadian People. Ottawa: Queen's Printer. Pp. 412.
Langelier, R.
'L'Evolution des origines sociales des finissants en médecine de l'Université Laval de 1948 à 1965.' Thèse de licence, Univ. Laval.
Ryan, C.
'Ce que société attend d'une faculté de médecine,' *Laval Méd.* XXXVIII, 252-57.
Université Laval.
Rapport du Comité d'étude des relations entre l'Université Laval, la Faculté de Médecine et les hôpitaux d'enseignement. Quebec: L'Université. Pp. 245.
1968 **Canada, Department of National Health and Welfare.**
Provincial Health Services by Program. Ottawa: The Department. Pp. 37.
Cathcart, L. M.
'The Millis and Willard Reports,' *B.C. Med. Jour.* X, 15-17.

1968 **Copping, J. D.**
'L'Evolution de l'enseignement médical sur les hôpitaux d'enseignement et ses répercussions,' *Can. Hosp.* XLV (11), 53-56.
Copping, J. D.
'The Impact of Rapid Changes in Medical Education on Teaching Hospitals,' *Can. Hosp.* XLV (11), 41-44.
'Educational Issues,' *Can. Med. Assoc. Jour.* XCVIII, includes:
F. Hould, 'L'Affiliation des Hôpitaux d'enseignement,' 725-29;
J. Brunet, 'L'Enseignement de la médecine et les sciences de la santé ...' 730-31; R. M. Cherniack, 'The Correlation of Structure and Function in Medical Education,' 738-43.
Genest, J.
'La Recherche médicale au Canada français,' *Act. Nat.* LVIII, 114-28.
MacDonald, R. M.
'The Role of the University in Training of Personnel in the Health Sciences,' *N.S. Med. Bull.* XLVII (2), 29-31.
McKendry, J. B. R.
'Practitioner-Associates and the Medical Manpower Problem,' *Ont. Med. Rev.* XXXV, 455-57, 461.
Patterson, F. P.
'On Medical Education, Practice and Organization – 1968,' *B.C. Med. Jour.* X, 96-102.
St-Arnaud, P.
'Pour une sociologie de la pratique médicale au Québec,' *Recherches Soc.* IX, 281-97.

1969 **Blishen, B. R.**
Doctors and Doctrines: the Ideology of Medical Care in Canada.
Toronto: U. of T. Press. Pp. 202.
Brunet, J.
'Les Sciences de la santé et le nouveau programme des études à la Faculté de Médecine de l'Université Laval,' *Can. Med. Assoc. Jour.* C, 653-56.
Chevalot, T.
'Le Monople de la médecine: comment les médecins bloquent l'assurance maladie,' *Cah. Cité Libre* XIX (6). Montreal: Editions du Jour. Pp. 192.
Chipman, M. L., G. G. Clarke and J. W. Steiner.
'Career Choice Within Medicine: A Study of One Graduating Class at the University of Toronto,' *Can. Med. Assoc. Jour.* CI, 646-51.

1969 **Grove, J. W.**
Organized Medicine in Ontario: a Study for the Committee on the Healing Arts. Toronto: Queen's Printer. Pp. 327.
Marceau, G.
'La Réforme de l'enseignement médical,' *Laval Méd.* XL, 167-70.
McCreary, J. F.
'The Role of the Practising Physician in Medical School Recruitment,' *Can. Med. Assoc. Jour.* XCII, 728-31.
McWhinney, I. R.
'The Foundations of Family Medicine,' *Can. Family Physician* XV (4), 13-27.
Read, J. H. and J. L. Strick.
'Medical Education and the Native Canadian: An Example of Mutual Symbiosis,' *Can. Med. Assoc. Jour.* C (11), 515-20.
Rice, D. I.
'The College of Family Physicians of Canada,' *Can. Family Physician* III (9), 104-05.
Trout, F.
'The Nurse and the Family Physician,' *Can. Family Physician* XV (6), 23-28.
Van Staalduinen, W. J.
'A Study of Licensing in the Medical Profession in Canada.' Unpublished M.A. thesis, Carleton Univ.
Warwick, O. H.
'A University View of the Delivery of Health Care,' *Bus. Q.* XXIV (3), 72-74.
1970 **Committee on the Healing Arts.**
Report of the Committee on the Healing Arts. Toronto: Queen's Printer. 3 vols.
Duff, S. L. and D. G. Fish.
'Canadian Trained Physicians in the United States, Internships and Residencies: "Operation Retrieval" and Report of Statistics, 1966-68,' *Can. Med. Assoc. Jour.* CII, 291-95.

Historical Development : Développement historique

1860 **MacCallum, D. C.**
'Introductory Lecture Delivered at the Opening of the Faculty of Medicine, University of McGill College, November 5, 1860,' *British American Journal* I, 481-92.

1909 Scugog [J. F. W. Ross].
A Medical Student's Letters to his Parents. Toronto. Pp. 139.
1911 *Jour. Can. Med. Assoc.* I, contains the following editorials or reports bearing on the reaction of the various medical schools to the Flexner Report of 1910 (*Medical Education in the United States and Canada*): Queen's and the Carnegie Report, 62-64; The Halifax Medical College, 64-70; Medical Teaching in Halifax, 983-85; The Vindication of Laval, 354-56; Manitoba Medical College, 988-91; Western University, 993-94; The Proprietary School, 1091-93.
1916 Shortt, E. S.
Historical Sketch of Medical Education of Women in Kingston. Ottawa. Pp. 13.
1925 Flexner, A.
Medical Education: A Comparative Study. New York: Macmillan. Pp. 334.
1928 Gibson, T.
'Notes on the Medical History of Queen's,' *Can. Med. Assoc. Jour.* XVIII, 331-34, 446-51.
1932 Massicotte, E.-Z.
'Chirurgiens médecins et apothicaires sous le régime français,' *Bull. Recherches Hist.* 515-22.
1934 Weiskotten, H. G. et al.
Medical Education in the United States 1934-1939. Chicago: American Medical Association. Pp. 259.
1938 Auclair, E.-J.
'L'Ecole Victoria de Montréal,' *Mém. S.R.C.* sect. 1, 1-20.
1943 Dibrick, H.
'The Old Days at Toronto: Further Reminiscences concerning Faculty Members of the Medical School of the University of Toronto at the Turn of the Century,' *Hist. Bull. Calgary Clinic* VII (4), 6-9.
1944 Stanley, G. D.
'Dr. John Rolph: Medicine and Rebellion in Upper Canada,' *Hist. Bull. Calgary Clinic* IX (1), 1-13.
1945 Routley, T. C.
'Volume One, Number One of the Canadian Medical Association Journal,' *Hist. Bull. Calgary Clinic* X (1), 10-16.
1946 McKenzie, K. A.
'The Dalhousie Medical School,' *Hist. Bull. Calgary Clinic* XI, 78-81.
1947 Jutras, A.
'La Médecine français au Canada,' *Jour. Hôtel-Dieu* XV, 85-105.

1947 **Mitchell, R.**
'Manitoba's Medical School,' *Hist. Bull. Calgary Clinic* XII, 66-69.
1948 **Clarkson, F. A.**
'The Medical Faculty of the University of Toronto,' *Hist. Bull. Calgary Clinic* XIII, 21-30.
Crane, J. W.
'The University of Western Ontario Medical School,' *Hist. Bull. Calgary Clinic* XIII, 1-3.
1949 **Johnson, G. R.**
'McGill University – Medical Faculty,' *Hist. Bull. Calgary Clinic* XIV, 41-47; XV, 1-7.
Neatby, H.
'The Medical Profession in the North West Territories,' *Sask. Hist.* II, 1-15.
Parent, A.-M.
'Laval Medical School – Quebec,' *Hist. Bull. Calgary Clinic* XIV, 1-5.
Revell, D. G.
'The Medical Faculty – University of Alberta,' *Hist. Bull. Calgary Clinic* XIII, 65-75.
1951 **Ranta, L. E.**
'The Medical School of British Columbia,' *Hist. Bull. Calgary Clinic* XVI, 1-9.
1952 **Anderson, A. L.**
'The School of Medical Sciences and the Medical College of the University of Saskatchewan,' *Hist. Bull. Calgary Clinic* XVII, 1-9.
Cameron, M. H. V.
'Medical Education in Toronto,' *Hist. Bull. Calgary Clinic* XVII, 71-74.
Cleveland, D. E. H.
'The Edinburgh Tradition in Canadian Medical Education,' *Bull. Vancouver Med. Assoc.* XXVIII, 216-20.
1953 **Jobin, P.**
'Cent ans d'anatomie,' *Laval Med.* XVIII, 538-55.
1955 **Mitchell, R.**
Medicine in Manitoba: the Story of Its Beginnings. Winnipeg: Stovel-Advocate Press. Pp. 141.
Shields, H. J.
'The History of Anaesthesia in Canada,' *Can. Anaesth. Jour.* II, 301-08.
1956 **McKenzie, K. A. and C. B. Stewart.**
'Canadian Medical Faculties through the Years: Dalhousie University,' *Can. Med. Stud. Jour.* XI, 78-81.

1957 Boucher, R.
'La Médecine au Canada; de Jacques Cartier à la fondation du Collège des Médecins et Chirurgiens (1534-1847),' *Médecine de France* LXXXVII, 12-16.

1959 White, G. M.
'The History of Obstetrical and Gynaecological Teaching in Canada,' *American Jour. Obstetrics Gynecology* LXXVII, 465-74.

1963 Scott, J. W.
The History of the Faculty of Medicine of the University of Alberta 1913-1963. Edmonton: Univ. of Alberta. Pp. 43.

1964 Greenland, C.
'Richard Maurice Bucke, M.D.: A Pioneer of Scientific Psychiatry,' *Can. Med. Assoc. Jour.* XCI, 385-91.

Hewitt, R. M., J. R. Eckman and R. D. Miller.
'The Mayo Clinic and the Canadians,' *Can. Med. Assoc. Jour.* XCI, 1161-72.

1966 Desjardins, E.
'L'Existence simultanée à Montréal de quatre écoles de médecine,' *Union Méd.* XCV, 1425-28.

Godfrey, C. M.
'Trinity Medical School,' *App. Therapeutics* VIII, 1024-28.

Greenland, C.
'C. K. Clarke: A Founder of Canadian Psychiatry,' *Can. Med. Assoc. Jour.* XCV, 155-60.

Mitchell, R. and T. K. Thorlakson.
'James Kerr, 1848-1911 and Harry Hyland Kerr, 1881-1963: Pioneer Canadian American Surgeon,' *Can. Jour. Surgery* IX, 213-20.

Seguin, R.-L.
'L'Apprentissage de la Chirurgie en Nouvelle-France,' *Rev. Hist.* XX, 593-99.

Wasteneys, H.
'A Brief History of the Faculty of Medicine,' [University of Toronto] *Med. Grad.* XII (3), 6-7, 13.

1967 Appleton, V. E.
'Psychiatry in Canada a Century Ago,' *Can. Psych. Assoc. Jour.* XII, 345-61.

Cameron, I.
'One Hundred Years of Dalhousie,' *Dalhousie Med. Jour.* XXI (1), 5-9.

Curtiss, J. F.
'The First Medical School in Upper Canada,' *Ont. Med. Rev.* XXXIV, 449-52.

1967 **Godfrey, C. M.**
'King's College: Upper Canada's First Medical School,' *Ont. Med. Rev.* XXXIV, 19-22, 26.
Jacques, A.
'Anaesthesia in Canada, 1847-1967: The Beginnings of Anaesthesia in Canada,' *Can. Anaesth. Jour.* XIV, 500-10. See also H. R. Griffith, 'The Development of Anaesthesia in Canada,' 510-19.
Laurin, C.
'Evolution de l'enseignement de la médecine au Québec,' *Union Méd.* XCVII, 1424-30.
MacDermot, H. E.
One Hundred Years of Medicine in Canada (1867-1967). Toronto: McClelland & Stewart. Pp. 224.
Parks, A. E.
'The Evolution of Canadian Medical Practice during the Last Century,' *Mod. Med. Canada* XXII (7), 41-90.
'Struggle for Progress in the Faculty of Medicine at Laval University'/'L'Histoire de l'Université de Laval,' *Can. Med. Stud. Jour.* New Series I (1), 44-46.

1968 **Lemieux, G.**
'L'Enseignement de la médecine au Canada français,' *Union Méd.* XCVIII, 172-83.
Medical Research Council of Canada.
Canadian Medical Research: Survey and Outlook (M.R.C. Report no. 2). Ottawa: Queen's Printer. Pp. 416.
Stewart, C. B.
'One Hundred Years of Medical Education at Dalhousie,' *N.S. Med. Bull.* XLVII (5), 149-52.

1969 **Defries, R. D.**
The First Forty Years, 1914-1955: Connaught Medical Research Laboratories, University of Toronto. Toronto: U. of T. Press. Pp. 342.

1970 **Beatty, J. D.**
'History of Medical Education in Toronto,' *Univ. Toronto Med. Jour.* XLVII, 152-57.
Committee on the Healing Arts.
Report of the Committee on the Healing Arts. Toronto: Queen's Printer. 3 vols.
MacNab, E.
A Legal History of the Health Profession in Ontario. Toronto: Queen's Printer. Pp. 152.

1970 **Wilt, J. C.**
'The History of Medical Microbiology at the University of Manitoba,'
Man. Med. Rev. L (3), 16-21.

The M.D. Programme : Doctorat en Médecine

1912 **McPhedran, A.**
'Undergraduate Training and the Requirements for the License to Practise,' *Jour. Can. Med. Assoc.* II, 1-7.

1952 **Fish, F. M.**
'Medical Education in Canada,' *Hist. Bull. Calgary Clinic* XVII, 45-54.

1954 **Robertson, J. K.**
'An Experiment in Medical Education,' [at Queen's Univ.] *Brit. Jour. Radiology* XXVII, 593-603.
'Vancouver: Developments in Medical Education,' *Mod. Med. Canada* IX (5), 31-33.

1962 **Hamilton, J. D.**
'The Future of Medical Education at the University of Toronto,'
Med. Grad. VIII (1), 2-9.
Martin, J. K. *et al.*
'Curriculum Planning - University of Alberta,' *Can. Med. Assoc. Jour.* LXXXVI, 630-35.

1964 **Anderson, D. O.**
'The Premedical Student: His Identity; Characteristics of a Cohort of Premedical Students at the University of British Columbia,' *Jour. Can. Med. Assoc.* XCI, 1011-18.
Bergeron, G.-A.
'Un Système tutorial à Laval,' *Laval Méd.* XXXV, 963-65.
Botterell, E. H.
'Problems of Medical Education in Canada,' *Med. Grad.* X (2), 2-4.
Chute, A. L.
'Lecture on Medical Education,' *Can. Med. Stud. Jour.* XXIII (2), 26-33.
Coutu, L. L.
'Education Médicale Sous-graduée,' *Can. Med. Stud. Jour.* XXIII (2), 19-25.
'Educational Issue,' *Can. Med. Assoc. Jour.* XCI, includes:
H. Jason, 'A Study of the Teaching of Medicine and Surgery in a Canadian Medical School,' 813-19; S. L. Vanderwater, 'The Place of Anesthesiology in Undergraduate Medical Education,' 851-52;
H. R. Griffith, 'Medical Education and Anesthesiology,' 852-53;
J. W. Scott, 'Medicine as a General Education,' 869-71.

1964 Gurd, F. N.
'L'Education médicale contemporaine au Canada,' *Union Méd.* XCIII, 334-36.
McCreary, J. F.
'The Education of Physicians in Canada,' *Can. Med. Assoc. Jour.* XCI, 1215-21.
Nanson, M.
'Some Views on Medical Education,' *Can. Med. Stud. Jour.* XXIII (1), 5-8.
Nice, P. O.
'Seeds of Discontent,' *Can. Med. Stud. Jour.* XXIII (2), 5-11.
Rice, D. T.
'The Role of the General Practitioner in Undergraduate Medical Education,' *Coll. Gen. Practice Jour.* X (6), 23-26.
Sloane, R. B.
'Psychiatry in Undergraduate Education,' *Can. Med. Assoc. Jour.* XCI, 845-51.
U'ren, R.
'Liberal Education and the Student of Medicine,' *Can. Med. Stud. Jour.* XXIII (2), 12-18.

1965 'Educational Issue,' *Can. Med. Assoc. Jour.* XCII, includes: D. G. Fish and J. W. MacLeod, 'A Pilot Study of Applications to the Four Ontario Medical Schools for Admission to the First Professional Year,' 698-707; D. Anderson, E. Rickes and R. K. Evans, 'The Premedical Student, his Progress: A Study of a Cohort of Premedical Students at the University of British Columbia,' 717-22; J. M. Mather, *et al.*, 'Markings of a Class: the Statistical Trail Left by the First Graduating Class in Medicine, University of British Columbia,' 723-27; R. C. A. Hunter, 'Some Factors Affecting Undergraduate Academic Achievement,' 732-36; G. Gingras, 'Quelques considerations sur l'enseignement de la médecine physique et de la rehabilitation,' 756-57.
Garlick, J. K.
'Race for Teaching Space Blossoms Across Canada,' *Can. Doctor* XXXI (2), 25-29.
Gingras, R.
'L'Hôpital et l'enseignement clinique,' *Laval Méd.* XXXVI, 453-65.
Hall, G. W.
'... But a Preparation: A Report on Premedical Education,' *Can. Med. Stud. Jour.* XXIV (4), 47-73.

1965 **Hunter, R. C. A.**
'Youth and the Study of Medicine,' *Queen's Q.* LXXII, 435-41.
Klonoff, H.
'Psychology in Medical Schools and Teaching Hospitals: a Survey,' *Can. Psych.* VIa, 259-65.
'Medical Education in Canada,' *Can. Med. Assoc. Jour.* XCIII, 324-26.
Sipherd, R. S. and R. T. Chambers.
'On Premedical Education,' *Can. Med. Stud. Jour.* XXIV (2), 32-38.
Therrien, L.
'Enquête menée chez les externes, internes et résidents sur la valeur educative des différents cas cliniques,' *Laënnec Méd.* XVII (1), 19-26.
Yonge, K. A.
'The Use of Closed Circuit Television for the Teaching of Psychotherapeutic Interviewing to Medical Students,' *Can. Med. Assoc. Jour.* XCII, 747-51.

1966 **Association des Etudiants en Médecine de l'Université Laval.**
'Mémoire soumis ... aux membres de la Commission Bonneau,' *Laënnec Méd.* XVIII (2), 21-25.
'Educational Issue,' Part I, *Can. Med. Assoc. Jour.* XCVI, includes: S. M. Hunka, D. F. Cameron and J. A. L. Gilbert, 'Selection of Students for Admission to Medical School: a Two-Class Decision Approach,' 708-11; C. Buck, M. Schofield and O. H. Warwick, 'A Survey of Women Graduates from a Canadian Medical School,' 712-16; J. H. Mount and D. G. Fish, 'Canadian Medical Student Interest in General Practice and the Specialties,' 723-28; E. R. Smith, 'The Status of Medical Education: a Student's Viewpoint,' 729-34.
Fish, D. G. and B. I. Brown.
'A Comparison of Applicants and Applications to Canadian Medical and Dental Schools, 1965-66,' *Can. Med. Assoc. Jour.* XCV, 68-71.
Mather, J. M.
'Random Thoughts on a Department of Preventive Medicine in a Canadian Medical School,' *Can. Med. Assoc. Jour.* XCV, 1309-10.
'The Med School Dilemma,' *Can. Doctor* XXXII (11), 42-45; XXXIII (1), 46-48.

1967 **Anderson, D. O. and E. Riches.**
'Some Observations on Attrition of Students from Canadian Medical Schools,' *Can. Med. Assoc. Jour.* XCVI, 665-74.
Bergeron, G.-A.
'L'Enseignement médicale,' *Laval Méd.* XXXVIII, 245-48.

1967 **Bullman, M.**
'Concepts behind U.B.C.'s New Medical Complex, and the Role of Rehabilitation Medicine in Such a Complex,' *Can. Physiotherapy Jour.* XIX, 16-19.
'Educational Issues,' *Can. Med. Assoc. Jour.* XCVI, include:
D. Waugh, 'Experiences with Evaluation Procedures in Pathology Teaching at Dalhousie University,' 947-53; R. H. More, 'Depth in Training in Academic Pathology Including Teaching and Research,' 953-57; H. C. Soltan, 'Thoughts on Learning and Teaching in the First Two Years of the Medical Curriculum,' 965-71; G. C. Clarke and D. G. Fish, 'The Premedical Education of the First-Year Class in Canadian Medical Schools, 1965-66,' 1019-26; R. B. Goldbloom and G. M. Jones, 'The Role of a Tutorial System in Undergraduate Medical Education,' 1027-31.
Evans, R. K. and D. O. Anderson.
'The Selection of Medical Students in Western Canada,' *Can. Med. Assoc. Jour.* XCVI, 473-80.
Gingras, R.
'Les Admissions à la faculté de médecine de l'Université Laval,' *Laval Méd.* XXXVIII, 262-71.
Haynes, E. R.
'The Orientation of Medical Students to Total Health Care,' *Can. Family Physician* XIII, 36-41.
Hunter, A. T.
'Family Medicine in a Changing Profession,' *Can. Family Physician* XIII, 49-52.
Macleod, J. W.
'The Maladies of Medical Education: Palliative Medicine or Radical Surgery?'/'Les Maladies de l'education médicale ...' *Can. Med. Stud. Jour.* New Series I (1), 41-43.
Macleod, J. W. and S. Duff.
'The Forces Reshaping Our Medical Education,' *Can. Doctor* XXXIII (7), 35-38.
McInnes, R. R., ed.
'Workshop on Medical Education,' *Dalhousie Med. Jour.* XXI (1), 29-35.
Miller, J. R.
'A Genetics Program for Undergraduate Medical Students at the University of British Columbia,' *Journal of Medical Education* [U.S.] XLII, 371-73.

1967 Read, J. G.
'The Medical Student and Hospital Organizations,' *Can. Hosp.* XLIV (4), 41-45.
Ross, M. G.
'Medicine and the Social Sciences,' *Can. Med. Assoc. Jour.* XCVII, 965-69.

1968 Botterell, E. H.
'Current Concepts Regarding Education of Medical Students,' *Can. Hosp.* XLV (11), 45-48.
Canadian Medical Association.
'Audiovisual Aids in Medical Teaching,' *Can. Med. Assoc. Jour.* XCVIII, 1079-114, 1123-50.
Cochrane, W. A.
'Philosophy and Program for Medical Education at the University of Calgary Faculty of Medicine,' *Can. Med. Assoc. Jour.* XCVIII, 500-05.
Davidson, A. G. F. and W. J. Dube.
'Role of Research in the Undergraduate Medical Curriculum, An Account of Three Summers of Undergraduate Research in Physiology,' *Can. Med. Assoc. Jour.* XCVIII, 692-95.
'Developments at Western,' *Can. Family Physician* II (9), 11-74.
'Educational Issues,' *Can. Med. Assoc. Jour.* XCVIII, include:
D. V. Bates, 'Physiology and the Teaching of Medical Students,' 665-69; D. Waugh, 'Preventive Education: a Prospective Program to Reduce Academic Failure and Poor Performance,' 669-73; H. C. Barrows, 'Simulated Patients in Medical Teaching,' 674-76.
Fish, D. G., C. Farmer and R. Nelson-Jones.
'Some Social Characteristics of Students in Canadian Medical Schools, 1965-66,' *Can. Med. Assoc. Jour.* XCIX, 950-54.
Gibson, D. A.
'The Audio-Visual Division of Dalhousie Medical School,' *N.S. Med. Bull.* XLVII (3), 91-93.
Hamilton, J. D.
'College of Health Sciences,' *Can. Univ.* III (1), 42-43.
Hunter, A. T.
'Training the Family Physician,' *Can. Doctor* XXXIV (5), 63-68.
Jobin, J.-B.
'Quelques aspects de l'enseignement médical à l'Université Laval,' *Laval Méd.* XXXIX, 248-55.

1968 McCreary, J. F.
'Teaching Medical School Practice and Patients,' *Can. Med. Assoc. Jour.* XCVIII, 810-11.
'Medical Education: The Revolution Has Already Begun,' *Can. Doctor* XXXIV (6), 44-47.
Mustard, J. F.
'Wanted: New Approaches to Medical Education,' *Sci. Forum* I (1), 29-32.
Patterson, F. P.
'On Medical Education, Practice and Organization – 1968,' *B.C. Med. Jour.* X, 96-102.
Rice, D.
'Education of the Family Physician,' *Can. Doctor* XXXIV (6), 50-54.
Robinson, S. C.
'Medical Education at Dalhousie,' *Dalhousie Med. Jour.* XXI (4), 107-13.
Sanazaro, P. J.
'Emerging Patterns in Medical Education,' *Alta. Med. Bull.* XXXIII (2), 48-53.
Shepley, D. J.
'Medical Education and the Computer,' *Can. Family Physician* XIV (3), 25-28.
'Training in Family Medicine,' *Can. Doctor* XXXIV (6), 29-36.
Wilson, D. L.
'The Ambulator Clinic in a Teaching Hospital,' *Can. Med. Assoc. Jour.* XCVIII, 812-14.

1969 Bergeron, G.-A.
'Le Premier cycle de l'enseignement de la médecine,' *Laval Méd.* XL, 734-39.
Bryans, A. M.
'The Summer School of Frontier Medicine, CAMSI [Canadian Association of Medical Students and Interns] Exchange – Inwick 1969,' *Can. Med. Assoc. Jour.* C, 512-15.
'Changing Climate for Learning – Toronto's Faculty of Medicine Streamlines Its Curriculum with Systems Teaching Approach,' *Hosp. Admin. in Canada* XI (12), 41-44.
Dawson, J.
'The Primary Care Physician – A Student's Viewpoint,' *B.C. Med. Jour.* XI, 239-40.
Dickson, A. D. *et al.*
'Planning for Medical Education at the University of Calgary,' *Can. Med. Assoc. Jour.* C, 665-69.

1969 **Dymond, M. B.**
'Higher Aims for Medical Schools,' *Ont. Med. Rev.* XXXVI (1), 15-18.
'Educational Issues,' *Can. Med. Assoc. Jour.* C, includes:
A. D. Dickson, 'The Place of Anatomy in a New Canadian Medical School,' 611-14; C. P. Shah, G. C. Robinson and C. Kinnin, 'An Ambulatory Pediatric Teaching Program for Final-Year Medical Students: Report of a Study of Student Attitudes,' 615-19;
J. A. Romeyn, 'What is the Matter with Medical Education.'
Gutelius, J. R. and J. Mathieu.
'Undergraduate Clinical Education,' *Can. Med. Assoc. Jour.* CI, 601-02.
LeClair, M. A., A. Trias and M. L. Munam.
'The Medical School of Sherbrooke and the Undergraduate Education,' *Can. Med. Assoc. Jour.* C, 657-58.
Lewis, D. J., C. Scriver and N. MacDonald.
'Behaviour Growth and Development Course, First Year Medicine, McGill University,' *Laval Med.* XL, 910-17; 'A Behaviour Growth and Development Course in First-Year Medicine,' *Can. Med. Assoc. Jour.* C, 613-45.
MacEwan, C. J. Zylak and R. J. Walton.
'Organization of Undergraduate Radiologic Teaching in a Small Medical Centre,' *Can. Radiol. Jour.* XX, 206-09.
McCreary, J. F.
'The Concepts behind the Health Sciences Centre (at U.B.C.),' *Can. Jour. Occup. Therapy* XXXVI (2), 49-55.
McKendry, J. B. J.
'The Medical Student and His Clinician,' *Alta. Med. Bull.* XXXIV (1), 3-6. Also in *Med. Grad.* XV (1), 6-9.
Nelson-Jones, R. and D. G. Fish.
'Medical Student Enrolment in Canada,' *Can. Med. Assoc. Jour.* C (14), 646-52.
Rose, B.
'Medical Schools and Teaching in Immunology,' *Can. Med. Assoc. Jour.* CI, 96-97.
Spaulding, W. B.
'The Undergraduate Medical Curriculum: McMaster University,' *Can. Med. Assoc. Jour.* C (14), 659-64.
Sumner, J.
'The Family Physician and the Medical Student,' *Can. Family Physician* XV (8), 23-26.

1969 Ward, L. K.
'Medical Curricula and the Medical Student,' *Alta. Med. Bull.* XXXIV (1), 8-9.
Waugh, D. and C. A. Moyse.
'Oral Examinations: A Videotape Study of the Reproductibility of Grades in Pathology,' *Can. Med. Assoc. Jour.* C, 635-40.
1970 Brown, D. C.
'Family Medicine Training at Dalhousie,' *N.S. Med. Bull.* XLIX, 112-13.
Nelson-Jones, R. and D. G. Fish.
'Canadian and Landed Immigrant Applicants to Canadian Medical Schools for 1968-1969,' *Can. Med. Assoc. Jour.* CII, 186-91.
Nelson-Jones, R. and D. G. Fish.
'Canadiens et Immigrants étudiant dans les facultés francophones de médecine au Canada,' *Laval Méd.* XLI, 360-69.

Internship and Residence : Internat et résidence

1964 Wilson, D. L.
'The Place of Internships and Residencies in Medical Education,' *Ont. Med. Rev.* XXXI, 195-202, 275-79.
1966 Fish, D. G.
'The Resident's View of Residency Training in Canada,' *Can. Med. Assoc. Jour.* XCIV, 800-05.
Steeves, L. C.
'Current Trends in Intern and Residency Education,' *Dalhousie Med. Jour.* XX (1), 7-9.
1967 Steinmetz, N.
'Pediatric Services and Residency Training in the Canadian Arctic,' *Can. Jour. Pub. Health* LVIII, 461-63.
1968 Adamson, J. D., H. Prosen and W. Bebchuk.
'Training in Formal Psychotherapy in the Psychiatric Residence Program,' *Can. Psych. Assoc. Jour.* XIII, 445-54.
Andrew, R. B.
'O.M.S.I.P. and the Intern,' *Ont. Med. Rev.* XXXV, 357-58, 360.
Rigley, F. N.
'Internship for General Practice and Relationship to Undergraduate Education and Residency Training,' *Can. Family Physician* XIV (2), 33-37.

1969 **Derbez, R.**
'Psychiatric Residency Training at McGill University,' *Laval Méd.* XL, 983-85.
'Educational Issues,' *Can. Med. Assoc. Jour.* C, includes:
C. H. McGuire, 'A Scientific Approach to Problems of Professional Assessment,' 593-98; J. S. Millis, 'The Objectives of Residency Training,' 599-602; C. H. Hollenberg, 'The Training of the Physician Scientist,' 603-05; J. Genest, 'Some Thoughts on Residency Training,' 606-08.
MacEwan, D. W. and J. M. Tichler.
'Organization of a University Oriented Diagnostic Radiology Residency Program in a Small Medical Centre,' *Can. Radiol. Jour.* XX, 142-46.
Parkhouse, J.
'Residence in Perspective'/'Residence en Perspective,' *Can. Anaesth. Jour.* XVI, 447-53.
Trout, E. D.
'A New Approach to Recruitment of Residents in Radiology,' *Can. Radiol. Jour.* XX, 138-41.

Specialization : Spécialités

1964 **Bates, D. and J. Genest.**
'The Education of the Clinical Scientist,' *Can. Med. Assoc. Jour.* XCIV, 765-68.
Cappon, D., S. Neiger and O. White.
'Possible Predictors in the Training of Psychiatrists,' *Jour. Med. Ed.* [U.S.] XXXIX, 860-63.
Coutu, L. L.
'L'Education médicale post-gradué,' *Union Méd.* XCIII, 322-33.
1965 **Jason, H.**
'Medical Teaching as a Professional Pursuit,' *Queen's Q.* LXXII, 425-34.
Lindenfield, R.
'The Teaching Program in a Psychiatric Setting: Its Implications for Patients, Trainees and Staff,' *Can. Med. Assoc. Jour.* XCII, 752-55.
Rice, D.
'The Programme for Advanced Training in General Practice of the College of General Practice in Canada,' *Alta. Med. Bull.* XXX, 87-99.
1966 **Blain, G.**
'University Studies in Hospital and Health Administration,' *Can. Jour. Pub. Health* LVII, 504-09.

1966 **Martin, J. K.** et al.
'The Teaching of Psychiatry as Applied to Pediatrics,' *Can. Med. Assoc. Jour.* XCIV, 789-91.
McLean, J. D.
'Psychiatric Education for Family Practitioners,' *Can. Mental Health* XIV (5), 2-22.

1967 **Beck, R. P.**
'Current Problems in Postgraduate Medical Education,' *Ont. Med. Rev.* XXXIV, 747-50.
Bertho, E.
'Conception actuelle d'un hôpital universitaire et de l'enseignement de la chirurgie au Canada français,' *Union Méd.* XCVI, 191-94.
Foulkes, R. G.
'Family Practice: A New Challenge in Graduate Education,' *Can. Doctor* XXXIII (11), 53-56.
Gordon, R. A.
'The Canadian Contribution to the Anaesthesia Training Programme of the World Federation of Societies of Anaesthesiologists,' *Can. Anaesth. Jour.* XIV, 495-500.
Graham, J. R.
'A Description of Teaching Programs in Psychiatry,' *Can. Psych. Assoc. Jour.* XII, 505-14.
Hall, L. W.
'What Does a G.P. Accomplish in a Six-Month Postgraduate Course?' *Can. Family Physician* XIII (August), 7-8.
Villancourt, de G.
'Enseignement médicale postuniversitaire,' *Union Méd.* XCVI, 310-11.

1968 'Educational Issues,' *Can. Med. Assoc. Jour.* XCVIII, include:
I. A. Riegh and G. C. Robinson, 'The Planning of a University Pediatric Teaching Practice,' 677-81; R. Gariepy, 'Enseignement postgradue en chirurgie orthopedique ...' 682-83; A. T. Hunter, 'Graduate Training for Family Practice: Experience in a Pilot Programme,' 721-24.
Foulkes, R. G.
'Physician, Key Member of Mental Retardation Team,' *Can. Doctor* XXXIV, 69-72.
Graham, J. R.
'Defining Educational Objectives in Psychiatry,' *Can. Psych. Assoc. Jour.* XIII, 433-39.

1968 **Hunter, R. C. A. and D. H. Frayn.**
'A Survey of Postgraduate Psychiatric Education in Canada, 1966-1967,' *Can. Psych. Assoc. Jour.* XIII, 417-23.
Kaufman, M. R.
'Psychiatry in Medical Education,' *Can. Psych. Assoc. Jour.* XIII, 399-409.
Silver, D.
'The Role of Surgery in the Education of the Specialist in Community Health,' *Man. Med. Rev.* XLVIII, 100-03.

1969 **Beck, J. C.**
'Graduate Medical Education-Crisis and Challenge,' *Can. Med. Assoc. Jour.* C, 670-78.
Cockings, E. C. and G. M. Wyant.
'Anaesthesia and Medical Education,' *Can. Anaesth. Jour.* XVI, 187-94.
Gelber, H.
'Identification with the Instructor as a Factor in the Teaching of Psychiatry to Medical Students,' *Laval Méd.* XL, 918-20.
Jacoby, A.
'Mental Health Education,' *Can. Mental Health* XVII (2), 26-31.
'Postgrad Study Formula: Cash, Time, Incentives and the Will to Learn,' *Can. Doctor* XXXV (2), 29-30.
Turcot, J.
'Concepts nouveaux dans l'enseignement des spécialités,' *Union Méd.* XCVIII, 601-08.

1970 **McWhinney, I. R.**
'Postgraduate Education for Family Medicine: Surely We Can Do Better'/'L'Enseignement postdoctoral en médecine familiale ...' *Can. Family Physician* XVI (1), 15-18.
Minuck, M.
'Future Manpower Needs in Anaesthetic Practice,' *Can. Anaesth. Jour.* XVII, 1-3.
Villeneuve, A. and C. Sterlin.
'La Recherche psychiatrique au Québec: état actuel et perspectives d'avenir,' *Laval Méd.* XLI, 551-52.

Continuing Education : Education permanente

1964 **Kling, S.**
'The Challenge of Continuing Medical Education,' *Alta. Med. Bull.* XXIX, 2-10.

1964 **Williams, D. H.**
'Physicians and "Life-Long Learning,"' *Jour. Ed. (B.C.)* no. 10, 60-71.
1965 'Educational Issues,' *Can. Med. Assoc. Jour.* XCII, includes:
L. C. Steeves, 'The Need for Continuing Medical Education,' 758-61;
P. Jobin, 'Enseignement medicale permanent a Laval,' 762-64;
D. G. Cameron, 'Continuing Medical Education: Some Thoughts on Sponsorship,' 765-66.
1967 'Educational Issues,' *Can. Med. Assoc. Jour.* XCVI, includes:
P. Jobin, 'L'Enseignement médicale continu – y'a-t-il encombrement?' 971-72; D. H. Williams, 'A Taxonomy of Continuing Medical Education,' 1040-44; D. V. Bates, 'Advanced Professional Training,' 1057-61.
1968 **Bell-Irving, R. W.**
'The Threat of Obsolescence,' *B.C. Med. Jour.* X, 221-23.
Hunter, A. T.
'The Use of Broadcast Television in Continuing Medical Education,' *Can. Med. Assoc. Jour.* XCVIII, 34-39.
'The Physician's Education – Can Sabbaticals Help?' *Can. Med. Assoc. Jour.* XCVIII, 1198-1200.
Routley, J. V.
'The Medical Audit Is Continuing Education,' *B.C. Med. Jour.* X, 13-14.
Yates, D. E.
'Periodic Return of the Physician to the Teaching Hospital Environment,' *Can. Med. Assoc. Jour.* XCVIII, 732-33.
1970 **Des Rosiers, G.**
'Continuing Medical Education,' *Can. Family Physician* XVI (6), 94-97.

NURSING : NURSING

1926 **Hurley, E. B.**
'Preparation for Public Health Nursing in the Province of Quebec,' *Modern Hospital* XXVII, 110-11.
1939 **Baudoin, J. A.**
'L'Ecole d'hygiene sociale appliquée,' *Rev. Trim. Can.* XXV, 198-217.
1940 **Gowan, Sister M. Oliva.**
'Report of a Survey of L'Ecole d'Hygiène Sociale Appliquée, Université de Montréal, Montréal, Canada, August 19, 20, 21, 1940.' Typewritten manuscript, Catholic Univ. of America, Washington, D.C.
1944 **Fidler, N.**
'The Preparation for Professional Nursing,' *Can. Nurse* XL, 621-26.

1945 **Bennett, H.**
'Preparation for University Nursing,' *Can. Nurse* XLI, 539-45.
1949 **Russell, E. K.**
'The Teaching of Nursing' in *Papers for the Biennial Meeting of the International Council of Nurses, Sweden, 1949.* Reprinted in *Can. Nurse* XLV, 820-25.
1951 **Emory, F. H.**
'Preparation for Administration and Supervision in Public Health Nursing,' *Can. Nurse* LVII, 418-20.
1955 **Carpenter, H. M.**
'Basic Degree Course in Nursing,' *Can. Nurse* LI, 200-02.
1956 **Carter, G. B.**
'Some Considerations on the Basic Nursing Curriculum,' *Can. Nurse* LII, 357-61.
1960 **Mussallem, H. K.**
Spotlight on Nursing Education, The Report of the Pilot Project for the Evaluation of Schools of Nursing in Canada. Ottawa: Canadian Nurses' Association. Pp. 141.
1964 **Beaudoin, F.**
'Securité et estime de soi, critères de l'identité de l'etudiante infirmière,' *Bull. Inf. Cath.* XXXI, 105-18.
Brown, M. C.
'The Library and Nursing Education,' *Can. Nurse* LX, 350-52.
Cranstaun, J.
'The Changing Concept of Nursing,' *Can. Hosp.* XLI (12), 40-42, 47.
Gagnon, J.
'Nouvelles Tendances en education des infirmières au cours de base,' *Bull. Inf. Cath.* XXXI, 55-59.
Hamilton, W.
'Continuing Education,' *Can. Nurse* LX, 29-33.
Jameson, E. E. and E. J. Mackie.
'Reorganization of a Department of Nursing,' *Can. Nurse* LX, 566-71.
Jourard, S.
'Let's Look at the Teacher,' *Can. Nurse* LX, 471-74.
Jourard, S.
'Personal Contact in Teaching,' *Can. Nurse* LX, 556-59.
Laycock, S. R.
'The Teaching of Nursing Ethics,' *Can. Nurse* LX, 1153-56.
Morley, T. P.
'The Need for Nursing Reform in Ontario,' *Can. Med. Assoc. Jour.* XCI, 684-86.

1964 **Morrison, R. M.**
'Public Health Nursing in the Nursing Curriculum,' *Can. Nurse* LX, 1081-85.
Mussallem, H. K.
A Path to Quality. A Plan for the Development of Nursing Education Programs within the Central Educational System of Canada. Ottawa: Canadian Nurses' Association. Pp. 208.
Naegele, K. D.
'Study of Nursing Education,' *Can. Nurse* LX, 865-69.
Nobert, R.
'La Bibliothéque au service de l'infirmière,' *Bull. Inf. Cath.* XXXI (1), 26-29.
Rowles, D.
'A Comparison of the Daytime Activities Performed by Student Nurses and by Staff Nurses in two Medical-Surgical Units of one General Hospital.' Unpublished M.A. thesis, Univ. of Toronto.
Wedgery, A. W.
'Le Nursing masculin,' *Cah. Nursing* XXXVII (2), 21-25.

1965 **Béland, N.**
'L'Infirmière et la Rehabilitation,' *Bull. Inf. Cath.* XXXII, 120-23.
Canadian Nurses' Association.
Statistical Data on Schools of Nursing in Canada 1964. Ottawa: The Association. Pp. 31.
Franchea, M. and T. Castonguay.
'Improving Diploma Programs,' *Can. Nurse* LXI, 533-36.
Klonoff, H. and A. M. Marcus.
'An Innovation in Nursing Education,' *Can. Nurse* LXI, 455-57.
MacLaggan, K.
Portrait of Nursing. A Plan for the Education of Nurses in the Province of New Brunswick. Ottawa: Canadian Nurses' Association. Pp. 146.
Mussallem, H. K.
Nursing Education in Canada. Ottawa: Queen's Printer. Pp. 139.
[Study prepared for Royal Commission on Health Sciences.]

1966 **Association des Gardes-Malades Auxiliaires.**
'Mémoire au Comité des Bills publics sur la suggestion de former un Conseil supérieur des professions infirmières et para-médicales,' *Cah. Nursing* XXXIX (5), 5-15.
Bissonnier, H.
'Pédagogie de l'élève infirmière en vue d'une intégration de sa personalité,' *Bull. Inf. Cath.* XXXIII, 29-35.

1966 **Bureau, R.**
'Syndicalisme et Nursing dans le Province de Quebec,' *Bull. Inf. Cath.* XXXIII, 139-44.
Carpenter, H. M.
'Nursing Education in Canada,' *International Nursing Review* [Switzerland] XII (5), 29-35.
'Compte rendu d'une session d'étude sur le méthodologie de l'enseignement organisée par La Commission des Ecoles de Gardes-Malades Auxiliaires de la Province de Québec,' *Cah. Nursing* XXXIX (4), 17-19.
Fahmy, P.
'La Perception de soi à travers leur future profession chez les étudiantes infirmières en 1ère annee, de la ville de Québec.' Thèse de licence, Univ. Laval.
Flaherty, M. J.
'An Enquiry into the Need for Continuing Education for Registered Nurses in the Province of Ontario.' Unpublished M.A. thesis, Univ. of Toronto.
Lebel, M.
'La Formation sociale et culturelle des infirmières,' *Bull. Inf. Cath.* XXXIII, 74-93.
Loyer, M. A.
'Should Nursing Education be under the Domain of Hospitals?' *Can. Nurse* LXII (4), 25-26.
McMillan, E. and Y. Marie.
'Schools of Nursing Should Be Independent,' *Can. Nurse* LXII (7), 32-33.
Rowsell, G. S.
'University Nursing Education – Facts and Trends,' *Can. Nurse* LXII (12), 31-33.
St. Louis, Sister.
'Investigation into Regional Planning for Nursing Education,' *Can. Nurse* LXII (6), 40-43.
Sutherland, R. W.
'Needed: Nurses Who Are Clinical Specialists,' *Can. Nurse* LXII (8), 26-28.
Telnes, L.
'As Others See Us,' *Can. Nurse* LXII (9), 49-54.
Tunis, Barbara L.
In Caps and Gowns: The Story of the School for Graduate Nurses McGill University 1920-1964. Montreal: McGill Univ. Press. Pp. 154.

1966 **Wallace, M. B.**
'Hospitals Should Retain their Schools of Nursing,' *Can. Nurse* LXII (2), 27-28.
Weir, J. M.
'A Refresher Course for Public Health Nurses,' *Can. Jour. Public Health* LVII, 260-68.
Wood, V.
'Measurement and Evaluation in Nursing Education,' *Can. Nurse* LXII (4), 54-58.

1967 **Allen, M.**
'Health Service within the Context of Social Security-Nursing,' *Can. Jour. Public Health* LVIII, 69-72.
Bulletin des Infirmières catholiques du Canada XXXIV inclut:
K. M. Straub, 'Hospital Nursing,' 199-208; E. Sheehan, 'Public Health Nursing,' 209-11; M. John, 'Psychiatric Nursing,' 212-16; P. T. Verhonick, 'Teaching and Research in Nursing,' 217-24; D. Lalancette, 'Ecole des Sciences Infirmières, Université Laval,' 283-84; 'Ecoles des Sciences Hospitalières, Université de Moncton,' 127-29; 'Université de Montréal, Faculté de Nursing,' 34-37.
Callin, M.
'Inservice Education,' *Can. Nurse* LXIII (8), 32-34.
Good, S. R.
'Considerations for Nurse Recruitment,' *Can. Nurse* LXIII (12), 31-32.
Long, L.
'Tomorrow's Nursing Education in Saskatchewan,' *Can. Nurse* LXIII (4), 30-33.
Milord, R.
'Principes de base dans l'éloboration d'un programme d'orientation,' *Bull. Inf. Cath.* XXXIV, 27-34.
Morison, J. D.
'Teaching Nursing in a Child Health Program,' *Can. Jour. Public Health* LVIII, 518-19.
Sagar, M.
'Education and Training of Nurses in a Child Health Program,' *Can. Jour. Public Health* LVIII, 464-66.

1968 'L'Avenir de la profession infirmière et son contexte,' *Bull. Inf. Cath.* XXV, 171-74.
Blais, N. and N. Beaudry-Johnson.
'Nursing Education in Quebec – A New Era,' *Can. Nurse* LXIV (5), 60-62.

1968 **Hudon, L.-N.**
'L'Enseignement d'hier et d'aujourd'hui,' *Cah. Nursing* XLI, 140-42.
Hudon, L.-N.
'Les Etudiants d'hier et d'aujourd'hui,' *Cah. Nursing* XLI, 68-70.
LaRose, P. E.
'Condition de la démocratisation: revalorisation de l'enseignement technique et professionnel,' *Cah. Nursing* XLI, 291-93.
Robinson, S. C.
'A Doctor Looks at Nursing Education,' *Can. Nurse* LXIV (7), 38-40.
'The Role of the University in Training of Personnel in the Health Sciences,' *N.S. Med. Bull.* XLVII (2), 29-31.
Steed, M. E.
'Trends in Diploma Nursing Education,' *Can. Nurse* LXIV (2), 40-41.

1969 **Allen, D. E.**
'A Comparison between Television Instruction and Conventional Methods in Teaching Medical Isolation-Gown Procedure: an Experimental Study.' Unpublished M.Ed. thesis, Univ. of New Brunswick.
Buckland, J. K.
'An Institute as an Educational Experience in the Continuing Education of a Selected Population of Nurses.' Unpublished M.A. thesis, Univ. of British Columbia.
Costello, C. G. and Sister T. Castonguay.
'Two-Year versus Three-Year Programs,' *Can. Nurse* LXV (2), 62-64.
'La Jeunesse dissidente,' *Cah. Nursing* XLII, 265-73.
Kergin, D.
'Nurses and Educational Change,' *Can. Nurse* LXV (12), 28-30.
Ontario Department of Health, Communications Branch.
Report of the Ontario Council of Health on Education of the Health Disciplines. Toronto: Queen's Printer. Pp. 79. See especially 43-53.
Post, S.
'Inservice for Teachers, too?' *Can. Nurse* LXV (9), 29-30.
Post, S.
'Nursing Education and Service Cannot be Separated,' *Can. Hosp.* XLVI (9), 35-37.
Royce, M.
Continuing Education for Women in Canada Trends and Opportunities. Toronto: Ontario Institute for Studies in Education. Pp. 167.
Trout, F.
'The Nurse and the Family Physician,' *Can. Family Physician* XV (6), 23-28.

1970 **Innis, M. Q., ed.**
Nursing Education in a Changing Society. Toronto: U. of T. Press. Pp. 244.
Murray, V. V.
Nursing in Ontario: a Study for The Committee on the Healing Arts. Toronto: Queen's Printer. Pp. 284.
'University Schools of Nursing in Canada,' *Can. Nurse* LXVI (4), 41-51.

PHARMACY : PHARMACIE

1932 **Massicotte, E.-Z.**
'Chirurgiens, médecins et apothicaires sous le régime français,' *Bull. Recherches Hist.* XXXVIII, 515-22.

1955 **Swartz, S. G.**
'Pharmaceutical Education in Ontario, 1900-1950.' Unpublished B.Sc. thesis, Faculty of Pharmacy, Univ. of Toronto.

1964 **Archambault, A.**
'En Juin la Faculté de Pharmacie est en plein évolution,' *Rev. Pharm.* XV, 220-22. Voir aussi J. A. Mockle, 'Nouvelle Bibliothèque de Pharmacie,' 224-25.
Morrison, F.
'Continuing Education for the Pharmacist,' *Can. Pharm. Jour.* XCVII, 470-71.
Nairn, J. G. and D. R. Kennedy.
'Continuing Education for the Pharmacist,' *Ont. Coll. Pharm. Bull.* XIII, 26-28.
Walker, G. C.
'The Faculty of Pharmacy, University of Toronto,' *American Jour. Pharm. Ed.* XXVIII, 360-77.

1965 **Duff, J. G.**
'Pharmaceutical Education in the Maritimes: A Brief History,' *Can. Pharm. Jour.* XCVIII, 6-8, 24.
Guillot, M.
'Culture générale et pharmacie,' *Rev. Pharm.* XVI, 250-53.
Paterson, G. R.
'The Participation of Pharmaceutical Chemists in a Continuing Education Program,' *American Jour. Pharm. Ed.* XXIX, 785-93.
Riedel, B. E.
'Biochemistry in a Pharmaceutical Chemistry Course,' *American Jour. Pharm. Ed.* XXIX, 743-57.

1965 **Teare, F. W.**
'A Course in Quantitative Pharmaceutical Analysis,' *Amer. Jour. Pharm. Ed.* XXIX, 721-30.

1966 **Committee of Presidents of Universities of Ontario, Presidents'** Research Committee.
The Health Sciences in Ontario Universities: Recent Experience and Prospects for the Next Decade. Toronto: The Committee. Pp. 26.
Des Roches, B. P.
'Suggestions for Use in a Practical Training Program,' *Ont. Coll. Pharm. Bull.* XV, 87-96.
Nayler, M. J. V.
'A Report on the New Pharmacy Internship Programme as Conducted at St. Joseph's Hospital, Hamilton,' *Ont. Coll. Pharm. Bull.* XV, 26-29.
Ross, T. M.
Pharmacist Manpower in Canada. Ottawa: Queen's Printer. Pp. 136.

1967 **Archambault, A.**
'Pharmaceutical Education: A Dual Challenge,' *Can. Pharm. Jour.* C, 142-43, 163.
Archambault, A.
'Pharmaceutical Education: A Look at the Future,' *Can. Pharm. Jour.* C, 480-83, 499.
Archambault, A.
'Where Pharmaceutical Education is Going,' *Proc. Can. Pharm. Fac.* XXIV, 96-106.
Bain, J.
'A Course in Therapeutics for Pharmacy Students,' *Proc. Can. Conf. Pharm. Fac.* XXIV, 164-68.
Baxter, R. M.
'Where the Profession is Going,' *Proc. Can. Conf. Pharm. Fac.* XXIV, 20-27.
Can. Pharm. Jour. C, includes article, on history of pharmacy in each Province, e.g. 'The History of Pharmacy in Manitoba,' 5-9.
Collins, A. L.
'Methods Used in the Practical Training of the Student in Hospital Pharmacy,' *Ont. Coll. Pharm. Bull.* XVI, 2-5.
Des Roches, B. P.
'Philosophy of the Practical Training Programme,' *Ont. Coll. Pharm. Bull.* XVI, 89-97.
Dooley, J. E.
'A Course in Computer Programming and Applications for Pharmacy Students,' *Proc. Can. Conf. Pharm. Fac.* XXIV, 169-78.

1967 **Gaudry, R.**
'The Relation of Pharmaceutical Education to the Quality Assurance of Pharmaceutical Products,' *Med. Services Jour.* XXIII, 367-80.
Hughes, F. N.
'The Practice of Pharmacy: the Eleventh Hour?' *Ont. Coll. Pharm. Bull.* XVI, 65-72.
Liquori, Sister M.
'The Hospital Pharmacist as an Educator,' *Can. Pharm. Jour.* C, 520-22, 524.
Paterson, G. R.
'Canadian Pharmacy in Preconfederation Medical Legislation,' *Can. Pharm. Jour.* C, 476-78, 500-01.
Wood, J. A.
'New Pharmacy Facilities at University of Saskatchewan,' *Can. Pharm. Jour.* C, 23-29.

1968 **Baxter, R. M.**
'Early Developments in Pharmaceutical Education,' *Can. Pharm. Jour.* CI, 96-100, 117.
Baxter, R. M.
'Where the Profession is Going,' *Ont. Coll. Pharm. Bull.* XVII, 21-26.
Bell, P. W.
'Pharmacy Administration: "Quo Vadis,"'*Ont. Coll. Pharm. Bull.* XVII, 53-55.
Murray, D.
'Pharmaceutical Research,' *Can. Pharm. Jour.* CI, 219-23, 233.
Waller, R. H.
'Pharmacy as the New Grad Sees It,' *Can. Pharm. Jour.* CI, 483-84, 493.

1969 **Sonnedecker, G., E. W. Stieb and D. R. Kennedy.**
One Hundred Years of Pharmacy in Canada. Toronto: Canadian Academy of the History of Pharmacy. Pp. 38.
Tremblay, J.
'Le Pharmacien doit se spécialiser et démontrer sa compétence,' *Pharm.* XLIII (10), 38-40, 44.

1970 **Granger, W. E.**
'Pharmacy Education in the 70's,' *Drug Merchandising* LI (6), 12-16, 24.
Hlynka, J. N.
'Clinical Pharmacy: Myth or Must,' *Can. Pharm. Jour.* CIII, 40-43.
Lamonde, A. et J. M. Gariepy.
'Le Stage du pharmacien dans l'industrie,' *Pharm.* XLIV (6), 25-26.

1970 Miller, B. and R. Merrett.
'Pharmacy Education: A Need for Bifurcation,' *Ont. Coll. Pharm. Bull.* XIX (2), 40-42.
'New Internship Program for Alberta Pharmacy Students,' *Can. Pharm. Jour.* CIII, 105-08.
Segal, H. J.
'A Concept of Social Management and Practice,' *Ont. Coll. Pharm. Bull.* XIX, 12-16.

OPTOMETRY : OPTOMÉTRIE

1945 Bourcier, C.
'L'Optométrie dans son évolution,' *Act. Univ.* XI (10), 69-71.
1965 Langlois, R.
'Optométrie et orientation professionnelle,' *Orient. Prof.* I, 182-84.
1966 'Report of a Committee to Investigate Education of Optometry in Canada,' *Can. Jour. Optometry* XXIX, 107-36.
1967 Fisher, E. J.
'Optometrical Education in Canada,' *Can. Jour. Optometry* XXIX, 81-98.
Messier, J. A.
'Ecole d'Optométrie Université de Montréal,' *Can. Jour. Optometry* XXIX, 99-105.
University of Waterloo, Senate Committee on Optometric Education.
'Report of ...' *Can. Jour. Optometry* XXIX, 107-36.

PHYSICAL AND HEALTH EDUCATION : EDUCATION PHYSIQUE

1929 Hussey, Christopher.
Tait McKenzie: A Sculptor of Youth. London: Country Life. Pp. 107.
1944 Lamb, A. S.
'Tait McKenzie in Canada,' *Jour. Health, Physical Recreation* [U.S.] XV, 69-70, 85.
Munro, I.
'Physical Education and the University,' *Jour. Ed. (N.S.)* XV, 547-50.
1948 Mercier, A.
Le Problème de l'Education Physique dans les Universités canadiennes-françaises. Montréal: Université de Montréal. Pp. 97.
1956 Meagher, J. W.
'Physical Education Teacher Training at McGill: an Historical, Interpretative and Evaluative Study.' Unpublished doct. dissertation, Pennsylvania State Univ.

1964 **Eaton, J. D.**
'The Life and Professional Contributions of Arthur Stanley Lamb, M.D. to Physical Education in Canada.' Unpublished doct. dissertation, Ohio State Univ.

1965 **Cunningham, D. A.**
'Physical Education as an Academic Discipline,' *Can. H.P.E.R. Jour.* XXXI, 21-22.

Potts, R. E.
'The Development of Physical Education in Nova Scotia Schools.' Unpublished M.Ed. thesis, Acadia Univ.

Tranchemontagne, R.
'L'Education physique a l'Université d'Ottawa,' *Can. H.P.E.R. Jour.* XXXI, 28.

West, N. W.
'Althouse College of Education,' *Can. H.P.E.R. Jour.* XXXII (2), 13, 28-29.

1966 **Keyes, M. E.**
'John Howard Crocker LL.D. 1870-1959,' *Western Ontario History Nuggets* no. 32. Pp. 96.

Marshall, J. M.
'Teacher Preparation in Health and Health Education in Canada,' *Can. Jour. Public Health* LVII, 458-63.

Pennington, G.
'Some Values of Research to the Physical Educator,' *Can. H.P.E.R. Jour.* XXXII (3), 15, 30-31.

Schegel, R. P.
'Factors Influencing the Decision to Major in Physical Education.' Unpublished M.Sc. thesis, Univ. of Illinois.

Wipper, K. A. W.
Retrospect and Prospect. A Record of the School of Physical and Health Education 1940-1965. Toronto: Privately printed. Pp. 47.

1967 **Brown, L. E.**
'The Preparation of Teachers in Health Education – Implications,' *Can. H.P.E.R. Jour.* XXXIII (5), 17-19.

Canadian Association for Health, Physical Education and Recreation.
Physical Education and Athletics in Canadian Universities and Colleges: A Statement of Recommended Policies and Standards/Education physique et sport dans les universités et collèges du Canada: Exposé des mesures et normes recommendées. Toronto: The Association. Pp. 108.

1967 **Korchinsky, N. W.**
'Qualifications, Responsibilities and Programs of High School Physical Education Teachers in the Province of Alberta.' Unpublished M.A. thesis, Univ. of Alberta.

1968 **Brown, S. R.**
'Physical Education and Athletics in the University,' *Can. H.P.E.R. Jour.* XXXIV (4), 3-4.
Lewis, J. A.
'Preparation of Physical Education Teachers,' *Man. Jour. Ed. Res.* III (2), 42-48.
Nash, J. C.
'Health - An Academic Discipline,' *Can. H.P.E.R. Jour.* XXXIV (5), 21-23.
'The Role of the University in Training of Personnel in the Health Sciences,' *N.S. Med. Bull.* XLVII (2), 29-31.

1969 **Bisakowski, K.**
'A Summary of the History of Athletics and Physical Education at Dalhousie University,' *Can. H.P.E.R. Jour.* XXXV (6), 26-28.
Paul, T. and J. E. Welch.
'Selective Retention of Physical Education Major Students,' *Can. H.P.E.R. Jour.* XXVI (6), 29, 35.
Simond, G.
'L'Education physique et sportive dans l'enseignement collégial au Québec,' *Prospectives* V, 179-84.
Ziegler, E. F., M. Spaeth and G. Paton.
'A Plan for the Preparation of Administrators in Physical Education and Athletics,' *Can. H.P.E.R. Jour.* XXXVI (1), 5-8, 36.

1970 **Davidson, C. L.**
'The Faculty: the Heart of the Program or Criteria for Excellence in Physical Education,' *Can. H.P.E.R. Jour.* XXXVI (4), 23-25.
Montoye, H. and H. G. Welch.
'Some Thoughts on the Training of Physical Education Teachers - Part I,' *Can. H.P.E.R. Jour.* XXXVI (4), 6-8.

PHYSICAL AND OCCUPATIONAL THERAPY :
THÉRAPEUTIQUE PHYSIQUE ET PROFESSIONNELLE

1964 'Students in Hospital'/'L'Internat en physiothérapie,' *Can. Physiotherapy Jour.* XVI, 226-31; XVII, 10-19.

1964 **Sutherland, J. B.**
'Occupational Therapy in the Re-establishment of the Physical Handicapped,' *Can. Jour. Occup. Therapy* XXXI, 143-46.

1965 **Ferland, M.**
'Physiothérapie au Canada,' *Can. Physiotherapy Jour.* XVII, 154-63.
Gingras, G.
'Quelques considerations sur l'enseignement de la médecine physique de la rehabilitation,' *Can. Med. Assoc. Jour.* XCII, 756-57.

1966 **Catterton, M. M.**
'Dimensions of Occupational Therapy,' *Can. Jour. Occup. Therapy* XXXIII, 153-64.
Forbes, J. M.
'The School's Expectations of the Clinical Training Centre,' *Can. Jour. Occup. Therapy* XXXIII, 15-18.
Gault, H. M.
'The Shortage of Qualified Physiotherapists in Canada,' *Can. Physiotherapy Jour.* XVIII, 149-54.

1967 **Buchan, M.**
'The Benefits of Interning,' *Can. Physiotherapy Jour.* XIX, 11-15.
Bullman, M.
'Concepts behind U.B.C.'s New Medical Complex, and the Role of Rehabilitation Medicine in Such a Complex,' *Can. Physiotherapy Jour.* XIX, 16-19.
'On Becoming a Physiotherapist,' *Can. Physiotherapy Assoc. Jour.* XIX, 8-10.

1968 **Driver, M. F.**
'A Philosophic View of the History of Occupational Therapy in Canada,' *Can. Jour. Occup. Therapy* XXXV (2), 53-60.
Pearson, W. W.
'New Perspectives on the Role of Occupational Therapists in an Age of Automation,' *Can. Jour. Occup. Therapy* XXXV (1), 6-8.
Truelove, J. H. and M. B. Spence.
'Post-graduate Education in Physiotherapy,' *Can. Physiotherapy Jour.* XX, 255-57.

1969 **Bernd, J.**
'Have You a Responsibility?' *Can. Jour. Occup. Therapy* XXXVI (1), 6-8.

1969 Evans, D. E.
'A Philosophy of Physiotherapy,' *Can. Physiotherapy Jour.* XXI (1), 36-38.
McCreary, J. F.
'The Concepts Behind the Health Sciences Centre [at U.B.C.],' *Can. Jour. Occup. Therapy* XXXVI (2), 49-55.
1970 Allbon, L. G. and B. Fifield.
'Activity Aids,' *Can. Jour. Occup. Therapy* XXXVII (1), 11-18.
Gingras, G.
'Teaching of Rehabilitation Medicine,' *Can. Med. Assoc. Jour.* CII, 1385-87.

PUBLIC HEALTH : HYGIÉNE PUBLIQUE

1939 Baudoin, J. A.
'L'Ecole d'Hygiène Sociale Appliquée de l'Université de Montréal,' *Rev. Trim. Can.* XXV (1939), 198-216.
1951 Emory, F. H.
'Preparation for Administration and Supervision in Public Health Nursing,' *Can. Nurse* LVII, 418-20.
1964 Mackenzie, C. J. C.
'Continuing Role of the University in the Education of Public Health Workers,' *Can. Jour. Public Health* LV, 489-96.
Rhodes, A. J.
'Recent Revisions in Basic and Advanced Courses in Public Health Offered in Toronto,' *Can. Jour. Public Health* LV, 435-44.
Troupin, J. L.
'Education for Public Health,' *Can. Jour. Public Health* LV, 417-23.
1965 Hall, E. M.
'Whither Public Health?' *Can. Jour. Public Health* LVI, 421-29.
O'Hara, A. S.
'Educational Development of the Public Health Inspector,' *Can. Jour. Public Health* LVI, 65-69.
Pett, L. B.
'Operational Research and Health Services,' *Can. Jour. Public Health* LVI, 457-62.
1966 Mather, J. M.
'Random Thoughts on a Department of Preventive Medicine in a Canadian Medical School,' *Can. Med. Assoc. Jour.* XCV, 1309-10.

1967 Aujaleu, E.
'La Recherche en santé publique,' *Can. Jour. Public Health* LVIII, 158-62.
Gilbert, J.
'The Grandeur and Decadence of Health Education,' *Can. Jour. Public Health* LVIII, 355-58.
Josie, G. H.
'Need and Opportunity for Public Health Research,' *Can. Jour. Public Health* LVIII, 163-66.
Palko, M. E.
'Significant Developments in Canadian Health Education,' *Med. Services Jour.* XXIII, 1053-68.
Sagar, M.
'Education and Training of Nurses in a Child Health Program,' *Can. Jour. Public Health* LVIII, 464-66.

1968 MacDermott, H. E.
'Pioneering in Public Health,' *Can. Med. Assoc. Jour.* XCIX, 267-73.
Sanazaro, P. J.
'Emerging Patterns in Medical Education,' *Alta. Med. Bull.* XXXIII (2), 48-53.

1969 Brown, K. H., D. J. Yeo and K. F. Pownall.
'Attitudinal Roadblocks and Dental Programs: Opinions of Dental Students, Dentists and Ten Other Health Disciplines,' *Can. Jour. Public Health* LX, 442-46.
Brunet, J.
'Les Sciences de la santé et le nouveau programme des études à la Faculté de Médecine de l'Université Laval,' *Laval Méd.* XL, 147-51.
Defries, R. D.
The First Forty Years, 1914-1955: Connaught Medical Research Laboratories, University of Toronto. Toronto: U. of T. Press. Pp. 342.
Hastings, J. E. F.
'Some Plain Thoughts on the State of the Public Health,' *Can. Jour. Public Health* LX, 97-103.
House, D.
'Program Planning in Health Education,' *Can. Jour. Public Health* LX, 391-94.
'Public Health – the Career with Personal Satisfaction,' *Can. Doctor* XXXV (9), 52-57.
Smith, E. S. O.
'Can We Make Public Health More Attractive?' *Can. Jour. Public Health* LX, 378-84.

1969 Trout, F.
'The Nurse and the Family Physician,' *Can. Family Physician* XV (6), 23-28.
1970 Tyler, R. W.
'The Education of Health Personnel to Meet the Needs of the Child in Contemporary Society,' *Cah. Jour. Public Health* LXI, 31-36.

SOCIAL WORK : SCIENCES SOCIALES

1961 MacLean, F.
'The Maritime School of Social Work,' *Atlantic Advocate* LI (9), 74-76.
1964 Denault, H.
'The Profession of Social Work in the Quebec of the Future,' *Soc. Worker* XXXII, 5-12.
Hamel, R.
'L'Administration en service social,' *Service Social* XIII, 78-85; J. de la Chevrotière, 'Commentaire,' 86-88.
Leigh, A.
'Viewpoint on Canadian Social Work and the Changing Times,' *Soc. Worker* XXXII, 36-40.
Lindenfield, R.
'The New Look in Mental Health Services: Its Implication for Social Work,' *Canada's Mental Health* XII (6), 10-16.
Martin, J.-P.
'Le Role de l'université et de l'école de service social dans le développement du bien-être au Québec,' *Service Social* XIII, 108-18.
Morgan, J. S.
'In-Service Training and Staff Development' in *Training for Social Welfare: Proceedings of the Workshop on Staff Training* (Ottawa: Canadian Welfare Council), 10-17.
Zay, N.
'La Recherche et les écoles de service social,' *Service Social* XIII, 89-104; M.-S. Blais-Grenier, 'Commentaire,' 105-07.
1965 Splane, R. B.
Social Welfare in Ontario 1791-1893. Toronto: U. of T. Press. Pp. 305.
Stott, M. M.
'Community Development – Adult Education or Social Work?' *Continuous Learning* IV, 31-34.
1966 Gifford, C. G.
'L'Apprentissage des relations humaines et le service social professionnel,' *Service Social* XV, 25-43.

1966 **Govenlock, S.**
'Ecole de service social: perspectives d'avenir,' *Soc. Worker* XXXIV, 12-15.
Stubbin, H.
'The Undergraduate Social Worker and the Manpower Crisis,' *Soc. Worker* XXXIV, 256-59.

1967 **Association of Universities and Colleges of Canada.**
Manpower Needs in the Field of Social Welfare. Papers Presented at a Conference on Manpower Needs and Education in the Field of Social Welfare. Ottawa, November, 1966. Pp. 144. Bound with *Le Besoin de personnel dans le domaine du bien-être social, allocations presentées à la conference ... Ottawa, Novembre, 1966.* Pp. 144. Ottawa: The Association.
Gagne, J.
'Education en Service Social,' *Soc. Worker* XXXV, 182-90.
Katz, M.
'The Profession Looks Ahead at Practice and Manpower,' *Soc. Worker* XXXV, 211-17.
Knight, B.
'An Undiscovered Conflict in Social Work,' *Soc. Worker* XXXV, 54-56.
Sirota, D.
'The Use of the Combined-Methods Placement in Field Instructing,' *Soc. Worker* XXXV, 273-75.
Stubbin, H.
'The Professions Expectations of Undergraduate Education,' *Soc. Worker* XXXV, 64-70.

1968 **Blais-Grenier, M.-S.**
'Perspectives de le recherche dans les agences de service social,' *Service Social* XVII, 49-64.
McClellan, G.
'Education for the Social Services in Community Colleges,' *Soc. Worker* XXXVI, 191-94.
Mohr. J.
'La Science sociale et le traitment social,' *Bien-être* XX, 42-46.
Zay, N.
'La Recherche dans les agences de service social,' *Service Social* XVII, 5-13.

1969 **Turner, F. J.**
'Some Observations on the Doctoral Degree in Social Work,' *Soc. Worker* XXXVII, 197-202; 'Some Further Observations ...' 261-63.

TEACHER TRAINING AND EDUCATION :
FORMATION DES ENSEIGNEMENTS ET ENSEIGNEMENT

1952 **Hutton, H. K.**
'French Canadian Normal Schools: an Historical, Interpretative and Evaluative Study.' Unpublished doct. dissertation, Penn. State Univ.

1940 **Cook, J. T.**
'Teacher Training in the Province of New Brunswick: An Historical and Analytical Study of Its Evolution.' Unpublished doct. dissertation, Univ. of Southern California [reported incorrectly in 1965 *Supplement* as Harvard Univ.].

1953 **Way, H. H.**
'An Experiment in Teacher Education,' *Jour. Ed. (N.S.)* II (3), 34-37.

1954 **Hickman, G. A.**
'A Guide to the Improvement of the Pre-Service Programme of Teacher Education in Newfoundland.' Unpublished doct. dissertation, Columbia Univ.

McGuigan, D.
'Teacher Training in Prince Edward Island.' Unpublished M.Ed. thesis, Univ. of New Brunswick.

1955 **McCarthy, J. P.**
'One Hundred Years of Teacher Education,' *Jour. Ed. (N.S.)* v (1), 5-20; v (2), 3-18.

1956 **Aikenhead, J. D.**
'To Teach, Or Not to Teach,' *Alta. Jour. Ed. Research* II (3), 173-85.

Dunlop, G. M.
'A Challenge to the Faculty of Education,' *Alta. Jour. Ed. Res.* II (2), 71-78.

Ford, E. K.
'The Training Program for Vocational School Teachers in Nova Scotia,' *Jour. Ed. (N.S.)* VI (1), 33-38.

1957 **Cann, M. M.**
'Have the Aims of Teacher Education Changed in Nova Scotia?' *Jour. Ed. (N.S.)* VI (3), 18-21.

1959 **Black, D. B.**
'Why Did They Differ? Study of Two Groups,' *Alta. Jour. Ed. Res.* v (2), 119-29.

Sparby, H. T.
'The Inter-Disciplinary Approach in the Training of School Administrators,' *Alta. Jour. Ed. Res.* v (2), 87-90.

1960 **Langley, G. J.**
'Philosophy of Teacher Training in Saskatchewan in Historical Perspective' in *Papers Presented at the Fifth Annual Conference of the Canadian Association of Professors of Education* (Toronto), 26-43.

1961 **McLuhan, H. M.**
'The New Media and the New Education,' *Bas. Teacher* VI, 93-100.

1963 **Downey, L.**
'The Education of Secondary School Teachers,' *Can. Admin.* III (1), 1-4.

Housego, I. E.
'How a Decision was Made: A Study of the Teacher Training Issue in Saskatchewan.' Unpublished doct. dissertation, Univ. of Alberta.

1964 **Bailey, A. W.**
'The Professional Preparation of Teachers for the Schools of the Province of New Brunswick 1784 to 1964.' Unpublished doct. dissertation, Univ. of Toronto. See also *Ont. Jour. Ed. Research* VII, 1-10, 231-39.

Chorny, M. and A. G. Storey.
'Towards the Improvement of Methods Courses and Practice Teaching,' *Alta. Jour. Ed. Res.* X (3), 153-57.

Coutts, H. T. and B. E. Walker.
'The Faculty of Education at the University of Alberta,' *Sch. Prog.* XXXIII (9), 31-37, 50.

Coutts, H. T. and B. E. Walker.
G. Fred: The Story of G. Fred McNally. Toronto: J. M. Dent. Pp. 118.

McIntosh, J. R.
'The Effectiveness of In-Term Block Practice Teaching,' *Can. Ed. Research Digest* IV, 34-42.

Philip, Brother.
'Educational Psychology and the Teachers,' *Bas. Teacher* VIII, 353-60.

Scarfe, N. V.
'In Pursuit of Teacher Excellence,' *Tor. Ed. Q.* IV (1), 7-11.

Toombs, M. P.
'A Saskatchewan Experiment in Teacher Education 1907-17,' *Sask. Hist.* XVII, 1-12.

Yolande-de-l'Immaculée, Soeur.
'Le Collège bilingue de pédagogie d'Edmonton: un example concret de bi-culturalisme,' *Humanities Association Bulletin* XV (1), 17-23.

1965 **Bertrand, J.**
'Enquête auprès des professeurs; le service pédagogique,' *Rev. Scolaire* XVI (June-July), 28-29.

1965 **Chorny, M. and A. G. Storey.**
'A Team Approach to Student Teaching,' *Can. Ed. Research Digest* v, 60-65.
Cruickshank, W. A. and T. J. Wigney.
A Follow-up Study of Atkinson Students Who Became Secondary School Teachers. Atkinson Study of Utilization of Student Resources, Report no. 12. Toronto: Ontario College of Education. Dept. of Educational Research. Pp. 116.
Earl, S. A.
'An Examination of Selected Opinions on Teacher Internship in the Province of Alberta, 1964.' Unpublished doct. dissertation, Montana State Univ.
Goodland, J. I.
'The Academician, Friend or Foe of Teacher Education?' *Jour. Ed. (B.C.)* no. 11, 37-43.
MacIntosh, A. G.
'The Development of Teacher Education in Nova Scotia.' Unpublished M.A. thesis, Saint Mary's Univ.
McCurdy, S. G.
'The Function of the University and the Department of Education in Improving the Teaching of Reading in Newfoundland Schools,' *Nfld. Dept. of Education Newsletter* XVI (Feb.), 3-5; (Mar.), 4-5.
McCurdy, S. G.
'The Legal Status of the Canadian Teacher.' Unpublished doct. dissertation, Univ. of Alberta.
McIntosh, R. G.
'The Saskatchewan Internship Program: An Experiment in Teacher Education,' *Arbos* I (3), 12-16.
McKinnon, A. R.
'Notes on Teacher Education at Simon Fraser University,' *B.C. School Trustee* XXI (Winter-Spring), 16-18.
Newnham, W. T. and A. S. Nease.
The Professional Teacher in Ontario. Toronto: Ryerson. Pp. 233.
Orris, B. D.
'Are we Teaching Intelligently?' *Bas. Teacher* IX, 449-61.
Smith, C. E.
'Necessary Learning for the Beginning Teacher,' *Jour. Ed. (B.C.)* no. 11, 3-16.
Viswanathan, K.
'Interest Measurement with Particular Reference to the Kuder Preference Record and Its Use in the Selection of Student Teachers.' Unpublished M.A. thesis, McGill Univ.

1965 **Wisenthal, M.**
'Programmed Instruction and Teacher Education,' *Can. Ed. Research Digest* V, 66-76.

1966 **Aikenhead, J. D.**
Problems in Student Teaching. Ottawa: Canadian Council for Research in Education. Pp. 15.
Audet, L.-P.
'Les Cadres scolaires' in G. Sylvestre, ed., *Structures sociales du Canada français* (Toronto: U. of T. Press), 29-66.
Barbeau, M.
'L'Université, clef de voute de la formation des maîtres,' *Can. Ed. Research Digest* VII, 191-204.
Bassett, G. W.
'Teacher Education in Canada as seen by an Australian Observer,' *Can. Ed. Research Digest* VII, 1963-73.
Borrowman, M.
Clinical Aspects of Teacher Education. Edmonton: Alberta Teachers' Association. Pp. 11.
Borrowman, M.
Teacher Education and the Making of Educational Policy. Edmonton: Alberta Teachers' Association. Pp. 21.
Heming, H.
Challenges to Teacher Education in the Sixties. Ottawa: Canadian Council for Research in Education. Pp. 6.
Horowitz, M.
Effect of Student Teaching Experiences on Attitudes of Student Teachers. Ottawa: Canadian Council for Research in Education. Pp. 19.
Marshall, J. M.
'Teacher Preparation in Health and Health Education in Canada,' *Can. Jour. Public Health* LVII, 458-63.
McGechaen, J. and P. G. Penner.
Teacher Education at the University of British Columbia 1956-1966. Vancouver: Faculty of Education, U.B.C. Pp. 99.
Ontario Department of Education.
Report of the Minister's Committee on the Training of Elementary School Teachers 1966. Toronto: The Department. Pp. 70.
Paton, J. M.
Current Thinking on Teacher Education. Toronto: Gage. Pp. 56.
Ratsoy, E. W.
'Professional Attitudes of Prospective Teachers,' *Can. Admin.* V (8), 31-34.

1966 Scarfe, N. V.
Principles of Teacher Education. Toronto: Gage. Pp. 7.
Ziel, H. R.
'Training Vocational Teachers,' *Sch. Prog.* xxxv (6), 44-45, 58.

1967 Belth, M.
Priority in Teacher Education: the Problem of Identity. Toronto: W. J. Gage. Pp. 20.
Brown, L. E.
'The Preparation of Teachers in Health Education – Implications,' *Can. H.P.E.R. Jour.* xxxiii (5), 17-19.
Caisman, N.
'De la Pratique à la formation psycho-pédagogique du maître,' *Can. Ed. Research Digest* vii, 67-74.
Canadian Teachers' Federation.
Foundations for the Future: A New Look at Teacher Education and Certification in Canada. Ottawa: The Federation. Pp. 153.
Ellis, M. D., M. Gill and H. W. Savage.
Elementary School Teachers-in-Training: Their Qualifications and Success at Teachers' College. Toronto: Ontario Institute for Studies in Education. Pp. 65. Atkinson Study of Utilization of Student Resources Report no. 13.
France, N.
'Teachers in Canada: Supply and Demand,' *Can. Ed. Research Digest* vii, 47-58.
Horowitz, M.
'Project MEET [McGill Elementary Education Teaching Teams],' *McGill Jour. Ed.* ii, 183-85.
Horowitz, M.
'Role Theory: One Model for Investigating the Student-Teacher Process,' *McGill Jour. Ed.* ii, 38-44.
Howsam, R. B.
'Needed: a Revolution in Teacher Education,' *Can. Ed. Research Digest* vii, 195-208.
Wisenthal, M.
'Linear Programme Writing and Teacher Education,' *McGill Jour. Ed.* ii, 14-24.

1968 French, D.
High Button Bootstraps: Federation of Women Teachers' Association of Ontario, 1918-1968. Toronto: Ryerson. Pp. 208.

1968 **Hardy, T. A.**
'Student and Teacher Perception of the Occupation of Teaching as a Source of Need Satisfaction.' Unpublished M.A. thesis, Univ. of Toronto.
King, A. J. C. and R. A. Ripton.
Audio-Visual Feedback-Counselling: an Experimental Evaluation of the Use of Video-Tape Recordings in the Training of Student Teachers. Kingston: Queen's Univ. Pp. 48.
King, A. J. C. and R. A. Ripton.
A Paradigm for Change: Reaction to Innovation in a Teachers' College. Ottawa: Canadian Council for Research in Education. Pp. 16.
Lewis, J. A.
'Preparation of Physical Education Teachers,' *Man. Jour. Ed. Res.* III (2), 42-48.
Macdonald, J.
Discernible Teacher: Three Essays on Teacher Education. Ottawa: Canadian Teachers' Federation. Pp. 81.
Masson, L. I. and E. Ryan.
The Selection of Student Teachers. Calgary: Univ. of Calgary. Pp. 38.
'Project MEET: McGill Launches Intern Teaching Teams,' *Sch. Prog.* XXXVII (4), 46-47, 66.
Staples, L. A.
Ratings of Students who Attended Teachers' College. Hamilton, Ont.: Board of Education. Pp. 112.
Sutherland, N.
'The "New" Social Studies and Teacher Education,' *McGill Jour. Ed.* III (2), 168-80.

1969 **Dupuis, P.**
'Administration Scolaire,' *ACFAS* XXXVI, 105.
Duval, R.
'La Reforme des éducateurs professionnels commence à l'Université reformée,' *Orient. Prof.* V, 85-96.
Gravel, C.
'Comment voulons-nous former nos enseignement de demain?' *Technique* XLIII (3), 2-6.
Herbert, J. and D. P. Ausubel.
Psychology in Teacher Preparation. Toronto: Ontario Institute for Studies in Education. Pp. 128.
Kaplan, D. L.
'New Needs for Future Teachers of Music,' *Ed. Can.* IX (3), 37-42.

1969 **Ross, V.**
'La Structure idéologique des manuels de pédagogie québécois,' *Recherches Soc.* X, 171-96.
Smith, G. I. H.
'Expectations and Perceptions of the Intern Teacher.' Unpublished M.A. thesis, McGill Univ.
Soule, L.
'A Canadian View of Teacher Education in the U.K.,' *Ed. Canada* IX, 22-27.
Steinhauer, D.
'The Professional Training of Teachers of Modern Languages at the Elementary Level,' *Can. Mod. Lang. Rev.* XXV (2), 22-30.
Topley, D. N.
'The Professional Policies of the Ontario Secondary School Teachers' Federation, 1919-1966.' Unpublished doct. dissertation, Univ. of Toronto.
University of British Columbia, Commission on the Future of the Faculty of Education.
The COFFE Report. Vancouver: The University. Pp. 125.

1970 **Branscombe, F. R.**
'Educational Media and Teacher Training,' *Sch. Prog.* XXXIX (1), 'Why Bother,' 38-41; (2), 'Where Are We Going?' 32-35; (3), 'Where Should We Go From Here?' 48-51, 72-73.
Carter, R. P. and V. M. Short.
'In-Service Teacher Training for Adult Literacy Programs,' *Jour. Ed. (N.S.)* XIX (2), 3-6.
France, N.
'Teachers in Canada: Supply and Demand for the '70's,' *Ed. Canada* X (1), 3-7.
Horner, L. T.
'Broader Participation in Foreign Language Teacher Training,' *Mod. Lang. Jour.* LIV, 250-52.

THEOLOGY : THEOLOGIE

1821 **McCulloch, T.**
'A Lecture Delivered at the Opening of the First Theological Class in the Pictou Academy' in W. McCulloch, *The Life of Thomas McCulloch D.D.* (Truro: privately printed, 1920), 197-215.

1909 Scott, E. F.
'The Place of Theology (Inaugural Address),' *Queen's Q.* XVI, 205-12.
1942 Beauregard, L.
'Le Part de M. Desaulniers à l'introduction du Thomisme au Canada, vers l'époque de la renaissance religieuse,' *Soc. Can. Hist. Eglise Catholique,* 1941-42, 77-89.
1946 Falconer, J. W. and W. G. Watson.
A Brief History of Pine Hill Divinity Hall and the Theological Department at Mount Allison University. Halifax: privately published. Pp. 55.
Holy Heart Seminary.
An Album Commemorating the Fiftieth Anniversary of Holy Heart Seminary. Halifax: J. T. McNally. Pp. 93.
1953 Lachance, E.
Paul Lecourtois, eudiste, Directeur du Grand Séminaire, 1863-1951. Québec: Geo. E. Grandbois. Pp. 88.
1958 Clebsch, W. A.
'The Mission of the Church as the Context of Theological Education,' *Can. Jour. Theology* IV, 246-54.
1959 Conway, J. S.
'The Universities and Religious Studies,' *Can. Jour. Theology* V, 269-72.
1960 Kelly, J. M.
'Theology in our Colleges and Universities,' *Bas. Teacher* V, 71-76.
McCorkell, E. J.
'The Spirit of the Pontifical Institute,' *Bas. Teacher* V, 37-40.
1962 Hughes, D.
'Theology: Core and Catalytic of Intellectual Integration,' *Bas. Teacher* VII, 100-08.
1963 Campeau, L.
'Le Séminaire de Québec dans le plan de Monseigneur de Laval,' *Rev. Hist.* XVII, 315-24.
Principe, W. H.
'The Priest-Teacher: A Theological Evaluation,' *Bas. Teacher* VIII, Supplement, 60-85.
Provost, H.
'Le Séminaire de Québec - premièr logiment, premier esprit,' *Rev. Univ. Laval* XVII, 787-97.
St. Augustine's Seminary.
50 Golden Years 1913-1963. Toronto: St. Augustine's Seminary. Pp. 59.

1964　**Langis, J.**
'Les Débuts de St Sulpice à Montréal (1657-1688),' *Can. Cath. Hist. Report*, 15-22.
Nicholls, W.
'The Role of a Department of Religion in a Canadian University' in K. R. Bridston and D. W. Calver, eds., *The Making of Ministers: Essays on Clergy Training Today* (Minneapolis: Augsburg Publishing House), 72-90.
Provost, H.
Le Séminaire de Québec: documents et biographies. Québec: Archives du Séminaire de Québec. Pp. 542.

1965　**Drolet, J.-C.**
'Les Débuts du Séminaire de Chicoutimi (1873-88),' *Can. Cath. Hist. Report*, 29-36.
Savard, P.
'Le Journal de l'abbé Benjamin Paquet, Etudiant à Rome 1863-1866,' *Culture* XXVI, 64-83.

1966　**Bater, R.**
'Canadian Lay Training Centres and Renewal,' *Continuous Learning* V (Religion and Adult Education Section), xxix-xxxiv.
Feilding, C.
'Twenty-Three Theological Schools: Aspects of Canadian Theological Education,' *Can. Jour. Theology* XII, 229-37.
Lebel, M.
'Les Cadres religieux' in G. Sylvestre, ed., *Structures sociales du Canada français* (Toronto: U. of T. Press), 14-28.
Maloney, D. A.
'Theology in the University,' *Bas. Teacher* X, 278-88.
Pickering, W. S. F.
'Pastoral Planning Studies: the North American Approach,' *Can. Jour. Theology* XII, 98-109.

1967　**Lessard, M.-A. et J.-P. Montminy.**
'Les Religieuses du Canada: âge, recrutement et persévérance,' *Recherches Soc.* VIII, 15-48.

1968　**Allen, E. B.**
'The Roman Catholic Seminary: Changing Perspectives in Theological Education,' *Can. Jour. Theology* XIV, 159-68.
Doerksen, J. G.
'Mennonite Brethren Bible College and College of Arts: Its History, Philosophy and Development.' Unpublished doct. dissertation, Univ. of North Dakota.

1968 **Fairweather, E. R.**
'Perspectives and Problems: Scholarship and Practicality in Theological Education,' *Can. Jour. Theology* XIV, 147-48.
Langevin, G.
'L'Evolution récente et l'état actuel de l'enseignement de la théologie au Canada français: Dossier,' *Can. Jour. Theology* XIV, 169-79.
Routier, F. et G. Tremblay.
Le Profil sociologique du séminariste québécois. Quebec: Univ. Laval. Pp. 165.
Wagner, N. E. and A. J. Siirala.
'Theological Education as Ministry,' *Can. Jour. Theology* XIV, 149-59.
1969 **Légaré, J.**
'Les Religieuses du Canada: leur évolution numérique entre 1965 et 1980,' *Recherches Soc.* X, 7-21.

VETERINARY MEDICINE : MÉDECINE VÉTÉRINAIRE

1960 **Marois, P.**
'Le Médicin vétérinaire devant son destin,' *Can. Vet. Jour.* I, 87-93.
1961 **Saint-Georges, J.**
'75ᵉ Anniversaire de l'Ecole de Médecine Vétérinaire de la Province de Québec et 12 ièmes Journées Vétérinaires du Collège,' *Can. Vet. Jour.* II, 340-44.
Whenham, G. R.
'Veterinary Medicine in Alberta-Historical Notes,' *Can. Vet. Jour.* II, 226-28.
1962 **Gattinger, F. E.**
'History is the Map of Time,' *Can. Vet. Jour.* III, 331-39. [Address on the occasion of the Ont. Vet. College Centennial, July 15, 1962.]
1964 **Mullens, J. E.**
'Thoughts on the Alliance of Veterinary and Human Medicine,' *Can. Vet. Jour.* IV, 12-15.
1965 **Ferrando, R.**
'Les Sciences vétérinaires face à leur destin,' *Can. Vet. Jour.* VI, 63-77.
Jones, T. L.
'Facilities for Veterinary Education,' *Can. Vet. Jour.* VI, 147-50.
Phaneuf, L. P.
'Report of the Royal Commission on Education in Quebec – Possible Effects on Veterinary Teaching,' *Can. Vet. Jour.* VI, 143-46.

1966 **Henderson, J. A.**
'Trends in Veterinary Education,' *Can. Vet. Jour.* VII, 51-53.
Jones, T. L.
'Veterinary Education of the Future,' *Can. Vet. Jour.* VII, 138-41.
McElroy, L. W.
'The Veterinarian and Animal Production,' *Can. Vet. Jour.* VII, 66-68.
Pritchard, W. R.
'Veterinary Medical Education for the Next Decade,' *Can. Vet. Jour.* VII, 55-61.
Smith, D. L. T.
'The Western Canadian Veterinary College – Its Philosophy,' *Can. Vet. Jour.* VII, 62-65.
Soltys, M. A.
'The Veterinary Teacher, His Duties and His Problems,' *Can. Vet. Jour.* VII, 277-79.
1968 **Soltys, M. A.**
'Suggested Changes in Veterinary Education,' *Can. Vet. Jour.* IX, 3-6.
1969 **Fraser, C. M.**
'Formal Recognition of Veterinary Clinical Competence,' *Can. Vet. Jour.* X, 59-60.
Howell, D. G.
'The Veterinary School at the Close of the Second Millennium,' *Can. Vet. Jour.* X, 153-58.

VOCATIONAL GUIDANCE : ORIENTATION PROFESSIONNELLE

1930 **Henry, G. M.**
'Vocational Guidance in Elementary and Secondary Schools with Special Reference to Canada.' Unpublished M.A. thesis, McMaster Univ.
1964 **Auger, L.**
'Vers une Conception dynamique de l'orientation,' *Coll. et Fam.* XXI (1), 12-16.
Beauchemin, J.-M.
'L'Orientation: processus de maturation,' *Bull. Fed. Coll.* IX (4), 6-9.
Duval, R.
'L'Evolution de l'orientation professionnelle aux points de vue historique, méthologique et légal dans la province de Québec et ses implications futures,' *Orient. Prof.* I (2), 3-21.

1964 **Perkins, S. A.**
'A Study of the Duty of Counsellors in the Secondary Schools of British Columbia.' Unpublished M.Ed. thesis, Western Washington State College.
Super, D. E.
'The Psychology of Careers,' *Continuous Learning* III, 106-15.

1965 **Chard, W. D.**
'The Evolution of Guidance in the Schools of Nova Scotia.' Unpublished M.A. thesis, St. Mary's Univ.
'Counselling and Guidance for Educational and Vocational Development,' *Jour. Ed. (N.S.)* XV (2), 3-4.
Parmenter, M. D.
Blueprint for Guidance in Canadian Schools. Toronto: Crest Publishing Co. Pp. 74.
Pelletier, D.
'Le Monde du travail et l'orientation professionnelle,' *Orient. Prof.* I, 237-44.
Wyspianski, J. O.
'Guidance Re-Examined,' *Proc. Can. Assoc. Student Services* 48-51.

1966 **Adkins, A. A.**
'Predicting Success in a Counselling Internship,' *Proc. Can. Assoc. Student Services* 27-31.
Bellerive, A.
'La Formation des conseillers d'orientation face à l'école nouvelle québécoise [rapport de discussion],' *Orient. Prof.* II, 407-10.

1967 **Lubick, E. E.**
'Guidance Services at a Community College,' *School Guidance Worker* XXII (June), 25-34.
Slater, E.
'Le Role et la formation du professeur d'information,' *Orient. Prof.* IV, 55-58.

1968 **Thompson, S. D.**
'Some Personality Characteristics of Student Teachers of Guidance.' Unpublished doct. dissertation, Univ. of British Columbia.

1969 **Bannen, J.**
'Organization and Administration of Guidance Services in Canada,' *Man. Jour. Ed.* IV (2), 5-13.
Bedal, C.
'Renaissance of Vocational Guidance,' *Can. Couns.* III (4), 26-33.

1969 **Dion, G.**
'La Raison d'être de la clinique d'orientation de l'Université Laval,' *Orient. Prof.* v, 103-07.
Fraser, J. A. H.
'Evaluation of a High School Counselling Programme,' *Can. Couns.* III (1), 41-46.
Gauthier, A.
'L'Ecole et la formation professionnelle,' *Orient. Prof.* v, 32-40.
LeBlanc, P. B.
'The Concept of Privileged Communication in Selected Professions with Particular Reference to the Field of School and University Counselling in Canada.' Unpublished M.A. thesis, McGill Univ.
Nevison, M.
'Evolving Patterns of Counsellor Education,' *Can. Couns.* III (1), 59-62.
Storey, A. G., W. McCormick and J. Loken.
'The Counsellor's Role as Perceived by Counsellor, Teacher, and Counsellee,' *Can. Couns.* III (3), 49-53.
1970 **Clark, R. C.**
'The Emerging Counsellor in Canada,' *Can. Couns.* IV (1), 5-9.
D'Oyley, V.
'Canadian Post-Secondary Institutions: A Challenge to Counsellors,' *Can. Couns.* IV (2), 87-97.

G. GRADUATE STUDIES : ETUDES POST-UNIVERSITAIRES

1898 **Dearness, J.**
'The Post-Graduate Training of Teachers,' *Proc. Dominion Educational Assoc.* 1898, 75-82.
1956 **Deane, S. G.**
'Financial Assistance Available for Graduate Study in the Field of Education,' *Alta. Jour. Ed. Res.* II (3), 156-72.
1960 **Stock, E. H. and P. J. Beaulieu.**
'Science Postgraduates of Canadian Universities,' *Can. Public Admin.* III, 326-30.
1965 **Cragg, L. H., M. G. Ross and E. F. Sheffield.**
Canadians in U.S. Graduate Schools: a Rich Pool of Potential Canadian University Teachers and Research Workers. Ottawa: Canadian Universities Foundation. Pp. 12.

1965 Jackson, R. W. B.
'The Ontario Institute for Studies in Education,' *Ont. Jour. Ed. Res.* VIII, 173-81.
Poole, C. F.
'The Ph.D. as a Qualification for University Teachers,' *C.A.U.T. Bull.* XIV (2), 61-64.

1966 Eastman, H. C.
'The Master of Philosophy Degree,' *C.A.U.T. Bull.* XV (1), 85-90.
Edwards, R.
On the Teaching of Methods of Educational Research: a New Dimension? Ottawa: Canadian Council for Research in Education. Pp. 12.
Manning, T. W.
'Graduate Education in Agricultural Economics,' *Can. Jour. Agric. Econ.* XIV (2), 1-14.
Organization for Economic Cooperation and Development.
Training of and Demand for High-Level Scientific and Technical Personnel in Canada. Paris: The Organization. Pp. 136.
Risi, J.
'Le Gradué, la recherche et l'Université,' *Rev. Univ. Laval* XX, 603-17.
Robinson, A. J.
'The Bladen Commission and Graduate Education,' *Can. Jour. Econ. Pol. Sci.* XXXII, 520-25.
Rothrock, G. A.
'The Ph.D.: Academic License or Status Symbol,' *C.A.U.T. Bull.* XIV, 43-45.
Sheffield, E. F. and M. M. McGrail, eds.
La Récupération des gradués canadiens étudiant à l'étranger/The Retrieval of Canadian Graduate Students Abroad. Ottawa: Assoc. of Universities and Colleges of Canada. Pp. 82.

1967 Corry, J. A.
'The Spinks Report,' *Univ. Affairs* VIII (3), 3-5.
Gingras, B. A. and T. W. West.
'National Research Council of Canada: Fifty Years of Scholarships,' *Eng. Jour.* L (11), 15-18.
Spinks, J. W. T.
'Ontario Graduate Commission Report,' *Univ. Affairs* VIII (3), 1-2.
Spinks, J. W. T.
'The Spinks Report,' *Can. Univ.* II (2), 51-52.

1968 **Dupuis, J. R. P.**
'A Study of the Rate-of-Return on Investment in Graduate Studies in Educational Administration.' Unpublished doct. dissertation, Univ. of Alberta.
Genest, B.-A.
'Une Décision importante: la poursuite d'etudes post-universitaires,' *Ing.* LIV (235), 22-25.
Lapointe, M.
'Conseil des Arts du Canada: Humanities et Sciences Sociales 1966-67,' *C.A.U.T. Bull.* XVI (4), 29-38.
Mardiros, A. M.
'Let's Abolish the PH.D.,' *Can. Dimension* V (4), 32-34.
Pavalko, R. M.
'Talent Migration: Canadian Students in the United States,' *International Review of Education* [Germany] XIV, 300-24.
Sirluck, E.
'The Future Development of Graduate Programmes in Ontario,' *Queen's Q.* LXXV, 195-207.
Smith, D. C.
'The Preparation of College Teachers: Towards a Rationale for Instruction,' *Can. Ed. Research Digest* VII, 230-44.

1969 **Barker, B.**
'A Plan to Keep Canada's Scientists at Home,' *Can. R. and D.* II (6), 26-28.
Carter, R. P. and V. M. Short.
'Selection and Training of Adult Educators,' *Jour. Ed. (N.S.)* XIX (1), 33-36.
Fisher, E. A.
International Market for Graduates. Ottawa: Canadian Council for Research in Education. Pp. 8.
Jackson, R. W. B. and J. Andrews.
'O.I.S.E.,' *Ed. Canada* IX (1), 58-66.
Smith, D. C.
'The Future of International Studies in Teacher Education,' *McGill Jour. Ed.* IV (2), 141-49.

1970 **Goddard, G. V.**
'PH.D. Training: The End of an Era,' *Can. Psych.* XI, 133-36.
Ontario Council on Graduate Studies.
The First Three Years of Appraisal of Graduate Programmes. Toronto: Committee of Presidents of Universities of Ontario. Pp. 17.

1970 Wake, F. R. and D. B. Harris.
'The Natural Development of a Graduate Student,' *Can. Psych.* XI, 48-56.

H. ADULT EDUCATION : EDUCATION DES ADULTES

1939 Eastman, S. M.
'Workers' Education in Canada,' *International Labour Review* [Switzerland] XL, 320-37.
1944 Smyth, D. M.
'The Need for Adult Education,' *Jour. Ed. (N.S.)* XV, 29-35.
1945 Henson, G.
'Adult Education and Farm People,' *Jour. Ed. (N.S.)* XVI, 811-18.
1957 Cormier, H.
'Is Adult Education Making an Effective Contribution?' *Atlantic Advocate* XLVII (8), 17-18.
1958 Porter, M.
'The Great Back-to-School Boom,' *Maclean's* LXXI (6), 22, 38-42.
Waters, B. E.
'The Development of Adult Education in British Columbia.'
Unpublished doct. dissertation, Oregon State College.
1961 Ritchie, R. S.
'The Need for Continuing Education,' *Can. P. R. Jour.* VIII (4), 19-23.
Shand, G. V.
'Adult Education among the Negroes of Nova Scotia,' *Jour. Ed. (N.S.)* X (1), 11-21.
1963 Corbett, E. A.
'Atkinson College,' *Continuous Learning* II, 22-25.
Rank, I.
'Adult Education, Part I,' *Can. Lib. Assoc. Bull.* XX, 113-17; 'Part II,' 320-24.
Thomas, A. M.
'Continuing Education and the Professions,' *Continuous Learning* II, 179-84.
1964 Canadian Association for Adult Education.
'The Annual Review,' *Continuous Learning* III, 200-05.
MacKenzie, N. A. M.
'Adult Education Extension Work and the New Universities,' *Continuous Learning* III, 9-17. See also G. Selman, 63-67 and A. S. R. Tweedie, 115-21.

1964 **McLean, I.**
'University Extension Students and the Public Libraries,' *Ont. Lib. Rev.* XLVIII, 143-45.
McNeil, D. R.
'Attitudes of Extension Personnel about Their Jobs,' *Continuous Learning* III, 198-206.
Roby, Y.
Alphonse Desjardins et les caisses populaires, 1854-1920. Montréal: Fides. Pp. 149.
Selman, G.
'University Extension 1914-1963,' *Jour. Ed. (B.C.)* no. 10, 17-25.
Timmons, H. P.
'Adult Education and Community Developments,' *Jour. Ed. (N.S.)* XIII (2), 47-49.

1965 **Campbell, S. S.**
Continuing Education for Women in Metropolitan Toronto. A study prepared for Atkinson College. Toronto: York Univ. Pp. 28.
Canadian Association for Adult Education.
'The Annual Review,' *Continuous Learning* IV, 193-97.
Canadian Association for Adult Education.
'The Mature Student Clause,' *Continuous Learning* IV, 205-15.
Canadian Association for Adult Education.
Report of the Conference on Adult Education in Community Colleges. Toronto: The Association. Pp. 51. See also 'Adult Education and the Community College in Canada: Report on the C.A.A.E. National Conference,' *Continuous Learning* IV, 155-70.
Hawkins, G. R. S.
'The Adult Education Responsibilities of a Provincial Department of Education; a Study of Saskatchewan, 1944-1963.' Unpublished M.A. thesis, Univ. of Toronto.
Stott, M. M.
'Community Development – Adult Education or Social Work?' *Continuous Learning* IV, 31-34.

1966 **Blakely, R. J.**
'Is Adult Education Developing as a Profession?' *Continuous Learning* V, 153-58.
Canadian Association for Adult Education.
'The Annual Review,' *Continuous Learning* V, 193-99. See also 'Community Colleges 1966,' 221-26.

1966 **Canadian Association for Adult Education.**
A White Paper on the Education of Adults in Canada: A Canadian Policy for Continuing Education. Toronto: The Association. Pp. 8.
Institut Canadien d'Education des Adultes.
Quelles sont nos responsabilités en éducation des adultes? Montréal: L'Institut. Pp. 42.
Kidd, J. R.
The Implications of Continuous Learning. Toronto: Gage. Pp. 122.
La Fountaine, M. E.
'Adult Education – A Gross Illusion,' *Continuous Learning* v, 5-12.
Laliberté, J.
'En Marge d'un colloque de l'I.C.E.A.: l'enterprise et l'éducation des adultes,' *Prospectives* II, 34-38.
Lefebvre, J.-P.
Les Adultes à l'école. Montréal: Editions du Jour. Pp. 122.
Lefebvre, J.-P.
'L'Entreprise et l'éducation des adultes,' *Relations Ind.* XXI, 235-42.
Lefebvre, J.-P.
'The Role of Industry in Adult Education,' *Continuous Learning* v, 75-83.
Miller, L.
'Canada' in B. Groombridge, ed., *Adult Education and Television* (London: National Institute of Adult Education in collaboration with UNESCO), 9-54.
Mutchler, P.
'Seminar Reflects Changing Approach to Adult Education,' *Ont. Lib. Rev.* L, 134-37.
Selman, G.
A History of Fifty Years of Extension Service by the University of British Columbia, 1915-1965. Toronto: Can. Assoc. for Adult Education. Pp. 60.

1967 **Andrew, G. C.**
'What's Past is Prologue,' [Address at the opening of Corbett House] *Continuous Learning* IV, 5-15. See also 15-27.
Canadian Association for Adult Education.
'The Annual Review,' *Continuous Learning* VI, 271-77.
Cavanagh, D. A.
'Continuing Education and Training Hold Key to Canada's Future,' *Can. P. and R. Jour.* VIX (4), 43-44.

1967 **Draper, J. A.**
'A Proposal for Systematically Collecting and Reporting Research Relating to Adult Education in Canada,' *Continuous Learning* VI, 211-14.
Gunn, C. R.
'The Role of the Atlantic Provincial Governments in Adult Education.' Unpublished doct. dissertation, Univ. of Toronto. Summary in *Jour. Ed. (N.S.)* XVII (1), 16-24.
Maisey, D. P.
'A Study of Students Enrolled in the Adult Education Evening Program of the Lethbridge Junior College.' Unpublished M.Ed. thesis, Univ. of Alberta.

1968 **Armstrong, D. P.**
'Corbett's House: the Origins of the Canadian Association for Adult Education and Its Development during the Directorship of E. A. Corbett, 1936-1951.' Unpublished M.A. thesis, Univ. of Toronto.
Blaney, J. P.
A Staff Development Program for the Extension Department, the University of British Columbia. Vancouver: Univ. of British Columbia, Department of University Extension. Pp. 19. Occasional Paper in Continuing Education, no. 2.
Canadian Association for Adult Education.
A Report to the Canadian People on Manpower Development. Toronto: The Association. Pp. 28.
Dorais, L. A.
'The Next Decade in University Adult Education,' *Continuous Learning* VII, 205-06, 225-31.
Flaherty, M. J.
'The Prediction of College Level Academic Achievement in Adult Extension Students.' Unpublished doct. dissertation, Univ. of Toronto.
Institut Canadian d'Education des Adultes.
Le Centre des Dirigeants d'Enterprise et l'éducation des adultes. Montréal: L'Institut. Pp. 185.
Institut Canadien d'Education des Adultes.
L'Education des adultes et les problèmes de main-d'oeuvre. Montréal: L'Institut. Pp. 183.
Institut Canadien d'Education des Adultes.
Rapport de la Première Conference Nord-Americaine sur l'éducation des adultes. Montréal: L'Institut. Pp. 104.

1968 James, L.
'Will Scarborough College "Flunk Out?"' *Continuous Learning* VII, 198-202.
Kauffmann, J.-P.
'SESAME: Une porte s'ouvre sur une nouvelle formation des adultes,' *Technique* XLII (3), 2-6.
Selman, G.
'The Next Decade in University Adult Education,' *Continuous Learning* VII, 204, 220-24.
Smith, M. E.
'Community Co-Ordination in Adult Education,' *Continuous Learning* VII, 137-40.
Thomas, A.
'The Media Lag in Adult Education,' *Can. Audio-Visual Rev.* IV (5), 4-5, 14.
Tough, A.
'Adult Education as a Field of Study in Canada,' *Continuous Learning* VII, 4-14. See also *ibid.*, 15-33.
Tweedie, A. S. R.
'Some Thoughts of an Adult Educator,' *Continuous Learning* VII, 123-31.
Vuo, F. E. W.
'Some Administrative and Organizational Aspects of University Adult Education.' Unpublished M.A. thesis, Dalhousie Univ.

1969 Beauchamp, C.
'L'Institut Coopératif Desjardins,' *Technique* XLIII (3), 14-18.
Brooke, W. M.
'The Adult Basic Education Teacher in Ontario: His Background, Problems and Need for Continuing Professional Education.' Unpublished M.A. thesis, Univ. of Toronto.
Canadian Association for Adult Education.
Report of the Committee on the Philosophy, Structure and Operation of the Canadian Association for Adult Education. Toronto: The Association. Pp. 34.
Carter, R. P. and V. M. Short.
'Selection and Training of Adult Educators,' *Jour. Ed. (N.S.)* XIX (1), 33-36.
Dickinson, G. and C. Verner.
Community Structure and Participation in Adult Education. Vancouver: Univ. of British Columbia. Pp. 43.

1969 **Gauthier, G.**
'L'Observation de l'interaction entre le professeur et l'étudiante adulte,' *Prospectives* V, 249-58.
Kidd, J. R.
'You Can't Tear Up the Seamless Robe of Learning,' *Sch. Prog.* XXXVIII (9), 58-62.
Légaré, T.
'Le Recyclage professionnel et academique des femmes mariées, rêve et réalité,' *Orient. Prof.* V, 228-37.
MacDonald, A. A.
Extension Philosophy and Operation: The Antigonish Concept. Antigonish: St. Francis Xavier Univ. Pp. 13.
Niemi, J. A. and D. Anderson.
'Remedial Adult Education – An Analytical Review of Evaluation Research,' *Continuous Learning* VIII, 90-94.
Royce, M.
Continuing Education for Women in Canada Trends and Opportunities. Toronto: Ontario Institute for Studies in Education. Pp. 167.
Vernon, F.
'The Development of Adult Education in Ontario 1790-1900.' Unpublished doct. dissertation, Univ. of Toronto.

1970 **Bélanger, P. and P. Pacquet.**
'Problématique de l'éducation des adultes dans les CEGEP,' *Prospectives* VI, 104-21.
Carter, R. P. and V. M. Short.
'In-Service Teacher Training for Adult Literacy Programs,' *Jour. Ed. (N.S.)* XIX (2), 3-6.
Draper, J. A. and F. Yadao, Jr.
'Adult Education as a Field of Study in Canada,' *Continuous Learning* IX, 65-82.
Ohliger, J.
'Integrating Continuing Education,' *Continuous Learning* IX, 101-06.

I. ADMISSIONS : INSCRIPTIONS

1956 **Smith, S.**
'Does More Money than Brains Go to College?' *Maclean's* LXIX (19), 4, 40-43.
1958 **Evenson, A. B. and D. E. Smith.**
'A Study of Matriculation in Alberta,' *Alta. Jour. Ed. Res.* (2), 67-83.

1958 **Wilson, L.**
'How Many Alberta Matriculants Register as Freshmen at the University of Alberta,' *Alta. Jour. Ed. Res.* IV (2), 108-13.
1959 **Black, D. B.**
'Why Did They Differ? Study of Two Groups,' *Alta. Jour. Ed. Res.* V (2), 119-29.
1962 **Baskerville, W. R.**
'Admission of Foreign University Students to Canada,' *Univ. Affairs* III (4), 4-5.
Mowat, A. S. and J. A. Ross.
Loss of Student Potential and Predication of University Success. (C.A.C. High School Testing Project, Report no. 2.) Halifax: Central Advisory Committee on Education in the Atlantic Provinces. Pp. 150.
Picard, G.
'De l'Accessibilité à l'enseignement universitaire chez les fils d'ouvriers.' Thèse de licence, Univ. Laval.
1963 **Black, D. B.**
'A National Testing Program for University Admission,' *Alta. Jour. Ed. Research* IX (1), 3-12.
Graham, E. S.
'Advanced Placement,' *Univ. Affairs* V (2), 3-4.
1964 **Kierman, O. B.**
'Who Should Go to College?' *Sch. Prog.* XXXIII (10), 40-41.
Mowat, A. S., ed.
Where Are They Now? Able Students Who Did Not Proceed to University, Teachers' College or School of Nursing. (C.A.C. High School Testing Project, Report no. 3.) Halifax: Central Advisory Committee on Education in the Atlantic Provinces. Pp. 70.
1965 **Beaulieu, Y.**
'Etude sur la valeur et la justification de la sélection universitaire.' Mémoire en orientation professionnelle, Univ. Laval.
Brochu, A.
'Cas de conscience: orientation et selection,' *Orient. Prof.* I, 268-72.
Knowles, D. W.
'The Influence of Faculty, High School Size, and Sex in the Prediction of Success Using Departmental and Principal's Rating Grade XII Scores.' Unpublished M.Ed. thesis, Univ. of Alberta.
Knowles, D. W.
'Problems of Admission to the University of Alberta,' *Alta. Jour. Ed. Res.* XI (1), 3-16.

1965   **Knowles, D. W. and D. B. Black.**
'Factors Influencing the Prediction of Freshman Success at the University of Alberta, Edmonton,' *Alta. Jour. Ed. Res.* XI (2), 71-82.
Viswanathan, K.
'Interest Measurement with Particular Reference to the Kuder Preference Record and Its Use in the Selection of Student Teachers.' Unpublished M.A. thesis, McGill Univ.
Watson, C. and P. M. Lyle.
Ontario Grade 13: Three Studies. Toronto: Ontario Institute for Studies in Education. Pp. 149.

1966   'Admissions Service Proposed,' *Can. Univ.* I (2), 30-31.
Black, D. B.
'Methods of Predicting Freshman Success: Summary and Evaluation,' *Alta. Jour. Ed. Res.* XII, 111-126.
Fish, D. G. and B. I. Brown.
'A Comparison of Applicants and Applications to Canadian Medical and Dental Schools, 1965-66,' *Can. Med. Assoc. Jour.* XCV, 68-71.
Gadbois, L. et J. Bordeleau.
'Les Examens d'admissions dans les universités et les écoles professionnelles,' *Orient. Prof.* II, 428-31.
Hunka, S. M., D. F. Cameron and J. A. L. Gilbert.
'Selection of Students for Admission to Medical School: a Two-Class Decision Approach,' *Can. Med. Assoc. Jour.* XCVI, 708-11.
Ontario Institute for Studies in Education and The University of Guelph.
The Students of the 1966 Spring Admission Programme at the University of Guelph: Who are They? Why did They Come? The Guelph Spring Admission Research Project: Study no. 1. Guelph: Univ. of Guelph. Pp. 81.

1967   **Chipman, M. L. and J. W. Steiner.**
'An Attempted Simulation by Computer of a Committee on Admissions,' *Can. Med. Assoc. Jour.* XCVI, 936-41.
Evans, R. K. and D. O. Anderson.
'The Selection of Medical Students in Western Canada,' *Can. Med. Assoc. Jour.* XCVI, 473-80.
Gingras, R.
'Les Admissions à la faculté de médecine de l'Université Laval,' *Laval Méd.* XXXVIII, 262-71.
Lamontagne, L.
'The Service for Admission to College and University,' *Can. Ed. Research Digest* VII, 269-82.

1968 **Porter, J.**
'Inequalities in Education,' *Can. Counsellor* II, 136-47.
Rocher, G.
'Le Droit à l'éducation,' *Bien-être* XX, 109-15, 123.
1969 **Canadian Education Association. Information Division.**
Requirements for Secondary School Leaving Certificates, Admission to University and Admission to Teacher Training. Toronto: The Association. Pp. 44.
Clark, E., D. Cook, G. Fallis and M. Kent.
'Student Aid and Access to Higher Education in Ontario.' Mimeograph report issued by Prof. R. W. Judy, Univ. of Toronto. Pp. 259.
Khan, S. B.
A Factor Analytic Study of the Ontario Tests for Admission to College and University. Toronto: Dept. of Measurement and Evaluation, Ontario Institute for Studies in Education. Pp. 8 and 6 tables.
Khan, S. B., P. Ransom and M. Herbert.
Prediction of First-Year Achievement in Ontario Universities.
Toronto: Dept. of Measurement and Evaluation, Ontario Institute for Studies in Education. Pp. 18 and 68 tables.
Lamontagne, L.
'Les Problèmes de la sélection au niveau collégial et universitaire,' *Orient. Prof.* IV, 464-76.
More, A.
'The Relation of High School Grades, Achievement and Intelligence Test Scores to Success in Dental School,' *Can. Counsellor* III (1), 56-58.
Perkins, S. A.
An Examination of Five Different Groups of First-Year Students at the University of Lethbridge on the College Qualification Test and Grade Point Average, 1967-68. Ottawa: Canadian Council for Research in Education. Pp. 30.
1970 **Joly, J.-M.**
'Le Service d'admission au collège et à l'université (SACU),' *Prospectives* VI, 150-54.
Maher, D.
'Discriminatory Requirements on University Admission Forms' in *Studies on the University, Society and Government* ... (Ottawa: Univ. of Ottawa Press. 2 vols.), I, 435-62.
Vaselenak, M.
'Admission of Mature Non-Matriculated Students into a Degree Program,' *McGill Jour. Ed.* V (1), 85-96.

J. EVALUATION AND GRADING :
EVALUATION ET CLASSEMENT

1964 **Endler, N. S.**
'Factors Related to the Prediction of Academic Success,' *Ont. Jour. Ed. Res.* VII (2), 147-54.
Endler, N. S. and L. S. Snyder.
'Anxiety, Aptitude, and Academic Achievement,' *Ont. Jour. Ed. Res.* VI, 85-91.

1965 **McCormack, P. D.**
'The Evaluation of Student Achievement,' *Can. Ed. Research Digest* V, 77-82.

1966 **Black, D. B.**
'Methods of Predicting Freshman Success: Summary and Evaluation,' *Alta. Jour. Ed. Res.* XII, 111-126.
Brown, D. W. R.
'An Analysis of the Achievement of Junior College Students at the University of Calgary.' Unpublished M.Ed. thesis, Univ. of Calgary.
Payne, R. W., P. O. Davidson and R. B. Sloane.
'The Prediction of Academic Success in University Students: A Pilot Study,' *Can. Jour. Psych.* XX, 52-63.

1968 **Charette, R., D. Bedard and C. Hamel.**
'Aspects du sous-rendement chez un groupe d'étudiants du niveau universitaire,' *Can. Counsellor* II, 261-68.
Ross, I. and G. F. McGuigan.
'The War Against Exams and Lectures,' *Can. Univ.* III (1), 63, 88.

1969 **Franke, W.**
'Measurement Complex [is] Stifling Academic Freedom,' *Can. Univ. & Coll.* IV (9), 30-31, 59.
Waugh, D. and C. A. Moyse.
'Oral Examinations: A Videotape Study of the Reproducibility of Grades in Pathology,' *Can. Med. Assoc. Jour.* C, 635-40.

1970 **Gagné, F. and M. Chabot.**
'PERPE [Perceptions Etudiantes de la Relation Professeur-Etudiante], une conception neuve du perfectionnement pédagogique,' *Prospectives* VI, 160-81.

K. INSTRUCTIONAL AIDS : AIDES DIDACTIQUES

1961 'More Education on Television Channels: Here's What Canadian Universities Are Doing,' *Can. Bus.* XXXIV (2), 26-27.

1963   **Bindra, D.**
'Exploring the Newer Technological Aids to Instruction at McGill,'
Univ. Affairs IV (4), 3-4.
Dansereau, J.
'Sus au joual; l'électronique vient au secours des professeurs,'
Mag. Maclean III (9), 28-29, 55-57.
Fawdry, K.
'Possibilities et limites de la télévision au service de l'Education,'
Rev. Scolaire XIV, 100-02, 163-65.

1964   **Beauregard, L.**
'Géographie télévisé,' *Cah. Géog.* XVI, 297-303.
Fraser, D. C.
'Teaching Machines,' *Continuous Learning* III, 74-80.
Juneau, M. P.
'Les Moyens audio-visuels et le système scolaire,' *Rev. Scolaire* XIV, 269-71.

1965   **Beckel, W. E.**
'Some Aspects of Teaching Aids,' *American Journal of Pharmaceutical Education* XXIX, 774-80.
Jason, H.
'Programmed Instruction: New Bottle for Rediscovered Wine,'
Can. Med. Assoc. Jour. XCII, 711-16.
Kennedy, R.
'Educational Television in Canada and Abroad,' *Can. Ed. Research Digest* V, 122-33.
Yonge, K. A.
'The Use of Closed Circuit Television for the Teaching of Psychotherapeutic Interviewing to Medical Students,' *Can. Med. Assoc. Jour.* XCII, 747-51.

1966   'ETV – Pandora's Box or Panacea for Lecturers?' *Can. Univ.* I (2), 17-21.
Jeanes, R. W. and D. A. Massey.
'Language Labs – A New Look,' *Can. Mod. Lang. Rev.* XXII (2), 40-50.
Knowles, A. F.
'Notes on a Canadian Mass Media Policy,' *Continuous Learning* V, 251-61.
Miller, L.
'Canada' in B. Groombridge, ed., *Adult Education and Television* (London: National Institute of Adult Education in collaboration with UNESCO), 9-54.

1966 **Preuter, K. F.**
'L'Enseignement et la nouvelle technologie scolaire,' *Technique* XL (6), 18-27.
Slade, M.
'Studying Film and Television,' *Continuous Learning* V, 203-09. See also 269-75.

1967 **Fremont, C.**
'L'Enseignement télévisé à l'Université Laval,' *ACFAS* XXX, 169 (Resumé).
Knowles, A. F.
'Educational Television – Laboratories of Fun!' *Continuous Learning* VI, 163-66. See also 167-74.
'The Media Explosion Hits Higher Education,' *Can. Univ.* II (2), 36-47.
Plante, L.
'La Téléprojection à la relève de l'enseignement,' *Technique* XLI (10), 29-32.
Rosen, E., ed.
Educational Television, Canada. Toronto: Burns & MacEachern. Pp. 101.

1968 **Canadian Medical Association.**
'Audiovisual Aids in Medical Teaching,' *Can. Med. Assoc. Jour.* XCVIII, 1079-114, 1123-50.
Dixon, R. C.
'Constitutional Issues of Educational Television,' *Man. Law Jour.* III, 75-86.
Gibson, D. A.
'The Audio-Visual Division of Dalhousie Medical School,' *N.S. Med. Bull.* XLVII (3), 91-93.
Guay, J.
'Le Chef Labrie, un écolier parmi 35,000,' *Mag. Maclean* VIII (6), 14-17, 24-25.
Hunter, A. T.
'The Use of Broadcast Television in Continuing Medical Education,' *Can. Med. Assoc. Jour.* XCVIII, 34-39.
King, A. J. C. and R. A. Ripton.
Audio-Visual Feedback-Counselling: an Experimental Evaluation of the Use of Video-Tape Recordings in the Training of Student Teachers. Kingston: Queen's Univ. Pp. 48.
Pappert, E. C.
'Cooperation in Production Exchange and Distribution of Educational Television,' *Continuous Learning* VII, 117-22.

1968 **Reid, I.**
'E.T.V.? Disaster Deliverance,' *Can. Consulting Eng.* X (4), 47-52.
Ryan, E. F.
'Television and the Law Schools – a Preliminary Appraisal,' *Chitty's Law Jour.* XVI, 293-98.
Wilson, W. R.
'Changing Technology and Educational Television,' *Continuous Learning* VII, 213-19.

1969 **Allen, D. E.**
'A Comparison between Television Instruction and Conventional Methods in Teaching Medical Isolation-Gown Procedure: an Experimental Study.' Unpublished M.Ed. thesis, Univ. of New Brunswick.
Eshelman, W.
'Orchestrating Media Sub-Systems,' *Can. Univ. & Coll.* IV (4), 38-42.
Grégoire, R.
'L'Irruption de la technologie dans l'éducation et les attitudes à développer par l'éducateur,' *Prospectives* V, 119-27.
Knowles, A. F.
'Canadian Education – And Television,' *Continuous Learning* VII, 113-20.
O'Brien, J. E.
'The Impact of Mass Media on Education,' *McGill Jour. Ed.* IV (1), 40-47.
'Teaching Media Set CES [Canadian Education Showplace] Pace,' *Can. Univ. & Coll.* IV (12), 19-21.
Thomas, W. K.
'The Medium Helps the Message,' *English Q.* II, 57-62.

1970 **Branscombe, F. R.**
'Educational Media and Teacher Training,' *Sch. Prog.* XXXIX (1), 'Why Bother,' 38-41; (2), 'Where Are We Going?' 32-35; (3), 'Where Should We Go From Here?' 48-51, 72-73.
'ETV Agreement Ends Three Years of Uncertainty,' *Univ. Affairs* XI (1), 25-28.
Scanlon, T. J.
'Sweep of Color: Adding Dimension to the Language of Learning,' *Can. Univ. & Coll.* V (4), 27-29.

Research and scholarship
Recherche et études

A. GENERAL : GÉNÉRALITÉS

1946 **Speakman, H. B.** *et al.*
Research in Canada: Planning for the Coming Years: Papers Given at the Symposium of the Chemical Institute of Canada, Quebec City, June 1945. Toronto: Imperial Oil Ltd. Pp. 160. Includes:
R. K. Stratford, 'The Coordination of Research in Canada,' 7-14;
D. L. Thomson, 'The Role of the Universities in Research,' 21-26;
C. J. MacKenzie, 'Government Sponsored Research,' 33-42;
J. M. Swaine, 'The Coordination of Agricultural Research,' 45-53;
E. F. Palmer, 'Horticultural Research in Ontario and Its Practical Application,' 55-62; G. E. Jackson, 'The Provision of Manpower in Research in Canada,' 63-84.

1963 **Andrews, J. H. M.**
'The Practical Function of Research,' *Can. Ed. Research Digest* III, 169-80.
Canada, Dept. of National Health and Welfare, Research Development Section.
Research Assisted under the National Health Grants Programme. Ottawa: Queen's Printer. Pp. 68.
Moorey, C. M.
'Research under National Health Grants,' *Can. Psych.* IVa, 143-48.
Nicholls, R. W.
'Research and Canadian Industry,' *Bus. Q.* XXVIII (3), 12-29.

1964 **Lebel, M.**
'On the Meaning of Research – or the Genesis and Evolution of the Nature of Research,' *Trans. R.S.C.* 3-20.

1965 **Hume, J. N. P.**
'Putting Computers on-line with Research,' *Trans. R.S.C.* sect. III, 293-300.

1966 **Medical Research Council of Canada.**
Survey of Research Personnel in the Medical Sciences in Canada 1965-66. (Report no. 1.) Ottawa: The Council. Pp. 33.
Milhiot, B.
'Le "Sondage d'opinions": instrument de recherche ou technique d'infruition?' *Bull. Inf. Cath.* XXXIII, 11-14.

1966 'University Research,' *Chem. Can.* XVIII (1), 43-52.
1967 **Downs, R. B.**
Resources of Canadian Academic and Research Libraries. Ottawa: Association of Universities and Colleges of Canada. Pp. 301.
Engineering Institute of Canada.
A Canadian Policy for Research and Development as suggested by the Engineering Institute of Canada. Montreal: The Institute. Pp. 35.
Joly, J.-M.
'Research and Innovation: Two Solitudes,' *Can. Ed. Research Digest* VII, 184-94.
Repo-Davis, M.
'Easier Shelved than Done,' *This Magazine* I (4), 104-11.
Wright, D. T.
'Remark on Research Policies,' *Univ. Affairs* IX (1), 10-11.
1968 **Beaudoin, L.**
La Recherche au Canada-français. Montréal: Presses Univ. Montréal. Pp. 161.
Canada, Dept. of the Secretary of State, Education Support Branch.
Federal Expenditures on Research in the Academic Community 1966-67, 1967-68. Ottawa: Queen's Printer. Pp. 113.
Chapman, J. H.
'Joint Research in Canada,' *Trans. R.S.C.* 77-83.
Duckworth, H. E.
'University Research and Governments,' *Trans. R.S.C.* 43-52.
Gaudry, R.
'Les Relations entre la recherche universitaire et l'industrie,' *Trans. R.S.C.* 53-64.
Guindon, R.
'L'Université et la recherche,' *Trans. R.S.C.* 65-71.
Mattaisson, J. S.
'My Discipline is Better than Your Discipline: Some Barriers to Interdisciplinary Research,' *Can. Rev. Soc. Anthrop.* V, 263-75.
Medical Research Council of Canada.
Canadian Medical Research: Survey and Outlook. (M.R.C. Report no. 2.) Ottawa: Queen's Printer. Pp. 416.
Mordell, D. L.
'Basic Changes Needed in Research Policy,' *Can. Bus.* XLI (4), 48-54.
'The New I.R.I.'s: University Help for the Small Firm,' [I.R.I.: Industrial Research Institute] *Can. R. and D.* I (1), 34-35, 60.

1969 **Law, C.**
'More Support Urged for University Research,' *Can. Univ. & Coll.*
IV (5), 41-44, 61-62.
Macdonald, J. B.
'The Macdonald Report: the Federal Role in University Research,'
Science Forum II (3), 3-6. See also L.-P. Dugal, 'The Minority Report:
Too Little Attention to Quebec's Problems,' 6-7; H. G. Thode, 'A
Courageous Report Which Will Spark Both Discussion and Dissent,'
8-12; J. Brazeau, 'A Social Scientist's View: Much Useful Information
but Too Radical Advice.'
Macdonald, J. B. *et al.*
*The Role of the Federal Government in Support of Research in
Canadian Universities.* Special Study no. 7 of the Science Council
of Canada. Ottawa: Queen's Printer. Pp. 361.
'The Macdonald Report – Science Gets a Challenge,' *Can. R. and D.*
II (3), 31-36.
McCarter, J. H.
'Why Not Nationalize the Universities? A Researcher's View,'
Sci. Forum II (1), 21-23.
Ross, V.
'Les Instituts de recherche,' *Rev. Univ. Moncton* II, 43-44.
Vogt, E. N.
'The Macdonald Report – Federal Research in the Universities,'
Physics in Canada XXV, 61-63.

1970 **Grove, J. W.**
'The Place of Universities in Supporting Scientific Research in
Canada' in *Studies on the University, Society and Government ...*
(Ottawa: Univ. of Ottawa Press. 2 vols.), II, 137-80.
Halpenny, F. G.
'Of Time and the Editor,' *Scholarly Publishing* I, 159-69.
Jeanneret, M.
'Information Retrieval and the Decision to Publish,' *Scholarly
Publishing* I, 229-43.
McCausland, I.
'Research vs. Teaching: New Insights into an Old Problem,'
Sci. Forum III (1), 17-19.
Spencer, E. Y.
'Relations between Universities and Government-Supported Research
Institutes and Organizations' in *Studies on the University, Society
and Government ...* (Ottawa: Univ. of Ottawa Press. 2 vols.), II, 227-78.

B. HISTORICAL DEVELOPMENT : DÉVELOPPEMENT HISTORIQUE

1923 **Adams, F. H.**
'Industrial Research in Canada,' *Annals of American Academy of Political and Social Science* CVII (May 1923), 115-19.
Hopkins, E. S.
'Agricultural Research in Canada: Its Origin and Development,' *Annals of American Academy of Political and Social Science* CVII (May 1923), 82-87.

1929 **Coats, R. H.**
'The Place of Statistics in National Administration – Function and Organization of Statistics – Scope and Method of the Dominion Bureau of Statistics,' *Trans. R.S.C.* sect. II, 81-93.

1939 **Boyle, R. W.**
'Promotion of Research within the University and Interuniversity Cooperation,' *National Conference of Canadian Universities Proceedings* 79-93.

1942 **Bazett, H. C.**
'The Contributions of Canadian Scientists to Aviation Medicine,' *Proc. N.C.C.U.C.* 24-40.

1958 **Hart, J. L.**
Biological Station, St. Andrews, N.B.: 1908-1958. Ottawa: Fisheries Research Board of Canada. Pp. 35.
Rigby, M. S. and A. G. Huntsman.
'Materials Relating to the History of the Fisheries Research Board of Canada (formerly the Biological Board of Canada) for the Period 1898-1924.' Ottawa: Fisheries Research Board of Canada. Pp. 272. Mimeo.

1963 **Falardeau, J.-C.**
'Le Sens de l'oeuvre sociologique de Léon Gérin,' *Recherches Soc.* IV, 265-89.

1965 **Hachey, H. B.**
'History of the Fisheries Research Board of Canada.' Manuscript Report Series (Biological). No. 843. Ottawa: Fisheries Research Board of Canada. Pp. 499. Typescript.

1966 **Thistle, M.**
The Inner Ring: The Early History of the National Research Council of Canada. Toronto: U. of T. Press. Pp. 435.

1966 **Wiggins, G. B., ed.**
Centennial of Entomology in Canada 1863-1963: A Tribute to Edmund M. Walker. Toronto: U. of T. Press. Pp. 94.
1967 **Brown, J. A.**
Ideas in Exile. Toronto: McClelland & Stewart. Pp. 372.
Gingras, B. A. and T. W. West.
'National Research Council of Canada: Fifty Years of Scholarships,' *Eng. Jour.* L (11), 15-18.

C. IN THE SCIENCES : SCIENCES

1963 **Spinks, J. W. T.**
'Development of Basic Research in Radiation Chemistry at the University of Saskatchewan,' *Can. Nuclear Tech.* II (1), 31-39.
1964 **Anderson, D. V.**
Geophysical Research on the Great Lakes. Toronto: Ontario Dept. of Lands and Forests. Pp. 39.
Gill, J. E.
'Research in the Geological Sciences,' *Trans. R.S.C.* sect. III, 197-204.
Mackenzie, C. J.
Report to Prime Minister on Government Science. Ottawa: Queen's Printer. Pp. 36.
Symposium on 'Organization and Support of Basic Scientific Research in Canada,' *Trans. R.S.C. 1964* includes:
J. W. T. Spinks, 'The National Research Council Forecast for Support Needed for Basic Research in Canadian Universities,' 327-38;
H. G. Thode, 'Basic Scientific Research – Its Importance and Support,' 339-48; F. R. Hayes, 'Co-operation Between Universities and Government,' 349-54; C. M. Drury, 'A Partnership in Science Between Government, Industry and the Universities,' 355-61.
1965 **Babbitt, J. D., ed.**
Science in Canada: Selections from the Speeches of E. W. R. Steacie. Toronto: U. of T. Press. Pp. 198.
Baxter, S. D.
'Computers and the National Research Council,' *Trans. R.S.C.* sect. III, 301-16.
1966 **Bonn, G. S.**
Science-Technology Literature Resources in Canada: Report of a Survey for the Associate Committee on Scientific Information. Ottawa: National Research Council. Pp. 80.

1966 Savile, D. B. O.
'Unity for Diversity in Biological Research,' *Trans. R.S.C.* sect. IV, 245-51.
1967 Dugal, L.-P.
'La Valeur culturelle de la recherche scientifique (surtout de la recherche désinteressée),' *Univ. Affairs* IX (1), 12-13.
Rigaud, M.
'L'Université et la recherche scientifique dans le monde d'aujourd'hui,' *Ing.* LIII (219), 31-33.
1968 Gaudry, R.
'Les Problèmes de la recherche universitaire en sciences naturelles,' *A.U.C.C. Proc. 1967* II, 98-100.
Gaudry, R.
'Les Relations entre la recherche universitaire et l'industrie,' *Trans. R.S.C.* 53-64.
Lapointe, M.
'Subventions du Conseil Naturale de Recherches 1964-1965, 1965-66, 1966-67,' *C.A.U.T. Bull.* XVI (4), 39-69.
Macdonald, J. B.
'Science Education: Backdrop for Discovery,' *Jour. Dental Research* [U.S.] XLVII, 855-59.
McTaggart-Cowan, I.
'Problems of Research in the Natural Sciences,' *A.U.C.C. Proc. 1967* II, 101-04.
1969 Barker, B.
'A Plan to Keep Canada's Scientists at Home,' *Can. R. and D.* II (6), 26-28.
Hannell, F. G.
'Research in Urban Climate at McMaster University,' *Climatology Bull.* no. 5, 51-53.
1970 Doern, G. B.
'"Big Science" and the Relations between Governments and Universities in Canada: The Case of "ING" and Nuclear Physics' in *Studies on the University, Society and Government ...* (Ottawa: Univ. of Ottawa Press. 2 vols.), II, 181-226.
Trainor, L.
'Science in Canada – American Style' in I. Lumsden, ed., *Close the 49th Parallel etc.: The Americanization of Canada* (Toronto: U. of T. Press), 241-56.

D. IN THE HUMANITIES AND SOCIAL SCIENCES :
HUMANITÉS ET LES SCIENCES SOCIALES

1961 **Harris, R. F.**
'Prospects for Business Research in Canadian Universities,'
Proc. Schools Bus. 103-07.

1964 **Lebel, M.**
'Bibliographie des mémoires relatifs à l'antiquité,' *Culture* xxv, 213-22.
Sydiaha, D.
'Academia and Social Change,' *Can. Dimension* I (7), 14-15.

1965 **Binhammer, H. H. and M. Booth.**
'Research Assistance in the Humanities and Social Sciences,'
C.A.U.T. Bull. xiii (2), 23-26.
Klink, C. F. ed.
Literary History of Canada: Canadian Literature in English (Toronto: U. of T. Press), includes:
K. N. Windsor, 'Historical Writing in Canada [to 1920],' 208-50;
J. A. Irving, 'Philosophical Writings (to 1910),' 431-44; W. M. Kilbourn, 'The Writing of Canadian History [since 1920],' 495-518; J. A. Irving, 'The Achievement of G. S. Brett,' 576-85; A. H. Johnson, 'Other Philosophers,' 586-97; M. Maclure, 'Literary Scholarship,' 529-50;
J. S. Thomson, 'Religion and Theological Scholarship,' 551-95.

1966 **Johnson, H. G.**
'The Social Sciences in the Age of Opulence,' *Can. Jour. Econ. Pol. Sci.* xxxii, 423-42.
Tremblay, L.-M.
'La Recherche en relations industrielles dans les universités canadiennes depuis 1960,' *Relations Ind.* xxi, 485-507.
Trudel, M.
'Des Sujets de recherche pour un siècle ou deux ...' *Rev. Hist.* xx, 228-35.

1967 **Garigue, P.**
'Les Problèmes de la recherche en sciences sociales dans le universités francophones du Québec,' *ACFAS* xxxiv, 207 (Resumé).
Lamb, W. K.
'Seventy-Five Years of Canadian Bibliography,' *Trans. R.S.C.* sect. ii, 1-11.
Mackey, W.
'The International Center for Research on Bilingualism,' *Univ. Affairs* viii (4), 1-3.

1967 **Slater, D.**
'Economic Policy and Economic Research in Canada since 1950,' *Queen's Q.* LXXIV, 1-20.

1968 **Hubbard, R. H., ed.**
Scholarship in Canada, 1967: Achievement and Outlook. Toronto: U. of T. Press. Pp. 104.
Lapointe, M.
'Conseil des Arts du Canada: Humanities et Sciences Sociales 1966-67,' *C.A.U.T. Bull.* XVI (4), 29-38.
Menard, J., ed.
Recherche et littérature canadienne-français. Ottawa: Presses Univ. d'Ottawa. Pp. 297.
Oliver, M.
'Research in the Social Sciences,' *A.U.C.C. Proc. 1967* II, 113-22.
Pacey, D.
'Research in the Humanities,' *A.U.C.C. Proc. 1967* II, 133-50.
Smith, A. J. R.
'The Social Sciences and the "Economics of Research,"' *Trans. R.S.C.* 21-33.
Timlin, M. F. and A. Faucher.
The Social Sciences in Canada: Two Studies/Les Sciences sociales au Canada: deux études. Ottawa: Social Sciences Research Council. Pp. 136.

1969 **Lemieux, V.**
'L'Etat de la recherche politique au Canada français,' *ACFAS* XXXVI, 129.
Schindeler, F. and C. M. Lanphier.
'Social Science Research and Participatory Democracy in Canada,' *Can. Public Admin.* XII, 481-98.
Silvers, R. J.
'In Defense of Socially Irrelevant Scientifically Significant Research,' *Can. Rev. Soc. Anthrop.* VI (1), 58-61.
Stanford, L.
'Ivory to Replace Brass?' *Can. Public Admin.* XII, 566-71.
Willson, J. D.
'Alberta's Human Resources Research Council,' *Ed. Canada* IX (3), 18-22.

E. IN EDUCATION : ENSEIGNEMENT

1962 **Coutts, H. T. and D. B. Black.**
'The Carnegie – University of Alberta Joint Project on Educational Research: A Report after Five Years,' *Alta. Jour. Ed. Res.* VIII (3), 133-46.

1963 **Brehaut, W.**
'Educational Research in Canada, 1959-1961,' *Can. Ed. Research Digest* III, 128-31.
Robinson, F. G.
'Research and Educational Decision-Making,' *Ont. Jour. Ed. Res.* VI, 155-63.
Rocher, G.
'La Sociologie de l'éducation dans l'oeuvre de Léon Gérin,' *Recherches Soc.* IV, 291-312.

1964 **Council for Research in Education.**
Proceedings of the Third Canadian Conference on Educational Research held at MacDonald College, Ste.-Anne-de-Bellevue, June 3-5, 1964. Ottawa: The Council. Pp. 276.
Macdonald, J.
A Feasibility Study Conducted for the Canadian Council for Research in Education. Ottawa: Canadian Council for Research in Education. Pp. 30.
Moffatt, H. P.
'The Role of the Canadian Council for Research in Education,' *Ont. Jour. Ed. Res.* VI, 119-28.
Robinson, F. G. and E. Haltrecht.
'Staff Research in Canadian Degree-Granting Universities and Colleges.' (Status of Education Research in Canada, Preliminary Paper no. 1.) Ottawa: Canadian Council for Research in Education. Pp. 54. Mimeo.

1965 **Davis, W. G.**
'The Ontario Institute for Studies in Education' in *Education in Ontario* (Toronto: Ontario Dept. of Education), 31-36.
Fleming, W. G.
'A Milestone in Educational Research: the Ontario Institute for Studies in Education,' *Man. Jour. Ed. Res.* I (1), 14-19.
Garstin, L. G.
'What's Wrong with Educational Research?' *B.C. Teacher* XLV (Sept.), 14-15.

1965 Jackson, R. W. B.
'The Ontario Institute for Studies in Education,' *Ont. Jour. Ed. Res.* VIII, 173-81.
Le Sieur, A.
'Administration de la recherche pédagogique dans les universités de l'ouest canadien,' *Can. Ed. Research Digest* V, 233-47.
Robinson, F. G.
'Educational Research in Canada - A New Frame of Reference,' *Man. Jour. Ed. Res.* I (1), 5-13.
Robinson, F. G.
Educational Research - a Parent's Concern. Ottawa: Canadian Council for Research in Education. Pp. 32.
Whitworth, F. E.
'A Hard Look at Research in Education,' *Can. Ed. Research Digest* V, 219-32.

1966 Fleming, W. G.
'The Ontario Institute for Studies in Education - A Serious Canadian Investment in the Scientific Study of Education,' *Can. Ed. Research Digest* VII, 18-25.
Hutchison, H.
'Research in Education - Characteristics and Directions,' *Man. Jour. Ed. Res.* II (1), 61-71.
Webster, D. A.
Can Research in Education at the Master's Level be More than an Academic Exercise? Ottawa: Canadian Council for Research in Education. Pp. 6.

1967 Buchanan, B. H.
'Cybernetics and Educational Research,' *Ont. Jour. Ed. Res.* X, 73-82.
Card, B. Y.
Possibilities and Problems of Research Collaboration by Educators and Sociologists in Canada. Ottawa: Canadian Council for Research in Education. Pp. 9.
Katz, M.
'In Defense of OISE,' *This Magazine* I (4), 63-67. See also 68.
Stager, D. A.
'OISE: The New Look in Educational Research,' *Can. Forum* XLVI, 268-69.
Whitworth, F. E. and R. Marineau.
Publication of Educational Research in Canada: a Survey/La Publication de la recherche ... Ottawa: Canadian Council for Research in Education. Pp. 24.

1968 **Edwards, R.**
'Educational Research and the Training of Researchers in Canada,'
Can. Ed. Research Digest VII, 307-27.
Fleming, W. G.
'No Isolation for Research and Development Organizations,'
Can. Ed. Research Digest VII, 133-40.
Whitworth, F. E.
On Organizing R & D in Education. Ottawa: Canadian Council for Research in Education. Pp. 136.

1969 **Brehaut, W.**
'Trends in Education Theses in Canada: 1962-67,' *Ed. Canada* IX (2), 33-36.
Desjardins, L.
'L'Enseignement et la recherche en docimologie,' *ACFAS* XXVI, 101-02.
Katz, J.
'Canadian Educational Research Follows instead of Leads,' *Ed. Canada* IX (1), 3-9.
Ontario Institute for Studies in Education.
OISE: the First Phase; Some Programs and Projects in the First Stage of Organization. Toronto: The Institute. Pp. 8.

1970 **Chase, F. S.**
'Some Thoughts on Educational Research and Development,' *Orbit* I (2), 20-21.
Knell, W. D.
'Information Storage and Retrieval for Educational Research: A Progress Report,' *Alta. Jour. Ed. Res.* XVI (1), 23-27.

F. LIBRARIES : BIBLIOTHEQUES

1877 **Turcotte, L. P.**
'Les Archives du Canada,' *Annuaire de l'Institut Canadien de Québec* no. 4, 151-63.

1898 **Bain, J.**
'Public Libraries in Canada,' *Proc. Royal Institute of Canada* 95-101.
Gould, C. H.
'Description of Important Libraries in Montreal with Remarks upon Departmental Libraries,' in *Transactions and Proceedings of the 2nd International Library Conference* (London, July 13-16, 1897), 154-57.

1908 **Burpee, L. J.**
'Canadian Libraries of Long Ago,' *American Library Association Bull.* II, 136-43.

1916 **Fauteux, A.**
Les Bibliothèques canadiennes, étude historique. Montréal. Pp. 45.

1927 **Van Pratten, N.**
'College and University Libraries of Ontario,' *Library Jour.* [U.S.] LII, 457-61.

1940 **Drolet, A.**
'Le Bibliothèque du Séminaire de Québec et son catalogue de 1782,' *Canada Français* XXVIII, 261-66.

1942 **Lomer, G. R.**
'The Redpath Library: Half a Century, 1892-1942,' *McGill News* XXIV, 9-13.

1947 **Massicotte, E.-Z.**
'Bibliothèques d'autrefois à Montréal,' *Cah. Dix.* XII, 9-16.
Pearce, C. A.
'The Development of Special Libraries in Montreal and Toronto.' Unpublished M.L.S. thesis, Univ. of Illinois.

1950 **Redmond, D. A.**
'Some College Libraries of Canada's Maritime Provinces: Selected Aspects.' Unpublished M.L.S. thesis, Univ. of Illinois. (Abridgement published in *College and Research Libraries* [U.S.] XI, 355-62, Oct. 1950.)

1952 **Drolet, A.**
'La Bibliothèque de l'Université Laval,' *Rev. Univ. Laval* VII, 34-41.

1954 **Redmond, D. A.**
'Curriculum and Library in our Colleges,' *Atlan. Prov. Lib. Bull.* XIX, 5-7.

1955 **Drolet, A.**
'Les Ouvrages scientifiques dans la bibliothèque du Collège de Québec, 1635-1799,' *Nat. Can.* LXXII, 102-07.
Redmond, D. A.
'Engineering Students and Their College Libraries,' *Atlan. Prov. Lib. Bull.* XX, 6-8.

1961 **Drolet, A.**
'La Bibliothèque du Collège des Jésuites: essai de reconstruction,' *Rev. Hist.* XIV, 487-544.

1962 **Benjamin, M.**
'The McGill Medical Librarians 1829-1929,' *Bull. Medical Library Assoc.* [U.S.] L, 1-16.

1962 **Drolet, A.**
'La Bibliothèque de l'Université Laval,' *Rev. Univ. Laval* VII, 34-41.
Williams, E. E.
Resources of Canadian Libraries for Research in the Humanities and Social Sciences. Ottawa: Assoc. of Univs. and Colleges. Pp. 87.

1963 **Gifford, H.**
'The MacOdrum Library of Carleton University,' *College and Research Libraries* [U.S.] XXIV, 43-46.

1964 **Giles, L. G. and P. Medland.**
'Hospital Medical Libraries,' *Can. Hosp.* XLI (3), 57-58.
Jutras, J.-G.
'Bibliothèques scolaires,' *Rev. Scolaire* XIV, 309-12.
Simon, B. V.
Library Support of Medical Education in Canada: Report of the Medical College Libraries of Canada ... Ottawa: Assoc. of Medical Colleges. Pp. 132.

1965 **Beckman, M.**
'Size and Library Research Collections,' *Atlan. Prov. Lib. Bull.* XXIX, 143-49.
Bissell, C. T.
'Libraries in the Life of the Nation,' *Can. Library* XXII, 78-83.
Bregzis, R.
'Ontario New Universities Library Project: an Automated Bibliographic Data Control System,' *College and Research Libraries* [U.S.] XXVI, 495-508.
Canadian Association of College and University Libraries.
Guide to Canadian University Library Standards: Report of the University Library Standards Committee. Ottawa: The Association. Pp. 53.
Carrier, L. J.
'Are University Reserve Collections Justified?' *Atlan. Prov. Lib. Bull.* XXX, 85-88, 99-103.
Desrochers, E.
'Aurons-nous d'authentiques bibliothèques universitaires?' *Relations* no. 298, 295-96.
Drolet, A.
Les Bibliotheques Canadiennes 1604-1960. Ottawa: Cercle du Livre de France. Pp. 234.
Gattinger, F. E.
'Reclassification - Are You Converted Yet?' *Atlan. Prov. Lib. Bull.* XXIX, 16-19, 21-22.

1965 **Gattinger, F. E.**
'Reclassification in Canadian Academic Libraries,' *Atlan. Prov. Lib. Bull.* XXIX, 62-68.
Hussain, M. R.
'Photocopying in Atlantic Provinces University Libraries,' *Atlan. Prov. Lib. Bull.* XXIX, 91-98.
St. John, F. R. *et al.*
Ontario Libraries: A Province-wide Survey and Plan. Toronto: Ontario Library Association. Pp. 182.
Sherwood, B.
'The University Librarian – Complacent or Dynamic?' *Ont. Lib. Rev.* XLIX, 176-78.
Williams, M.
'Reclassification Program at Memorial University of Newfoundland,' *Atlan. Prov. Lib. Bull.* XXIX, 99-104.

1966 **Blackburn, R. H.**
'Planning Academic Libraries,' *R. Arch. Inst. Can. Jour.* XLIII (2), 33-34.
Bonn, G. S.
Science-Technology Literature Resources in Canada; Report of a Survey for the Associate Committee on Scientific Information. Ottawa: National Research Council. Pp. 80.
Bregzis, R.
'The Library – From Books to Information,' *R. Arch. Inst. Can. Jour.* XLIII (2), 37-40.
Ellsworth, R. E.
'Elements in Planning a Library Building Program,' *R. Arch. Inst. Can. Jour.* XLIII (2), 25-28.
Hailand, S.
'The Canadian University Library,' *R. Arch. Inst. Can. Jour.* XLIII (2), 29-31.
Hall, M. M.
'Theoretical Considerations of Selection Policy for University Libraries,' *Can. Library* XXIII (Sept.), 89-98.
'Money Alone Won't Cure Library Ills,' *Can. Univ.* I (3), 17-20.
Peel, B.
'Problems of Canadian Academic Libraries,' *C.A.U.T. Bull.* XIV (4), 7-14.
Wilkinson, J. P.
'A History of the Dalhousie University Main Library, 1867-1931.' Unpublished doct. dissertation, Univ. of Chicago.

1967 **Downs, R. B.**
Resources of Canadian Academic and Research Libraries. Ottawa: Association of Universities and Colleges of Canada. Pp. 301.
Glazier, K. M.
'United States Influence on Canadian Universities and Their Libraries,' *College and Research Libraries* [U.S.] XXVIII, 311-16.
Griffin, M.
'Automation in Libraries: A Projection,' *Can. Library* XXIII, 360-67.
Hanlon, P.
'Needed: Student Key to Library Resources,' *Can. Library* XXIII, 270-71.
Kippen, M. R. L.
'University Librarians' Attitudes toward Librarianship.' Unpublished M.Ed. thesis, Univ. of Saskatchewan.
Ng, T. K.
'The Birth and Growth of an East Asian Vernacular Library: Being the Asian Studies Division of the University of British Columbia Library,' *Canadian Library Association Occasional Paper* LIII, 1-5.
Ridge, A. D.
'The McGill University Archives,' *Archives* [U.K.] VIII (37), 16-23.
'Tomorrow's Libraries: You Won't Recognize Them,' *Can. Univ.* II (6), 27-35.

1968 **Brault, J. R.**
'La Bibliothèque du CEGEP,' *Bull. Bibl.* XIV (March), 16-21.
Cartwright, M. J.
'Survey of the History of Academic Libraries in Canada,' *Can. Library* XXV, 98-102.
Dawson, B.
'Can the Academic Library Do More to Help Students Who Feel They are Being "Cooled Out?"' *Sask. Lib.* XXII (1), 10-33.
Ettlinger, J. R. T.
'Through a Glass Darkly – Academic Book Selection in Crisis,' *Atlan. Prov. Lib. Bull.* XXXII, 32-40.
Henderson, G. F.
'The Royal Commission Collection at Queen's University Library,' *Douglas Library Notes* XVI (3), 20-23.
'The Impact of Technology on the Library Building,' *Can. Arch.* XIII (7), 29-34.
James, J. V.
'Faculty Status for Librarians,' *Sask. Lib.* XXI (2), 27-34.

1968 **Lamb, W. K.**
'Present Holdings [of Canadian University Libraries] and Future Developments' in R. H. Hubbard, ed., *Scholarship in Canada, 1967* (Toronto: U. of T. Press), 3-10.
McIntyre, H. C.
'The Downs Report: $300 Million Urged for University Libraries,' *Can. Univ.* III (3), 58-59.
Ontario Council of University Librarians.
Inter-University Transit System Anniversary Report. Toronto: Committee of Presidents of Universities of Ontario. Pp. 20.
Parker, M. L.
'Photocopying in University Libraries and the Canadian Laws of Copyright,' *Atlan. Prov. Lib. Bull.* XXXII, 41-50.
Raymond, B. and D. Francis.
'Is This Trip Really Necessary?' *Can. Library* XXV, 35-37.
Warner, R. M.
'The Status of College and University Archives,' *American Archivist* XXXI (3), 235-37.

1969 **Astbury, E. C.**
'Library Technicians and the Reference Service,' *Can. Library Jour.* XXVI, 54-57.
Bjorgo, M.
'Technicians in Reference Service – Another View,' *Can. Library Jour.* XXVI, 58-60.
Blackburn, R. H. and R. B. Downs.
Financial Implications of the Downs Report on Canadian Academic and Research Libraries/Répurcussions financières ... Ottawa: Association of Universities and Colleges of Canada. Pp. 42.
Campbell, H.
Canadian Libraries. Toronto: McClelland & Stewart. Pp. 90.
Francis, D. and B. Raymond.
'University Librarians: Shepherds of Books or Disseminators of Information?' *Can. Library Jour.* XXVI, 144-47.
Kikauka, T.
'Halls of Silence,' *Can. Univ. & Coll.* IV (4), 45-47.
Morley, W. F. E. and V. E. Empery.
'Survey of Canadian Library Rare-Book Departments and Special Collections,' *Can. Library Jour.* XXVI, 109-25.
O'Connell, T. F.
'The Creation of a Canadian Research Library,' *Can. Library Jour.* XXVI, 132-35.

1969 **Piekarski, H.**
'Acquisition of Out-of-Print Books for a University Library,'
Can. Library Jour. XXVI, 346-52.
Ready, W.
'Bibliocentre: an Essay in Central Processing at College Level,'
College and Research Libraries [U.S.] XXXI (1), 50-54.
Ready, W.
'The C.A.T.T.S. Bibliocentre: Personal Beginnings,' *Inst. Prof. Lib. Ont. Newsletter* X, 115-19.
Ready, W.
'McMaster's Acquisition of the Russell Papers,' *Can. Library Jour.* XXVI, 136-39.
Riddell, W. A.
'Library Development in the Prairie Universities,' *Lib. Assoc. Alta. Bull.* I (2), 3-9.
Stokes, R. B.
'The Library's Role in the Academic Community,' *B.C. Lib. Q.* XXXIII (1), 11-22.
Thomson, J.
'Cataloguing of Large Works on Microfilm in Canadian University Libraries,' *Can. Library Jour.* XXVII, 446-52.
Vagianos, L.
'New Look for Library Cooperation in Nova Scotia,' *Can. Univ.* IV (1), 21-23.
White, D.
'Academic Status: Right or Rite?' *Can. Library Jour.* XXVI, 287-89.

1970 **Bignell, D. C.**
'Do We Need a Reserve Book Collection?' *Sask. Lib.* XXIII (2), 2-22.
Burgis, G. C.
'The Contemporary University Library Learning Resource Technology and Techniques,' *Can. Library Jour.* XXVII (1), 24-28.
Hotimsky, C. M.
'Slavic Studies and Libraries,' *Can. Library Jour.* XXVII (2), 119-23.
Law, H.
'Library Automation: Things are Humming in the Halls of Silence,' *Can. Univ. & Coll.* V (1), 15-17.
McLennan, D.
'The McMaster University Rare Maps Collection,' *McMaster Lib. News* I (4), 1-17.
O'Connell, T. F.
'Undergraduate Library?' *Can. Library Jour.* XXVII, 278-82.

1970 'Standardization in Canadian University Libraries – an Approach and a Prospect,' *Atlan. Prov. Lib. Bull.* XXXIV (1), 6-14.

G. MUSEUMS AND ART GALLERIES : GALERIES D'ART ET LES MUSEES

1903 **Merrill, F. J. H.**
'Natural History Museums of the United States and Canada,' *New York State Museum Bull.* 62. Albany: Univ. of the State of New York. Pp. 333.

1933 **Falconer, R.**
'The Royal Ontario Museum and other Museums in Canada,' *Univ. Tor. Q.* II, 168-85.
Miers, H. A. and S. F. Markham.
Directory of Museums and Art Galleries in Canada, Newfoundland, Bermuda, the British West Indies, British Guiana. London: Museums Assoc. Pp. 92.

1948 **Edgar, P.**
'The Royal Ontario Museum,' *Univ. Tor. Q.* XVII, 168-78.

1956 **Currelly, C. T.**
I Brought the Ages Home. [Royal Ontario Museum.] Toronto: Ryerson. Pp. 312.

1964 **Brown, F. M.**
Breaking Barriers: Eric Brown and the National Gallery. Toronto: Society for Art Publications. Pp. 113.
Dow, H. J.
'Mount Allison's Owens Museum: a Look at 19th Century Values,' *Can. Art* XXI (2), 76-79.

1965 **Hubbard, R. H.**
'The Early Years of the National Gallery of Canada,' *Trans. R.S.C.* sect. 2, 121-30.

1966 **Heinrich, T. A.**
'The National Gallery and Education,' *Can. Art* XXIII (2), 16-19.
Pare, J.
'Un Musée qui n'est plus provincial,' *Mag. Maclean* VI (5), 23-26, 42, 44.

1970 **Boggs, J. S.**
'The National Gallery,' *Arts Can.* XXVI (1), 3-7.

H. LEARNED AND PROFESSIONAL SOCIETIES : SOCIETES SAVANTES ET PROFESSIONNELLES

1874 **Turcotte, L. P.**
'L'Institut Canadien de Québec,' *Annuaire de l'Institut* ... no. 1, 5-20.

1885 **Harper, J. M.**
'The Annals of an Old Society [Lit. & Hist. Soc. of Quebec],' *Trans. R.S.C.* sect. 11, 55-65.

1924 **Quebec Literary and Historical Society.**
The Centenary Volume, 1824-1924. Quebec: L'Evénement. Pp. 196.

1929 **Lattimer, J. E.**
'Organization of the Canadian Society of Agricultural Economics' in *Contributions to Canadian Economics* II (Toronto: U. of T. Press), 11-13.
MacGibbon, D. A.
'The Meeting of Canadian Economists at Ottawa' in *Contributions to Canadian Economics* II (Toronto: U. of T. Press), 7-10. [The meetings of May 22-23, 1929, which led to the revival of the Can. Political Science Assoc.]

1930 **Ferguson, J.**
History of the Ontario Medical Association 1880-1930. Toronto: Murray. Pp. 142.

1932 **Burpee, L. J.**
'Introduction' to *Royal Society of Canada Fifty Year Retrospect, Canada 1882-1932* (Toronto: Ryerson), 1-8. See also R. Falconer, 'The Intellectual Life of Canada as Reflected in Its Royal Society,' 8-25.

1935 **MacDermot, H. E.**
History of the Canadian Medical Association 1867-1921. Toronto: Murray. Pp. 209.

1936 **Morin, V.**
'Les Dix,' *Cah. Dix.* I, 7-36. Describes origins and objectives of Les Dix at Montreal 1935. Also refers to Le Club des Dix constituted at Ottawa in 1882 (A. DeCelles, B. Sulte *et al.*) and Le Cercle des Dix constituted at Quebec in 1893 (J.-M. Le Moine, J.-E. Roy, Faucher de Saint-Maurice *et al.*).

1937 **Morin, V.**
'Les Origines de la Société Royale,' *Cah. Dix* II, 157-98.

1938 **Hudon, T.**
L'Institut canadien de Montréal et l'Affaire Guibord. Montréal: Librairie Beauchemin. Pp. 172.

1943 **Morin, V.**
'L'Odyssée d'une société historique,' [Société Historique de Montréal] *Cah. Dix* VIII, 13-54.
1947 **Bruchesi, J.**
'L'Institut Canadien de Québec,' *Cah. Dix* XII, 93-144.
Lesage, A.
Le College de Médecins de Québec, 1847-1947. Montreal: Pp. 87.
1948 **Morin, V.**
'Clubs et Sociétés notoires d'autrefois,' *Cah. Dix* XIII, 109-38.
1949 **Desilets, A.**
Les Cent ans de l'Institut Canadien. Québec: L'Institut. Pp. 252.
Wallace, W. S.
'A Sketch of the History of the Royal Canadian Institute, 1849-1949' in *Royal Canadian Institute Centennial Volume* (Toronto: The Institute), 123-67.
Warrington, C. J. S. and R. V. V. Nicholls.
'Chemical Institutions and Journals' in *A History of Chemistry in Canada* (Toronto: Chemical Institute of Canada), 393-408.
1950 **Bancroft, L. I.**
'The Literary and Historical Society of Quebec; an Historical Outline from the Sociological Point of View.' Thèse de license, Univ. Laval.
1952 **Guillett, D. W.**
'Notes on the Development of the Canadian Dental Association,' *Can. Dent. Assoc. Jour.* XVIII, 303-07.
1953 **Colgate, W.**
'The Toronto Art Students' League, 1896-1904,' *Ont. Hist.* LXV, 1-26. [Includes reference to Toronto Society of Artists (1847) and Royal Canadian Academy of Arts (1882).]
1955 **Dandurand, M.**
'Les Premières difficultés entre Mgr. Bourget et l'Institut Canadien de Montréal (1844-1865),' *Rev. Univ. Ottawa* XXV, 145-65, 273-307.
1957 **Bray, M.**
'The History of the Canadian Association for Health, Physical Education and Recreation.' Unpublished M.A. thesis, Univ. of Oregon.
Camu, P.
'La Quatre-Vingtième anniversaire de la Société de Géographie de Québec,' *Cah. Géog.* III, 135-41.
Frewin, M.
'A History of the Canadian Pharmaceutical Association, Inc., 1907-57,' *Can. Pharm. Jour.* XC, 588-602.

1960 Guillet, E. C.
In the Cause of Education: Centennial History of the Ontario Education Association 1861-1960. Toronto: U. of T. Press. Pp. 472.

1961 Hamelin, L.-E.
'Une Association canadienne des géographes ou plusieurs groupements de géographes au Canada?' *Cah. Géog.* v, 289-92.
Pouliot, L.
'L'Institut Canadien de Montréal et l'Institut National,' *Rev. Hist.* xiv, 481-86.

1962 Lewis, D. S.
The Royal College of Physicians and Surgeons of Canada 1920-1960. Montreal: McGill Univ. Press. Pp. 291.
Paton, J. M.
The Role of Teachers' Organizations in Canadian Education. Toronto: Gage. Pp. 89.

1963 Rodwell, L.
'The Saskatchewan Association of Music Festivals,' *Sask. Hist.* xvi, 1-21.

1964 Carrière, G.
'Nos Archives et la Société Canadienne d'Histoire de l'Eglise Catholique,' *Rev. Univ. Ottawa* xxxiv, 73-96.
Community Planning Review (Revue Canadienne d'Urbanisme) xiv (2), devoted to 'History of cpac [Community Planning Association of Canada].'

1965 **Canadian Cultural Information Centre.**
Some Canadian Cultural Organizations. Ottawa: Le Droit. Pp. 72.
Myers, C. R.
'Notes on the History of Psychology in Canada,' *Can. Psych.* via, 4-19. [re: Canadian Psychological Association.]

1966 Gagnon, J.-A.
'La Société canadienne d'Orientation et de Consultation,' *Orient. Prof.* ii, 210-13.

1967 Keeping, E. S.
Twenty-One Years of the Canadian Mathematical Congress 1945-1966. Montreal: Can. Mathematical Congress. Pp. 22.
Kenyon, R.
The Ontario Dental Association: a Profile, The First One Hundred Years. Toronto: Ontario Dental Assoc. Pp. 32.
Kirkconnell, W.
'Organizing the Humanities [especially Humanities Research Council of Canada]' in *A Slice of Canada: Memories* (Toronto: U. of T. Press), 233-48.

1967 **McAllister, J.**
'History of C. Ph. A. Affiliated Organizations and other Related Pharmacy Groups,' *Can. Jour. Pharm.* C, 506-16.
McAllister, J.
'The 60-year History of the Canadian Pharmaceutical Association,' *Can. Pharm. Jour.* C, 237-79. See also A. V. Raison, 'Profiles of Founding Fathers of C.P.A.,' 280-84.
Northcott, R. J.
'The Growth of the R.A.S.C. and Its Guiding Mentor, C. A. Chant,' *R. Astron. Soc. Jour.* LXI, 218-25.
Taylor, K. W.
'The Founding of the Canadian Political Science Association,' *Can. Jour. Econ. Pol. Sci.* XXXIII, 581-85.
Woycenko, O.
'Learned Societies' in *The Ukrainians in Canada* (Winnipeg: Canada Ethnic Press Federation), 149-51.

1968 **Desrochers, E.**
'The Canadian Association of Library Schools,' *Can. Library* XXIV, 518-19.
Gill, M. S.
'C.L.C. to C.L.A.' in B. Peel, ed., *Librarianship in Canada, 1946-1967* (Victoria, B.C.: Can. Library Assoc.), 11-19. Also F. S. Waldon, 'The C.L.A. – The First Twenty Years,' *ibid.*, 22-37.
MacMillan, K.
'National Organizations' in A. Walter, ed., *Aspects of Music in Canada* (Toronto: U. of T. Press), 288-318.
'Proceedings of the First Annual Meeting of the Canadian Institute of ONAMASTIC SCIENCES,' *Onamastica* no. 36, 7-12.

1969 **Farine, A.**
'La Raison d'être de la SCECI,' [Société Canadienne d'Education Comparée et Internationale], *Comp. International Ed. Soc. Canada Papers* 100-03.

I. LEARNED AND PROFESSIONAL JOURNALS :
   REVUES PROFESSIONNELLES

1930 **MacDermot, H. E.**
A Bibliography of Canadian Medical Periodicals with Annotations.
Montreal: Renouf. Pp. 21.

1936 **Groulx, L.**
Dix Ans d'Action Française. Montréal: Lévesque. Pp. 273.
1943 **Calvin, D. D.**
'Queen's Quarterly, 1893-1943,' *Queen's Q.* L, 117-29.
1945 **Routley, T. C.**
'Volume One, Number One of the Canadian Medical Association Journal,' *Hist. Bull. Calgary Clinic* X (1), 10-16.
1954 **Conacher, W. M.**
'A Chronicle of Queen's Quarterly,' *Queen's Q.* LX, 554-57.
1959 **McDougall, R. L.**
'The University Quarterlies,' *Can. Forum* XXXVIII, 253-55.
1961 **Harman, E., ed.**
The University as Publisher (Toronto: U. of T. Press) includes: M. Jeanneret, 'The University as Publisher,' 3-19; E. Harman, 'Founding a University Press,' 19-58; F. Halpenny, 'The Scholarly Books of the University of Toronto Press,' 59-62; E. Harman, 'The Scholarly Journals of the University of Toronto Press,' 63-66.
1962 **Savard, L.**
'"Cité Libre" et l'idéologie monolithique du vingtième siècle au Canada français.' Thèse de licence, Univ. Laval.
1967 **MacDermot, H. E.**
'Medical Journals' in his *One Hundred Years of Medicine in Canada 1867-1967* (Toronto: McClelland & Stewart), 156-66.
White, M.
'Phoenix: the First Twenty Years,' *Phoenix* XX, 273-84.
1968 **Bilodeau, R.**
'Les Vingt ans de la *Revue d'Histoire de l'Amérique Français*,' *Rev. Hist.* XXI, 1-12. See also 13-15.
1969 **Shortt, S. E. D.**
'The Progressive Mind in Academic Canada: *The University Magazine*, 1907-1914.' Unpublished M.A. thesis, Carleton Univ.

The student and student services
L'étudiant et les services aux étudiants

A. GENERAL : GÉNÉRALITÉS

1959 **Gzowski, P.**
'The Gay and Gutsy World of the College Press,' *Maclean's* LXXII (3), 22, 34-35.

1961 **Swan, P. J. M.**
'Student Attitudes – What Are We Doing to Augment Them?' *Bas. Teacher* VI, 64-68.

1963 **Kelly, J. M.**
'Educational Purpose and the Modern Student,' *Bas. Teacher* VII, 204-09.

1964 **Anderson, D. O.**
'The Premedical Student: His Identity; Characteristics of a Cohort of Premedical Students at the University of British Columbia,' *Can. Med. Assoc. Jour.* XCI, 1011-18.

1965 **Archambault, J. G.**
'University-Student Relations,' *Proc. Assoc. Stud. Services* 14-17.
Fleming, W. G.
Characteristics and Achievement of Students in Ontario Universities.
Toronto: Atkinson Study Report, no. 11. Pp. 197.
Loisel, J.
'Etude de la masculinité-feminité chez les étudiants universitaires.'
Thèse de licence, Univ. Laval.

1966 **Fahmy, P.**
'La Perception de soi à travers leur future profession chez les étudiantes infirmières en 1ère annee, de la ville de Québec.' Thèse de licence, Univ. Laval.
Harp, J. and P. Taietz.
'Academic Integrity and Social Structure: A Study of Cheating Among College Students,' *Soc. Problems* [U.S.] XIII, 365-73.
Judy, R. D.
'A Saggital Section: the Good Life Seen from the Viewpoint of the Entering Student,' *Culture* XXVII, 447-56.
McDonough, G.
'The Law and Student Drinking,' *Proc. Assoc. Stud. Services* 48-51.

1966 **Rabinovitch, R.**
An Analysis of the Canadian Post-Secondary Student Population; Part I: a Report on Canadian Undergraduate Students. Ottawa: Canadian Union of Students. Pp. 101.
Tyler, F. T.
Scholarship Students in College: Their Ideas about Academic Freedom and Their Correlates. Ottawa: Canadian Council for Research in Education. Pp. 9.
1967 **Breton, R. and J. C. McDonald.**
Career Decisions of Canadian Youth, vol. 1 – 1967. Ottawa: Queen's Printer. Pp. 203.
Duncan, A. R. C.
'The Problem of the Rootless Student,' *Queen's Univ. Alumni Rev.* XLI (2), 32-39, 55-56.
Gifford, L. D.
'The Student and Drug Use,' *Proc. Assoc. Stud. Services* 21-23.
Marshall, D.
'Campus "67,"' *Maclean's* LXXX (11), 11-13, 44-48.
1968 **Arsenault, F.**
'Valeurs des jeunes et renouveau de l'instruction,' *Rev. Univ. Moncton* I (1), 22-25.
Letts, A.
'The Characteristics of Students in Alberta Junior Colleges.' Unpublished M.Ed. thesis, Univ. of Alberta.
Ross, I. and G. F. McGuigan.
'The War Against Exams and Lectures,' *Can. Univ.* III (1), 63, 88.
University of Western Ontario.
President's Committee of Inquiry into Social Behaviour (A. W. R. Carrothers, Chairman), *Report of ... : Let Right Be Done.* London: The University. Pp. 55.
1969 **Beaudry, R. et Guindon, H.**
Attentes et satisfactions d'un groupe d'étudiants de niveau collégial. Montréal: CADRE. Pp. 218.
Clark, E., D. Cook, G. Fallis and M. Kent.
'Student Aid and Access to Higher Education in Ontario.' Mimeograph report issued by Prof. R. W. Judy, Univ. of Toronto. Pp. 259.
Friesen, D.
'A Semantic Differential Study of Attitudes Held by University Students Toward Educational Administration,' *Alta. Jour. Ed. Res.* XV (2), 103-15.

1969 Gadbois, L.
'De l'Etude et des relations humaines comme valeurs opposées dans l'école,' *Prospectives* V, 283-98.
Parent, A.-M.
'Relations professeurs-étudiants à l'ère technologique,' *Mém. S.R.C.* sect. 1, 93-96.

1970 **Black, A. and D. Black.**
'The University, the Student and the Rules' in *Studies on the University, Society and Government* ... (Ottawa: Univ. of Ottawa Press. 2 vols.), I, 463-544.
Diemer, A. H. and M. L. Dietz.
'Canadian University Students' Stereotypes of Canadians and Americans,' *McGill Jour. Ed.* V (1), 29-37.
Université de Montréal.
Les Etudiants et leurs préoccupations: annexes au Rapport de la Commission Conjointe du Conseil et de l'Assemblée Universitaire, Université de Montréal. Montréal: Presses Univ. Montréal. Pp. 334.

B. POLITICAL AND SOCIAL INVOLVEMENT :
ENGAGEMENT POLITIQUE ET SOCIALE

1964 **Bouvier, E.**
'Le Syndicalisme étudiant,' *Rev. Univ. Sherbrooke* V, 17-26.
Collège et Famille XXI (2-3), Numéro spécial, 'La Jeunesse étudiante du Québec en 1964,' inclut:
P. Mondon, 'Leur Engagement politique?' 90-100; G. Gaudreau, 'Leur Avenir professionnel?' 111-16; J. Genest, 'Que pensant-ils de leurs études?' 143-56.

1965 **Dubreuil, J.-C.**
'Le Syndicalisme étudiant,' *Rev. Scolaire* XV, 302-03.
Goodings, S.
'Students and Social Action,' *Univ. Affairs* VI (4), 5-6.
Goodings, S.
'Two Student Majorities,' *Can. Forum* XLV, 6-8.
Joyal, S.
'Student Syndicalism in Quebec,' *Can. Dimension* II (3), 20-21.
Mathews, R. D.
'University Crisis and the Common Weal,' *Can. Forum* XLV, 32-34.

1965 **Scott, N.**
'The Canadian Union of Students,' *C.A.U.T. Bull.* XIII (2), 5-10.
1966 **Buller, H.**
'Young French Canada and the Student Left,' *Can. Jewish Outlook* IV (8), 5-7.
Laliberté, J.
'Les Travailleurs étudiants du Québec,' *Our Generation* IV, 3, 32-38. See also F. Dansereau, *ibid.*, 38-39.
Laxer, J. and A. Pape.
'The New Left as It Sees Itself,' *Can. Dimension* III (6), 14-15.
Laxer, J. and A. Pape.
'Youth and Canadian Politics,' *Our Generation* IV (3), 15-21.
Lemay, L.
'Les Valeurs d'étudiant en mouvement,' *Proc. Assoc. Stud. Services* 61-66.
Nelson, R., D. Ward, L. Lemay and J. F. Leddy.
'Student-University Relationships/Relations entre les étudiants et l'université,' *A.U.C.C. Proc.* 89-112; 217-40.
Rowat, D. C.
'Democracy in the University Community: C.U.S. Eighth Seminar,' *C.A.U.T. Bull.* XIV (4), 36-42.
Swilley, L. C.
'Evaluating Student Protest,' *Bas. Teacher* X, 37-42.
Thompson, D. N.
'Revolution on the Campus,' *Atlantic Advocate* LVI (9), 33-39.
1967 **Brayton, F.**
'Two Student Revolts in Montréal,' *Our Generation* V (3), 91-97.
Favreau, R.
'The Quandary of L'Union Générale des Etudiants du Québec,' *Our Generation* V (1), 93-101.
Hodgetts, J. E.
'Some Hints on De-Coding "Student Power,"' *Univ. Affairs* IX (2), 10-11.
Reamsbottom, G.
'Student Motion in B.C.,' *Our Generation* V (1), 87-92.
Ship, S.
'Students Question the University,' *Can. Jewish Outlook* V (12), 4-5.
Szabo, D.
'Aliénations, révolte inadaptation de la jeunesse: Quelques aspects nouveau d'un vieux problème,' *Bien-être* XIX, 69-74.

1968 **Buller, H.**
'The New Proletariat,' *Can. Jewish Outlook* VI (10), 8-10.
Committee of Presidents of Universities of Ontario, Subcommittee on Research and Planning.
Student Participation in University Government. Toronto: The Committee. Pp. 21.
Corry, J. A.
'Student Involvement is Better than Student Indifference,' [Convocation Address, University of Manitoba] *Queen's Univ. Alumni Review* XLII (1), 6-10.
Drache, D.
'Canadian Students: Revolt and Apathy,' *Can. Dimension* V (7), 24-26.
Frye, H. N.
'Student Unrest Questions Our Vision of Society,' *Sch. Prog.* XXXVII (11), 18-19, 88-89.
Hoch, P.
'The French Thing and Canadian Radicals,' *This Magazine* II (3), 37-43.
McDonough, G.
'Student Power,' *Jour. Council Student Services* III (1), 35-38.
McGuigan, G. F., G. Payerle and P. Horrobin, eds.
Student Protest. Toronto: Methuen. Pp. 285. Includes:
G. F. McGuigan, 'The Search of Issues,' 13-50; D. Zunbelt, 'A Student Manifesto [at U.B.C.] 53-61; J. Harding, 'From the Midst of Crisis: Student Power in English-Speaking Canada,' 90-102; D. LaTouche, 'The Quebec Student Movement ...' 113-31; N. Kelly, 'The Pragmatic Pursuit of Happiness or Anatomy of Establishment,' 236-58.
Villeneuve, P.
'Une Canadienne dans les rues de Paris pendant la révolte étudiante, mai 1968,' *Cah. Cité Libre* XIX (4). Montréal: Editions du Jour. Pp. 192.
Whitelaw, J. A.
'The CEGEP Revolt and After,' *Can. Univ.* III (9), 30-33.

1969 **Adelman, H.**
The Beds of Academe: a Study of the Relations of Student Residences and the University. Toronto: Praxis Press. Pp. 258.
Altmann, H. A.
'Changing Perceptions of the University of Calgary Students over a One-Year Period,' *Can. Counsellor* III (3), 38-41.

1969 **Baby, A., P. W. Belanger, R. Ouellet and Y. Pepin.**
Nouveaux Aspects du problème de la démocratisation de l'enseignement dans les CEGEP. Quebec: Universite Laval. Pp. 32. See also *L'Orientation Professionelle* V (2).
Bedard, P. et C. Charron.
'Les Etudiants Québeçois: La Contestation Permanente,' *Noir et Rouge* no. 2, Edition Spéciale. Pp. 72.
Benjamin, C. et al.
'Rapport du comité d'étude de la contestation étudiante,' *Prospectives* V, 229-48.
Bissell, C. T.
'Academic Freedom: The Student Version,' *Queen's Q.* LXXVI, 171-84.
Bissell, C. T.
'Institutions of Higher Education in Canada: Some Recent Developments' in W. R. Niblett, ed., *Higher Education: Demand and Response* (London: Tavistock), 139-51.
Buller, H.
'Roots of Revolt,' *Can. Jewish Outlook* VII (5), 8-10, 15.
Cole, R. F.
'A Study of the Factors Influencing Students Attitudes towards Participation in University Affairs.' Unpublished M.Ed. thesis, Univ. of Calgary.
Compton, N.
'Sir George Williams Loses Its Innocence,' *Can. Forum* XLIX, 2-4.
Compton, N.
'What Do Young People Want?' *Can. Forum* XLIX, 51-53.
Fairweather, G.
'Youth and Responsibility,' *Can. Bus.* XLII (1), 34-40.
Field, J., S. Langdon and B. Keith.
'Why Are Many Students So Hostile to Science? Three Give Their Reasons,' *Sci. Forum* II (4), 11-15.
Frye, H. N.
'The University and Personal Life: Student Anarchism and the Educational Contract' in W. R. Niblett, ed., *Higher Education: Demand and Response* (London: Tavistock), 35-51.
Geoffroy, M.
'La Contestation,' *Act. Nat.* LVIII, 507-16.
Goldstick, D.
'The Student Left Today,' *Can. Jewish Outlook* VII (10), 5-6, 12.

1969 Harding, J.
'What's Happening at Simon Fraser University?' *Our Generation* VI (3), 52-64.
Kreutwieser, E. et al.
'Student Dissent,' *Can. Univ. & Coll.* IV (7), 11-16.
Laxer, J.
'The Student Movement and Canadian Independence,' *Can. Dimension* VI (3), 27-34; (4), 69-70.
Lloyd, T.
'Students and Research: A Critical Analysis of the Reformers' Demands,' *Sci. Forum* II (4), 7-10.
Macpherson, C. B.
'The Violent Society and the Liberal,' *C.A.U.T. Bull.* XVIII (1), 7-15.
McIntyre, H. C.
'The Sir George Williams Story,' *Can. Univ. & Coll.* IV (4), 48-53.
Rae, R.
'What Do Students Want? A Student's Answer: Genuine Influence,' *Sci. Forum* II (4), 3-6.
Rajan, V.
'The Challenge of Youth,' *Can. Bus.* XLII (9), 30-37.
Reid, T. and J. Reid, eds.
Student Power and the Canadian Campus. Toronto: Peter Martin. Pp. 226.
Sauvé, J.-C.
'Le Syndicalisme étudiant se meurt ... et c'est dommage,' *Prospectives* V, 71-73.
Sheps, G. D.
'The Apocalyptic Fires at Sir George Williams University,' *Can. Dimension* V (8), 6-7, 52-53.
Spinks, S.
'Notes on McGill and Sir George,' *This Magazine* III (2), 135-44.
Young, I.
'Against Student Power,' *Catalyst* II (3), 6-10.
Zoll, D. A.
'The Student as Trade Unionist,' *Laur. Univ. Rev.* II (4), 92-96.
1970 Adelman, H.
'A Decade of Protest: Coroner's Report,' *Can. Forum* LXIX, 258-60.
Lauzon, A.
'The New Left in Québec,' *Our Generation* VII (1), 14-30.

1970 **Laxer, J.**
'The Americanization of the Canadian Student Movement' in
I. Lumsden, ed., *Close the 49th Parallel etc.: The Americanization of Canada* (Toronto: U. of T. Press), 275-86.
Lazure, J.
'Les Jeunes Québécois encore à l'âge métaphysique,' *Prospectives* VI, 31-45.
Ratner, R. S. and R. J. Silvers.
'Three Cultures and the Student Revolution' in *Studies on the University, Society and Government* ... (Ottawa: Univ. of Ottawa Press. 2 vols.), I, 167-204.
Resnick, P.
'The New Left in Ontario,' *Our Generation* VII (1), 32-50.
Roussopoulos, D.
'C.E.G.E.P.S., Charlebois, Chartand; The Quebec Revolution Now,' *This Magazine* IV (2), 58-76.
Rusk, B., T. Hardy and B. Tooley.
The Student and the System: Proceedings of the Conference Sponsored by the Graduate Students Association, O.I.S.E., November, 1969. Toronto: Ontario Institute for Studies in Education. Pp. 78.
Thompson, R.
'The New Left in Saskatchewan,' *Our Generation* VII (1), 52-66.

C. FINANCIAL AID : AIDE FINANCIÈRE

1963 **Garneau, J.**
'Bourses en faveur de la communauté culturelle française,'
Univ. Affairs V (2), 1-2.
1965 **Ryan, E. F. and B. V. Slutsky.**
'Canada Student Loans Act – Ultra Vires?' *U.B.C. Law Rev.* II, 299-306.
1966 **Adam, W. G.**
'Financial Aid to New Brunswick High School Graduates for University Education.' Unpublished M.Ed. thesis, Univ. of New Brunswick.
Burns, M. D.
'Clothing Expenditures by Women University Students in Manitoba,' *Can. Home Econ. Jour.* XVI, 19-20.

1969 Clark, E., D. Cook, G. Fallis and M. Kent.
'Student Aid and Access to Higher Education in Ontario.' Mimeograph Report issued by Prof. R. W. Judy, Univ. of Toronto. Pp. 259.
New Brunswick Higher Education Commission.
Investing in the Future: a Programme for Government Assistance to Universities, Technical Schools and Their Students. Fredericton: The Commission. Pp. 67.
Pike, R. M.
'Public Financial Aid to Undergraduates in Canadian Universities for the Year 1969-70,' *Univ. Affairs* x, Supplement. Pp. 6.
1970 Primeau, W. J.
'Public Financial Aid to Undergraduates in Canadian Universities for the Year 1970-71 / Aides financières des gouvernements ...' *Univ. Affairs* xi (6), 1-6; 11-16.

D. HOUSING : LOGEMENT

1961 Lussier, C. A.
'The Canadian Students' Home in Paris,' *Univ. Affairs* ii (4), 1-2.
1966 Bland, J. and N. Schoenauer.
Student Housing in Canada. Montreal: McGill Univ. Press. Pp. 135.
Stager, D. A.
'New Patterns in Student Housing,' *Can. Univ.* i (4), 28-31.
Wilkinson, W. K.
'Residence Culture: A Descriptive Study of the Culture of the Lister Hall Residence Complex, University of Alberta, Edmonton.' Unpublished M.Ed. thesis, Univ. of Alberta.
1967 'Luxury Living on Campus,' *Can. Univ.* ii (4), 28-33.
1968 Parisel, C.
'Le Logement étudiant,' *Architecture* xxiii (268), 32-37; (269), 35-
'Student Housing: The Great Residence Gap,' *Can. Univ.* iii (8), 29-38.
1969 Adelman, H.
The Beds of Academe: a Study of the Relations of Student Residences and the University. Toronto: Praxis Press. Pp. 258.
'Blueprint for Student Living,' *Can. Univ. & Coll.* iv (11), 19-27.
Klein, J. and H. Sears.
Room to Learn; a Study on Housing for the Canadian Student. Ottawa: Association of Universities and Colleges of Canada. Pp. 141.

1969   **Pendakur, V. S. and N. M. Dempsey.**
'How Students Choose Housing,' *Can. Univ.* IV (2), 34-37, 50.
1970   **Spinks, S.**
'Dreaming in the Beds of Academe,' *This Magazine* IV (1), 80-108.

E. COUNSELLING AND GUIDANCE : ORIENTATION

1961   **Andoff, J. E.**
'Student Problems of Transition to University,' *School Guidance Worker* XVI (7), 25-33.
Moon, B. and D. L. Stein.
'The Anxious Years of an Undergraduate,' *Maclean's* LXXIV (21), 13, 81-83.
1963   **Becker, P., ed.**
Proceedings of a Conference on Student Mental Health Held at Queen's University, Kingston, Ontario, May, 1963. Toronto: World Univ. Service of Canada. Pp. 133.
1964   **Schwarz, C. J.**
'A Psychiatric Service for University Students,' *Can. Psych. Assoc. Jour.* IX, 232-38.
1965   **Fair, D. C.**
'The Importance of Positive Diagnosis in Counselling,' *Proc. Assoc. Stud. Services* 20-23.
Rose, B.
'New Spectre on the Campus; Student Crackups,' *Maclean's* LXXVIII (24), 9, 28-32.
Waldie, A. C.
'Functional Illness in the University Student,' *Coll. Gen. Practice Jour.* XII (2), 37-39.
1966   **Appley, D. G.**
'Presenting Problems of Self-Referred University Students – Theory and Fact,' *Proc. Assoc. Stud. Services* 32-43.
Boyce, R. M.
'Psychiatric Problems of University Students,' *Can. Psych. Assoc. Jour.* XI, 49-56.
Brodeur, C. C.
'The Foreign Student Advisor,' *Jour. Assoc. Student Services* I (1), 8-15.

1966 **Gifford, L. D.**
'Orientation for What?' *Proc. Assoc. Stud. Services* 67-71.
Hale, J. P.
'Initial Problems in Establishing a University Guidance Service,'
Proc. Can. Assoc. Student Services 90-95.
Maranda, A.
'Mieux connaître pour mieux choisir,' *Jour. Assoc. Student Services*
I (1), 16-22.
Pavalko, R. M. and D. R. Bishop.
'Peer Influences on the College Plans of Canadian High School
Students,' *Can. Rev. Soc. Anthrop.* III, 191-200.

1967 **Baby, A.**
'Du Collège à l'université: un penible arrimage,' *Cah. Cité Libre* V,
18-34.
Isabelle, L.
'Vingt-cinq ans en orientation à l'Université d'Ottawa,' *Jour. Assoc.
Student Services* III (1), 15-22.
Schwarz, C. J.
'A Survey of Health and Psychiatric Services on Canadian Campuses,'
Can. Med. Assoc. Jour. XCVI, 1361-66.

1968 **Appley, D. G., R. Heinz and R. M. Lee.**
'Counselling Services in Canadian Universities,' *Jour. Council Student
Services* III (1), 3-24.
Moncion, D.
'Les Services personnels aux étudiants,' *Bien-être* XX, 13-15.
Peavy, R. V.
'Mental Health Crises of University Students,' *Can. Mental Health*
XVI (3), 15-17.
'Les Priorités [en orientation scolaire] de l'heure au post-secondaire,'
Orient. Prof. IV (5), inclut:
L. Gadbois, 'L'Articulation des études et de l'orientation entre le
secondaire et le collégial,' 414-28; J.-A. Gagnon, 'Les Relations entre
l'Institut et l'Université du point de vue de l'orientation et du
counseling,' 429-35; A. Bellerive, 'Les Processus de décision de
l'école secondaire a l'Université,' 436-42.
Rainey, C. A.
'A Behaviourally-Oriented Approach to Counselling Problems,'
Proc. Assoc. Stud. Services 40-49.
Rempel, P. P., P. Sartoris and A. Vanderwell.
'The University Counselling Service: A Model,' *Jour. Council Student
Services* III (1), 25-34.

1969 **Conklin, R. C. and L. C. Handy.**
'Client Problems as Perceived by Counsellors,' *Jour. Council Student Services* IV (1), 14-25.
Dion, G.
'L'Orientation dans un Québec qui cherches à se définer,' *Orient. Prof.* V, 330-38.
Dion, G.
'La Raison d'être de la clinique d'orientation de l'Université Laval,' *Orient. Prof.* V, 103-07.
Hudson, R. I.
'The University Counselling Service: as Alternate Model,' *Jour. Council Student Services* IV (1), 6-13.
LeBlanc, P. B.
'The Concept of Privileged Communication in Selected Professions with Particular Reference to the Field of School and University Counselling in Canada.' Unpublished M.A. thesis, McGill Univ.
Pratte, C.
'L'Orientation dans les CEGEP,' *Orient. Prof.* V, 238-45.
1970 **Wrenn, C. G.**
'Group Counselling and Problems of Communication in the Large Universities,' *Can. Counsellor* IV (2), 117-27.

F. PLACEMENT : EMPLOI

1963 **MacLean, M.**
'An Investigation of the Factors Influencing the Occupational Choice of Selected College Students.' Unpublished doct. dissertation, Fordham Univ.
1965 **Stapleford, A. C. and A. Brown.**
'The Problem of Graduate Turnover,' *Proc. Assoc. Stud. Services* 39-43.
1966 **Bradford, K.**
'The Company Interviewer in the Role of Educator,' *Jour. Assoc. Student Services* I (2), 3-7.
Chartier, R.
'Company Planning for University Recruitment,' *Can. P. R. Jour.* XIII (2), 45-58.
Elliott, J. W.
'How Do Canadian Companies Attract and Recruit?' *Proc. Assoc. Stud. Services* 17-26.

1967 Dick, W. W.
'Clarity of Self-Concepts in the Vocational Development of Male Liberal Arts Students.' Unpublished doct. dissertation, Univ. d'Ottawa.
Flohil, R.
'How *Not* to Hire College Grads,' *Plant Admin. Engin.* XXVIa (2), 46-47, 73-74.
Flohil, R.
'Why Industry's Losing the Race for College Grads,' *Plant Admin. Engin.* XXVIa (1), 24-27, 58.
Muir, J. D.
'How to Recruit Business Graduates,' *Can. Bus.* XL (9), 42-51.
Peitchinis, S. G.
'The Economic Value of Education,' *Bus. Q.* XXXII (1), 59-67.

1969 Chipman, M. L., G. G. Clarke and J. W. Steiner.
'Career Choice Within Medicine: A Study of One Graduating Class at the University of Toronto,' *Can. Med. Assoc. Jour.* CI, 646-51.
Goodman, F. V. S.
'The Supply of and Demand for Graduates of Post-Secondary School Institutes in the Next Decade,' *Jour. Council Student Services* IV (2), 20-26.
Gross, A. C.
'Education, Employment and Utilization Patterns of French-Canadian and English-Canadian Engineering Graduates,' *Relations Ind.* XXIV, 559-78.
Kothari, V.
'L'Evaluation d'un placement,' *Rev. Univ. Moncton* II, 91-98.

1970 Schiele, R.
'Company on Campus: Student Manpower for Hire,' *Can. Bus.* XLIII (4), 74-78.

G. EXTERNAL ORGANIZATIONS :
ORGANISATIONS EXTERIEURES

1964 Becker, J.
'Report from the Frontiers of Friendship,' [re: Canadian University Students Overseas] *Maclean's* LXXVII (11), 18-19, 29-30, 32.
Lyon, P. V.
'Comparing Canada's Peace Corps – CUSO,' *Canadian Commentator* VIII (2), 6-7.

1965 **Company of Young Canadians.**
A Report of the Organizing Committee of the Company of Young Canadians to the Prime Minister. Ottawa. Pp. 35.
Fleck, P.
'The World University Service of Canada,' *C.A.U.T. Bull.* XIII (2), 11-20.

1966 **Harding, J.**
'An Ethical Movement in Search of an Analysis: the Student Union for Peace Action in Canada,' *Our Generation* IV (1), 20-29.

1968 **Ashley, C. A.**
'The Company of Young Canadians,' *Comm. Jour.* 15-20.
Harkleroad, P.
'Peace Corps Volunteer,' *Comparative International Ed. Society of Canada Paper* 1968, 73-75. See also B. Bailey 'C.U.S.O. Volunteer Teacher, 75-77; B. A. Geddes, 'C.U.S. Volunteer Teacher, 77-79; R. McCombs, 'Independent World Traveler,' 79-82; J. I. Prattis, 'V.S.O. Government Officer,' 82-86.
McWhinney, W. and D. Godfrey, eds.
Man Deserves Man: CUSO in Developing Countries. Toronto: Ryerson. Pp. 461.

1969 **Benning, J. A.**
'Canadian University Service Overseas and Administrative Decentralization,' *Can. Public Admin.* XII, 515-50.

The professor and conditions of work
Le professeur et les conditions de travail

A. GENERAL : GÉNÉRALITÉS

1964 **Drummond, I. M.**
'The Robbins Commission and the Canadian Scene,' *Can. Forum* XLIII, 265-68.

1965 **Floch, W. and C. Watson.**
The Ontario Data of the Canadian Universities Foundation Survey of the Movement of University Teaching Staff. Toronto: Ontario College of Education, Department of Educational Research. Pp. 118.
Johnson, H. G.
'The Economics of the "Brain Drain": The Canadian Case,' *Minerva* [U.K.] III, 299-311.
Scott, P. D.
'Professors as Reformers: a Canadian Pattern,' *Can. Forum* XLV, 149-50.

1966 **Audet, L.-P.**
'Les Cadres scolaires' in G. Sylvestre, ed., *Structures sociales du Canada français* (Toronto: U. of T. Press), 29-66.
Chabassol, D. J.
'Research, Publication and Teaching,' *Alta. Jour. Ed. Res.* XII (1), 55-62.
Johnson, H. G.
'The Social Sciences in the Age of Opulence,' *Can. Jour. Econ. Pol. Sci.* XXXII, 423-42.
Morin, F.
'Les Services essentiels des professeurs de l'Etat,' *Relations Ind.* XXI, 442-47.
Moxham, R.
'Memo from an Expatriate Canadian,' *Univ. Affairs* VII (3), 1-3.
Monahan, E. J. *et al.*
'The North Hatley Conference on the Future of the C.A.U.T.,' *C.A.U.T. Bull.* XV (2), 4-41.
National Research Council, Office of Economic Studies.
Some Characteristics of University Teachers in the Biological and Physical Sciences 1958-59 to 1963-64. Ottawa: The Council. Pp. 55.

1966 **Robson, R. A. H.**
Sociological Factors Affecting Recruitment into the Academic Profession/Elements sociologiques ... Ottawa: Association of Universities and Colleges of Canada. Pp. 46.
Rothrock, G. A.
'The Ph.D.: Academic License or Status Symbol?' *C.A.U.T. Bull.* XIV (4), 43-45.

1967 **Brunet, M.**
'Le Professeur des universités franco-québécoises, évolution de son rôle au sein de notre société,' *Cah. Cité Libre* V, 12-17.
Cohn, W.
'Publication and Due Process,' *C.A.U.T. Bull.* XVI (2), 44-53.
Sasnett, M.
'Equivalences of Degrees,' *McGill Jour. Ed.* II, 145-55.
Scott, A.
'The Recruitment and Migration of Canadian Social Scientists,' *Can. Jour. Econ. Pol. Sci.* XXXIII, 494-508.

1968 **Brown, D. J.**
'The Productivity of University Educators.' Unpublished M.A. thesis, Univ. of British Columbia.
Lee, D.
'Getting to Rochdale,' *This Magazine* II (5), 72-96. Also in H. Adelman and D. Lee, eds., *The University Game* (Toronto: Anansi, 1968), 69-94.

1969 **Beauregard, C.**
'Congédiements de professeurs: au delà des mécanismes, un climat à restaurer,' *Prospectives* V, 139-41.
Burgess, J. P.
'Canadianizing the University,' *Can. Forum* XLIX (582), 77-79.
Canadian Association of University Teachers, Executive and Finance Committee.
'"Canadianization" and the University/"Canadianisation" et l'université,' *C.A.U.T. Bull.* XVIII (1), 42-43. See also (3), 47-54.
Canadian Association of University Teachers and the Ontario Universities' Television Council.
'Copyright and Higher Education,' *C.A.U.T. Bull.* XVIII (1), 64-96.
Ontario Confederation of University Faculty Associations.
'Interim Guidelines on Professional Ethics for Academics,' *OCUFA Newsletter* III (1), 24-27.

1969 **Ontario Confederation of University Faculty Associations.**
'What is OCUFA?/L'UAPUO, Qu'est-ce que c'est?' *OCUFA Newsletter* III (1), 1-6.
Parent, A.-M.
'Relations professeurs-étudiants à l'ère technologique,' *Mém. S.R.C.* sect. 1, 93-96.

1970 **Jowett, G.**
'The Dossier as Hornet's Nest,' [Three Reviews of Mathews and Steele, *The Struggle for Canadian Universities*] *Can. Rev. Amer. Studies* I (1), 48-56. See also J. Gold, 'We Stand on Guard for Thee?' *ibid.*, pp. 56-62 and R. Bates, 'Who's Afraid of Cultural Identity? or, Stand Up and Be Counted Down,' *ibid.*, 62-68.
Kay, Z. and J. B. Marshall.
'Academic Public Servants and University Faculty: A Comparative Note' in *Studies on the University, Society and Government ...* (Ottawa: Univ. of Ottawa Press. 2 vols.), II, 279-304.
Lumsden, I.
'American Imperialism and Canadian Intellectuals' in I. Lumsden, ed., *Close the 49th Parallel etc.: The Americanization of Canada* (Toronto: U. of T. Press), 321-36.
Mathews, R.
'Science Policy, Teaching, and the Non-Canadian,' *Sci. Forum* III (1), 24-25.

B. PROFESSOR AS TEACHER :
LE PROFESSEUR COMME ENSEIGNANT

1961 **Fischette, R. M.**
'College Pedagogy,' *Bas. Teacher* V, 225-30.

1962 **Smith, P. D.**
'Instructors for Evening and Summer Courses,' *Univ. Affairs* III (4), 3-4.
Woodside, M. St. A.
'A Critical Examination of University Methods of Instruction' in R. deChantal and D. Edmonds, eds., *The University in Canadian Life* (Ottawa: National Federation of Canadian Students), 42-49.

1963 **MacDonald, W. R.**
'The Training of College Teachers,' *Can. Ed. Research Digest* III, 221-29.

1965 **Miller, G. E.**
'On Training Medical Teachers,' *Can. Med. Assoc. Jour.* XCII, 708-11.
Poole, C. F.
'The Ph.D. as a Qualification for University Teachers,' *C.A.U.T. Bull.* XIV (2), 61-64.

1966 **Chabassol, D. J.**
'Research, Publication and Teaching,' *Alta. Jour. Ed. Res.* XII (1), 55-62.
Kinley, C. E. and G. R. Langley.
'Observations on a Medical Teacher Training Programme,' *Can. Med. Assoc. Jour.* XCIV, 785-88.
Stensland, P. G.
'The University Teacher,' *C.A.U.T. Bull.* XV (1), 59-65.
Toussaint, M. F.
'Quelques Aspects de la tâche des enseignants du Québec,' *Can. Ed. Research Digest* VII, 284-300.
Webb, C. W.
'The Ph.D. Octopus Tightens Its Grip,' *Toronto Globe and Mail*, Feb. 17, 1966. Page 7.

1967 **Rocher, G.**
'Le Professeur d'université: un enseignant pas comme les autres?' *Cah. Cité Libre* V, 5-11.

1969 **Flower, G.**
'Teaching: the Forgotten Role,' *Laur. Univ. Rev.* II (4), 75-83.
Lorin, J. C.
'Comment améliorer notre enseignement,' *Rev. Univ. Moncton* II, 36-38.
Smith, J. P.
'Teach - Or Get Lost,' *C.A.U.T. Bull.* XVII (4), 2-19.

1970 **McCausland, I.**
'Research vs. Teaching: New Insights into an Old Problem,' *Sci. Forum* III (1), 17-19.

C. ACADEMIC FREEDOM : LIBERTES UNIVERSITAIRES

1919 **Taylor, R. B.**
'Academic Freedom,' *Queen's Q.* XXVII, 1-11.

1934 **Underhill, Frank H.**
'A Letter to the *Winnipeg Free Press* on Academic Freedom' (March 1, 1934) in *In Search of Canadian Liberalism* (Toronto: Macmillan, 1961), 110-13. See also 'On Professors and Politics,' 107-09.

1937 **Beatty, E.**
'Freedom and the Universities,' *Queen's Q.* XLIV, 463-71.
1961 **Lavery, C. J.**
'Lay Professors on the Catholic Campus,' *Bas. Teacher* V, 111-15.
1962 **Kaplan, J. G.**
'Problems of Freedom in the University' in R. de Chantal and D. Edmonds, eds., *The University in Canadian Life* (Ottawa: National Federation of Canadian Students), 64-70.
1963 **Schoeck, R. J.**
'The Catholic Scholar and the Intellectual Life,' *Bas. Teacher* VIII, 23-31.
1964 **Canadian Assoc. of University Teachers.**
'C.A.U.T. Statements of Policy,' *C.A.U.T. Bull.* XII (3), 72-78.
Freedman, S.
'The Right to Practise One's Profession,' *Can. Med. Assoc. Jour.* XCI, 862-68.
Lower, A. R. M.
'Administrators and Scholars,' *Queen's Q.* LXXI, 214-25.
Thompson, W. P.
'A University in Trouble,' *Sask. Hist.* XVII, 81-104.
Turner, G. H.
'Academic Freedom and Tenure: Notes on Investigational Procedures,' *C.A.U.T. Bull.* XII (3), 48-54.
1965 **Bergeron, V. et A. DesMarais.**
'Statut du professeur: conditions de vie et de travail,' *C.A.U.T. Bull.* XIV (2), 25-38.
Fellman, D.
'Academic Freedom' (an address delivered before the Annual Dinner of the C.A.U.T.), *C.A.U.T. Bull.* XIV (1), 34-42.
Skora, S. J.
'Notes on the Freedom of the Scholar and the Authority of the Church,' *Rev. Univ. Ottawa* XXXV, 198-206.
Soberman, D. A.
'Tenure in Canadian Universities, A Report/La Stabilité de l'emploi dans les universités canadiennes, rapport,' *C.A.U.T. Bull.* XIII (3), 5-36; 37-73.
Turner, G. H. et al.
'Comments on Tenure in Canadian Universities,' *C.A.U.T. Bull.* XIII (3), 77-90. See also 'Soberman Replies to Collier,' XIV (1), 43.

1966 Howard, H. W.
'Academic Freedom,' *Bas. Teacher* x, 125-32.
Hurtubise, R.
'Security of Tenure of University Teachers in the Province of Quebec/ La Stabilité d'emploi des professeurs d'universités de la province de Québec,' *C.A.U.T. Bull.* XIV (3), 4-21.
'Venture Capital and Academic Freedom,' *Can. Univ.* I (3), 21-24.

1967 **Canadian Assoc. of University Teachers, Academic Freedom and Tenure Committee.**
'Statement on the Williamson-Murray Case/Declaration ... Affaire Williamson-Murray,' *C.A.U.T. Bull.* XV (3), 32-43.

1968 **Haggar, G.**
'Academic Freedom and All That,' *Can. Dimension* V (6), 11-12.
Leblanc, S.
'Le Professeur sacrifié au béton,' *Maintenant* no. 77, 144-49.
Smith, J. P.
'Developments at Simon Fraser University,' *C.A.U.T. Bull.* XVII (1), 23-33.
Smith, J. P.
'Faculty Power and Simon Fraser,' *Can. Forum* XLVIII, 122-24.
Smith, J. P.
'The Work of the C.A.U.T. Committee on Academic Freedom and Tenure,' *C.A.U.T. Bull.* XVII (2), 2-11.

1969 **Berland, A.**
'A Report on the Strax Case at the University of New Brunswick,' *C.A.U.T. Bull.* XVII (4), 20-64.
Milner, J. B.
'The Strax Affair,' *C.A.U.T. Bull.* XVII (3), 36-42. See also 43-46.

1970 **Berland, A.**
'On the Present State of Academic Freedom,' *C.A.U.T. Bull.* XVIII (2), 2-11.
Mallock, A. and L. P. Taschereau.
'Le Cas de sociologie à l'Université de Moncton,' *C.A.U.T. Bull.* XVIII (3), 43-46.

D. SALARY AND BENEFITS : SALARIES ET BENEFICES

1942 **James, H.**
'The T.I.A.A. [Teachers' Insurance and Annuity Association] and Canadian Universities,' *N.C.C.U. Proc.* 42-50.

1964 **Canadian Assoc. of University Teachers.**
'Academic Salaries in Canadian Universities, Final Report of the Salary Committee, 1963-64,' *C.A.U.T. Bull.* XIII (1), 33-43.
Canadian Teachers' Federation, Research Division.
A Comparative Summary of Procedures for Determining Teachers' Salaries in Canada and 26 Other Countries. Ottawa: The Federation. Pp. 35.

1965 **Canadian Association of University Teachers.**
'Salaries of Full-Time Lay Teaching Staff at Canadian Universities and Colleges 1964-65,' *C.A.U.T. Bull.* XIII (2), 53-64.
Canadian Association of University Teachers.
'Salary Scales for Lay Staff at Canadian Universities and Colleges, 1964-65,' *C.A.U.T. Bull.* XIII (1), 44-53.
Monahan, E. J.
'Financing the C.A.U.T.,' *C.A.U.T. Bull.* XIII (2), 33-36.
Weynerowski, W.
'Canadian University Retirement Plans – an Appraisal of Change: 1956 to 1964,' *C.A.U.T. Bull.* XIII (2), 27-32.
Weynerowski, W.
'Selected Fringe Benefits Available in 1965 at Canadian Universities and Colleges,' *C.A.U.T. Bull.* XIII (4), 33-45.

1966 **Canadian Association of University Teachers.**
'Salary Scales for Lay Staff at Canadian Universities and Colleges, 1965-66,' *C.A.U.T. Bull.* XIV (1), 20-31.
Ingraham, M. H. and S. Eckler.
Faculty Retirement Systems in Canadian Universities: A Report to the Association of Universities and Colleges of Canada/Regimes de retraite ... (Toronto/Quebec: U. of T. Press/Presses Univ. Laval. Pp. 92.
Lapointe, M.
'Sommaire de l'étude des avantages sociaux offerts aux professeurs dans les universités du Canada: 1965-66,' *C.A.U.T. Bull.* XV (1), 67-84.

1967 **Baillie, D. C.**
'Thoughts on the Ingraham Report,' *C.A.U.T. Bull.* XV (4), 35-48.
Rosenbluth, G.
'The Structure of Academic Salaries in Canada,' *C.A.U.T. Bull.* XV (4), 19-23.

1968 **Robinson, A. J.**
'Would Collective Bargaining Increase Academic Salaries,' *C.A.U.T. Bull.* XVI (4), 70-79.

1969 **Lapointe, M.**
'A Comparison of Men's and Women's Employment Fringe Benefits in the Academic Profession: Pension Plans and Life and Long-Term Disability Insurance Plans, 1965-66 and 1968-69,' *C.A.U.T. Bull.* XVIII (1), 47-63.
Lapointe, M.
'Etude des avantages sociaux (Survey of Faculty Fringe Benefits) 1968-69,' *C.A.U.T. Bull.* XVII (4), 65-140.
Robson, R. A. H.
'A Comparison of Men's and Women's Salaries in the Academic Profession,' *C.A.U.T. Bull.* XVII (3), 50-75.

II Non-degree granting institutions
   Etablissements qui ne confèrent pas de grade

Non-degree granting institutions
Etablissements qui ne confèrent pas de grade

A. GENERAL : GÉNÉRALITÉS

1939 **Sexton, F. H.**
'Technical Education in Canada' in H. V. Usill, ed., *The Year Book of Education 1939* (London: Evans Brothers Limited), 604-34. See also *Year Book 1932*, 662-84; *1933*, 440-61; 519-31; *1934*, 87-90, 281-93, 547-606; *1935*, 46-59, 252-59; *1936*, 601-18; *1937*, 170-85, 294-307; *1938*, 154-71.

1941 **Johns, R. J.**
'Origin and Development of Technical Education in Canada.' Unpublished M.A. thesis, Colorado State Coll. of Agriculture and Mechanic Arts.

1960 **Mitchener, R. D.**
'The Junior College Idea in Canada,' *Univ. Affairs* I (3), 9-11.

1962 *School Progress* XXXI (May 1962). Issue devoted to Technical/Vocational Education.
Sinclair, S.
'Do-it-yourself Education: an Answer to Industry's Training Problem,' *Can. Bus.* XXXV (9), 42-52.
Sinclair, S.
'Technical and Vocational Training: Are We on the Right Road?' *Can. Bus.* XXXV (4), 42-44, 103-10; (5), 66-70, 73-77.

1963 *School Progress* XXXII (May 1963). Issue devoted to Technical/Vocational Education.
School Progress XXXII (July 1963). Issue devoted to a consideration of junior community colleges.

1964 **Glendenning, D. E. M.**
'Impact of Federal Financial Support on Vocational Education in Canada.' Unpublished doct. dissertation, Indiana Univ.
Glendenning, D. E. M.
Organization and Financing of Vocational Training in Canada. Ottawa: Dept. of Labour. Pp. 207.
Robinson, F. G.
Needed Research in the Field of Technical and Vocational Education. Ottawa: Canadian Council for Research in Education. Pp. 39.

1964 *School Progress* XXXIII (May 1964). Issue devoted to Technical/ Vocational Education.
1965 **Andrew, G. C.**
'What Kind of Colleges Do We Need?' *Univ. Affairs* VI (4), 3-4.
Arnett, J.
'What is a Community College?' *Information* XIII, 9-12+.
Canadian Association for Adult Education.
Report of the Conference on Adult Education in Community Colleges. Toronto: The Association. Pp. 51. See also 'Adult Education and the Community College in Canada: Report on the C.A.A.E. National Conference,' *Continuous Learning* IV, 155-70.
Gerrish, R. E.
'Teachers for Community Colleges,' *Sch. Prog.* XXXIV (7), 40-41, 51.
Grossman, H. J.
'Solving the Education Dilemma – The Community College,' *Continuous Learning* IV, 105-09.
Maltby, P.
'Financing the Community College,' *Continuous Learning* IV, 161-63.
Meltz, N. M.
Changes in the Occupational Composition of the Canadian Labour Force 1931-1961. Ottawa: Queen's Printer. Pp. 136.
1966 'The Annual Review,' [of the Canadian Association for Adult Education] *Continuous Learning* V, 193-99. See also 'Community Colleges,' V, 221-26.
DeNevi, D.
'The Growing Canadian Community College Movement,' *Educational Record* [U.S.] XLVII, 199-202.
Elston, A. J.
'Institutes of Technology: Key to Our Future or Keyhole View of Technology's Past?' *Sch. Prog.* XXV (6), 55-56.
Ford, C. R.
'The Personnel Man's Part in Canada's Technical and Vocational Education Program,' *Can. P. R. Jour.* XIII (2), 39-43.
Gayfer, M.
'What Role for the Community College?' *Sch. Prog.* XXXV (7), 22-24.
Hartle, D. G.
The Employment Forecast Survey. Toronto: U. of T. Press. Pp. 156.
Law, H.
'Community Colleges: Dead-End or Doorway?' *Can. Univ.* I (1), 32-35.

1966 **Law, H.**
'Community Colleges Search for an Identity,' *Can. Univ.* I (2), 26-29.
Mann, W. E.
'Adult Dropouts,' *Continuous Learning* v, 55-65. See also 127-43.
Parai, L.
Immigration and Emigration of Professional and Skilled Manpower during the Post-War Period. Ottawa: Queen's Printer. Pp. 248.
Seger, J. E. and G. L. Mowat, eds.
The Junior College: Report of the Lecture Series of the Banff Regional Conference of School Administration. Edmonton: Department of Educational Administration, Faculty of Education, Univ. of Alberta.
Stager, D. A.
'An Answer to: What Else Can They Do?' *Can. Forum* XLV, 227-29.
Thomas, A. M., ed.
Community Colleges 1966: A National Seminar on the Community College in Canada, May 30, 31 and June 1, 1966. Toronto: Canadian Assoc. for Adult Education. Pp. 114.
Wilson, H. V. and F. E. B. Markell.
'The Community College in Canada,' *Can. H.P.E.R. Jour.* XXXIII (1), 21-23.

1967 **Bortolazzo, J. L.**
'Junior Colleges: Bridging an Educational Gap,' *Alberta School Trustee* XXXVII, 16-18.
Canadian Association for Adult Education.
'A Report to the Canadian People on Manpower Development,' *Continuous Learning* VI, 242-53; 'Rapport aux citoyens canadiens concernant la formation de la main d'oeuvre,' 256-69.
Dineen, J. O.
'The Role and Objectives of Technological Institutes in Education Today,' *Can. Surveyor* XXI, 29-37.
Farquhar, H. E.
'The Role of the College in the System of Higher Education.' Unpublished doct. dissertation, Univ. of Alberta.
Grant, L. S.
'Canada's Evolving Two-Year Colleges,' *Junior College Journal* [U.S.] XXXVII (5), 25-27.
Hamilton, A. C.
'Objectives and Problems of the Institutes of Technology,' *Can. Surveyor* XXI, 74-92.

1967 **Hemphill, H. D.**
'Trends in Educational Finance and the Public Sector: 1946-60,'
Can. Ed. Research Digest VII, 334-48.
Jones, G. M.
'The Junior College: an Examination of Selected Aspects Related to Its Development, Present Status and Future Direction.' Unpublished M.A. thesis, Dalhousie Univ.
McBryde, W. A. E.
'Alternate Route to a University Degree,' *Chem. Can.* XIX (7), 26-28.
Page, G. T.
'Canada's Manpower Training and Education: Federal Policy and Programs,' *Can. Ed. Research Digest* VII, 283-98.

1968 **Adams, P. R.**
'Needed: More Effectively Trained Administrators for Post-secondary Education,' *Educational Administration Reporter* [U.S.] II (4), 2-3.
Canadian University III (4). Issue devoted to Survey of Technical and Applied Arts Education.
'Can Community Colleges Train Media Technicians?' *Can. Audio-Visual Rev.* IV (6), 6-7, 14-15.
'Community College Roundup,' *Sch. Prog.* XXXVII (8), 29-34.
Johnston, R. J.
'Counselling Services at Colleges of Applied Arts and Technology,' *School Guidance Worker* XXIV, 10-17.
Law, H.
'What's the Job Role for New Breed of Graduate?' *Sch. Prog.* XXXVII (8), 35, 52-53.
Neal, W. D.
'The Preparation of Community College Teachers' in *Transcript of Addresses of the Twenty-fourth Annual Secretaries' Short Course and Trustees' Seminar in School Administration* (Edmonton: The Department of Extension, Univ. of Alberta), 56-63.
'An Outbreak of Colleges,' *Monday Morning* II (5), 24-25.
Whitehouse, J. R. W.
'Toward a College-Centred Labour Studies Program,' *Continuous Learning* VII, 265-72.

1969 **Canada, Dept. of the Secretary of State, Education Support Branch.**
Federal Expenditures on Post-Secondary Education 1966-67, 1967-68.
Ottawa: Queen's Printer. Pp. 34.
Gwilliam, R. B.
'Community Colleges and a Commission,' *Continuous Learning* VIII, 289-92.

1969 **Lamontagne, L.**
'La Technologie et l'accès aux études post-secondaires,' *Mém. S.R.C.* sect. 1, 87-92.
1970 **Judge, D. et al.**
'Community Colleges: Are They Serving Community Needs Across Canada?' *Can. Univ. & Coll.* V (3), 21-38, 54-55.

B. NEWFOUNDLAND : TERRE-NEUVE

1963 **Ford, C. R.**
'The Emerging Concepts of Technical and Vocation Education,' *N.T.A. Journal* LV, 19-23.
1967 **Royal Commission on Education and Youth.**
Report of... St. John's, Newfoundland: Province of Newfoundland and Labrador. 2 vols.

C. PRINCE EDWARD ISLAND : ILE-DU-PRINCE-EDOUARD

1965 **Prince Edward Island. Royal Commission on Higher Education.**
Report of... Charlottetown: Queen's Printer. Pp.

D. NOVA SCOTIA : NOUVELLE-ECOSSE

1921 **Sexton, F. H.**
'Education for Industry in Nova Scotia,' *Dalhousie Rev.* I, 66-74.
1963 **Everett, D. J.**
'The Development of Vocational Education in Nova Scotia.' Unpublished M.Ed. thesis, St. Francis Xavier Univ.
1968 **Verma, D.**
'Medical Laboratory Technology Instruction in Nova Scotia.' Unpublished M.A. thesis, Saint Mary's Univ.
1969 **Chuk, J. E.**
'A College with a Difference,' *Atlantic Advocate* LXIX (9), 45-49.

E. NEW BRUNSWICK : NOUVEAU-BRUNSWICK

1963 **Milbury, J. C.**
'The Development of Vocational Education in New Brunswick.' Unpublished M.Ed. thesis, Univ. of New Brunswick.

1965 'Technical and Trade Training in New Brunswick Institutes of Technology and Trade Schools,' *Profile Ed. N.B.* IV (1), 14-16.
1966 **Ali, A. H.**
'Federal Aid to Education in New Brunswick: The Effects of Federal Aid on the Development of Technical and Vocational Education in New Brunswick.' Unpublished M.Ed. thesis, Univ. of New Brunswick.
1967 **Milbury, J. C.**
'Vocational Education in New Brunswick 1900-1967.' Unpublished M.Ed. thesis, Univ. of New Brunswick.
Sonier, H. *et al.*
'A Look at the Five Trade and Technical Schools,' *Profile Ed. N.B.* VI (1), 6-11.
1969 **New Brunswick Higher Education Commission.**
Investing in the Future: a Programme for Government Assistance to Universities, Technical Schools and Their Students. Fredericton: The Commission. Pp. 67.

F. QUEBEC : QUEBEC

1962 **Comité d'Etude sur l'Enseignement Technique et Professionnel.**
Rapport du ... Québec: Imprimeur de la Reine. 2 vols.
1964 **Angers, P.** *et al.*
La Structure du premier cycle universitaire. Montréal: Centre de Psychologie et de Pédagogie. Pp. 68.
'Un Problème crucial de notre enseignement: la structure du premier cycle universitaire,' *Act. Nat.* LIV, 413-25.
1966 **Hervieux, G.**
'Les Opérations financières courantes des collèges classique de 1960 à 1966,' *Prospectives* II, 254-57.
Savard, M.
'Le Niveau post-secondaire: ses objectifs, ses structures, ses méthodes,' *Prospectives* II, 92-98.
1967 **Beauregard, C.**
'Les Collèges d'enseignement général et professionnel: problèmes et perspectives,' *Prospectives* III, 225-28.
Beausoliel, J. et D. Massé.
Les Services aux étudiants dans la structure administrative des CEGEP. Montréal: Fédération des Collèges Classiques. Pp. 99.

1967 **Desbiens, J.-P.**
'Des Instituts aux CEGEP; du rapport Parent au Bill 21,' *Technique* XLI (7), 2-7.
Genest, J.
'Le Québec en marche et son système scolaire,' *Act. Nat.* LVII, 17-28.
Gillett, M.
'The New Look in Quebec Education,' *Comparative International Education Society of Canada Paper* 46-53.
Legroulx, L.
'L'Enseignement professionnel au nouveau cours collégial,' *Prospectives* III (3), 199-203.
Masson, C.
'L'Ecole de Métiers de Jacques-Cartier,' *Technique* XLI (6), 21-24.
Québec, Ministère de l'Education.
L'Enseignement collégial et les collèges d'enseignement général et professionnel. Documents d'Education, 3. Québec: La Ministère. Pp. 122.
Racette, J.
'La Philosophie dans les collèges autrefois dits classiques,' *Relations* no. 314, 66-69.
Savard, M.
'Les Programmes du collégial: une marche vers la confusion ou vers l'unification?' *Prospectives* III, 164-69.

1968 **Angers, P.**
'Les Disciplines obligatoires dans le collège public: leurs objectifs sont-ils valides?' *Prospectives* IV, 247-61.
Côté, F.
'Le Collège canadien des travailleurs,' *Technique* XLII (3), 14-20.
Côté, F.
'Une Nouvelle discipline au CEGEP: La météorologie,' *Technique* XLII (7), 8-10.
Dorais, F.
'Les CEGEP après un an,' *Relations* XXVIII, 212-15.
Dorais, F.
'Nos CEGEP à l'heure de l'occupation,' *Relations* XXVIII, 312-15.
Lavoie, B.
'Le CEGEP: au confluent de l'université et de l'industrie,' *Technique* XLII (1), 16-19.
Quebec, Department of Education.
College Education and the General and Vocational Colleges. Quebec: The Department. Pp. 122.

1968 **Whitelaw, J. H.**
'Quebec System Creates New Learning Level,' *Sch. Prog.* XXXVII (8), 36-38, 54.
Whitelaw, J. H.
'Quiet Revolution in Technical Education,' *Can. Univ.* III (4), 18-21.

1969 **Baby, A., P. W. Belanger, R. Ouellet and Y. Pepin.**
Nouveaux Aspects du problème de la démocratisation de l'enseignement dans les CEGEP. Québec: Université Laval. Pp. 32. See also *L'Orientation Professionelle* V (2).
Beauregard, C.
'Vers la Création d'une association canadienne au service des collèges?' *Prospectives* V, 82-83.
Dion, G.
'L'Orientation dans un Québec qui cherche à se définir,' *Orient. Prof.* V, 330-38.
Gauthier, A.
'Situation de l'enseignement professionnel dans les écoles secondaires et les CEGEP du Québec,' *Orient. Prof.* V, 97-102.
Gingras, P.-E.
La Vie pédagogique des collèges 1960-1970. Montréal: CADRE. Pp. 56.
Guay, J.
'A Quoi ça sert de s'instruire?' *Mag. Maclean* IX (1), 20-21.
Lauzon, A.
'The C.E.G.E.P. General Strike in Quebec,' *Our Generation* VI, 149-59.
'La Philosophie pour tous au CEGEP; nécessité ou perte de temps? *Maintenant* no. 89, 239-55.
Pratte, C.
'L'Orientation dans les CEGEP,' *Orient. Prof.* V, 238-45.
Thibault, M.
'Quelques Statistiques sur le personnel des institutions privées et collèges publics,' *Prospectives* V, 84-89.
Thibault, J.-L.
'L'Enseignement professionnel et le développement des resources humaines,' *Prospectives* V, 36-50.

1970 **Gingras, P.-E.**
'A la Recherche des objectifs de l'enseignement collégial,' *Prospectives* VI, 182-89.
Roussopoulos, D.
'C.E.G.E.P.'s, Charlebois, Chartand: The Quebec Revolution Now,' *This Magazine* IV (2), 58-76.

1970 **Thibault, M.**
'Etudiants et professeurs: combien sont-ils dans les institutions et les CEGEP?' *Prospectives* VI, 8-15.

G. ONTARIO

1934 **McQueen, J.**
'The Development of the Technical and Vocational Schools of Ontario.' Unpublished M.A. thesis, Columbia Univ.
1949 'The Ryerson Institute of Technology,' *Sch. Prog.* XVI (3), 30-33.
1956 **Beattie, E.**
'The Versatile College with the Concrete Campus,' [Ryerson Polytechnical Institute] *Maclean's* LXIX (23), 20-22, 34-37.
1959 **Montagnes, J.**
'Ryerson – a Training School for the Most-Wanted Men of the 20th Century,' *Can. Bus.* XXXII (9), 122-26.
1963 **Beattie, L. S.** *et al.*
A Study to Determine the Need for Technical Education in North York Township. Willowdale, Ontario: Board of Education for the Township of North York. Pp. 70.
1965 **Committee of Presidents of Provincially Assisted Universities and Colleges of Ontario.**
The City College. Toronto: The Committee. Pp. 15.
'Community Colleges (CAATs) in Ontario,' *Continuous Learning* IV, 228-32.
Davis, W. E.
'A Community College for the Ottawa Region,' *Continuous Learning* IV, 228-32.
Davis, W. G.
'Colleges of Applied Arts and Technology' in *Education in Ontario* (Toronto: Ontario Department of Education), 37-47.
Ontario, Department of Education.
Basic Documents Relating to Colleges of Applied Arts and Technology. Toronto: The Department. Pp. 20.
Semple, S. W.
'John Seath's Concept of Vocational Education in the School System of Ontario, 1884-1911.' Unpublished M.Ed. thesis, Univ. of Toronto.
1966 'Community Colleges (CAATs) in Ontario,' *Continuous Learning* V, 222-26.

1966 **Forsyth, G. R. and J. R. Niminger.**
Expanding Employability in Ontario: an Assessment of the Federal-Provincial Program for Training and Upgrading the Skills of the Unemployed and Its Implications for Government, Business and Labour. Toronto: Ontario Economic Council. Pp. 69.
Sisco, N. A.
'Two Comments on Ontario's Community Colleges,' *Continuous Learning* v, 222-26.

1967 **Brewin, M. J.**
'The Establishment of an Industrial Education System in Ontario.' Unpublished M.A. thesis, Univ. of Toronto.
'Bubbling Enthusiasm, Temporary Facilities Mark Opening of Second Community College,' [Lambton College of Applied Arts & Technology] *Can. Univ.* II (1), 43-45.
Forbes, W. G.
'Community Colleges in Ontario,' *Chem. Can.* XIX (8), 17-20.
'Ontario's Emerging C.A.A.T.S. ... A Survey and Progress Report,' *Can. Univ.* II (5), 60-64, 100.
Sisco, N. A.
'Canada's Manpower Training and Education: A View from Ontario,' *Can. Ed. Research Digest* VII, 299-304.

1968 **Gayfer, M.**
'How Cambrian Works As a Three-In-One CAAT College,' *Sch. Prog.* XXXVII (8), 39-42, 62.
Hoichberg, S. W.
'A Study of Relationships between a Student's Ontario High School Background and Performance in the Diploma Course in Agriculture at the Ontario Agricultural College.' Unpublished M.Sc. thesis, Univ. of Guelph.
Ontario Institute for Studies in Education.
Study for the Guidance of the Governors of the Colleges of Applied Arts and Technology of Ontario. Toronto: The Institute. Pp. 63.
Straka, M. K.
'The Colleges of Applied Arts and Technology,' *Ont. Math. Gaz.* VII (1), 3-12.
Sudar, D. D.
'Ontario's First Library Technology Course,' *Ont. Lib. Rev.* LII (1), 7-11.

1969 **Orlowski, S. T. and J. C. Simon with Leman-Sullivan, Architects and Planners.**
Colleges of Applied Arts and Technology Movement and Growth Patterns. Toronto: Ontario Department of Education. Pp. 28.
Orlowski, S. T., J. C. Simon, R. J. Stirling with Leman-Sullivan, Architects and Planners.
Colleges of Applied Arts and Technology Master Planning. Toronto: Ontario Department of Education. Pp. 36.
Ready, W.
'The c.a.t.t.s. Bibliocentre: Personal Beginnings,' *Inst. Prof. Lib. Ont.* x, 115-19.
Smith, R.
'Three-Year College Courses Planned to Meet Food Technician Shortage,' *Food in Canada* xxix (8), 42-43.
Wright, D. T.
'Ontario-Canadian Community Colleges' in *First Annual Conference, The Association of Colleges of Applied Arts and Technology of Ontario, Plenary Session Addresses* (Toronto: The Association), 1-13.

H. MANITOBA

1964 'The Manitoba Institute of Technology,' *Sch. Prog.* xxxiii (5), 42-44.
1967 **Driedger, L.**
'Developments in Higher Education Among Mennonites in Manitoba,' *Man. Jour. Ed. Res.* iii (1), 24-34.
Report on Post-Secondary Education Needs and Training in Manitoba, Part I: the Social and Economic Structure. Winnipeg: Manitoba Educational Research Council. Pp. 215.

I. SASKATCHEWAN

1955 **Jameson, G. B.**
'Some Aspects of Vocational Education in the North-West Territories from 1870 to 1905 and in the Province of Saskatchewan from 1905 to 1950.' Unpublished m.ed. thesis, Univ. of Saskatchewan.
1967 'Community College Blueprint Prepared for Saskatchewan,' *Canadian School Journal* xlv, 24-25.
'Community Colleges in Saskatchewan,' *Canadian School Journal* xlv, 24-25.

J. ALBERTA

1951 **Martorana, S. V.**
A Community College Plan for Lethbridge, Alberta. Lethbridge: Collegiate Institute.

1956 **Johns, W. H.**
'A Junior Community College as the University Sees It,' *The Alberta School Trustee* (Feb. 1956), 11-14.

1962 **Simon, F.**
'History of the Alberta Provincial Institute of Technology and Art.' Unpublished M.A. thesis, Univ. of Alberta.

1963 **Lowe, P. B.**
'Technical and Vocational Training in Alberta – A Descriptive Study of Its Development.' Unpublished M.A. thesis, Univ. of Alberta.

1964 **Coulson, W. G.**
'The Northern Alberta Institute of Technology,' *Sch. Prog.* XXXIII (5), 36-39.

1965 **Markle, A. G.**
'Genesis of the Lethbridge Public Junior College.' Unpublished M.Ed. thesis, Univ. of Alberta.

1966 **Brown, D. W. R.**
'An Analysis of the Achievements of Junior College Students at the University of Calgary.' Unpublished M.A. thesis, Univ. of Calgary.
Gunderson, H.
'Decision to Set Up Community College Delayed at Least One Year in Alberta,' *Can. Univ.* II (1), 4-5.
Loken, G.
'An Analysis of the Junior College in Alberta: Progress, Program and Prospect.' Unpublished M.Ed. thesis, Univ. of Alberta.
Robertson, C. S.
'Functional Analysis of an Agricultural and Vocational College in Alberta.' Unpublished M.A. thesis, Univ. of Calgary.
Stewart, A.
A Special Study on Junior Colleges. Edmonton: Queen's Printer. Pp. 81.

1967 **Farquhar, H. E.**
'The Role of the College in the System of Higher Education in Alberta.' Unpublished doct. dissertation, Univ. of Alberta.

1968 **Letts, A. B.**
'The Characteristics of Students in Alberta Public Junior Colleges.' Unpublished M.A. thesis, Univ. of Alberta, Edmonton.

1968 **Mase, D. J.**
'Meeting the Challenge – the Community College,' *Alta. Med. Bull.* XXXIII (3), 97-100.
Schindelka, D. J.
'The Characteristics of Students in the Alberta Institutes of Technology.' Unpublished M.A. thesis, Univ. of Alberta.

1969 **Robertson, C. S.**
'Olds Agricultural and Vocational College: Enrolment, Graduation and Employment Patterns.' Unpublished M.Ed. thesis, Univ. of Calgary.
Tod, A. J.
'A Survey of Staff Characteristics in Post-Secondary Institutions in Alberta.' Unpublished M.Ed. thesis, Univ. of Alberta.

K. BRITISH COLUMBIA : COLOMBIE-BRITANNIQUE

1963 **Beames, T. B. A.**
'The Needs for Technical Education in British Columbia – A Survey.' Unpublished M.A. thesis, Univ. of British Columbia.
British Columbia Teachers' Federation.
Community Colleges for British Columbia? Views and Points of View. Vancouver: The Federation. Pp. 21.

1965 **Academic Board for Higher Education in British Columbia.**
The Role of District and Regional Colleges in the British Columbia System of Higher Education. Vancouver: The Board. Pp. 28.
Bayley, C. M.
'Vancouver's City College: Education Insurance,' *Sch. Prog.* XXXIV, 38-39.
Hardwick, W. G. and R. J. Baker.
North Shore Regional College Study. Vancouver: Tantalus Research Ltd. Pp. 45.

1966 **Academic Board for Higher Education in British Columbia.**
College Standards. Victoria: The Board. Pp. 39.
Marsh, L. C.
A Regional College for Vancouver Island. Vancouver: Univ. of British Columbia, Faculty of Education. Pp. 181.

1967 **Academic Board for Higher Education in British Columbia.**
Guide to Post-Secondary Education in British Columbia. Vancouver: The Board. Pp. 26.

1968 **Cocking, C.**
'Whatever Happened to the Community Colleges?' *U.B.C. Alumni Chronicle* xx (3), 24-27.
Conway, C. B.
A Forecast of Potential Community College Enrolments, 1976. Victoria: B.C. Department of Education, Research and Standards Division. Pp. 51.
Dennison, J. D. and G. Jones.
A Statement of the Characteristics and Subsequent Performance of Vancouver City College Students who Transferred into The University of British Columbia in September 1967. Vancouver: U.B.C. and Vancouver City College. Pp. 77.
1969 **Academic Board for Higher Education in British Columbia.**
College-University Articulation. Vancouver: The Board. Pp. 51.

III Agencies and government departments
    Organismes et départements gouvernementaux

Agencies and government departments
Organismes et départements gouvernementaux

Dominion Bureau of Statistics/Bureau Federal de la Statistiques
Ottawa, Ontario

The majority of D.B.S. publications are published annually or biennially. The most recent volume in each series is noted in the following list. The catalogue number is given in parenthesis. All publications are bilingual with the exception of Post-Secondary Student Population, which is published in English and French editions.

Preliminary Statistics of Education	1968-69	(81-201)
Survey of Educational Finance	1966	(81-208)
Advance Statistics of Education	1969-70	(81-220)
Post-Secondary Student Population	1968-69	(81-543)
Salaries and Qualifications of Teachers in Universities and Colleges	1968-69	(81-203)
Survey of Higher Education		
PART I: Fall Enrolment in Universities and Colleges	1968-69	(81-204)
PART II: Degrees, Staff and Summary	1968-69	(81-211)
Canadian Universities: Income and Expenditure	1966-67	(81-212)
Tuition and Living Accommodation Costs at Canadian Degree-Granting Universities and Colleges	1966-67	(81-219)
Awards for Graduate Study and Research	1969	(81-527)
Survey of Libraries		
PART II: Academic Libraries	1967-68	(81-206)
University and College Libraries, Preliminary Release	1967-68	(81-218)
Museums and Art Galleries	1966	(81-529)
Survey of Vocational Education and Training	1967-68	(81-209)
Participants in Further Education in Canada	1959-60	(81-522)

AGENCIES AND GOVERNMENT DEPARTMENTS/278

Economic Council of Canada/Conseil Economique du Canada
Ottawa 4, Ontario

ANNUAL REVIEWS
1964   *Economic Goals for Canada in 1970.*
1965   *Towards Sustained and Balanced Economic Growth.*
1966   *Prices, Productivity and Employment.*
1967   *The Canadian Economy from the 1960's to the 1970's.*
1968   *The Challenge of Growth and Change.*
1969   *Perspective 1975.*
1970   *Pattern in Growth.*

STAFF STUDIES
No. 1   **Denton, F. T.** *et al.*
Population and Labour Force Projections to 1970.
No. 12 **Bartram, G. W.**
The Contribution of Education to Economic Growth.
No. 19 **Illing, W. M.**
Population, Family, Household and Labour Force Growth to 1970.
No. 20 **Illing, W. M. and Z. Zsigmund.**
Enrolment in Schools and Universities 1951-52 to 1975-76.
No. 25 **Zsigmund, Z. and C. Wenaas.**
Enrolment in Educational Institutions by Province, 1951-52 to 1980-81.
No. 27 **Cousin, J., J.-P. Fortin and C. J. Wenaas.**
Some Economic Aspects of Provincial Educational Systems.
No. 33 **Hettich, W.**
Expenditures, Output and Productivity in Canadian University Education.
No. 34 **Zur-Muehler, M. von.**
Development of Community Colleges in Canada.

SPECIAL STUDIES
No. 1   **Parai, L.**
Immigration and Emigration of Professional and Skilled Manpower during the Post-War Period.
No. 8   **Wilson, A. H.**
Science, Technology and Innovation.

Medical Research Council/Conseil des Recherches Médicales
National Research Bldg. M-58, Montreal Rd., Ottawa 7, Canada

1966 *Survey of Research Personnel in the Medical Sciences in Canada 1965-66.* Report No. 1, 33 pp.
Recensement du Personnel Employé dans le Domaine de la Recherche Médicale au Canada 1965-66. Rapport N°. 1, 33 pp.
1968 *Canadian Medical Research: Survey and Outlook,* Report No. 2, 416 pp.
L'Etat Actuel et l'Avenir de la Recherche Médicale au Canada. Rapport N°. 2, 474 pp.
Health Research Uses of Record Linkage in Canada. Report No. 3, 80 pp.
1970 *Research Trainees in the Health Sciences 1969-70.* Report No. 4, 1970. 86 pp. (Bilingual.)
Report of the President, 1969-70. 16 pp. (Bilingual.)
Grants and Award Guide. 99 pp. (Bilingual.)
Annual Review 1969-70. 167 pp. (Bilingual.)

National Research Council/Conseil National de Recherches
Ottawa 4, Ontario

Annual Report on Support of University Research 1965-66, 1966-67, 1967-68
1965 **Beaulieu, P. ed.**
Canadian Universities: Research in Science and Engineering.
1966 **Born, G. S.**
Science-Technology Literature Resources in Canada: Report of a Survey for the Associate Committee on Scientific Information. Pp. 80.
Graduate Students in Science and Engineering Registered in the Graduate Schools of Canadian Universities, 1965-55. Pp. 369.
Some Characteristics of University Teachers in the Biological and Physical Sciences 1958-59 to 1963-64. Pp. 55.
Statistical Summary of Students Registered in the Graduate Schools of Canadian Universities in Physical and Earth Sciences, in Architecture and Engineering, and in the Life Sciences, 1965-66. Pp. 79.
1967 **Levine, O. H.**
Graduate Students and Faculty Resources at Canadian Universities and Colleges. Pp. 38. Bound with *Etudiants diplômes et résources en personnel enseignant dans les établissments de haut savoir au Canada.* Pp. 40.
Expenditures on Research in Science and Engineering at Canadian Universities. Pp. 55.

AGENCIES AND GOVERNMENT DEPARTMENTS/280

1967 *Graduate Students at Canadian Universities in Science and Engineering 1966-67.* Pp. 104
Statistical Summary of Graduate Students at Canadian Universities in Science and Engineering, 1966-67. Pp. 87.
1968 *Graduate Students at Canadian Universities in Science and Engineering 1967-68/Etudiants gradués en science et en génie dans les universités canadiennes 1967-68.* Pp. 398.
Support of Research in Canadian Universities by the National Research Council of Canada. Pp. 54. Bound with *Aide finançière fournie par le Conseil National de Recherches du Canada aux universités canadiennes.*
1969 **Levine, O. H.**
Profiles and Characteristics of Graduate Students Enrolled for the Doctorate in Science and Engineering at Canadian Universities. Pp. 48.
Projections in Manpower Resources and Research Funds 1968-72: Science and Engineering Research in Canadian Universities. Pp. 104.

Science Council of Canada/Conseil des Sciences du Canada
150 Kent Street, Ottawa 4

First Annual Report 1966-67
Second Annual Report 1967-68
Third Annual Report 1968-69
Fourth Annual Report 1969-70

REPORT

No. 1 A Space Program for Canada
No. 2 The Proposal for an Intense Neutron Generator
No. 3 A Major Program of Water Resources Research in Canada
No. 4 Towards a National Science Policy for Canada
No. 5 University Research and the Federal Government
No. 6 A Policy for Scientific and Technical Information Dissemination
No. 7 Earth Sciences Serving the Nation – Recommendations

SPECIAL STUDY

No. 1 Upper Atmosphere & Space Program for Canada
No. 2 Physics in Canada
No. 3 Psychology in Canada
No. 4 The Proposal for an Intense Neutron Generator
No. 5 Water Resources Research in Canada
No. 6 Background Studies in Science Policy: Projections of R & D Manpower and Expenditure
No. 7 The Role of the Federal Government in Support of Research in Canadian Universities

No. 8 Scientific and Technical Information in Canada Part II
        Chapter 1 (Government Departments and Agencies)
        Chapter 2 (Industry)
        Chapter 3 (Universities)
        Chapter 4 (International Agencies and Foreign Countries)
        Chapter 5 (Techniques and Sources)
        Chapter 6 (Libraries)
        Chapter 7 (Economics)
No. 9 Chemistry and Chemical Engineering: A Survey of Research and Development in Canada

Association of Atlantic Universities/
L'Association des Universities de l'Atlantique
P.O. Box 24, Halifax, N.S.

1965 **Somers, H. J.**
Education in the Atlantic Provinces: a Report Submitted to the Commission on the Financing of Higher Education. Pp. 77.
1969 **Crean, J. F., M. M. Ferguson and H. J. Somers.**
Higher Education in the Atlantic Provinces: a Study. Prepared under the auspices of the Association of Atlantic Universities for the Maritime Union. Pp. 14.

Prince Edward Island Commission on Post-Secondary Education
Box 335, Charlottetown, P.E.I.

1970 **Arnold, M. H.**
'Interprovincial Grants and Payments in Support of Post-Secondary Education in the Atlantic Region (with Special Reference to Prince Edward Island.' Pp. 28. (Mimeograph.)
First Annual Report covering the Period to December 31, 1969. Pp. 28.

University Grants Committee of Nova Scotia
5413 Spring Garden Road, Halifax

Annual Reports entitled *Higher Education in Nova Scotia* 1963, 1964, etc. have been published each year since 1964.

AGENCIES AND GOVERNMENT DEPARTMENTS/282

New Brunswick Higher Education Commission
Fredericton, N.B.

1968 *First Annual Report (1967-68).* Pp. 20.
'Current Level of Government Assistance for Universities, Colleges and Students.' Pp. 23. (Mimeograph.)
'Level of Operating Grants for New Brunswick Universities.' Pp. 3. (Mimeograph.)
1969 *Investing in the Future: a Programme for Government Assistance to Universities, Technical Schools and Students.* Pp. 67.
Second Annual Report (1968-69). Pp. 30.
Duffie, Donald C.
Teacher Education and Training. Pp. 39.

Commission de l'enseignement superieur du Nouveau-Brunswick
Fredericton, N.B.

1968 *Premier rapport annuel (1967-68).* Pp. 20.
'Niveau courrant d'assistance gouvernementale aux universités, collèges et étudiants.' Pp. 29. (Autocopiste.)
'Niveau des subventions de fonctionnement accordées en 1968-1969 aux universités du Nouveau-Brunswick.' Pp. 3. (Autocopiste.)
1969 *Un regard vers l'avenir.* Pp. 72.
Deuxieme rapport annuel (1968-69). Pp. 30.
Duffie, Donald C.
Formation pédagogique. Pp. 39.

Centre d'animation de developpement et de recherche en education
1940 est, boulevard Henri-Bourassa, Montréal 360

1965 *Prospectives: Revue d'information et de recherche en éducation.*
1967 **Beausoleil, J. et D. Masse.**
Les Services aux étudiants dans le structure administrative des CEGEP. Pp. 99.
1969 **Bauman, A.**
Rapport analytique de l'exercice financier 1968-69 dans les institutions membres de l'AIES et de l'ACQ. Pp. 19. (A.F. 500.)

1969 **Beaudry, R. et H. Guindon.**
Attentes et satisfactions d'un groupe d'étudiants de niveau collegial.
Pp. 218. (E.D. 201.)
Gingras, P.-E.
La vie pedagogique des collèges 1960-1970. Pp. 56. (P.D. 600.)
Une liste du nombre considérable des publications de la Fédération des Collèges Classiques (1957 à 1967) peut être obtenir de CADRE.

La Conference des Recteurs et des Principaux des Universités du Québec/
Conference of Rectors and Principals of Quebec Universities
6600 Chemin de la Côte des Neiges, Montréal 249, Québec

1969 *Rapport Annuel.*
Martin, S.
'Public Policy Regarding Private Support of Universities.' Pp. 12.
Segal, M.
'Programme Budgeting and the Ministry Formulae.' Pp. 41.
1970 **Bordeleau, J., A. P. Contandriopoulos et N. Hung.**
'Etudes et proportions en vue de la mise en place d'une echelle normée des traitements pour les professeurs des universités du Québec.' Pp. 213.
Bordeleau, J. et J. Legare.
'Les Méthodes de previsions de population étudiante au niveau universitaire.' Pp. 33.
Proulx, P.-P.
'Collective Negotiations in Higher Education – Canada.' Pp. 28.
Segal, M.
'The Political Economy of Resource Distribution in Quebec Universities.' Pp. 430.

Conseil Supérieur de l'Education/Superior Council of Education
Hôtel du Gouvernement, Québec

1966 *La Participation au plan scolaire.* Rapport annuel 1964/1965 du Conseil superieur de l'Education. Pp. 213.
Participation in Educational Planning. Annual Report 1964/1965 of the Superior Council of Education. Pp. 213.
1968 'L'Enseignant face à l'évolution sociale et scolaire.' Rapport 1965/66-1966/67 du Conseil superieur de l'Education. Pp. 389.

AGENCIES AND GOVERNMENT DEPARTMENTS/284

1968 **Superior Council of Education.**
'The Teacher Faces Social and Educational Change.' Report 1965/66-1966/67 of the Superior Council of Education. Pp. 365.
1970 **Conseil superieur de l'Education.**
Rapport d'activités, 1967/68-1968/69 du Conseil superieur de l'Education. Pp. 363.
Superior Council of Education.
Activity Report, 1967/68-1968/69 of the Superior Council of Education.

Committee of Presidents of Universities of Ontario/
Comité des Présidents d'Universités de l'Ontario
230 Bloor Street West, Toronto 181

1963 Post-Secondary Education in Ontario 1962-70. Pp. 44.
The Structure of Post-Secondary Education in Ontario. Pp. 30.
1965 The City College. Pp. 15.
University Television: Report of the Subcommittee on Television ... Pp. 28.
1966 From the Sixties to the Seventies: an Appraisal of Higher Education in Ontario by the Presidents' Research Committee for the Committee of Presidents of Universities of Ontario. Pp. 101.
The Health Sciences in Ontario Universities: Recent Experience and Prospects for the Next Decade. Pp. 26.
1967 Systems Emerging: First Annual Review (1966-67) of the Committee of Presidents of Universities of Ontario. Pp. 59.
1968 Collective Autonomy: Second Annual Review, 1967-68. Pp. 68.
Student Participation in University Government: a Study Paper Prepared for the Committee of Presidents by its Subcommittee on Research and Planning. Pp. 21.
1969 **Ontario Council of University Librarians.**
Inter-University Transit System Anniversary Report, 1967-68. Pp. 20.
Campus and Forum: Third Annual Review, 1968-69. Pp. 75.
1970 **Ontario Council on Graduate Studies.**
The First Three Years of Appraisal of Graduate Programmes. Pp. 17.

Committee on University Affairs (Ontario)
481 University Avenue, Toronto

1963   *Ontario University Affairs.* Statement by the Honourable John P. Robarts, Prime Minister of Ontario. Delivered in the Ontario Legislature, March 21, 1963. Pp. 14.
1964   *Report on University Affairs.* Pp. 24.
1966   *Report of the Commission to Study the Development of Graduate Programmes in Ontario Universities.* Pp. 110.
1967   *Report,* 1967. Pp. 36.
1968   *Report on the Organizational Structure and Administration of the Ontario College of Art* by Douglas T. Wright. Pp. 23.
1969   *Report,* 1968-69. Pp. 38.
       Final Report of Subcommittee on Regional Computing Centres. Pp. 7.

Department of University Affairs of Ontario
481 University Avenue, Toronto

1965 – *Horizons:* a Guide to Educational Opportunities in Ontario Beyond the Secondary School Level. *Annual.*
       Statutes Governing the Provincially Assisted Universities of Ontario.
1966   *University Affairs in Ontario:* Statement by the Honourable William G. Davis, Minister of University Affairs, in Presenting the Estimates to the Legislative Assembly of Ontario. Pp. 21.
1967   *Higher Education in Ontario:* Statement by the Honourable William G. Davis, Minister of University Affairs, in Presenting the Estimates to the Legislative Assembly. Pp. 10.
1968   'Statement by the Honourable William G. Davis, Minister of University Affairs, in Presenting the Estimates to the Legislative Assembly.' Pp. 34. (Mimeograph.)
       Report of the Minister of University Affairs of Ontario, 1967. Pp. 130.
1969   'Selected Enrolment Data from Computer Reports Prepared by the Education Data Centre for the Provincially-Assisted and Church-Related Institutions of the Province of Ontario – 1969-70 Actual and 1970-71 Projected.' Annual. Pp. 34. (Mimeograph.)
       Report of the Minister of University Affairs of Ontario, 1968-69. Pp. 120.
       'Statement by the Honourable William G. Davis, Minister of University Affairs, in Presenting the Estimates to the Legislative Assembly.' Pp. 30. (Mimeograph.)

1970 *Manual of Costs of University Buildings and Cost Analyses since 1964.*
Recipients of Grants-in-Aid of Research 1969-70. Annual.
Statutes Governing the Provincially Assisted Universities of Ontario.
2nd edition.

Universities Grants Commission of Manitoba
10 - 395 Berry Street, Winnipeg 12

1968 *Annual Report for the Year Ending March 31, 1968.*
1969 *Annual Report for the Year Ending March 31, 1969.*

Alberta Colleges Commission
11160 Jasper Avenue, Edmonton, Alberta

STUDY COMMITTEE REPORTS
1969 *The Edmonton College:* Report of the Planning Committee to the Board of Post-Secondary Education. Pp. 72.
1970 *The Fairview Agricultural and Vocational College:* Report of a Study Conducted by the Minister of Education and the Minister of Agriculture. Pp. 124.

RESEARCH STUDY SERIES
1970 **Atherton, P. J.**
Alberta Junior College Cost Studies: Mount Royal College. (No. 1), Pp. 94.
Hanson, E. J.
Population Analysis and Projections: College Areas in Alberta. (No. 2), Pp. 103.
Letts, A.
The Characteristics of Students in Alberta Agricultural and Vocational Colleges. (No. 3), Pp. 91.
Schindelka, D. J.
The Characteristics of Students in the Alberta Institutes of Technology. (No. 4), Pp. 102.
Atherton, P. J.
Alberta Junior College Cost Studies: Grande Prairie Junior College. (No. 5), Pp. 31.

1970 **Atherton, P. J.**
Alberta Junior College Cost Studies: Financing Junior Colleges in Alberta. (No. 6), Pp. 154.
Tod, A. J.
Staff Characteristics in Post Secondary Institutions in Alberta. (No. 7), Pp. 163.
Falkenberg, E. E.
A Study of the Success of Alberta Junior College Transfer Students to Selected Alberta Universities. (No. 8), Pp. 212.

The Alberta Universities Commission
11111 87th Avenue, Edmonton 61, Alberta

1970 *1968-69 Annual Report of the Alberta Universities Commission.* Edmonton: Alberta Universities Commission.

Academic Board for Higher Education in British Columbia
3611 West 16th Avenue, Vancouver 8, B.C.

1965 *The Role of District and Regional Colleges in the British Columbia System of Higher Education.* Pp. 28.
1966 *College Standards.* Pp. 39.
1967 *Guide to Post-Secondary Education in British Columbia.* Pp. 26.
1969 *College-University Articulation.* Pp. 51.

Index

Abbott, R. D. 30, 141
Ackland, J. H. 126
Ackroyd, A. O. 49
Adam, W. G. 71, 243
Adams, F. H. 216
Adams, P. R. 66
Adams, T. 16
Adamson, J. D. 164
Adaskin, M. 102
Adelman, H. 61, 65, 240, 242, 244
Adelman, M. 119
Adeney, M. 102
Adkins, A. A. 196
Aganier, H. 17
Ahrendt, K. M. 56
Aikenhead, J. D. 185, 188
Ajaleu, E. 182
Albert, G. 132
Albrant, R. J. 70
Alexander, W. 18, 87
Ali, A. H. 12, 266
Allbon, L. G. 181
Allen, A. D. 120
Allen, C. 29
Allen, D. E. 173, 212
Allen, E. B. 193
Allen, M. 172
Allen, R. T. 60
Allenby, O. C. W. 119
Allison, L. M. 13
Altmann, H. A. 240
Anctil, P. 121
Anden, T. M. 84
Anderson, A. L. 48, 154
Anderson, C. P. 104
Anderson, D. 205
Anderson, D. O. 106, 149, 157, 158, 159, 160, 207, 236
Anderson, D. V. 217
Anderson, R. N. 75
Andoff, J. E. 245
Andrew, G. C. 59, 69, 71, 76, 78, 202, 262
Andrew, R. B. 164
Andrews, J. 199
Angers, F.-A. 79, 100

Angers, P. 17, 87, 136, 266, 267
Anglin, G. 38
Anselm, Sister 11
Appleton, V. E. 155
Appley, D. G. 245, 246
Appley, M. H. 112
Archambault, A. 174, 175
Archambault, J. G. 236
Archambault, J. L. 140
Arès, R. 95
Armstrong, D. E. 129, 130
Armstrong, D. P. 203
Armstrong, H. S. 149
Arnett, J. 262
Arnison, D. 144
Arnold, M. H. 5, 281
Arsenault, F. 237
Arthur, A. Z. 113
Arvidson, R. M. 51, 112
Ashley, C. A. 249
Astbury, E. C. 228
Atherton, P. J. 286, 287
Auclair, E.-J. 16, 153
Audet, L.-P. 25, 134, 188, 250
Auger, L. 195
Austman, H. H. 124
Ausubel, D. P. 113, 190
Ayert, R. M. 129
Aylwin, U. 95
Azard, P. 143

Babbitt, J. D. 115, 217
Baby, A. 241, 246, 268
Backman, L. B. 91
Bailey, A. G. 13
Bailey, A. W. 186
Bailey, B. 249
Baillie, D. C. 256
Bain, James 223
Bain, Jerald, 175
Bakan, D. R. 84, 113
Baker, R. J. 56, 273
Baldwin, C. H. 143
Baldwin, J. M. 102, 110
Ball, S. 11, 133
Ballantyne, P. M. 31

Bancroft, L. I. 232
Bannen, J. 196
Barbeau, M. 188
Barbeau, V. 99
Barbin, R. 104
Baril, G. 24
Barker, B. 199, 218
Barradas, R. G. 120
Barrosse, T. 104
Barrows, H. C. 161
Barry, W. F. 111
Bartram, G. W. 278
Baskerville, W. R. 206
Bassett, G. W. 188
Bater, R. 193
Bates, D. V. 161, 165, 168
Bates, I. 147
Bates, R. 63, 252
Baudoin, J. A. 23, 168, 181
Baudoin, L. 142
Bauman, A. 282
Baurno, A. N. 120
Baxter, R. M. 175, 176
Baxter, S. D. 217
Bayefsky, A. 90
Bayley, C. M. 273
Bayne, J. 33
Bazett, H. C. 216
Beames, T. B. A. 273
Beamish, F. E. 120
Beattie, E. 269
Beattie, L. S. 269
Beatty, E. 254
Beatty, J. D. 41, 156
Beauchamp, C. 204
Beauchemin, J.-M. 17, 69, 195
Beaudoin, F. 169
Beaudoin, L. 214
Beaudry, R. 237, 283
Beaudry-Johnson, N. 172
Beaugrand-Champagne, P.-P. 23
Beaulieu, P. 279
Beaulieu, P. J. 197
Beaulieu, Y. 206
Beauregard, C. 17, 251, 266, 268
Beauregard, L. 103, 108, 192, 210
Beauregard, M. 27
Beausoliel, J. 266, 282
Beaver, B. 5
Bebchuk, W. 164
Beck, J. C. 167
Beck, R. P. 166
Beckel, W. E. 61, 85, 210
Becker, J. 248

Becker, P. 245
Beckman, M. 225
Bedal, C. 196
Bedard, D. 209
Bedard, P. 241
Beeson, E. W. 141, 142, 145
Begg, R. W. 48, 65, 76
Beissel, H. 51
Beland, N. 170
Belanger, G. 82
Belanger, L. 140
Belanger, P. W. 205, 241, 268
Bell, J. J. 33
Bell, P. W. 176
Belleau, H. G. 143
Bellerive, A. 196, 246
Bell-Irving, R. W. 168
Belshaw, C. S. 106, 129
Belth, M. 189
Benjamin, C. 241
Benjamin, M. 224
Benjamin, S. 126
Bennett, H. 169
Bennett, P. H. 71
Benning, J. A. 249
Berdahl, R. O. 65
Bergeron, G.-A. 157, 159, 162
Bergeron, V. 254
Berland, A. 14, 57, 67, 255
Berlyne, D. E. 83, 105
Bernard, A. 8
Bernard, J. 180
Bernier, A. 46
Berry, D. G. 110, 111
Bertho, E. 166
Bertin, B. L. 39
Berton, P. 21
Bertram, G. W. 81
Bertrand, J. 186
Beschel, R. E. 35, 119
Bewley, L. M. 147
Bignell, D. C. 229
Billinton, R. 48
Bilodeau, R. 235
Bilsland, J. W. 90, 94
Biname, J.-J. 91
Bindra, D. 22, 210
Binhammer, H. H. 105, 219
Bisakowski, K. 10, 179
Bishop, D. R. 246
Bishop, O. B. 145
Bissell, C. T. 4, 28, 40, 58, 59, 61, 65, 225, 241
Bissonnier, H. 170

Bjorgo, M. 228
Black, A. 238
Black, C. 134
Black, D. 238
Black, D. B. 50, 84, 185, 206, 207, 209, 221, 238
Black, J. L. 31, 62, 98, 99
Blackburn, R. H. 226, 228
Blackie, W. V. 135
Blackmore, W. R. 130
Blackwell, K. M. 103
Bladen, V. W. 69, 70
Bladon, L. W. 133
Blain, G. 149, 165
Blain, M. 87
Blair, A. M. 109
Blais-Grenier, M.-S. 183, 184
Blais, N. 172
Blake, V. R. 116
Blakeley, P. 9, 10
Blakely, R. J. 201
Blanar, J. A. 129
Bland, J. 125, 244
Blaney, J. P. 85, 203
Blishen, B. R. 151
Bliss, J. M. 100
Blum, F. 112
Boggs, J. S. 90, 230
Boissonault, C.-M. 99
Boivin, A. 123
Bolstad, W. G. 131
Bonenfant, J.-C.
Bonn, G. S. 116, 217, 226
Bonn, W. 24
Bonneau, L.-P. 20, 65, 71
Bono, J. D. 89, 92
Booth, A. D. 134
Booth, M. 105, 219
Bordan, J. 136
Bordeleau, J. 207, 283
Born, G. S. 279
Borror, M. J. 138
Borrowman, M. 188
Bortolazzo, J. L. 263
Bosa, R. 146, 147
Botterell, E. H. 157, 161
Bouchard, R. 104
Boucher, G. 73
Boucher, J. 105
Boucher, R. 155
Boulay, D. 8
Bourcier, C. 177
Bourgault, R. 86
Bouvier, E. 238

Bowser, W. E. 124
Boyce, R. M. 245
Boyd, J. B. 111
Boylan, D. B. 144
Boyle, R. W. 216
Bradford, K. 247
Brady, A. 128
Brandenberger, A. J. 135
Branscombe, F. R. 191, 212
Brault, J. R. 227
Bray, M. 232
Brayton, F. 239
Brazeau, J. 14, 74, 215
Brecher, I. 96
Brecher, R. A. 96
Breckon, S. W. 123
Bredin, G. 54
Bregzis, R. 225, 226
Brehaut, W. 103, 221, 223
Breton, A. 104, 122
Breton, R. 237
Brett, G. S. 3
Brewer, A. W. 122
Brewin, M. J. 270
Briemberg, M. 57, 68
Bringmann, W. G. 44, 113
Brison, D. W. 111
Brochu, A. 206
Brodeur, C. C. 245
Brooke, W. M. 204
Brossard, R. 122
Brown, A. 247
Brown, A. M. 102, 247
Brown, B. I. 132, 159, 207
Brown, D. C. 164
Brown, D. J. 251
Brown, D. W. R. 52, 209, 272
Brown, F. M. 230
Brown, H. K. 132, 182
Brown, J. A. 217
Brown, L. 71
Brown, L. E. 178, 189
Brown, M. C. 169
Brown, S. R. 179
Brown, W. J. 47, 109
Bruchesi, J. 232
Brunet, J. 20, 24, 118, 151, 182
Brunet, M. 3, 15, 73, 77, 99, 251
Bryans, A. M. 162
Buchan, M. 180
Buchanan, B. H. 222
Buck, C. 159
Buckland, J. K. 173
Buckley, P. 135

Bucknall, B. D. 143
Bulani, W. 44, 135
Buller, H. 22, 239-41
Bullman, M. 55, 160, 180
Burchill, C. S. 99
Bureau, R. 171
Burgess, J. P. 251
Burgis, G. C. 229
Burnham, S. 29
Burns, M. D. 243
Burpee, L. J. 9, 18, 224, 231
Burton, G. F. A. 130
Burton, I. 108
Butler, R. M. 119
Buyniak, V. O. 98
Byleveld, H. 71, 72
Byrd, K. F. 129

Cailleux, A. 20, 110
Caisman, N. 189
Calam, J. 62
Callard, K. B. 127
Callin, M. 172
Callwood, J. 38
Calvin, D. D. 235
Cameron, D. 159, 168, 207
Cameron, D. M. 73
Cameron, E. L. 11, 134
Cameron, I. 10, 155
Cameron, J. W. 129
Cameron, M. H. V. 38, 154
Cameron, P. 65
Campbell, A. B. 6
Campbell, H. 228
Campbell, S. S. 201
Campeau, L. 192
Camu, P. 108, 232
Cann, M. M. 185
Cappon, D. 165
Cappon, J. 34
Card, B. Y. 114, 222
Cardinal, J.-G. 76, 77, 143
Careless, J. M. S. 100, 101
Carmichael, M. M. 139
Caron, I. 16
Carpenter, H. M. 41, 169, 171
Carr, H. 104
Carrier, H. 63
Carrier, L. J. 225
Carrière, G. 32, 33, 233
Carroll, J. 30
Carrothers, A. B. B. 142
Carrothers, A. W. R. 44, 142, 237

Carrothers, F. 75
Carter, B. G. 169
Carter, R. P. 191, 199, 204, 205
Cartwright, J. R. 43
Cartwright, M. J. 227
Case, P. 139
Castonguay, T. 170, 173
Cathcart, L. M. 149
Catterton, M. M. 180
Cauchy, V. 103
Cavanagh, D. A. 202
Cerwin, V. B. 44, 111, 112
Chabassol, D. J. 250, 253
Chabot, M. 209
Chalmers, J. W. 49
Chambers, R. T. 159
Chant, D. A. 119
Chapais, T. 16
Chapman, J. D. 109
Chapman, J. H. 77, 214
Chapman, J. K. 14
Charette, R. 209
Charland, T.-M. 86
Charles, W. H. 143
Charron, C. 241
Chartier, R. 129, 247
Chartier, Y. 102
Chase, F. S. 223
Cheffins, R. I. 22, 141
Cherniak, R. M. 151
Chevalot, T. 151
Chipman, M. L. 41, 151, 207, 248
Chorny, M. 186, 187
Chown, A. A. 34
Chown, M. M. 35
Chronister, G. M. 56
Chuk, J. E. 265
Churchley, F. 102
Chusid, H. 90
Chute, A. L. 157
Cinq-Mars, E. 15
Clark, E. 73, 208, 237, 244
Clark, R. C. 197
Clarke, G. C. 160
Clarke, G. G. 41, 151, 248
Clarkson, F. A. 38, 154
Clarkson, S. 40
Clebsch, W. A. 192
Cleveland, D. E. H. 154
Coats, R. H. 121, 216
Cochrane, H. G. 11
Cochrane, W. A. 161
Cockburn, P. 81

Cocking, C. 274
Cockings, E. C. 167
Cohen, M. 141
Cohen, R. 40, 92, 93
Cohn, W. 251
Cole, R. F. 241
Cole, W. 94, 101, 107, 110
Coleman, A. J. 122
Coleman, S. J. 6
Colette, J. 130
Colgate, W. 232
Colin, M. L. 23
Collins, A. L. 175
Collins, R. 50
Colton, A. S. 89
Compton, N. 27, 241
Conacher, W. M. 235
Condon, T. J. 14
Conkie, W. R. 36, 123
Conklin, R. C. 247
Connell, W. T. 35
Contandriopoulos, A. P. 283
Conway, C. B. 274
Conway, J. S. 104, 192
Cook, D. 73, 208, 237, 244
Cook, G. R. 62, 100, 101
Cook, J. T. 185
Coons, W. H. 110, 112
Cooper, W. M. 75
Copp, T. 101
Copping, J. D. 151
Corbett, E. A. 44, 200
Corbett, R. 18
Cormier, H. 200
Corry, J. A. 36, 59, 60, 63, 66, 67, 71, 76, 77, 198, 240
Costello, C. G. 173
Côté, F. 123, 267
Côté, J. E. 141
Coté, R. 129
Cotter, E. 95
Coughey, D. J. 14
Coulson, W. G. 272
Courtney, J. C. 48, 66, 77
Courtney, R. 91
Cousin, J. 278
Cousineau, R. 18
Coutts, H. T. 50, 51, 186, 221
Coutts, W. B. 130
Coutu, L. L. 157, 165
Cragg, L. H. 13, 135, 197
Craigie, E. H. 40, 119
Crane, J. W. 43, 154

Cranstaun, J. 169
Crawford, D. H. 121
Crean, J. F. 281
Crean, J. G. 5
Creighton, D. G. 39
Creighton, R. A. 95
Crepeau, R. 27, 141
Cross, G. 121
Croteau, J. 80
Crowley, C. P. 137
Cruikshank, G. 63
Cruickshank, W. A. 187
Cunningham, D. A. 178
Currelly, C. T. 230
Curtis, G. F. 143
Curtiss, J. F. 155
Cutler, M. I. 90
Cyert, R. M. 65

Dadson, D. F. 29
Dagnaud, P.-M. 8
Dalbis, L. J. 115
Dales, J. H. 107
Dandurand, M. 232
Daniells, R. 39, 88, 115, 116
Dannenmaier, W. D. 84
Dansereau, F. 239
Dansereau, J. 210
Davey, K. W. 131
Davidson, A. G. F. 161
Davidson, C. L. 179
Davidson, P. O. 113, 209
Davies, R. 35
Davis, W. E. 75, 269
Davis, W. G. 221, 269, 285
Dawson, B. 227
Dawson, J. 162
Day, H. I. 113
Day, R. H. 138
Deane, S. G. 197
Dearness, J. 197
de Belleval, D. 140
Decarie, A. 88
De Chantal, R. 58
De Courbertin, P. 3
Defries, R. D. 41, 156, 182
de Grandpré, J. 73
De Hesse, C. 149
de la Chevrotière, J. 183
Dembrowski, P. 91
Dempsey, N. M. 245
Denault, H. 183
DeNevi, D. 262

Denis, L.-G. 26
Denison, S. 140
Dennis, L. G. 146
Dennison, J. D. 56, 274
Denton, F. T. 278
Derbez, R. 165
Desbarats, P. 28
Desbiens, J.-P. 267
Desilets, A. 232
Desjardines, E. 24, 155
Desjardins, L. 223
Desjarlais, L. 87
Desmarais, A. 119, 254
Despland, M. 104
Desrochers, E. 144, 146, 225, 234
Desrochers, R. D. 25, 122
Des Roches, B. P. 175
Des Rosiers, G. 168
Deutsch, J. 36, 77, 62
Deveau, A. 8
De Vos, A. 109
Dhalla, N. K. 60
Diamond, A. J. 51
Dibrick, H. 38, 153
Dick, W. W. 248
Dickinson, G. 135, 204
Dickinson, J. R. 131
Dickson, A. D. 52, 162, 163
Diemer, A. H. 238
Dietz, M. L. 238
Dineen, J. O. 135, 263
Di Norcia, V. 61
Dion, G. 197, 247, 268
Dixon, R. C. 211
Dobson, W.A.C.H. 92, 93
Dodwell, P. C. 83, 105
Doerksen, J. G. 193
Doern, G. B. 218
Dolman, C. C. 116
Dolores, Sister F. 144
Domaradzki, T. F. 97
Dooley, J. E. 175
Dorais, F. 267
Dorais, L. A. 27, 203
Doray, V. 90
Douglas, A. E. 117
Douglas, V. I. 110
Dow, H. J. 13, 230
Downee, J. 36, 136
Downey, L. 186
Downs, R. B. 227, 228
D'Oyley, V. 197
Doyon, J. 17

Drache, D. 240
Draper, J. A. 203, 205
Driedger, L. 45, 271
Driver, M. F. 180
Drolet, A. 19, 224, 225
Drolet, J.-C. 193
Drummond, I. M. 28, 59, 65, 71, 75, 79, 80, 250
Drury, C. M. 75, 115, 217
Dube, W. J. 161
Dube, Y. 70
Duceppe, G. 61
Duckworth, H. E. 77, 214
Duclos, G. C. 81
Duff, J. 65
Duff, J. G. 174
Duff, S. L. 152, 160
Duffie, Donald C. 282
Dufresne, R. R. 24
Dugal, L.-P. 73, 215, 218
Dumas, M. 27
Dumont, F. 114
Duncan, A. R. C. 237
Dunlop, G. M. 50
Dunn, W. J. 43, 131, 132
Dunton, A. D. 30
Dupuis, J. R. P. 199
Dupuis, P. 190
Durand, M. 25
Duval, l'Archevêque 87
Duval, R. 190, 195
Dymond, M. B. 163

Earl, S. A. 187
Eastman, H. C. 105, 198
Eastman, S. M. 200
Eaton, J. D. 178
Eber, D. 28
Eckler, S. 256
Eckman, J. R. 155
Edgar, P. 230
Edmonds, D. 58
Edwards, C. H. C. 143
Edwards, J. K. 28
Edwards, R. 198, 223
Elder, A. T. 94
Eliot, C. W. J. 54, 85
Elliott, J. W. 247
Elliott, L. G. 116
Elliott, S. 7
Ellis, M. D. 189
Ellis, R. G. 39, 132
Ellsworth, R. E. 226

Elston, A. J. 262
Emory, F. H. 169, 181
Empery, V. E. 228
Empey, E. 139
Endler, N. S. 209
English, H. E. 70
Erickson, A. 42, 62
Eshleman, W. 57, 212
Ettlinger, J. R. T. 227
Evans, D. E. 181
Evans, J. 149
Evans, R. K. 158, 160, 207
Even, A. 12
Evenson, A. B. 50, 205
Everett, D. J. 265

Fabre-Surveyer, E. 141
Fahidy, T. Z. 135
Fahmy, P. 171, 236
Fairbairn, L. S. 142
Fair, D. C. 245
Fairweather, E. R. 194
Fairweather, G. 241
Falardeau, J.-C. 104, 114, 216
Falconer, J. W. 9, 13, 192
Falconer, R. 230
Falkenberg, E. E. 287
Fallis, G. 73, 208, 237, 244
Fancott, E. 88
Farine, A. 234
Farmer, C. 161
Farquhar, H. E. 263, 272
Farrant, R. H. 31, 112
Faucher, A. 106, 107, 220
Fauteux, A. 224
Favreau, R. 239
Fawdry, K. 210
Fehr, R. C. 44, 113
Feilding, C. 193
Fellman, D. 254
Fenton, A. 22, 128
Ferguson, G. 11, 90
Ferguson, G. A. 110
Ferguson, J. 231
Ferguson, K. 36, 37, 100
Ferguson, M. F. 5
Ferguson, M. M. 281
Ferland, M. 180
Ferns, H. S. 38
Ferrando, R. 194
Fiander, R. W. 7
Fiddes, J. 48
Fidler, N. 168

Field, J. 117, 241
Fifield, B. 181
Firestone, O. J. 4
Fischette, R. M. 252
Fish, D. G. 132, 149, 158-61, 163, 164, 207
Fish, F. M. 157
Fisher, E. A. 82, 199
Fisher, E. J. 177
Fisher, G. L. 67
Flahault, J. 119
Flaherty, M. J. 171, 203
Fleck, P. 249
Fleming, R. J. 48
Fleming, W. G. 221-23, 236
Flexner, A. 153
Flock, W. 250
Flohil, R. 248
Flower, G. 253
Flowers, J. E. 149
Flynn, A. E. 133
Flynn, M. 66
Fogarty, D. 12, 86
Fogarty, W. P. 133
Folejewski, Z. 98
Foran, M. R. 133
Forbes, J. M. 180
Forbes, W. G. 270
Ford, C. R. 262, 265
Ford, E. K. 185
Ford, J. E. 131
Foreman, D. A. 126
Forsyth, G. R. 270
Forsythe, P. A. 122
Fortier, E. 104
Fortin, G. 114
Fortin, J. P. 278
Forward, F. 116
Foster, H. 110
Foster, M. 38
Foulkes, R. G. 166
Fournier, J.-L. 103
Fowke, D. V. 66
Fox, W. S. 43
France, N. 82, 189, 191
Franchea, M. 170
Francis, D. 228
Franke, W. 209
Franklin, S. 7
Fraser, C. M. 195
Fraser, D. C. 210
Fraser, D. G. L. 7
Fraser, J. A. H. 197

Fraser, W. H.   37, 93, 95, 96
Frayn, D. H.   167
Frazer, W. J.   47
Freedman, S.   65, 141, 149, 254
Fremont, C.   211
French, D.   189
Frenkel, V.   90
Frewin, M.   232
Friedman, H. M.   143
Friesen, D.   237
Frumhartz, M.   30, 85
Frye, H. N.   39, 62, 240, 241
Fuller, J. A.   128
Fyfe, W. H.   34
Fyles, T. W.   47

Gacratt, G. A.   137
Gadbois, L.   207, 238, 246
Gaddes, W. H.   110, 113
Gagné, F.   209
Gagne, G.   91
Gagne, J.   169, 184
Gagnon, C.   25, 59
Gagnon, J.   169
Gagnon, J.-A.   233, 246
Gagnon, L.   25
Gajadharsingh, J.   94
Galarneau, C.   18, 87
Gareau, E.   93
Gariepy, J. M.   176
Gariepy, R.   166
Garigue, P.   105, 219
Garlick, J. K.   158
Garneau, J.   243
Garnett, F. J.   46
Garnier, B. J.   22, 109
Garrard, J. G.   98
Garrard, R.   10
Garrow, P.   124
Garstin, L. G.   221
Gathercole, G. E.   127
Gattinger, F. E.   194, 225, 226
Gaudreau, G.   15, 238
Gaudron, E.   88, 116
Gaudry, R.   25, 76, 116, 176, 214, 218
Gault, H. M.   180
Gauthier, A.   197, 268
Gauthier, G.   72, 205
Gauthier, Monseigneur G.   23
Gauthier, Y.   8
Gautier, G.   72, 205
Gayfer, M.   262, 270
Geddes, B. A.   249

Gelber, H.   167
Genest, B.-A.   135, 199
Genest, J.   15, 151, 165, 238, 267
Geoffroy, M.   241
Georges, E.   8
Gerrish, R. E.   262
Gibson, D.   111
Gibson, D. A.   10, 161, 211
Gibson, J. A.   29, 59
Gibson, J. C.   125
Gibson, T.   34, 153
Gibson, W. C.   54, 55
Gifford, C. G.   183
Gifford, H.   30, 225
Gifford, L. D.   237, 246
Gignac, J.-P.   136
Giguere, G.-E.   100
Gilbert, J. A. L.   159, 182, 207
Giles, L. G.   225
Gill, C.   59, 70, 71
Gill, D.   110
Gill, J. E.   217
Gill, M.   189
Gill, M. S.   234
Gillett, M.   267
Gilley, J. R.   127
Gillis, A. A.   4
Gilmour, R. P.   68
Gilmour, C.   53
Gingras, B.-A.   120, 198, 217
Gingras, G.   158, 180, 181
Gingras, P.-E.   268, 283
Gingras, R.   158, 160, 207
Gingras, R.-E.   26
Girand, J.   108
Glazier, K. M.   227
Glendenning, D. E. M.   69, 261
Glibon, P.   108
Glover, T. R.   33
Gnyp, A. W.   120
Goddard, G. V.   113, 199
Godden, J. O.   149
Godfrey, C. M.   40, 155, 156
Godfrey, D.   249
Gold, J.   63, 252
Goldbloom, R. B.   160
Goldstick, D.   241
Gonick, C. W.   65
Good, S. R.   172
Goodings, S.   238
Goodland, J. I.   187
Goodman, F. V. S.   248
Goodwin, W. L.   137

Gordon, C. B.   86
Gordon, D. M.   34
Gordon, G.   113
Gordon, J. M.   45, 48, 49, 131
Gordon, J. R. M.   131
Gordon, P. J.   66
Gordon, R. A.   166
Gordon, S.   81
Gotlieb, C. C.   122
Goudge, T. A.   103
Gould, C. H.   223
Govenlock, S.   184
Gowan, M. O.   24, 168
Graham, E. S.   206
Graham, J. F.   5, 70, 105
Graham, J. R.   166
Grand'maison, J.   77
Granger, W. E.   176
Grant, G. M.   33
Grant, G. P.   60, 105
Grant, L. S.   263
Gravel, C.   190
Gray, W. A.   43
Grayhurst, D.   42
Grebenschikov, W.   97
Greco, J.   79
Greenland, C.   155
Greer, W. N.   126
Greer-Wooton, B.   109
Gregoire, G.-A.   87
Grégoire, R.   212
Grelton, R.   127
Grenier, F.   108, 109, 114
Grewe, W.   44, 112
Grey, J.   23
Griffin, M.   227
Griffith, H. R.   156, 157
Grime, A. R.   109
Groome, L. J.   89
Gross, A. C.   136, 248
Grossman, H. J.   262
Groulx, L.   24, 99, 235
Grove, J. W.   116, 152, 215
Guay, J.   211, 268
Guillet, E. C.   233
Guillett, D. W.   232
Guillot, M.   174
Guindon, H.   237, 283
Guindon, R.   4, 9, 12, 32, 61, 85, 214
Gulick, L.   127
Gullman, A. I.   72
Gunderson, H.   272
Gundy, H. P.   36

Gunn, C. R.   76, 203
Gunn, K. L. S.   85
Gunning, H. E.   117
Gurd, F. N.   158
Gutelius, J. R.   163
Gutteridge, D.   95
Gwilliam, R. B.   264
Gzowski, P.   236

Hachey, H. B.   119, 226
Haddock, P. G.   138
Haggar, G.   255
Hague, D.   43
Hailand, S.   226
Hale, C.   32, 128
Hale, J. P.   246
Hall, E. M.   181
Hall, G. W.   158
Hall, H.   27
Hall, L. W.   166
Hall, M. M.   226
Hall, O.   114
Halpenny, F. G.   215, 235
Haltrecht, E.   221
Ham, J. M.   135
Hamel, C.   209
Hamel, R.   183
Hamelin, J.-M.   104
Hamelin, L.-E.   20, 108, 110, 233
Hamell, L.   108
Hamilton, A. C.   263
Hamilton, J.   111
Hamilton, J. D.   38, 116, 149, 150, 157, 161
Hamilton, W.   169
Handa, V. K.   136
Handy, L. C.   247
Hanley, C.   39, 105
Hanlon, P.   227
Hannell, F. G.   218
Hanrahan, T. J.   99
Hanson, E. J.   71, 286
Hanson, F.   21, 101
Harbron, J. D.   130
Harding, J.   240, 242, 249
Hardwick, W. G.   273
Hardy, T. A.   190, 243
Hare, F. K.   67, 77, 108
Harkleroad, P.   249
Harlow, N.   145
Harman, E.   235
Harp, J.   236
Harper, J. M.   231

Harper, W. D.   127
Harris, D. B.   200
Harris, M.   147
Harris, R. F.   128, 219
Harris, R. S.   3, 4, 28, 29, 59, 61, 76
Harrop, T. J.   132
Harrower, G.   37, 86
Hart, J.   29, 65, 115, 117, 122
Hart, J. L.   216
Hart, P. W.   145
Hart, T.   46
Hartle, D. G.   81, 262
Hartung, H.   131
Harvey, J.   78, 80
Haskett, J.   43, 54, 128
Hastings, J. E. F.   182
Hatfield, S.   135
Hawkins, G. R. S.   201
Hawkins, S. C.   95
Hay, K. A. J.   82
Hayes, F. R.   75, 115, 217
Hayne, D. M.   95
Haynes, E. R.   160
Heard, J. F.   40, 118
Heasman, D. J.   128
Hébert, G.   22
Heeney, W. B.   79
Heinke, G. W.   137
Heinrich, T. A.   230
Heinz, R.   246
Heise, D. H.   111
Heming, H.   188
Hemphill, H. D.   72, 264
Henderson, B.   145
Henderson, G. F.   36, 227
Henderson, J. A.   195
Henderson, M. E.   146
Henne, F.   146
Hennuy, G.   62
Henry, G. M.   195
Henson, G.   200
Herbert, J.   113, 190
Herbert, M.   208
Hershfield, C.   137
Hertzman, L.   51, 62, 99
Hervieux, G.   18, 266
Hettich, W.   278
Hewitt, R. M.   155
Hewson, J.   79
Heyen, J.   93
Hickman, G. A.   185
Hicks, H.   58
Higenbottom, G. A.   142

Hill, J.   111
Hills, T. L.   109
Hiltz, M. C.   138
Hlynka, J. N.   176
Hoch, P.   240
Hodge, G.   109
Hodgetts, A. B.   100, 101
Hodgetts, J. E.   62, 107, 239
Hoffart, R.   126
Hogg, H. S.   40, 118
Hoichberg, S. W.   125, 270
Holbrook, G. W.   134
Hollenberg, C. H.   165
Holmes, E. L.   116
Holt, H. E.   15
Hopkins, E. S.   124, 216
Horne, E. B.   121
Horner, L. T.   92, 191
Horowitz, M.   188, 189
Horrobin, P.   240
Hosken, F.   76, 126
Hosking, D. J.   149
Hotimsky, C. M.   98, 229
Houde, R.   103
Hould, F.   151
House, D.   182
House, R. K.   133
Housego, I. E.   186
How, H. R.   42, 68
Howard, H. W.   255
Howarth, T.   127
Howe, C. D.   137
Howell, D. G.   195
Howlett, L. E.   61
Howsam, R. B.   189
Hoyt, R.   111, 112
Hubbard, R. H.   220, 230
Hudon, L.-N.   173
Hudon, T.   231
Hudson, R. I.   247
Hughes, D.   104, 192
Hughes, F. N.   176
Hughes, P.   63
Hume, J. N. P.   213
Humphreys, E. H.   89
Humphries, C. W.   41, 100
Hung, N.   283
Hunka, S. M.   159, 207
Hunter, A. T.   160, 161, 166, 168, 211
Hunter, R. C. A.   158, 159, 167
Huntingford, A.   65
Huntsman, A. G.   118, 216
Hurley, E. B.   168

Hurtubise, R.   17, 78, 255
Hussain, M. R.   226
Hussey, C.   20, 177
Hutchison, H.   222
Hutton, E.   3
Hutton, H. K.   185
Hyman, C.   4, 73

Iacobucci, N. E.   143
Illing, W. M.   278
Inglis, J.   111
Ingraham, M. H.   256
Innanen, K. A.   45, 118, 123
Innis, M. Q.   174
Ironside, R. G.   110
Irving, J. A.   219
Isabelle, L.   33, 112, 246
Isbister, F.   130

Jackman, S. W.   57
Jackson, A.   126
Jackson, B. W.   59
Jackson, G. E.   213
Jackson, J. H. M.   213
Jackson, R. L.   96
Jackson, R. W. B.   59, 198, 199, 222
Jacoby, A.   167
Jacques, A.   156
James, H.   255
James, J. V.   227
James, L.   41, 204
Jameson, E. E.   169
Jameson, G. B.   271
Jaques, L. B.   48
Jasmin, J.-J.   124
Jason, H.   157, 165, 210
Jeanes, R. W.   91, 210
Jeanneret, F. C. A.   29, 40
Jeanneret, M.   215, 235
Jeffel, R. R.   57
Jeffrey, R. L.   121
Jobin, F.   149
Jobin, J.-B.   161
Jobin, P.   154, 168
Johns, M.   123
Johns, R. J.   261
Johns, W. H.   51, 52, 272
Johnson, A. C.   44
Johnson, A. H.   219
Johnson, F. H.   53
Johnson, G. R.   21, 154
Johnson, H. G.   80, 105, 107, 219, 250
Johnson, L. P. V.   513

Johnson, W. S.   140
Johnston, D.   58
Johnston, R. J.   264
Joly J.-M.   208, 214
Jones, B. M.   107
Jones, G.   56, 274
Jones, G. M.   160, 264
Jones, J. R.   121
Jones, R.   58
Jones, T. L.   194, 195
Josie, G. H.   182
Jourard, S.   169
Jowett, G.   63, 252
Joyal, S.   238
Judek, S.   81
Judge, D.   265
Judy, R. D.   236
Judy, R. W.   70, 83, 84
Juneau, M. P.   210
Jung, J.   113
Jurkszus, J.   97
Jutras, A.   153
Jutras, J.-G.   225
Juvet, C. S.   128

Kaller, C. L.   48
Kaplan, D. L.   102, 190
Kaplan, J. G.   58, 254
Kaplan, M.   101
Kartzke, P.   121
Katz, J.   223
Katz, L.   122
Katz, M.   184, 222
Kauffmann, J.-P.   204
Kaufman, M. R.   167
Kay, Z.   252
Keeping, E. S.   122, 233
Keith, B.   117, 241
Kelley, M. I.   147
Kelly, J. M.   192, 236
Kelly, N.   240
Kelly, P.   122
Kennedy, D. R.   174, 176
Kennedy, G.   11
Kennedy, L. A.   78
Kennedy, R.   210
Kent, M.   73, 208, 237, 244
Kenyon, R.   132, 233
Kergin, D.   173
Kernaghan, D. K.   130
Kernaliguen, A.   138
Kerr, H. E.   58
Kerr, D.   106

Kerr, R. B. 149
Kesterton, W. H. 140
Keyes, M. E. 44, 178
Khan, S. B. 208
Kibauka, T. 117
Kidd, J. R. 202, 205
Kidd, K. E. 89
Kierman, O. B. 206
Kikauka, T. 228
Kilbourn, W. M. 100, 219
Kimble, G. H. T. 108
King, A. J. C. 190, 211
King, C. 48
King, D. B. 95
Kinley, C. E. 253
Kinnin, C. 163
Kippen, M. R. L. 227
Kirkconnell, W. 4, 7, 8, 32, 36, 47, 48, 88, 97, 233
Klein, J. 244
Kling, S. 167
Klink, C. F. 219
Klonoff, H. 111, 159, 170
Knell, W. D. 223
Knight, B. 184
Knight, V. 138
Knowles, A. F. 210, 211, 212
Knowles, D. W. 51, 206, 207
Kockebakker, J. 74
Kohn, R. 149
Konecny, G. 134
Korchinsky, N. W. 179
Kothari, V. 248
Krésic, S. 93
Kreutwieser, E. 242
Kruger, A. 81

Lachance, D. 19
Lachance, E. 192
Lacombe, T. 15, 67
Lacoste, P. 62
Lacourcière, H. 124
Laflamme, J. C. K. 115
La Fountaine, M. E. 202
La Framboise, J.-C. 32, 128
Lafrenière, A. 86
Laidlaw, J. C. 149
Lajoie, F. 143
Lakin, J. D. 143
Lalancette, D. 172
Laliberté, J. 202, 239
Lamarche, S. 27
Lamb, A. S. 21, 177

Lamb, W. K. 219, 228
Lamonde, A. 176
Lamontagne, L. 63, 207, 208
Lamontagne, M. 63, 265
Lanctôt, B. 26, 137
Land, R. B. 40, 146-48
Langdon, S. 117, 241
Langelier, R. 149
Langevin, G. 194
Langis, J. 25, 193
Langley, G. J. 186
Langley, G. R. 253
Langlois, R. 177
Langton, J. 115
Lanphier, C. M. 106, 220
Lapalme, M. 27
Lapointe, M. 199, 218, 220, 256, 257
Lapointe, S. 26, 123
LaRose, P. E. 173
Lasalle-Leduc, A. 102
Laserre, R. 125
Laskin, B. 45, 68, 70, 144
LaTouche 240
Lattimer, J. E. 231
Laurin, C. 156
Lauvrière, E. 8
Lauzon, A. 26, 67, 242, 268
Lavallée, J.-G. 19, 25, 90
Laverdière, C. 108
Lavery, C. J. 254
Lavoie, B. 267
Law, C. 215
Law, H. 229, 262-64
Law, J. T. 149
Lawson, G. 118
Laxer, J. 239, 242, 243
Laycock, S. R. 169
Layne, N. 115
Lazure, J. 243
LeBaron, H. R. 138
LeBel, E. C. 78
Lebel, Marc 17, 19, 103
Lebel, Maurice 15, 87-89, 116, 171, 193, 213, 219
LeBlanc, P. B. 197, 247
LeBlanc, R. 12
LeBlanc, S. 255
LeClair, M. A. 27, 163
Lecompte, E. 16
Leddy, J. F. 48, 58, 61, 88, 239
Lederman, W. R. 142
Lee, D. 61, 62, 251
Lee, R. M. 246

Lee, R. S. 22, 141
Lee, R. W. 140
Lefebvre, J.-P. 202
Lefoli, K. 24
Lefrançois, J.-J. 114
Légaré, J. 194, 283
Légaré, T. 205
Leger, Cardinal Paul-Emile 25
LeGresley, O. 8
Legroulx, L. 267
Lehrman, J. 127
Leigh, A. 183
Lemay, L. 239
Lemelin, R. 19
Lemieux, G. 156
Lemieux, V. 220
Le Moine, J. M. 98
Leon, P. 91, 92, 95, 96
LePan, D. V. 61, 66
Lesage, A. 232
Le Sieur, A. 222
Lesperance, J. 99
Lessard, M.-A. 193
Letendre, A. 17
Lettre, J.-P. 124
Letts, A. 286
Letts, A. B. 237, 272
Leung, S. W. 54, 131, 132
Levasseur, J. H. 17
Levesque, U. 17, 18
Levine, J. B. 70, 83, 84
Levine, O. H. 279, 280
Levy, K. L. 96
Lewis, D. J. 163
Lewis, D. S. 233
Lewis, J. A. 106, 179, 190
Lewis, M. 29
Lewis, W. B. 116
Liddell, T. 33
Liewinowicz, V. 97
Lindal, W. J. 47, 96
Lindenfield, R. 165, 183
Liquori, M. 176
Liswood, S. 73
Lithwick, N. H. 82
Livesay, D. 94
Lloyd, L. E. 139
Lloyd, T. 242
Lockquell, C. 103
Loisel, J. 236
Loken, G. 272
Loken, J. 197
Long, L. 172

Lomer, G. R. 20, 21, 224
Lorimer, J. 80, 83
Lorrain, P. 59
Lortie, L. 58, 87
Lortie, M. 138
Lotz, J. 62, 64
Loudon, J. 137
Lougheed, W. C. 71
Lowe, P. B. 272
Lower, A. R. M. 36, 41, 47, 48, 58,
    100, 254
Loyer, M. A. 171
Lubick, E. E. 196
Lukermann, F. 108
Lumsden, I. 64, 252
Lupul, M. R. 78
Lussier, C. A. 244
Lussier, I. 24
Lussier, J.-P. 25, 132
Lusztig, P. A. 43, 54, 129
Lyle, P. M. 207
Lynch, M. 11, 94
Lyon, P. V. 248

Maas, C. E. 22
MacCallum, D. C. 152
MacDermott, H. E. 156, 182, 231, 234,
    235
MacDonald, A. A. 11, 205
MacDonald, D. 85
Macdonald J. 190, 221
Macdonald, J. A. 34
Macdonald, J. B. 45, 48, 49, 53, 65, 71,
    73, 77, 78, 116, 215, 218
MacDonald, N. 163
MacDonald, R. M.
MacDonald, W. R. 252
MacEwan, C. 163
MacEwan, D. W. 165
MacFarlane, R. O. 30, 128
MacGibbon, D. A. 231
MacIntosh, A. G. 187
Macintosh, D. F. 49
Mackay, C. B. 70, 71, 73
Mackenzie, C. J. 115, 213, 217
Mackenzie, C. J. C. 181
Mackenzie, N. A. M. 10, 60, 200
Mackey, W. 20, 219
Mackie, E. J. 169
MacKinnon, A. R. C. 57, 187
MacKinnon, F. 58
MacKinnon, W. B. 70
MacKintosh, W. A. 35, 106, 107, 127

MacLaggan, K. 170
MacLean, F. 183
MacLean, H. R. 51, 132
MacLean, J. F. 69
MacLean, M. 247
MacLean, M. B. 133
MacLean, W. J. 136
MacLennan, D. A. 46, 47
MacLennan, H. 94
MacLeod, D. E. 10
MacLeod, J. W. 158, 160
MacLeod, S. 6
Maclure, M. 219
MacMillan, K. 234
MacNab, E. 156
Macpherson, C. B. 62, 63, 85, 242
Magnan, C. J. 114
Magnuson, R. 79
Maher, D. 208
Maheux, A. 19, 86
Mailhiot, B. 110
Maisey, D. P. 52, 203
Major, M. 58
Malloch, A. 13, 255
Maloney, D. A. 193
Maltby, P. 262
Mandel, E. 94
Mann, W. E. 263
Manning, T. W. 124, 198
Maranda, A. 246
Marceau, G. 152
Marcotte, N. 12, 136
Marcus, A. M. 170
Mardiros, A. M. 199
Mardon, E. G. 53
Marie, Y. 171
Marineau, R. 112, 222
Marion, L. 116
Markell, F. E. B. 263
Markham, S. F. 230
Markle, A. G. 52, 272
Marois, P. 194
Marquis, G. W. 54, 101, 102
Marsh, L. C. 273
Marshall, D. 61, 237
Marshall, J. 41, 145
Marshall, J. B. 41, 145, 146, 178, 188, 252
Marshall, J. M. 178, 188
Martin, J. K. 151, 166
Martin, J.-M. 15, 74, 127, 178, 188
Martin, J.-P. 183

Martin, L. 22, 61
Martin, S. 283
Martin, Y. 60, 114
Martineau, A. 18
Martorana, S. V. 272
Mase, D. J. 273
Massé, D. 266, 282
Massey, D. A. 91, 210
Massicotte, E.-Z. 153, 174, 224
Masson, C. 267
Masson, L. I. 190
Mather, J. M. 158, 159, 181
Mathews, R. D. 60, 63, 64, 75, 117, 238, 252
Mathews, W. H. 55, 136
Mathieu, J. 163
Matlik, C. 11
Mattaisson, J. S. 214
Mattessich, R. 131
Matthews, B. C. 125
Maura, Sister 10
Maurault, O. 23, 97
Maxwell, R. W. 124
Maxwell, S. R. 131
May, K. O. 122
Maybee, A. R. 70
Mayne, B. 94
Mayo, H. B. 65
McAllister, J. 234
McArthur, N. M. 37
McBrine, R. W. 10
McBryde, W. A. E. 264
McCarter, J. A. 63
McCarter, J. H. 215
McCarthy, J. P. 185
McCarthy, J. R. 76
McCausland, I. 215, 253
McClean, A. J. 142
McClellan, G. 184
McConnell, T. R. 75
McCombs, R. 249
McCorkell, E. J. 38, 39, 41, 49, 56, 192
McCormack, P. D. 46, 110, 209
McCormick, W. 197
McCreary, J. F. 56, 149, 158, 162, 163, 181, 192
McCue, G. 127
McCulloch, T. 191
McCurdy, S. G. 187
McDavid, R. I. 91
McDonald, J. C. 237
McDonough, G. 236, 240
McDougall, R. L. 235

McElroy, L. W. 195
McEown, A. C. 58
McGechaen, J. 55, 188
McGrail, M. M. 198
McGuigan, D. 185
McGuigan, G. F. 64, 209, 237, 240
McGuire, C. H. 165
McIlwraith, T. F. 39, 106
McInerney, H. O. 141
McInnes, R. R. 160
McIntosh, J. R. 186
McIntosh, R. G. 187
McIntosh, R. L. 117
McIntyre, H. C. 28, 228, 242
McKay, A. G. 93
McKendry, J. B. J. 151, 163
McKenzie, K. A. 9, 153, 154
McKenzie, R. T. 21
McKinna, Sister M. O. 6, 79
McLean, I. 201
McLean, J. D. 9, 132, 166
McLennan, D. 229
McLuhan, H. M. 186
McMillan, E. 171
McMurrich, J. P. 118
McNeil, D. R. 201
McNeill, K. G. 116
McNeill, W. E. 35
McPhedran, A. 157
McPherson, A. 145
McQueen, J. 269
McTaggart-Cowan, I. 117, 218
McWhinney, I. R. 152, 167
McWhinney, W. 249
Meagher, J. W. 21, 177
Medec, W. J. 130
Medieros-Gutierrez, M. A. 88
Medland, P. 225
Meltz, N. M. 80-83, 262
Menard, J. 96, 220
Mengall, C. 81
Mercier, A. 177
Merrett, R. 177
Merrill, F. J. H. 230
Messier, J. A. 26, 177
Meyer, J. 25, 129
Michael, Sister Alice 10
Michaud, L. 74, 80
Michelson, W. 114, 126
Mickleburgh, B. 94
Middaugh, D. G. 132
Miers, H. A. 230
Milbury, J. C. 265, 266

Milhiot, B. 213
Miller, B. 177
Miller, G. E. 253
Miller, J. R. 160
Miller, L. 202, 210
Miller, R. D. 155
Miller, R. S. 60
Millett, F. B. 35
Millis, J. S. 165
Milner, J. B. 14, 57, 67, 255
Milnes, H. 41
Milord, R. 172
Minuck, M. 167
Mitchell, R. 46, 47, 154, 155
Mitchener, R. D. 4, 77, 261
Mockle, J. A. 174
Moffatt, H. P. 69, 221
Mohr, J. 105, 184
Moir, J. S. 3
Mollica, A. 96
Monahan, E. J. 66, 67, 250, 256
Moncion, D. 246
Mondon, P. 15, 238
Monier, F. 23
Montagnes, I. 41
Montagnes, J. 269
Montague, J. H. 36, 123
Montgomery, S. J. 133
Montminy, J.-P. 193
Montoye, H. 179
Moon, B. 38, 44, 118, 245
Moore, A. M. 72
Moore, L. 130
Moore, R. K. 129
Moorey, C. M. 213
Mordell, D. L. 214
More, A. 132, 208
More, R. H. 160
Morgan, J. S. 183
Morin, F. 250
Morin, J.-Y. 75
Morin, V. 231, 232
Morison, J. D. 172
Morisset, A.-M. 33, 145, 146
Morley, T. P. 169
Morley, W. F. E. 228
Morrison, F. 174
Morrison, R. M. 170
Morrison, R. N. 23, 131
Morton, J. D. 142
Mount, J. H. 159
Mowat, A. S. 206
Mowat, G. L. 263

Mowat, J. 33
Mowatt, D. G. 91
Moxham, R. 250
Moyse, C. A. 164, 209
Mueller, R. H. 44, 113
Muir, J. D. 130, 248
Mulcahy, G. 129
Mullens, J. E. 194
Munam, M. L. 27, 163
Mungall, C. 42
Munro, I. 177
Munroe, D. 4, 9, 12, 61, 83
Murphy, J. F. 85
Murray, D. 176
Murray, F. B. 144
Murray, V. V. 174
Murray, W. J. 89
Murty, R. C. 122
Mussallem, H. K. 169, 170
Mustard, J. F. 149, 162
Mutchler, P. 202
Myers, B. 51
Myers, C. R. 111, 113, 233

Nadel, G. H. 99
Naegele, K. D. 170
Nagle, P. 56
Nairn, J. G. 174
Nanson, M. 158
Nash, J. C. 179
Nayler, M. J. V. 175
Neal, W. D. 264
Nease, A. S. 187
Neatby, H. 154
Neher, P. A. 82
Neiger, S. 165
Neilson, H. R. 139
Nelson, C. 127
Nelson, E. L. 71
Nelson, J. G. 49
Nelson, R. 239
Nelson, T. M. 51, 112
Nelson-Jones, R. 161, 163, 164
Nesbitt, H. H. J. 119
Neville, A. M. 134
Nevison, M. 197
Newbold, B. T. 13, 119
Newman, W. C. 142
Newnham, W. T. 187
Ng, T. K. 55, 93, 148, 227
Nice, P. O. 158
Nichol, D. S. 133
Nichol, J. 13

Nicholls, C. G. W. 79
Nicholls, R. V. V. 232
Nicholls, R. W. 45, 118, 123, 213
Nicholls, W. 54, 104, 193
Nicol, E. 22
Nicholson, N. L. 109
Niemi, J. A. 205
Nikolaiczuk, N. 125
Niminger, J. R. 270
Niven, I. 121
Nobert, R. 170
Normann, T. F. 101
Northcott, R. J. 118, 234
Northover, F. H. 121
Nosanchuk, T. A. 104
Nowlan, J. P. 120
Nursall, J. R. 60

O'Brien, J. E. 212
O'Connell, T. F. 45, 228, 229
Oglesby, J. C. M. 96
O'Hara, A. S. 181
Ohliger, J. 205
Oliver, Michael 105, 220
Oliver, M. J. 54
O'Neill, I. 129
Orchard, G. E. 98
Orlowski, S. T. 271
Orr, J. L. 81, 117
Orris, B. D. 187
Ostrey, B. 38
Ouellet, F. 99, 100
Ouellet, P. 114
Ouellet, R. 241, 268
Ouellette, G.-J. 125

Pacey, W. D. 14, 88, 220
Pacquet, P. 205
Page, G. T. 264
Page, J. E. 126
Painchaud, P. 107
Palko, M. E. 182
Palmer, E. F. 213
Pannu, G. S. 148
Pape, A. 39, 239
Pappert, E. C. 211
Paquet, J.-C.
Paradis, J. 148
Parai, L. 80, 263, 278
Pare, J. 230
Parent, A.-M. 4, 9, 12, 15, 19, 75, 154, 238, 252
Parisel, C. 244

Parker, G. 144
Parker, J. H. 96
Parker, M. L. 228
Parkhouse, J. 165
Parks, A. E. 156
Parmenter, M. D. 196
Parr, J. G. 116
Paterson, G. R. 174, 176
Paton, G. 179
Paton, J. M. 188, 233
Patterson, F. P. 151, 162
Patterson, I. W. 72
Paul, T. 179
Paul VI 33
Paulson, B. D. 51
Pavalko, R. M. 199, 246
Payerle, G. 240
Payne, R. W. 209
Paynter, K. J. 132
Peacock, G. 91
Pearce, C. A. 21, 24, 224
Pearson, W. W. 180
Peavy, R. V. 246
Peel, B. B. 51, 72, 147, 226
Peitchinis, S. G. 81, 248
Pelletier, D. 75, 196
Pelletier, G. 62
Pendakur, V. S. 245
Penfield, W. G. 21, 22, 149
Penland, P. R. 147
Penner, P. G. 55, 188
Pennington, G. 178
Pepin, Y. 241, 268
Perkins, S. A. 53, 196, 208
Perron, M. A. 124
Petch, H. E. 116
Peterson, P. L. 21
Petitpas, H. 61
Pétolas, J. P. 16
Pett, L. B. 181
Phaneuf, L. P. 194
Philip, Brother 186
Picard, G. 206
Picard, G. L. 55
Pichette, L. P. 149
Pickard, G. L. 55, 206
Pickarski, H. 229
Pickering, W. S. F. 193
Pickersgill, J. W. 30, 128
Pidhany, O. S. 14, 98, 99
Pierre, G. E. 27
Pike, R. M. 244
Pilisuk, M. 39

Pinard, A. 111
Pinder, K. L. 137
Piper, D. 42
Plante, A. 31, 86
Plante, L. 18, 87, 211
Poole, C. F. 88, 198, 253
Porter, A. 134
Porter, J. 64, 76, 78, 208
Porter, M. 200
Poser, E. G. 110
Post, S. 173
Potts, R. E. 178
Pouliot, L. 233
Pownall, K. F. 132, 182
Pratte, C. 247, 268
Pratte, Y. 19, 142
Prattis, J. I. 249
Prentice, J. D. 116
Preshing, W. A. 130
Preston, Adrian 37
Preston, R. A. 37, 100
Preuter, K. F. 211
Priest, R. 89
Priestley, F. E. L. 89
Primeau, W. J. 74, 244
Prince, G. H. 13, 120, 137
Prince, J.-E. 16
Principe, W. H. 192
Pritchard, W. R. 195
Prober, J. 143
Procter, G. A. 102
Prosen, H. 164
Proulx, P. P. 283
Provencher, L. 86, 118
Provost, H. 17-20, 192, 193
Purdy, C. E. 132
Pushie, G. 5
Pylyshyn, Z. W. 113

Quazi, S. 29
Quick, E. 109

Rabinovitch, R. 237
Racette, J. 103, 267
Radwanski, P. A. 98
Rae, R. 62, 242
Rainey, C. A. 246
Raison, A. V. 234
Rajan, V. 242
Rand, I. C. 141
Rank, I. 200
Ransom, P. 208
Ranta, L. E. 53, 154

Ratner, R. S. 243
Ratsoy, E. W. 188
Raveneau, J. 108
Rawlinson, H. E. 50
Raymond, B. 228
Raymond, Y. 81
Raymore, W. G. 126
Raynauld, A. 106
Read, J. G. 161
Read, J. H. 152
Ready, R. K. 129
Ready, W. 32, 229, 271
Reaman, G. E. 125
Reamsbottom, G. 239
Reaney, J. 39
Reder, F. M. 57
Redmond, D. A. 7, 9, 13, 14, 133, 224
Reed, J. 148
Reeds, L. G. 108
Régnier, P. R. 47
Reid, Escott, 45
Reid, E. H. 46
Reid, I. 212
Reid, J. 242
Reid, J. H. S. 58, 75
Reid, T. 242
Reigh, I. A. 166
Rempel, P. P. 246
Repo-Davis, M. 214
Resnick, P. 243
Revell, D. G. 50, 154
Reynar, A. H. 93
Rhodes, A. J. 181
Rice, D. 152, 158, 162, 165
Richard, B. 87
Richer, E. 96
Richer, L.-M. 87
Riches, E. 149, 158, 159
Rickwood, J. 112
Riddell, W. A. 229
Rideout, E. B. 73
Ridge, A. D. 22, 227
Riedel, B. E. 120, 174
Rigaud, M. 218
Rigby, M. S. 118, 216
Rimmington, G. T. 5, 7, 8
Rioux, B. 25, 79
Rioux, M. 114
Ripley, F. N. 164
Ripton, R. A. 190, 211
Risi, J. 198
Ritchie, E. M. 138
Ritchie, R. S. 200

Robarts, John P. 285
Robbins, J. E. 30
Roberts, W. G. 49
Robertson, C. S. 125, 162, 173, 272, 273
Robertson, J. K. 35, 157
Robinson, A. J. 72, 198, 256
Robinson, C. 5
Robinson, C. S. 272, 273
Robinson, E. S. 144
Robinson, F. G. 221, 222, 261
Robinson, G. C. 163, 166
Robinson, J. L. 109
Robinson, S. C. 10, 162, 173
Robson, J. M. (McGill) 123
Robson, J. M. (Toronto) 64
Robson, R. A. H. 251, 257
Roby, Y. 201
Rocher, G. 15, 63, 64, 114, 208, 221, 253
Rock, V. 94, 101, 107, 110
Rockman, A. 90
Rodenhizer, J. 56
Rodwell, L. 102, 233
Roe, P. H. 136
Rogers, G. W. 18
Rogers, M. A. 22, 132
Rombout, L. 11
Romeyn, J. A. 163
Rose, B. 163, 245
Rose, D. C. 123
Rose, W. J. 55, 97, 98
Rosen, E. 211
Rosenbluth, G. 70, 72, 83, 256
Ross, G. W. 37
Ross, I. 209, 237
Ross, J. A. 206
Ross, J. F. W. 153
Ross, M. G. 45, 61, 65, 76, 82, 105, 161, 197
Ross, T. M. 175
Ross, V. B. 13, 191, 215
Rothrock, G. A. 198, 251
Rothstein, S. 55, 144-46
Rotstein, A. 40, 41, 67
Roussopoulos, D. 243, 268
Routier, F. 194
Routley, J. V. 168
Routley, T. C. 153, 235
Rowat, D. C. 64, 66, 78, 128, 239
Rowe, F. W. 5
Rowles, D. 170
Rowsell, G. S. 171
Roy, J.-E. 16

Roy, M. 102
Roy, P.-G.
Royce, M. 173, 205
Ruddy, J. 57
Rule, J. C. 99
Rumball, W. G. 46, 47
Rumilly, R. 8, 26, 130
Rusk, B. 243
Russell, E. K. 169
Russell, J. A. 125
Ruth, N. J. 44
Ruth, Sister 41
Ruttan, R. F. 133
Ruzesky, N. 130
Ryan, C. 149
Ryan, D. 6
Ryan, E. 190
Ryan, E. F. 143, 212, 243
Ryan, W. F. 14, 142, 143
Ryder, D. 52

St.-Arnaud, P. 114, 151
St. Clair-Sobell, J. 97
St. John, F. R. 226
St. Louis, Sister 171
St.-Pierre, G. 91
St. Pierre, J. 65
Sagar, M. 172, 182
Saint-Georges, J. 194
Saint-Martin, L. P. 99
Saint Miriam, Sister 11
Saint-Yves, M. 108, 109
Sampson, G. 102
Samuel, S. 39
Sanazaro, P. J. 162, 182
Sandiford, P. J. 129
Sangster, M. 139
Sanssoucy, L. 16
Sarrazin, G. 79
Sartoris, P. 246
Sasnett, M. 251
Saucier, P. 77
Saunders, R. M. 100
Sauvageau, F. 140
Sauvé, J.-C. 242
Savage, D. C. 92
Savage, H. W. 189
Savard, L. 235
Savard, M. 87, 90, 266, 267
Savard, P. 20, 193
Savile, D. B. O. 119, 218
Savoie, A. 12
Sawyer, W. W. 121

Scanlon, T. J. 140, 212
Scarfe, N. V. 59, 186, 189
Scargill, M. H. 94
Scarlett, E. P. 21
Schafer, R. M. 90
Schegel, R. P. 178
Schiele, R. 248
Schiff, H. I. 121
Schindeler, F. 106, 220
Schindelka, D. J. 273, 286
Schlieper, H. C. 92, 99
Schneider, W. G. 77, 117
Schoenauer, N. 244
Schofield, M. 159
Schonfield, D. 110
Schurman, D. M. 59
Schwarz, C. J. 245, 246
Scott, A. 105, 251
Scott, D. H. 74, 84
Scott, D. S. 134
Scott, E. F. 192
Scott, James 42
Scott, J. W. 50, 155, 157
Scott, M. 141
Scott, N. 239
Scott, P. D. 75, 250
Scott, W. G. 68
Scriver, C. 163
Scugog 153
Sears, H. 244
Seary, E. R. 91, 94
Segal, H. J. 177
Segal, M. 283
Seger, J. E. 263
Seguin, R.-L. 155
Seguinot, A. 96
Selby-Smith, C. 74
Selman, G. 54, 55, 200-202, 204
Selye, H. 119
Semple, S. W. 269
Seville, B. 77
Sexton, F. H. 261, 265
Shah, C. P. 163
Shand, G. V.
Shaw, E. C. 31
Shaw, R. F. 148
Sheehan, E. 172
Sheffield, E. F. 64, 70, 71, 75, 82, 197, 198
Shein, L. J. 98
Sheldon, M. 16, 130
Shepley, D. J. 162
Sheps, G. D. 28, 242

Sherwood, B. 226
Shields, H. J. 154
Ship, S. 239
Shoeck, R. J. 254
Shook, L. K. 39
Shore, L. E. 125
Short, V. M. 191, 199, 204, 205
Shorthouse, T. 55
Shortreed, J. H. 135
Shortt, E. S. 34, 153
Shortt, S. E. D. 235
Shrum, G. M. 81
Shuh, J. E. 125
Siddall, J. N. 32
Siirala, A. J. 194
Silver, D. 167
Silvers, R. J. 220, 243
Simard, J. V. 17
Simon, B. V. 225
Simon, F. A. 52, 272
Simon, J. C. 271
Simond, G. 179
Simpson, E. C. R. 48, 138
Sinclair, G. 101, 107
Sinclair, Sol 138
Sinclair, Sonia 129, 261
Sipherd, R. S. 159
Sirluck, E. 60, 199
Sirota, D. 184
Sisam, J. W. B. 137
Sisco, N. A. 270
Skolnik, M. 74
Skora, S. J. 79, 254
Slade, M. 211
Slater, D. 220
Slater, E. 196
Slater, R. J. 149
Sloane, R. B. 158, 209
Slutsky, B. V. 243
Smart, R. G. 112
Smiley, D. V. 69, 107, 128
Smith, A. J. R. 82, 220
Smith, C. E. 187
Smith, D. 28, 42, 60
Smith, D. C. 199
Smith, D. E. 50, 205
Smith, D. L. T. 195
Smith, E. J. 125
Smith, E. R. 159
Smith, E. S. O. 182
Smith, G. I. H. 191
Smith, G. W. 46
Smith, J. H. G. 137

Smith, J. P. 57, 61, 66, 67, 76, 89, 253, 255
Smith, M. B. 88
Smith, M. E. 204
Smith, P. D. 252
Smith, R. 139, 271
Smith, S. 205
Smith, W. A. S. 51, 53, 63, 83
Smyth, D. M. 200
Smyth, F. 11
Snowland, C. P. 41, 61
Snyder, L. S. 209
Soberman, D. A. 36, 144, 254
Solandt, O. M. 117
Soltan, H. C. 160
Soltys, M. A. 195
Somers, H. J. 5, 76, 281
Sonier, H. 266
Sonnedecker, G. 176
Soudack, A. C. 134
Soule, L. 191
Spaeth, M. 179
Sparby, H. T. 185
Sparshott, F. E. 62, 67
Spaulding, W. B. 32, 163
Speakman, H. B. 213
Spence, M. B. 180
Spencer, E. Y. 215
Spensley, P. J. 91
Spicer, E. J. 148
Spinks, J. W. T. 49, 75, 115, 198, 217
Spinks, S. 23, 28, 64, 242, 245
Splane, R. B. 183
Spragge, G. W. 40
Stackpole, S. H. 3
Stager, D. A. 72, 82, 222, 244, 263
Stanford, L. 220
Stanley, G. D. 153
Stanley, G. F. G. 100
Stapleford, A. C. 247
Staples, L. A. 190
Steacie, E. W. R. 115, 217
Steed, M. E. 173
Steele, J. 63, 64
Steeves, L. C. 164, 168
Steffy, R. A. 112
Stein, D. L. 245
Steiner, J. W. 41, 151, 207, 248
Steinhauer, D. 92, 191
Steinmetz, N. 164
Stensland, P. G. 138, 253
Stephens, M. 42
Stephenson, B. 27

Sterlin, C. 167
Stern, H. H. 92
Stewart, A. 272
Stewart, C. B. 5, 9, 10, 149, 154, 156
Stewart, E. E. 29, 78
Stewart, F. K. 69
Stieb, E. W. 176
Stirling, R. J. 271
Stock, E. H. 197
Stock, V. 38
Stokes, R. B. 229
Stone, C. G. 46
Stone, F. R. 69
Storey, A. G. 186, 187, 197
Stott, M. M. 183, 201
Straka, M. K. 270
Strakhovsky, L. I. 97
Stratford, R. K. 213
Straub, K. M. 172
Strayer, B. L. 141
Strick, J. L. 152
Stubbin, H. 184
Styliarios, D. 126
Sudar, D. D. 270
Sullivan, A. D. 3, 79
Sullivan, H. M. 123
Sullivan, J. R. 85
Sumner, J. 163
Super, D. E. 196
Sutherland, J. B. 180
Sutherland, J. S. 111
Sutherland, N. 105, 190
Sutherland, R. W. 171
Sutherland, W. H. 64
Swaine, J. M. 213
Swan, P. J. M. 236
Swanson, D. R. 145
Swartman, R. K. 135
Swartz, S. G. 174
Swift, W. 76
Swilley, L. C. 239
Sydiaha, D. 111, 112, 219
Symons, T. H. B. 42
Szabo, D. 239

Taietz, P. 236
Tallen, G. P. R. 142
Tarnopolsky, W. S. 44, 144
Taschereau, L. P. 13, 255
Taylor, K. W. 80, 107, 234
Taylor, Lord 6
Taylor, M. G. 148
Taylor, R. B. 34, 253

Teare, F. W. 175
Telnes, L. 171
Theall, D. F. 63, 78
Therrien, L. 159
Thibaudeau, G. 31, 112
Thibault, A. 114
Thibault, J.-L. 268
Thibault, M. 268, 269
Thistle, M. 3, 36, 116, 216
Thode, H. G. 74, 75, 115, 215, 217
Thom, R. J. 42, 57
Thomas, A. M. 200, 204, 263
Thomas, C. E. 9
Thomas, E. L. 149
Thomas, L. H. 101
Thomas, W. K. 94, 212
Thompson, A. R. 142
Thompson, D. N. 239
Thompson, R. 243
Thompson, S. D. 196
Thompson, W. P. 49, 149, 254
Thomson, A. H. 133
Thomson, D. L. 213
Thomson, J. 229
Thomson, J. S. 219
Thorlakson, T. K. 47, 155
Thumm, W. 123
Tichler, J. M. 165
Tiger, L. 57
Tilly, C. 114
Timlin, M. F. 106, 220
Timmis, W. G. 131
Timmons, H. P. 201
Tod, A. J. 49, 273, 287
Tollefson, E. A. 149
Tomkins, G. 101
Tooley, B. 243
Toombs, M. P. 186
Toombs, W. M. P. 72, 186
Toombs, W. N. 3
Topley, D. N. 191
Tory, H. M. 50
Tough, A. 204
Toussaint, M. F. 253
Trainor, L. 118, 218
Tranchemontagne, R. 178
Tremblay, G. 194
Tremblay, J. 73, 81, 176
Tremblay, L.-M. 123, 219
Trembley, R. 123
Trias, A. 27, 163
Trigger, B. G. 40, 106
Trost, W. R. 115

Trotier, L. 108, 109
Trotter, B. 36
Troupin, J. L. 181
Trout, E. D. 165
Trout, F. 152, 173, 183
Trudel, M. 219
Truelove, J. H. 180
Trueman, K. R. 148
Tucker, A. W. 121
Tucker, F. 55
Tunis, B. L. 22, 171
Turcot, J. 167
Turcotte, L. P. 223, 231
Turgeon, H. 140
Turner, F. J. 184
Turner, G. H. 254
Turner, K. 144
Twaites, W. O. 81, 129, 134
Tweedie, A. S. R. 200, 204
Tyler, F. T. 237
Tyler, R. W. 183

Uffen, R. J. 119, 122, 136
Underhill, F. H. 253
Upton, L. F. S. 100
U'ren, R. 158

Vachon, A. 99
Vachon, L.-A. 19, 59, 75, 79, 87
Vagianos, L. 7, 229
Vaines, E. 139
Valdman, A. 92
Van Cleave, A. B. 116, 117
Van der Bellen, L. 26, 147
Vanderwater, S. L. 157
Vanderwell, A. 246
Van Pratten, N. 32, 34, 43, 224
Van Staalduinen, W. J. 152
Vaselenak, M. 208
Vaughn, W. N. 83
Verhonick, P. T. 172
Verma, D. 265
Verner, C. 204
Verney, D. V. 45
Vernon, F. 205
Verrier, W. L. 80
Vezina, R. 18
Villancourt, de G. 166
Villeneuve, A. 167
Villeneuve, Cardinal 23
Villeneuve, P. 240
Vinay, J.-P. 91, 97
Viswanathan, K. 187, 207

Vogt, E. N. 215
Vogt, E. W. 122
Von Meier, K. 90
Vuo, F. E. W. 204

Wagner, N. E. 194
Waines, W. J. 70
Wake, F. R. 200
Waldie, A. C. 245
Waldon, F. S. 234
Walker, B. E. 51, 186
Walker, G. C. 39, 174
Wallace, M. B. 172
Wallace, R. C. 34
Wallace, W. S. 232
Waller, R. H. 176
Walter, A. 102
Walters, J. 56, 138
Walters, S. Z. 134
Walton, R. J. 163
Ward, A. G. 116
Ward, D. 239
Ward, L. K. 164
Wardlaw, J. M. 139
Warner, R. M. 228
Warrian, P. 62
Warrington, C. J. S. 232
Warwick, O. H. 152, 159
Wasteneys, H. 40, 155
Waters, B. E. 200
Waterton, P. 85
Watkins, M. H. 82, 107
Watson, C. 29, 83, 105, 207, 250
Watson, D. L. 112
Watson, W. G. 9, 13, 192
Watt, L. A. K. 43, 68
Watt, T. B. 126
Waugh, D. 160, 161, 164, 209
Way, H. H. 7, 185
Wayman, T. 95
Webb, C. W. 61, 253
Webster, D. A. 222
Webster, S. 67
Wedgery, A. W. 170
Weetman, G. F. 137
Weidner, D. L. 92
Weir, J. M. 172
Weiskotten, H. G. 153
Welch, H. G. 179
Welch, J. E. 179
Wenaas, C. J. 4, 278
Wenckler, P. A. 148
Wendling, A.-V. 133

Wesbrook, F. F.   3
West, N. W.   178
West, P.   5
West, T. W.   120, 198, 217
Westman, A. E. R.   120
Weynerowski, W.   256
Whenham, G. R.   194
White, D.   229
White, G. M.   155
White, M.   93, 235
White, O.   165
White, P. H.   72
White, R. L.   94, 101, 107, 110
Whitehouse, J. R. W.   264
Whitelaw, J. A.   240
Whitelaw, J. H.   268
Whiteside, S.   10, 147
Whitney, J. P.   37
Whitworth, F. E.   60, 69, 81, 222, 223
Wickens, G. M.   40, 97
Wiedrick, S. G.   146
Wiggins, C. B.   217
Wigney, T. J.   187
Wiles, R. M.   88
Wilkinson, B. W.   81
Wilkinson, J. P.   9, 226
Wilkinson, W. K.   51, 244
Williams, D. C.   39, 62, 68
Williams, D. H.   168
Williams, E. E.   39, 225
Williams, M.   6, 226
Williamson, D.   134
Willis, J.   126
Willis, R. B.   69
Willson, J. D.   220
Wilson, A. H.   278
Wilson, D.   37
Wilson, D. L.   162, 164
Wilson, G. W.   81
Wilson, H. V.   263
Wilson, J. H.   139
Wilson, L.   50, 206
Wilson, R.   84
Wilson, W. R.   212
Wilt, J. C.   47, 157
Windsor, K. N.   100, 219
'Winstanley'   64
Winter, E.   109

Winter, F. E.   68
Winthrop, H.   114
Wipper, K. A. W.   178
Wisenthal, M.   188, 189
Wolfe, R. I.   109
Wolock, M.   92, 93
Wood, A. R.   131
Wood, J.   176
Wood, J. A.   49
Wood, V.   172
Woods, H. D.   129
Woodside, M. St. A.   252
Woodsworth, K. C.   143
Worthington, F. F.   22
Woycenko, O.   234
Wrenn, C. G.   247
Wright, D. T.   72, 76, 135, 214, 271, 285
Wright, M. J.   113
Wyant, G. M.   167
Wynne-Edwards, H. R.   117
Wyspianski, J. O.   196

Yadao, F. Jr.   205
Yates, D. E.   168
Yeh, M. H.   124
Yeo, D. J.   132, 182
Yi-t'ung Wang   54, 93
Yolande-de-l'Immaculée, Soeur   186
Yolles, M.   42
Yonge, K. A.   159, 210
Young, I.   242
Young, P.   67, 90
Young, W. G.   133

Zarb, G.   132
Zassenhaus, H.   121
Zay, N.   183, 184
Ziegler, E. F.   179
Ziel, H. R.   189
Zielinska, M. F.   146
Zoll, D. A.   242
Zolobka, V.   97
Zsigmond, Z. E.   4, 278
Zunbelt, D.   240
Zur-Muehler, M. Von   278
Zyla, W. T.   98
Zylak, J.   163